GALVESTON: A History

GALVESTON
A History

by David G. McComb

UNIVERSITY OF TEXAS PRESS
Austin

Copyright © 1986 by the University of Texas Press
All rights reserved
Printed in the United States of America
Second printing, 1991

Requests for permission to reproduce material from this work should
be sent to:
    Permissions
    University of Texas Press
    Box 7819
    Austin, Texas 78713-7819

Library of Congress Cataloging-in-Publication Data

McComb, David G.
    Galveston: a history.
    Bibliography: p.
    Includes index.
    1. Galveston (Tex.)—History.   2. Galveston
Region (Tex.)—History.   I. Title.
F394.G2M36   1986   976.4'139   85-20956
ISBN 0-292-72049-1
ISBN 0-292-72053-X (pbk.)

⊗ The paper used in this publication meets the minimum require-
ments of American National Standard for Information Sciences—
Permanence of Paper for Printed Library Materials, ANSI Z39.48-1984.

To my family and friends who, during the writing of this book, put up with me when I was there, and when I was not.

CONTENTS

Preface 1
1. The Edge of Time 5
2. The New York of Texas 42
3. The Oleander City 84
4. The Great Storm and the Technological Response 121
5. The Free State of Galveston 150
6. Galveston Island: Its Time Has Come . . . Again 188
Notes 216
Index 257

ILLUSTRATIONS

Maps
1. Map of Galveston Bay by Bénard de La Harpe, 1721   7
2. Galveston Bay Area   9
3. Plan of the City of Galveston by William H. Sandusky, 1845   46
4. Hurricane Damage, 1900   128

Figures
1. Galveston City Population, 1850–1980   66
2. Galveston-Houston Populations, 1850–1980   67
3. Seawall Construction Plans   141

Photo section following page 120.

GALVESTON: A History

PREFACE

Every historian has an ax to grind.—Frank Vandiver (1961)

What Frank Vandiver meant when he made that statement to a group of his graduate history students at Rice University was that everyone, even professional historians, carries a load of prejudices and biases. He was correct, of course. We all have our ideas about why something happened, or what is important, and this is what we write about. Hopefully, historians know their predilections and can forewarn readers. It is best for everyone to recognize the historical filter through which a writer views the past.

Although I lived for short periods in various parts of the city of Galveston and "down the island" at Jamaica Beach during the twelve years of research for this study, I could never be considered an insider. I am neither a BOI (Born on the Island), nor an IBC (Islander by Choice). Galvestonians tend to judge people on that basis. Worse, I grew up in Houston, the great rival and bête noire of Galveston history. My early memories, fragmented and distorted, include a ride to the beach over the unfinished Gulf Freeway in a 1946 Ford with my brother at the wheel and the windows rolled all the way down to circulate the oven-heat of the Texas summer. The white dust from the oyster shell foundation rose in a huge cloud behind us and drifted onto the low trees along the right-of-way. They remained white until the next rainfall.

There are also recollections of illegal beer gulped with youthful bravado; a Boy Scout troop sleeping on the sand, forgetting about the consequences of high tide; and a happy fire and warm date in the moonlight of West Beach. Sometime around my sophomore year at Lamar High School in Houston I began to suspect there was something else going on in Galveston. When the name of the island came up in conversation, adults raised their eyebrows and spoke with innuendoes, while my peers used crude jokes and leers.

Later, Galveston became interesting for academic reasons. While teaching at the University of Houston and working on *Houston, the Bayou City,* I visited the Rosenberg Library in search of materials. The new wing had not been built and I looked through yellowed business records in a close, dark-paneled room. Toward the end of my work there the assistant archivist, Bob Dalehite, said, "Come with me, I want to show you something," and led the way to the attic. It was filled with dusty cardboard boxes of unsorted letters, journals, and records scattered amidst old cannonballs and other artifacts of Galveston history. It was a treasure trove of items about the most important city of Texas during the nineteenth century. I was impressed, and for over a decade I pursued the history of the Island City whenever I could.

I teach, among other subjects, the history of technology. Some scholars have long known about the importance of technology in human life. The journal *Technology and Culture,* for example, goes back to 1959, and there have been many books published on the subject. Only recently, however, have historians begun the exploration of technology and the city.[1] Although no historian has yet advanced a thoroughgoing technological interpretation of history, there is power in the suggestion that technology is the dynamic element in human development. Anthropologists have long assumed this, and so did Walter Prescott Webb in his study of western America, *The Great Plains.* When motivated people use the resources of their environment with their knowledge of how to do things, change occurs. Change is history, and technology is an important dynamic element.

Such a theoretical approach to history demands a discussion of the environment—geography and natural resources—in order to explain how people interacted with the land to form a city. It is also necessary to know about the individuals who came to the site, their motivation, and the technological baggage which came with them. The history involves what historian Roy Lubove called "the process of city building over time."[2] It is important to know why some cities grow, as in the case of Houston; why some die, as in the case of Indianola; and why some stagnate, as in the case of Galveston.

There is something special, in addition, in regard to Galveston which has to do with the character of the city. "Character" is difficult to define, but it involves how people feel about a place. Analysis is not subject to social scientific techniques, although Kevin Lynch came close in *The Image of the City*. People dislike or like places because of their experiences. These vary with individuals, and so "character" falls into the humanist realm. The feeling is emotional. Galveston is unlike any other Texas city and visitors immediately sense it, but the dissimilarity is hard to define for the satisfaction of all people.

This history of Galveston, therefore, is a narration about the development of the city. There is a bias toward technological events, but there is also an attempt to explain how people working in the Gulf Coast environment gave Galveston its distinct character. Fortunately, there is a lot of information about the Island City. The *Galveston Daily News* has the longest run of any newspaper in the state, and it is a prime source—like a daily diary. It has its prejudices, of course. The paper, for instance, did not print pictures of black student graduates until 1962, although it had featured white students since 1907.[3] The minutes of the city government still exist, and the archivists at the Rosenberg Library moved the dusty boxes from the attic. They successfully built the best urban archives in Texas.

Over the years, moreover, there have appeared some fine books about the city. Among the best are Howard Barnstone, *The Galveston That Was*; Charles W. Hays, *Galveston*; Margaret Swett Henson, *Samuel May Williams*; Earl Wesley Fornell, *The Galveston Era*; Bradley Robert Rice, *Progressive Cities*; John Edward Weems, *A Weekend in September*; and Kenneth W. Wheeler, *To Wear a City's Crown*. There are other individuals who have contributed to the knowledge of Galveston history through articles, speeches, bibliographies, and oral history work. These include Paul Burka, Bob Dalehite, Maury Darst, Virginia Eisenhour, Robert L. Jones, and Robert A. Nesbitt. I have benefited from their efforts and interest in Galveston.

Some people have aided me directly with my research, guided me around pitfalls, and pointed the way. A special note of appreciation, therefore, should go to: Jane Kenamore, the archivist of the Rosenberg Library; Colleen T. Kain, the executive assistant of the Texas State Historical Association; and two anonymous critics who evaluated the manuscript for the University of Texas Press. They appropriately pointed out errors and suggested improvements. One of the points raised concerned the use of dialect in quotations. Various sources of information, such as letters, newspapers, and books, reported conversations in what would be now considered a patronizing manner. As a historian I should recount the past as accurately as possible, but what should I do about dialect? On the one hand, the reported conversation may be insulting. On the other hand, that was the way the information was recorded, and people do, after all, speak with dialects and colloquialisms, sure enough. So, throughout the book, I report the conversations, misspellings, and local dialects as written in the original sources. These include references to uneducated whites, pirates, blacks, Germans, children, and others of undefined origin. The statements of the elite, regardless of ethnic group, are treated the same way. This is the "stuff" of history, and I am hesitant to tamper with it. It is a reflection of the times, and should be treated with respect while recognizing the possible patronizing attitude with which it was recorded. I will trust the maturity of the reader to recognize my use of quotations, and also the possibility of inadvertent factual error. Such faults are not intended and rest on the shoulders of the author.

THE EDGE OF TIME

Chapter One

When one tugs at a single thing in nature, he finds it attached to the rest of the world.—John Muir, cited by John L. Tveten in *Coastal Texas*

Galveston! The name resonates in the chords of imagination. There are others in our language: Virginia City, Jackson Hole, Aspen, Las Vegas, Key West, Dodge City, St. Augustine, Taos, Santa Fe. These are places we have heard about; places that are lodged in vague memory; places we will visit when we have the time. Because of their link with the past they all possess a romantic magnet. We are drawn to them by curiosity. So it is with Galveston. It is a name of imagery which summons four centuries of adventure, hope, tragedy, sin, and death.

The Indian name for the island of Galveston was "Auia," but in the sixteenth century the first Spaniards called it "Malhado," the isle of doom.[1] Sailing under the French flag, Bénard de La Harpe entered Galveston Bay in 1721, and attempted to establish a fort and trading post. The hostility of the local Indians prevented the success of his mission, but he included a map of the bay area in his account of the expedition. This is the earliest known map of Galveston Bay and its configurations are clearly revealed, even though La Harpe left Galveston Island unnamed and called the bay "Port François." In 1785 José de Evia charted the Texas coast at the command of Count Bernardo de Gálvez, the viceroy of Mexico and the former Spanish governor of Louisiana. A tracing of his map at the Barker Texas History Center at the University of Texas at Austin shows the island labeled "Isla de San Luis" with the eastern tip called "Pt. de Culebras" (Snake Point). The bay to the north is labeled "Bd. de Galvestown." A copy of the Evia map, printed in 1799, at the Rosenberg Library of Galveston, leaves Galveston Island unlabeled, notes Snake Point as "Pd. [*sic*] de Culebras," and calls the area "Bahia de Galveztowm" [*sic*].[2]

Alexander von Humboldt in 1804 repeated the designations of "I. de S. Luis," and "Pte de Culebras" for the island, and called the bay "Bahia de Galveston." Stephen F. Austin also used this modern spelling of the name in his 1822 map of the coastline. He labeled the island "San Luis," noted the Bolivar Peninsula, which was named for the great South American liberator, and drew a series of small houses on the eastern end of the island as "Galveston." The David H. Burr map, "Texas," in 1833 changed the name of the island to "Galveston Island," and included Pelican Island.[3] The Galveston City Company which established the city in 1838 used the name "Galveston" and thus firmly anchored the name in time.[4]

The island is located on the northwest coast of the Gulf of Mexico, fifty miles southeast of Houston, Texas. It is 345 miles west of the Mississippi River and 280 miles from the Rio Grande, at 29°18'17" latitude and 94°46'30" longitude. It varies in width from one and one-half miles to three miles, and is twenty-seven miles long.[5] Lying parallel to the coast two miles away, Galveston stands as a guardian protecting the land and the bay from the Gulf. The long straight edge facing the sea, which was cut by several short bayous in early days, offers a smooth, sandy beach, while the side facing the mainland is serrated into salt marshes and tidal flats except where altered by humans.

To a geologist Galveston is a sand barrier island. Such islands line and protect the Texas coast. Sand and silt carried by currents from as far away as the Mississippi River move parallel to the shore. As waves reach shallow water and form breakers, they lose their capacity to carry a load. They dump the sand, and eventually an island forms. Sea level changes and catastrophic events, like hurricanes, also play a role. Storms pick up shells and rocks from as deep as eighty feet and deposit them on land. They submerge mud flats with new layers and rearrange shore lines. The 1900 hurricane, for instance, pushed the beach back several hundred feet. The northeast tip of the island has moved westward, and there is evidence from the exposed clay deposits on the Gulf side that the island is moving closer to land.

Pelican Island, the small isle to the north of Galveston, was a narrow marsh with only a hundred feet of dry soil in 1816. Pelican Spit, now a part of Pelican Island, was a tidal marsh and shoal as late as 1841. The spit and the island were silt catchers, and prime roosting grounds for seabirds. They gradually enlarged, joined, and emerged above the sea in the nineteenth century.[6]

Galveston Island essentially consists of gray, brownish-gray, and pale yellow fine sand to a depth of many feet. While drilling for water

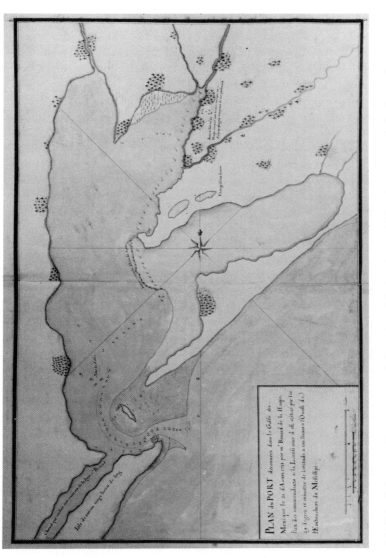

MAP 1. Galveston Bay. Map made by Bénard de La Harpe, 1721. Courtesy of the Rosenberg Library, Galveston, Texas.

in 1891, the workers took soil samples every 5 feet. To a depth of 1,500 feet the drill went through various layers of sand, clay, shell, sandstone, and shell conglomerates. From as deep as 900 feet the drill brought up fragments of wood. There was no underlying bedrock; it was truly an island of sand.[7] The water table lies within 4 feet of the surface and is brackish. Salt permeates the soil, and to the surprise of the new householders of the Lindale subdivision of the 1950's, their underground water pipes corroded to dust and had to be replaced.[8] Galvestonians, thus, have to import both water and topsoil.

The side of the island toward Galveston Bay consists of mud flats except where "improved" by human beings. Between Galveston and nearby Pelican Island is the Galveston channel, which was scooped out by a bay current. It formed a natural harbor for the sailing vessels and small steamers of the nineteenth century. It attracted early exploitation and was the major geographical feature which made the place desirable. An inner sandbar formed across the channel near its exit into the bay on the northeast end after 1843, and an outer bar, always there, obstructed the entrance from the Gulf into Galveston Bay. The outer bar stretched in horseshoe configuration with the arch pointed toward the sea for four miles between the eastern tip of Galveston Island and Bolivar Peninsula.[9] Still, this was the best natural port between New Orleans and Vera Cruz. "Galveston will be the sea Port sir, for this province," wrote a Texas pioneer in 1822, "water plenty, good Harbour, also an ancorage are exceled by non . . ."[10]

Extending to the north for thirty miles lies Galveston Bay. It is irregular in shape, about seventeen miles wide and generally seven to eight feet deep. It is the drainage basin for numerous small creeks and rivers. Dickinson Bayou, Clear Creek, and Buffalo Bayou are on the west; the San Jacinto River, Cedar Bayou, and the Trinity River are on the north. A large portion of the northeast quadrant is taken as the estuary of the Trinity River and forms Trinity Bay. South of that is East Bay, which Bolivar Peninsula separates from the sea. In the southwest quadrant is West Bay, which is formed by the two-mile expanse of water between Galveston Island and the mainland of Galveston County. Several small streams, including Halls Bayou and Highland Bayou, feed this portion. The gap between Galveston Island and Bolivar represents the main entryway into the bay, although there is an exit on the west end of Galveston Island called San Luis Pass. There was once an attempt to set up a rival town at that point, but the water was too shallow. The pass serves mainly as a tidal funnel for West Bay.

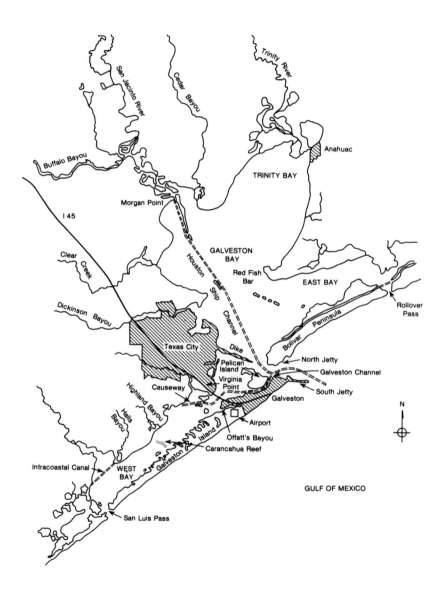

MAP 2. The Galveston Bay Area

The geological formation is relatively recent. The Gulf of Mexico appeared in the middle Mesozoic Era, about 180 million years ago. The sea advanced and retreated over the region at least nine times and left sedimentary deposits. The vast layers of sand and gravel put down at this time and later in the Cenozoic Era provided the basis for the artesian water and oil resources used in the twentieth century. Around Houston the deposits are twenty thousand feet thick. The youngest stratum is near the coast, and in the spoilage from the dredges at the Texas City dike are found the fossilized teeth and bones of ancient camels and horses. Throughout the area huge plugs of rock salt have punched through the sedimentary strata from salt beds far below. The bent edges of the rock layers caused folds and faults which trapped natural gas and petroleum. The domes also gave sulphur, salt, and gypsum.[11] What happened over 100 million years ago provided an environment of natural resources—salt, oil, gas, sulphur, water, rivers, and harbors—which combined in the twentieth century with the technology and ambition of human beings to establish a petrochemical industry that dominates the economic life of the region.

The land of the Gulf coastal plain slopes gently about two feet every mile. It is only forty feet above sea level in northwest Galveston County. The gradual descent continues into the water and then drops somewhat more rapidly to the edge of the continental shelf six miles from shore.[12] The soil on the mainland of Galveston County does not drain well. There are heavy clay subsoils which remain saturated with moisture for long periods. Portions, moreover, have high salt content, and the native vegetation is coarse grass and herbaceous plants. As a result, farming has never been particularly successful. Even as late as 1930, only 17 percent of the land was used for farming.[13]

An example of the difficulty with the land occurred in 1940–1941 when the federal government built an Army base near Highland Bayou. Camp Wallace had the advantages of proximity to the established base of Fort Crockett at Galveston, an urban water supply, and access to electricity. It possessed 1,600 acres, 161 barracks, a payroll of $150,000 per week, almost four hundred buildings, and a capacity for twelve thousand men. The disadvantages were weather and soil conditions which translated into drainage and flood-control problems. During construction the site flooded three feet deep after a nine-inch rainfall in November 1940. Roads washed away and the only way to move was with horses. There was brief consideration of a shift to higher ground, but the engineers persisted because of high land prices elsewhere. They emphasized the construction of ditches and the building of a railroad. Rail lines, historically, were the way to beat the mud of the area.

The engineers used draglines to dig ditches around the site and laid down three layers of planks to build a road. In December a six-inch rain flooded the site again. Draglines bogged in the mud and the plank road floated away. Soldiers worked knee deep at "Lake Wallace" to unload lumber from a spur track and to watch the material to be certain it did not drift away. The soldiers had to widen the bayou and place ditches throughout the campsite. Eventually they built shell roads with materials dredged from Galveston Bay. Even then roads had to be maintained by hand to remove the large clumps of waxy clay mud that dropped off the tires of trucks. Success came in May 1941, when a six-inch rain left only mud and no flooding.

Late in 1943 the Army left the site. The Navy took it over for a year as a boot camp, but after the war gave it up entirely. The government eventually divided it among Galveston County, the University of Houston, and the Hitchcock School District.[14] The story of Camp Wallace underscores the problems of land use in the coastal area. This environmental limitation also explains part of the success of Houston in the nineteenth century. In contrast to Galveston, Houston possessed a hinterland which produced cotton and other agricultural products. The surrounding land provided an agricultural base for a growing city. True, there was mud to overcome, but Houston merchants solved that with the widespread use of railroads.[15] Galveston lacked nearby farmland and had to span two miles of water and a county before reaching productive soil like that which encircled Houston.

The mud flats and salt marshes which rimmed the bay and the northern part of Galveston Island, nonetheless, are extraordinary. An acre of marsh produces ten times more protein than an acre of farmland. Cordgrass, sedges, and rushes with their roots in brackish water shelter, for example, frogs, spiders, snakes, bees, butterflies, herons, bitterns, blackbirds, mice, and ducks. Ninety percent of the coastal fish and shellfish depend upon the estuaries.[16] The marsh is intensely alive. A Rice University report on the wetlands of East Bay states:

> The plants, predominantly grasses, that flourish in this environment serve two biological functions: productivity and protection. From the amount of reduced carbon fixed by these plants during photosynthesis, this ecotone must be considered one of the most productive areas in the world and truly the pantry of the oceans. The dense stand of grass also represents a jungle of roots, stems, and leaves in which the organisms of

the marsh, the "peelers," larvae, fry, "bobs," and fingerlings seek refuge from predators. Organisms invade from both fronts, fresh and saline. Insects, spiders, birds, and mammals from the landward face. Crabs, clams, oysters, shrimp, and fish from the marine environment. The energy of the sun is trapped in the process of photosynthesis. Herbivors, the primary consumers devour these plants, and they in turn are eaten by other predators in the food chain.[17]

Alligators are common in the mainland marshes and show up once in a while on the island. In 1875 citizens observed a four-foot alligator comfortably walking along the street near Postoffice and 25th. In 1877 a seven-foot reptile was caught near the wharves, and in 1948 workers near John Sealy Hospital found a ten-foot beast in a drainpipe. In 1958 fishermen roped a 275-pound one in shallow water near the jetty on East Beach and towed it ashore. In East Bay in 1961 after Hurricane Carla men shot a twelve-foot, 400-pound alligator which had probably been dislodged by the storm.[18]

Much more common to Galveston and of greater danger are the rattlesnakes. The Indians feared them and avoided permanent settlement in part because of them. The early maps designate the eastern tip as the "Point of the Snakes." Every year, even now, doctors at the University of Texas Medical Branch treat twenty to thirty people for snakebite. These reptiles stay mainly in the marshes and the sand dunes of the west end, but sometimes show up in town. In 1964, for example, Willie Burns, the police chief at the time, was resting at home while his wife was working in the garden. He heard her scream, "Willie, it's a rattlesnake! Don't move! Call the police!" There was a five-foot rattler on the sidewalk. "Call the police?" he asked. "Why should I call the police? I am the chief of police." With that pronouncement, he killed the snake with a rake.[19]

There is food for humans in the flats, too, if they care to gather it. Green cattails can be eaten like corn on the cob and the roots crushed for flour. Quahog oysters and scallops can be harvested along with crabs and flounders.[20] More interesting, perhaps, are the ducks—especially to a hunter. As Joel Kirkpatrick, a journalist, explained:

> Well, every morning during the duck and goose hunting season, the sun brings the daylight, and sometimes it smears a salmon-colored sunrise along the horizon.
>   The wind frosts over the ponds with ripples and leaves its footprints on the marshgrass, and hunters crouch in blinds and look and listen for wildfowl, and breathe the fecund air of marshlands.

And finally, ducks come, wings whistling and cupped feet lowered, in to the decoys, and they're too beautiful to shoot—almost.[21]

Bolivar and the area of High Island and East Bay have long been prime hunting and poaching areas—Pelican Island, too, in the nineteenth century. The first seizure for illegal hunting came in 1912,[22] and the hunters, like the fishermen, liked to tell their tall tales. A hunter named Little John was bragging in a High Island cafe, "Why, with one shot I killed twenty-five ducks."

A stranger got up from a table, walked over, looked Little John in the eye, and asked, "Do you know who I am?"

"No."

"Well, I'm the new game warden, and what you did is illegal."

Little John paused and then said, "You know who I am?"

"No," the warden replied.

"I'm the biggest liar at High Island."[23]

Then there is the story of a hunter who flagged down the manager of a game preserve during the season and said, "I've shot some geese I can't identify. Can you help?"

"Sure," replied the manager as the hunter opened his trunk. He looked in at a pair of white birds and laughed, "Why man, you've shot seagulls."

The huntsman turned red and angrily retorted, "You can't fool me. These are geese! I'm a doctor from Galveston and I ought to know what seagulls look like!" He slammed the trunk and left. The manager could only wonder what the seagulls tasted like at the doctor's table.[24]

Other people come to watch Galveston's birds rather than shoot them. Some two thousand ornithologists visit each year, since the island is on a migratory flyway. At Galveston Island State Park, a two-thousand-acre preserve which includes wetlands, salt meadows, beach, dunes, and coastal prairie, the migratory birds include cuckoos, thrushes, orioles, warblers, tanagers, buntings, and grosbeaks. In 1962 an "extinct" Eskimo curlew was spotted and photographed. Permanent residents include the mockingbird, great blue heron, snowy egret, white ibis, mottled duck, bobwhite, mourning dove, red-bellied woodpecker, starling, red-winged blackbird, house sparrow, seaside sparrow, marsh wren, meadowlark, and horned lark, as well as the usual coastal birds such as sandpipers, gulls, plovers, rails, terns, and pelicans.[25]

The white pelican, a fresh-water migratory bird which winters in Galveston, has not had the trouble of the brown pelican, which lives there on a year-round basis. The browns were plentiful as late as 1955, when flocks of fifty to sixty at a time could be seen floating on the water. They proved to be extremely sensitive to the DDT they absorbed from the fish they ate. The eggshells of the young became thin and cracked, and after 1960 the brown pelican population went into a severe decline. The bird became an endangered species, and pelicans from Florida had to be brought to Galveston to reestablish the colony.[26]

Much more hardy are the seagulls; there are fifty-three species at Galveston. They are graceful, buoyant fliers, good swimmers, and poor walkers. Most gulls are scavengers and act like beach bums. They hover and pick up morsels wherever they can—the sanitation crew of the beach. The most common is the laughing gull, noted by its dark-red legs, thirty-two-inch wingspan, and raucous laugh. It lives for eight to fifteen years. There is also the Franklin gull with black head and black wing tips; the herring gull which has a fifty-four-inch wingspan and migrates to the South for the winter; and the ring-billed gull with yellow legs, a forty-eight-inch wingspan, and a black ring on its bill. In addition, the skimmer gull, northern gull, and various terns share the beach. The terns have narrower wings, cruise the waves, dive into the water, and live off fresh fish. It is considered an ill omen when the gulls fly in high, spiraling circles over the city. It is a sign of foul weather.[27]

The birds are at the top of the food chain. They all feed in their evolved manner and at their own depth; each has a distinct place on the tree of life. The plovers, for example, rush busily about picking up worms and crustaceans with their short beaks while the sandpipers probe the sand with their slender bills. There are all sorts of predators on the beach. Each species, seemingly, eats others while providing a meal for those which prey upon it. Some feed on plankton, others on algae. The moon snail drills into the shell of mollusks with its radula until it can reach and digest the inhabitant.[28]

There are sand dollars and seashells in abundance. Among the bivalves are clams, oysters, cockles, scallops, and mussels. They burrow into sand and cling to stone. The teredo, a wood-boring clam known as shipworm, destroys unprotected wooden pilings and ships within a few years. Galveston also has spiraled snail shells such as the wentletrap, olive, tulip, and whelks. In the rocky habitat of the jetties and groins are sponges, starfish, and sea urchins.[29]

Purple Portuguese men-of-war drift onto the beach with their dangerous trailing tentacles which can inflict a chemical type of burn on the unwary. Sargassum, a free-floating weed which harbors pipefish, flatworms, hydroids, and anemones, also floats ashore. In quantity both the men-of-war and the seaweed cause a stench while the sun and air decay them.[30] Blobs of tar, some as large as baseballs, wash ashore and melt in the sun to the distress of barefoot tourists. Ships and offshore oil drilling catch the blame. Coastal Indians, however, used the tar for decoration and waterproofing, and the de Soto expedition of the sixteenth century referred to it. The material likely comes from natural asphalt seeps along the Mexican coast. Kerosene easily removes it from the bottom of the feet.[31]

On occasion, in August or September, a "red tide" appears along the shoreline. This is caused by blue-green algae which make the water look red in the sunlight. It is harmless to humans, but hurtful to fish when it cuts off oxygen in narrow channels.[32] In 1909 another curiosity turned up in the form of schools of phosphorescent fish drawn by high tides into Galveston Bay. A good pair of eyes could read a newspaper by their light at two o'clock in the morning, so it was reported.[33] Turtles also have shown up. A large green turtle weighing forty pounds and caught with a hook and line was served at Peter Liselle's restaurant in 1872. A dozen two-hundred-pound sea turtles came ashore near 41st Street in 1880 presumably to lay eggs. They were captured. A shrimp boat brought in a two-thousand-pound leatherback turtle from the north jetty area in 1951. It managed to knock over a dock worker with a flipper before meeting its fate of steak and soup. In 1978 the National Marine Fisheries Service established a laboratory at Galveston to raise Ridley turtles to one year of age in order to give them a head start in life. They are an endangered species, and the scientists hoped to establish them on Padre Island. One of the tagged specimens turned up on a beach in France after 569 days.[34]

People have shown greater curiosity about the whales which become stranded every now and then. According to stories, three whales blew ashore in the storm of 1810, and a sixty-two-foot sperm whale in the storm of 1818. The latter killed a seventeen-year-old Portuguese sailor with a swat of its tail. There was also memory of a fifty-foot whale that washed up on the west end in 1848 and was melted down for oil. A whale discovered in the Galveston channel near Bolivar in 1875 brought a scramble for possession in which everyone lost except the catfish, which ate it. In 1916 two black men captured a sixty-foot Atlantic right whale with broken bones east of the south jetty. There had been a hurricane south of Corpus Christi, and supposedly it came from that area. The men towed it to a dock, covered it with canvas, and charged ten cents for the curious to view it. They later towed it back to the jetties for dissection. In 1951 sightseers paid twenty-five cents per adult and ten cents for a child to see a seventeen-foot finback whale on the beach at Bolivar. The specimen finally decomposed after 3,500 people saw it, and the exhibitors gave the money to a polio charity drive. Although there once was discussion in the early twentieth century about starting a whaling industry, nothing happened. There were just not enough whales in the Gulf of Mexico to support the enterprise.[35]

Away from the hard-packed surface of the shoreline, at the upper reaches of the beach, dunes form from dry, blowing sand. The dunes move and shift with the winds until covered with vegetation. Salty air dehydrates and stunts. Plants must have tough, wiry stems and thick leaves in this essentially desert habitat. Sea oats boldly thrust into the air, but most flora hug the ground like the beach morning glory. There are dove weeds, goatweeds, sunflowers, and all sorts of grasses. They stabilize the dunes and form a natural breakwater during storms. Left alone, the dunes grow naturally and acquire a covering of plants. At one time, before the residents of the city took the sand for filling purposes, Galveston dunes reached fifteen feet high. Nothing like that exists at present. Now, as then, however, the dunes provide a home for beetles, grasshoppers, katydids, lizards, ghost crabs, gophers, mice, rabbits, birds, and diamondback rattlers.[36]

Mosquitoes have always been around Galveston to annoy human beings. Even with current fogging techniques, an early morning jog across a grassy area will prove their hardiness. When the wind stops, the mosquitoes close in. Two boys who worked the cotton presses in 1875, for instance, took their girl friends for an early evening sail near Pelican Island. The wind dropped and they drifted ashore. They tried to sing songs, but insects "as big as sparrows" attacked, and they discovered that "love and musquitos will not harmonize." The boys prepared to swim for help, but the girls had a better idea of using the planks from the boat as paddles. After a forty-five-minute effort they reached the wharf well-bitten, but safe.[37]

Oscar M. Addison wrote to his mother in 1845:

> You may think you have some fleas "to hum," but were you to pass a few nights in this City, the conclusion would force itself upon your mind that there is none in comparison to what we have here, for sometime after I arrived here, sleep was almost impossible, and it is only by use that I have become accustomed to their disagreeable company. But Musquitoes and fleas united form a desperate anoyance and the poor fellow who has to sleep without a bar is in a "bad fix" and is really deserving of sympathy.[38]

In addition to all of these natural phenomena, there is something else that makes Galveston different. This can be seen, and felt, and heard at the beach. From two hundred yards away as you face the sea, you hear a steady whiffle of wind which usually blows at a rate ideal for kite flying. From one hundred yards you hear not only the wind, but also a steady, low, roar from the Gulf. Closer, at twenty-five yards, the sound becomes more complex. You can hear individual waves as they run with a shhhhh sound to the shore and then break with a ka-shhhh on the sand. They arrive in a rough cadence, one about every six seconds.

At Galveston the easy slope of the continental shelf and the small tides, which rarely rise over two feet, do not produce crashing surf. For the most part the waves are gentle, and somewhat inconsistent because of the variance of the wind. As a wave nears the shore the friction of the bottom causes the lower part of the wave to slow and the top portion to fall forward and break. The breaker then rushes foaming to the beach until its energy dissipates and the water slides back into the sea with a never-ending pulse.[39]

Even on the winter beach, when the wind comes from the north rather than from the usual southeast direction, the sonance of the waves continues. "The waves sounded on the beach with crisp and icy splashes," wrote a reporter in 1876, "and over the broad open area of sand from east to west, as far as the eye could reach, the north wind whistled with relentless viciousness, defying the glare of open-faced sol." Of the elemental sounds of nature, as Henry Beston once noticed about Cape Cod, the sounds of the ocean on the shore are the most varied.[40] There are roars, hisses, splashes, whispers, and hollow tumblings which change in accent and tempo. The sound can be soothing, slow, and lulling. In times of storm it can resound like a cannonade as the ancient war between land and sea reopens. To the listener it is a reminder that we, as human beings, long ago cast our destiny with the land. The voice of the storm king thundering on the beach raises a prehuman terror because we know that the sea has not forgiven our infidelity.

The beach invades our other senses as well. It is not just sound, but also sight, and smell, and feel. The air is heavy with salt and moisture. It coats the skin and films over glass surfaces. The air is highly corrosive, a solvent which attacks the technology of human-ity. Galveston always looks in need of a can of paint, and the people buy used cars to reduce the high cost of rust. The odor is salty, and sometimes fishy as well. If the sun is out and it is warm, the com-bination of air, smell, and feel is highly sensual. What is seen, too, is different. The haze produces pastel colors—lavender sunsets and misty, orange sunrises over the shore. The softness is addictive.

On the beach there is a strong, almost primordial urge to sit naked in the surfline and allow the warm water and sun to wash away the worries of life. It promises renewal. Here on the beach you stand at the edge of the world. Here is the border of the two primary divisions of earth and water. Here you can feel the heartbeat of the planet. Here the voice of creation can still be heard. Galveston Island is one of the youngest of nature's land children. It is still in formation. It stands on the edge of time, and time is new.

The edge of the sea and land is a gateway of evolution. Once the transition is accomplished, however, it is dangerous to linger. The edge is treacherous as well as nurturing. It is unstable and subject to more natural violence than older places. In shallow waters the salinity and temperature ranges are greater than elsewhere, and shoreline creatures must adapt to the constant smash and wet immersion. Such inhabitants develop hard shells and claws in order to hang on to their environment. Human beings, also, have found life on the edge difficult. The natural death toll by disease and storm has made Galveston in its short history one of the dramatic killing grounds of the Western Hemisphere. The four horsemen of the Apocalypse— fire, famine, war, and death—have thundered across the island and left their hoofprints in the sand.

Although the surrounding coastal land is comparatively unproductive, the bay and the sea provide a bountiful harvest. Fresh water from rivers and bayous reduces the salinity of the bay, supports marshlands, and provides nutriments for infant oysters and shrimp. Oysters prefer clean, shallow, diluted seawater, and in early days they flourished in the many bays along the Texas coast. Across Galveston Bay, cutting it in half, was a great oystershell reef called Red Fish Bar. It was a hazard to navigation, but a tribute to long centuries of industrious oysters. There were other oyster beds in the bay and along the lee shore of Galveston Island. Shell ridges once cut across the eastern end and midway down the island. Indians, thinking that the shell would keep the rattlesnakes away, preferred to camp on the ridge.[41]

In the nineteenth century the city developed a seasonal oyster industry which in 1885 employed five hundred men and shipped oysters throughout the Southwest. Reduced in size, the business continues to the present. It is hard, dirty work. Oyster gatherers use a broad, four-foot rake to scoop across a reef. With a winch it is raised to the boat and dumped upon a culling table. "Irons" which look like meat cleavers are used to sort out the shell, crabs, beer cans, and oysters less than three inches. These are thrown overboard, and the small oysters are allowed to grow to legal size. Dredging in the area has greatly reduced the extent of the oyster beds. Mud-shell became a useful substitute where gravel was scarce, and from 1880 it was used for paving streets, providing ballast for highways and railroads, producing lime, and improving chicken feed. Led by W. D. Haden and his successors, the shell industry removed 214,000,000 cubic yards from Texas shores during the half-century from 1912 to 1962.[42]

Brown and white shrimp also find existence in the shallow water. They spawn offshore; the babies hatch and migrate to the inlets and salt marshes. In two to three months they mature and return to the sea to start the cycle over again. Too much fresh water, too much salt, or too much pollution will diminish the numbers. At first shrimp fishers used seines, but after 1912 they adopted trawls, copied from those utilized by scientists working along the coast of North Carolina. The idea spread from Florida, where the first shrimp trawl was used, along the Gulf Coast. In 1955 shrimpers from Rockport, Texas, began using powerful two-rig trawls which increased the catch by one-third. On one- to five-day voyages the boats prowl the coastline and bays. Workers use a small "try" net to locate their prey and then deploy the large nets which are pulled along the bottom to capture the shrimp. The nets are opened on the deck of the boat and the trash separated. The shrimp are iced and brought to port for sale. During the late 1940's the catch of white shrimp from the bays declined. It was then that the shrimp boats began to venture into the Gulf in pursuit of brown shrimp, which now compose about 80 percent of the annual catch.[43]

The variety of sea life is enormous and has contributed not only to the dining tables of humans, but also to their entertainment and sport. The types of fish are like those of the South Atlantic Coast, and the markets in Galveston are similar to those of Charleston and Norfolk.[44] Flounder, redfish, Spanish mackerel, red snapper, sheepshead, croakers, and speckled trout are all-time favorites, while the silver king tarpon is the most exciting. Dave Huddleston holds the record with a 192-pound, seven-foot, four-inch silver king taken from the Galveston Ship Channel. Most weigh 125–150 pounds. All have a silvery appearance and the spectacular ability to leap five to six feet from the water when attempting to throw loose a hook. Silver kings have been characterized as having the "agility of the mountain trout, wisdom of the serpent, courage of the tiger, and the weight of a full-grown man."[45] No wonder they are a thrill to catch.

The best tarpon fishing occurred from 1938 until 1965, when it was possible to hook them from the piers and jetties. Even then you had to be patient; there were only one or two strikes per day. People blamed the decline in the 1960's on pollution and the dynamiting of fish for fertilizer on the Mexican coast. The blasting has stopped and it is hoped that the fish are recovering.[46]

Spanish mackerel, plentiful around the rock jetties, are among the more beautiful and graceful of game fish. They have burnished sides, silver flecked with gold, and are about two feet long with a row of dense spines. Also numerous around submerged structures are sheepshead. They are scrappy fighters and good eating, but they are hard to clean and have jaws and teeth which can cut through wire.[47] In 1887 "old darkies" were observed "crack fishing" through the planks on the New Wharf for such fish at the harbor. The men would lie on their stomachs and hold the line in their teeth. When one got a nibble he jerked his head and grabbed the line. Strangely enough, the technique was successful.[48]

Redfish runs in the surf after storms, especially in the early fall, are sensational. Redfish are bottom feeders and like rough, sandy water. It helps to be there at the right time, because the conditions do not last long. In 1967 people hauled in reds from the Flagship pier, some twenty-five feet above the water. The fish weighed up to forty pounds and there were broken lines with lost fish in the process. After Hurricane Cindy in 1964 about three thousand redfish were caught in Galveston waters.[49]

Then there are some oddballs caught every now and then. In 1887 a fisherman told of being towed two miles by a "granduquois." It was six feet long, resembled an alligator gar, and finally broke the line. The same man also pulled one into his rowboat. It flopped around, knocked him and his tackle over the side, tipped the boat over, and escaped. Jewfish, or junefish as they are sometimes called, also appear. They weigh as much as 700 pounds; measure six feet in length; are rough-scaled, sluggish, and dark green in color; and make a good ingredient for chowder. Sawfish sometimes surprise people. In 1962 two boys fishing near the concrete ship, a half-submerged vessel at the edge of the harbor, threw a fifteen-pound anchor overboard and hooked a ten-foot sawfish. The fish tore free as they tried to tow it to shore, but it left saw marks on the side of the boat. A seventeen-foot sawfish was caught from Kuhn's Wharf in 1860 by boys fishing for jewfish. Its bill was almost six feet long, and it took several rifle shots to kill it. Another one, twenty feet overall, was caught by hand in the surf in 1885 and hauled onto the sand. More recently, a shrimp fisherman caught a seventeen-and-a-half-foot sawfish weighing around 2,400 pounds in his net near Texas City.[50]

Devilfish, or rays, have shown up in the surf around the bathhouse piers. One captured in 1885 and brought up to the beach measured sixteen feet and had a mouth large enough for a flour barrel. Another, captured in 1910 with harpoons, rifle fire, and a forty-pound anchor used as a hook, was fourteen feet wide and weighed 2,000 pounds.[51] There have also been eels, sea horses, and porpoises, but those attracting the greatest and most persistent fascination have been the sharks.

There have always been a lot of sharks around Galveston. In 1856 a ten-and-a-half-foot shark with a mouth large enough to swallow a small boy was caught at the wharves. In 1868 an eight-foot one with a mouth large enough for a hamper basket was captured at the same place. Fishing for jewfish in 1873, John Benson hooked a twelve-foot shark that began towing him and his small boat to sea. The pilot boat came to his rescue, and the fish towed them both until killed with a harpoon. A ten-and-a-half-foot shark caught from the wharves in 1877 had a dog collar with rope attached in its stomach. From the wharves in 1890 fishermen caught a twelve-foot shark. "Black Tom," a twenty-one-foot shark with a black dorsal fin, lived for a while in the Galveston channel in the 1930's. People shot the fin and left it with white pock marks. Once, a band of twenty blacks on the dock hooked him. The tug of war ended when the inch-and-a-half manila rope broke with a crack and snapped back over the heads of the men to the top of a cotton shed. Then in 1947 an eight-and-a-half-foot, 240-pound sand shark was brought to land from the 25th Street pier. A five-gallon can would fit in its mouth, but sand sharks are not noted for eating humans.[52]

Galvestonians have often stated that the waters around the island are safe from shark attack. That information is reassuring to swimmers, and for the most part the claims are correct. Ben C. Stuart while a lad in Galveston in the late nineteenth century used to swim nude with other boys near the wharves at 16th Street. One of their thrills was to swim into the channel behind the steamboats and "take the wash" of the paddle wheels. The boys would also dive twelve to fourteen feet to the bottom to fetch mud with which to plaster their companions. They were never bothered by sharks and had more fear of the three-hundred-pound constable who tried to catch them and who chased them home in their "airy costume."[53]

In the 1940's, beachfront businesses sponsored long-distance swimming contests on the Gulf shore to demonstrate that there was no shark menace. There was never a problem, but it is doubtful that the athletes knew how they were being used. The director of the beach patrol in 1978, Bill Scott, stated that he had never heard of a shark attacking a swimmer at Galveston. Much more dangerous in his opinion were the Portuguese men-of-war and the powerful currents around the groins. "Floaters," bodies which drift into shore, moreover, do not show shark bites even though they have been weeks in the water.[54] Galvestonians make a convincing case, but there are, nonetheless, some isolated incidents.

At the turn of the century Judge George W. Baylor, a long-time fisherman who caught sharks from the wharves, recalled a deadly attack on a man trying to wade across San Luis Pass. A sailor who had been swimming around the docks at Texas City in 1911 experienced some minor wounds when a shark took a swipe at his feet dangling in the water. The most serious case, however, occurred in 1937. A police officer found a fourteen-year-old boy, wounded, in shallow water on the beach two miles west of 61st Street. He had been swimming in four-foot-deep water when struck. His lower right arm was gone, along with the flesh of his upper right leg. No one saw a shark, but they could see tooth marks. The boy died at the hospital. One cannot be certain that it was a shark, but it probably was.[55]

Farther offshore there is more evidence. A four-hundred-pound shark hoisted tail up aboard a boat two miles south of the south jetty regurgitated a human body. It had not been long since eaten. A day later, in 1976, a fishing boat caught a tiger shark, fourteen feet long, with a human skull inside, seven miles off Galveston. The discovery surprised the skipper, and he foreswore his habit of taking a noon-time recreational swim around his boat. In 1983 a windsurfer disappeared from Galveston waters. His leg with a Nike shoe still on the foot, severed by a shark, washed into Corpus Christi. The board was found thirty miles at sea from Sabine Pass.[56] The idea that sharks at Galveston are not dangerous, as local propaganda states, is just not true. There is danger in the water. For swimmers it is unlikely to come from a shark. But it can happen.

Commercial fishing, other than for oysters and shrimp, developed along with the sport fishing. There is an early story about a visit of a French admiral in 1839. While the mayor and other dignitaries visited the flagship, a fishing boat came alongside and sold a cargo of red snapper. The fish had been caught off some banks, but, unfortunately, the men neglected to note the location. It remained lost until 1868, when Captain "Dave" McCluskey discovered red snapper at the Campeche Banks of Mexico. In the same year Galveston fishermen began to catch snappers about forty miles out from Galveston.[57]

By the time of the First World War Galveston possessed a fishing fleet that regularly coursed the Campeche Banks. Small-scale fishing, meanwhile, kept Galveston markets well supplied with a variety of fish. Most often the fishers sold to a merchant, but others marketed in their own way. In 1875 a black fisherman brought to shore a 140-pound jewfish, still in the water, towed behind his boat. As he dickered with buyers on shore about the price, a twelve-foot shark came by and took all but the head. Everyone laughed except the fisherman, who turned to the last bidder and said, "I b'lieve you knowed dat shark was dere all de time."[58]

Fishing and fishermen always create exaggerated stories. Journalist Christie Mitchell recorded one in 1961. Two old fishermen were discussing their exploits. One claimed that he caught a six-foot, eighty-pound trout in front of the Galveston jetties. That had to be the biggest sea trout in the world, his companion noted, but he also had something to brag about. The second man claimed that while fishing near the concrete ship he pulled up a lantern just like the one his grandfather used a hundred years ago. The surprising thing was that the lantern was still lit. The first man heartily protested such a lie, so the second replied, "O.K. I'll make a deal with you. You can cut four feet off that trout and I'll blow the light out of the lantern."[59]

People also relate to the weather—probably the most talked-about subject in the world. The temperature at Galveston averages 49° F. in the winter and 87° F. in the summer. Forty-two to forty-seven inches of rain fall per year, and the wind blows from the southeast except in the winter months, when it comes from the north. In summer Galveston is cooler than most of Texas which gave the island an early reputation as a place to go to escape the heat. The water temperature shifts from 67° F. in the winter to 84° F. in the summer.[60] There can be extremes and unusual conditions, but for the most part the climate is mild.

The winter sometimes brings "blue northers" of great intensity. Robert H. Hunter recorded in his diary of the 1820's about being caught near Cedar Bayou:

> I got about half way home when the norther sprung up a fresh, rained and sleeted, and my lazy horse, I could not git him a long. And I got so cold that I had no fealing. The icicles hung to my hat brim so that I could hardly see my way. I finally got home, I rode up to the gate and Pa come out to git some wood and saw me. He cald me to git down. I heard him, but I could not speak. He came to me and took me off the horse and stude me on the ground and I fell over.[61]

The "blue norther" approaches Galveston as a heavy bank of dark, purple clouds on the northern horizon. It attacks with a whirring noise, bends trees, slams shutters, and lowers the temperature by as much as 24° F. in an hour.[62] It arrives either dry or wet, but always cold. As an editor commented in 1876, "The norther has many ways of demonstrating its affection for animal objects. It can come about as near getting over, and under, and around, and inside of a thinly clad specimen of the human species as almost anything else that the material universe has yet turned out in the long list of its prodigious productions."[63]

At times Galveston Bay has frozen. Jane Long experienced such a condition during her fruitless, lonely vigil on Bolivar in 1820–1821 waiting for her husband to return. In 1886, with temperatures a few degrees above zero, the bay froze five miles out to a thickness of two-and-a-half inches. Several schooners were caught and one captain died. A twelve-hour snowfall resulted in five-foot drifts and a frolic for the city folks. Improvised sleighs with crude slats to replace wheels appeared on the streets. Beaver hats became prime targets for snowballs, and the businessmen from the Strand turned out to have fun. An Englishman who tried to run a gauntlet with his umbrella for protection lost both his umbrella and his dignity. Upon complaint, a policeman explained to him, "Why, these are our representative citizens just indulging in a bit of a lark for the fun of the thing, you know."[64]

An aged black man on a dray, after receiving a merciless pelting, leaped from the wagon with a yell, ran, and collapsed in a snowdrift. The attack stopped, and someone said, "He's dead!" A young man, Johnny Moran, approached, gently called, and stooped to look at him. At that, the old man leaped up with a laugh and said, "Possum!" Moran could only say, "Dod bum it," at being fooled, but the crowd escorted the man back to the dray and gave him a cheer.

The most lively point of activity was the corner of Tremont and Market. Through this dangerous defile came a man casually driving a large wagon, and the snowball brigade saw him coming. They gathered ammunition and pelted the unconcerned driver in the slicker until he was close-by. "Up boys, and at 'em!" he shouted, and a gang of ten men rose from the wagon to fire back at the surprised multitude. The counterattack resulted in a rout. The wagon and its surprise cargo then calmly went in search of more prey.

The police finally had to break up the fun, but not before one intrepid character tried to get down the street with his head in a barrel for protection. The attackers found his rear exposed, and the adventurer could not get his head out of the barrel. In retreat he finally stumbled into a drugstore.[65]

In 1895 the same thing happened. The bay froze and the city received a fourteen-inch snowfall. Numbed fish floated in the surf, and plumbers working on the frozen pipes became heroes. The streetcars had to have snowplows affixed, and a fight between blacks and whites which began with snow degenerated into fists and bottles. On another occasion, in 1935, thousands of cattle died during a blizzard, and in 1951 people could dip stunned fish from the bay during a cold snap. In 1962 the same situation made fishing with nets easy; the ice reached fifty feet from the bay shore. Through these times the citizens had the good sense to insure survival with the insulation provided by the "hot Scotch" and warm "Tom and Jerries" served in the Galveston bars.[66]

There were also times of excessive rain which would flood the streets. A five-hour cloudburst in 1950 brought four feet of water and $400,000 in damages. A five-inch rain in 1973 pushed water up to the steps of the new ANICO Building. In 1843 there was so much rain in the region that sailors could dip fresh water from the bay for over a month.[67] The converse—a shortage of rain—also happened. An estimated thousand head of cattle died on the island because of lack of water in 1857. Some wandered into town searching for water, died, and had to be hauled away. In 1872 and 1876 the same thing happened, and this time the cisterns ran dry. Water sold for twenty-five cents per bucket. The city had no assured water supply and depended upon rainfall.[68]

The dense fogs of winter which immobilized the ships in the harbor also gave rise to tall tales. It seems, for example, that two men drove from Houston to Galveston in a Model-T Ford to go fishing in the surf. The fog became so thick that neither could see the road, and finally the driver stopped. He stepped out, sniffed, and reached for his gear. There was salt grass around and they were still on the highway. "Aren't you going to fish?" asked the driver as he baited a hook. "Hell no," was the incredulous reply. "I ain't never fished in a place like this before. We're nowhere's near the sea. I'm liable to hook a brahma bull." The driver, nonetheless, sent the line, hook, sinker, and bait into the fog with a whir and waited. There was no splash. Shortly, however, he reeled in an eight-pound redfish. The surprised companion quickly scrambled for his equipment and the two of them caught twenty-five fish before the fog lifted. Then they could see that they were fifteen miles from the Gulf and had been fishing in a fog bank. Galveston, indeed, produces thick fog.[69]

Of even greater density than the fogs are the waterspouts that touch Galveston once in a while. These tornadoes filled with water rarely cause damage, but they leave a wet trail across the land and thousands of dancing silvery minnows in the puddles. Two small ones crossing Bolivar in 1969, however, dumped over seven house trailers and injured one person. The folklore method for dispelling a waterspout is to make the sign of a cross, or shoot it with a shotgun or cannon. Having no artillery, a captain in 1890 ordered his seamen to pound the sides of his schooner while he maneuvered to avoid a spout one hundred feet in diameter. The tactic did not work, but the waterspout finally disappeared into the clouds, carrying fish and debris with it.[70]

More serious are the actual tornadoes that sometimes strike the island. Tornadoes injured thirty-three people in 1943 and five in 1961. In June 1981 a whirlwind skipped across the city from the southeast and over Offatt's Bayou while blowing out windows and taking off roofs. In September the same year seven tornadoes struck at dusk and caused $3 million in damages. One of them lifted an 8,139-ton ship and turned it 180 degrees.[71] These small, vicious destroyers whose winds reach 500 miles per hour often accompany hurricanes.

The West Indian hurricane is the most important weather phenomenon in Galveston history. People have known about these storms and feared them since the beginning of life on the island. No one knows why they form. Perhaps it is to release the heat of the tropics, since they originate in the central Atlantic Ocean near the entrance to the Gulf of Mexico during the summer and fall. Warm, moist air rises into the upper atmosphere like smoke going up a chimney. It can carry 17 billion tons of water and produce twenty-inch rainfalls. The storm develops an eye as the air funnels upward and the winds form a wall around the center. The rotation of the earth gives the winds a counterclockwise motion. The general course of the hurricane in the Gulf is northwestward, and it gathers strength as long as it remains over the water. The U.S. Weather Service calls an area of unsettled weather a tropical disturbance, but when the storm becomes a closed low-pressure system with winds up to 39 miles per hour, it is classified as a tropical depression. Between 39 and 73 MPH it becomes a tropical storm; at 74 MPH and faster, it is a hurricane. Great storms range upward from 120 MPH and push a dome of water fifty miles wide called a storm surge. Hurricane Camille produced a tide of twenty-five feet; Carla reached twenty-two feet, resulting in Texas floods ten miles inland.

Because of the counterclockwise wind motion, the highest tides are usually east of the center, along with most of the tornadoes. Camille spawned one hundred tornadoes and Carla gave birth to twenty-six. The worst situation for Galveston City—as was the case with Alicia in 1983—occurs when the eye crosses at San Luis Pass, the extreme western end of the island. The slower the storm moves, the higher the tide. The lower the barometric pressure, the higher the tide. A five-foot surge will flood much of Galveston; a fifteen-foot tide will cover 90 percent of the island.[72]

During the nineteenth century hurricanes struck Galveston at least eleven times. There was only passing reference to a tempest in 1810, but the local Indians suffered its wrath. Joseph O. Dyer, who first visited the island in 1874 and wrote about its history, interviewed some of the early inhabitants. Colonel Warren D. C. Hall told him an old squaw referred to that early storm which drowned the Indians who had taken refuge on the shell ridge midway down the island. Dyer also reported a storm in October 1815 which disrupted the formation of a revolutionary army at Bolivar. Out of sixty-seven people, only eleven men and one woman survived. A conflicting report by Hall, however, indicated that this preliminary effort by Henry Perry failed when the main supply ship foundered in the Bolivar breakers after being lost in a fog.[73] A hurricane may have caused the trouble, but the record is unclear.

Refugees from the unsuccessful French colony on the Trinity River, Champ d'Asile, described the cyclone of 1818. Through the indulgence of Jean Laffite, who then controlled the island, the refugees set up a temporary camp. As the two-day storm surged landward the sky darkened, the wind rose with a sound like cannons, and the seabirds sought inland safety. The salt water flowed over Galveston to a depth of four feet. Only six houses endured, including that of the pirate chieftain. Laffite lost four of his ships. Three of them dragged their anchors and foundered with the loss of all on board. The fourth traversed the bay and broke up at Virginia Point. Later, artillery from this ship was found and salvaged.[74]

In 1837, while Galveston was being used as a base after the Texas Revolution, the wrath of the sea came once more. An eyewitness commented, "In the month of October, during the storm which laid waste the whole southern coast, from Mobile to Vera Cruz, and still further south, it was my lot to witness vessels of considerable tonnage floating over the foundations of the future city." The turbulence lasted three days and nights. "It appeared . . . as if the heavens were making battle with the earth." Although people floated about on boards, only one died. Eight ships ended up on dry land, and there were shattered masts and rigging everywhere.[75]

Another observer, Amasa Turner, said that only one house survived, the old Mexican customhouse which he had converted to his home. "After this," recorded Turner, "many felt discouraged and left Galveston, thinking it would always be subject to such storms, while others maintained that this one was an exception."[76] The new Texas customshouse built under the orders of the customs agent, Gail Borden, Jr., was gone. It was but two days old. Borden moved to a beached brig for the next year, but reconstruction by others began quickly with the arrival of building materials. Joseph Ehlenger, a local carpenter, suggested that Borden place the rebuilt customs-house on four-foot pilings to keep it above flood waters. The practice of placing buildings and houses on stilts thus became a Galveston style.[77]

The hurricanes by this time had given Galveston a deadly reputation. Samuel Swartwout wrote to James Morgan one month later, on November 3, 1837, "I take for granted that Galveston is done up. . . . The roads may be well enough for vessels to ride in, but the land will hereafter, be regarded as a dangerous place for a city or even a residence." Swartwout was attempting to build a rival town and in 1842 wrote to Morgan, "Clear out Red-Fish Bar, & that would in time, become the commercial Emporium, for as sure as there is a God, the whole of Galveston will be swept away within ten years."[78]

It did not happen quite according to that prediction, but in 1842 a cyclone banged the ships about the harbor, flooded the business district, and knocked the Episcopal Church off its high blocks. In 1854 another storm ravaged Matagorda, flooded the Strand, and broke a steamer in two pieces.[79] Much worse was the hurricane of 1867. It submerged and tore up all but one of the Galveston docks, inundated the business area with two to four feet of water in the lower floors, sank a steamer so completely that even the smokestack was beneath the surface, left two ships upside down on the wharves, and deposited the schooner *Julia* at the corner of the Strand and 26th Street. It drove four ships with anchors dragging and catching across the tracks of the railroad bridge and left only the pilings. The city government forgave the $240,000 debt owed by the railroad company in exchange for its rebuilding the bridge. It took over a month to get the gaslights on again, and over a year to completely restore the wharves. The Houston and Texas Central Railway began to argue at this time for a ship channel to Houston to gain safety from coastal destruction.[80]

Galveston experienced three "hurricanes" in 1871. The first two, in June, were closely spaced. On June 4 the *Galveston Daily News* reported heavy rain and minor damages. A storm had been noted in Key West and, therefore, so the newspaper thought, traveled seven hundred miles in thirty hours. The courageous rescue of fourteen sailors clinging to the rigging of the bark *Virginia Dare* as it foundered on the outer bar merited a gold watch from the citizens for Captain R. Irvine. Although the storm was designated a hurricane, the barometer dropped only to 29.51 and the wind blew only thirty-nine miles per hour.

Six days later a second storm arrived with winds over fifty miles per hour and a barometer reading of 29.58. It drove various small craft ashore and left three sloops and one schooner on 19th Street. The railroad bridge held up, but St. Patrick's Church fell down. Two men died.[81] One of the interesting features of these 1871 storms was the increased sophistication in measuring the ferocity of the tempests with wind gauges and barometers. The U.S. Weather Service was just beginning to function.

In early October the city took another weatherbeating. The barometer dropped to 29.68 and wind velocity reached sixty miles per hour. Pushed by north winds, the bay backed into the city and there was widespread small damage. During the cleanup workers found the bodies of two blacks on the beach, a sloop across the railroad track near the depot, and more damage to the railroad bridge.[82]

Except for a few high spots, water again covered the town in 1875. "The storm is now raging with terrible violence," stated a report on September 15. "The east end of the city is submerged, and the small houses in that locality are being washed away. . . . At the City Hospital the waves are breaking against the building. . . . The wharves are submerged and freight much damaged."[83] The Weather Service reported a low reading of 29.04 on the barometer. The tide was thirteen-and-a-half-feet above normal in Galveston Bay, and six people died. Among the lost were Dr. George W. Peete and his grandson. They were unable to escape from the U.S. Quarantine Station, which he directed. The waves destroyed the station, and Peete's body was found later floating in the bay in three feet of water.

On the mainland a Houston reporter saw a thirty-ton schooner lying three hundred yards from the bay. At Galveston he observed little damage to the business section, but massive destruction, "pitiable to see," on the Gulf side of the island. Some five hundred houses had been smashed, and looters threatened those who tried to stop them. The storm made deep cuts into the land at 20th, 25th, and 29th streets. The city government reacted but slowly to the emergency needs of the destitute—the mayor was out of town and the aldermen were so split over a gaslight contract that they were unable to function. Finally, after nine days the mayor appointed a committee to distribute relief funds and allowed the use of beach sand to fill in the holes.[84]

The Morgan steamer *Harlan*, meanwhile, sailed into Galveston with its flag at half-mast. It carried the news of the complete devastation of Galveston's rival, Indianola. There, water poured over and through the low-lying city for eighteen hours while the flooded prairies and lakes behind the city prevented escape for the people. Over a hundred buildings were gone, and only twelve remained. In the following days ships in the Gulf found bits of furniture, pieces of buildings, trees, and the bodies of animals. The death list amounted to 270 recovered corpses. Most of the survivors wanted to move the town, but the Morgan Line refused to change locations. Indianola struggled on, the lesson yet unlearned.[85]

At Galveston, citizens began to talk about protection from storms, and the city asked the state legislature to finance the construction of a breakwater. Representatives argued that Galveston provided one-eighth of the state's taxes, and, therefore, the state should protect Galveston just as it protected people living on the frontier. Opponents said that Galveston contributed to its own problem by taking sand from the beaches, and that it would be better if the Gulf covered up the island. The port would then be located inland and closer to the people. The bill never passed. Lamely, in 1878, the city responded to the problem and planted salt cedars along the line of the old sand dunes. It was hoped that the tough plants would form a network of roots, accumulate sand, rebuild the dunes, and form a natural breakwater to protect the city.[86]

In 1886 the storm god struck again. A small hurricane in June knocked over trees, blew off roofs, and flattened fences. There was minor flooding and damage to the wharves. It was not too bad. "The town got a pretty thorough drenching and a good shaking up, but is doing business at the old stand, as gay as a lark and as spruce as a grass widow," so judged the *Galveston Daily News*. The wind blew eighteen miles per hour at Indianola.[87]

A second storm came in August. Flooding of one to four feet brought salt water into the lower floors of Galveston's business buildings and floated away the wooden blocks used for paving. There occurred an estimated $150,000 in damages, a few deaths, and more talk about protection. At Indianola the hurricane repeated the destruction of 1875, and fire from a broken kerosene lamp added to the loss. Before this storm, both Indianola and Galveston had received warning from the weather station at Key West. At Indianola, moreover, people had learned to rely on a new system of warning flags begun shortly after the storm of 1875. The hurricane, nonetheless, destroyed the place, and the citizens, this time, decided to move. They abandoned the site, and the town died.[88]

Such a lesson should have been plain for Galveston. It was not. People demonstrated a cavalier attitude. "Yesterday's squall," wrote the editor of the *Galveston Daily News* the day after the hurricane, "frightened a good many people of Galveston at first and subsequently entertained them. A couple of feet of salt water here and there on some of the principal streets was a curiosity."[89] A letter to the editor argued that Galveston could never suffer like Indianola because it only happened where the storm surge hit a solid object like the mainland. The bay would absorb the shock for Galveston.[90] Although there was some discussion in 1886–1887 about building a seawall, nothing was accomplished.[91]

Worse yet, Matthew F. Maury, a national authority, famous for navigational observations, stated that Galveston was exempt from the force of destructive hurricanes. It was located in a "cove of safety," protected by shallow water and sandbars running parallel to the shore. Inhabitants need not be apprehensive, he said, because the storm waves could never reach the shore in full force. One of the more articulate local writers, H. M. Stringfellow, repeated Maury's argument and commented that when he moved to Galveston from Houston a dozen friends warned him that the place was dangerous and that it was only a matter of a few years before it was washed away. Stringfellow's reaction was that citizens of Galveston had nothing to fear and the "periodical overflow joke is getting just a little stale."[92]

In consideration of a century of opposing evidence and experience, such talk and response was not only foolish, but also reckless. The people of Galveston lived on the border of land and water where the power of nature was strong, and they placed themselves in harm's way. The next storm, in 1900, was the greatest natural disaster in the history of the United States. It was a profound event which not only molded the mind and character of modern Galveston, but also provided a demonstration of the distinguishing characteristics of Western civilization. It is a story for a later point in Galveston history; first comes settlement and development.

The first humans to utilize the resources of Galveston Island were the Karankawa Indians. Our earliest knowledge of them comes through the report of Alvar Núñez Cabeza de Vaca, who landed with a thump on the Texas coast in November 1528. He was second in command of the ill-fated Spanish expedition of Pánfilo de Narváez. After failure in Florida, the starving explorers floated westward along the Gulf Coast in makeshift barges. Eighty to ninety survivors eventually landed on the island they called "Malhado," and Cabeza de Vaca recorded:

> As we drifted into shore, a wave caught us and heaved the barge a horse-shoe-throw out of the water. The jolt when it hit brought the dead-looking men to. Seeing land at hand, they crawled through the surf to

some rocks. Here we made a fire and parched some of our corn. We also
found rain water. The men began to regain their senses, their locomo-
tion, and their hope.[93]

There is some debate among historians about the location of
Cabeza de Vaca's Malhado. He was imprecise, and his dimensions do
not fit, but otherwise, it appears that the Spaniards landed on Galveston. The relationship of the island to the major rivers he described places it in the correct position.[94] Considering the passage of
four centuries and the effect of storms on sand barrier islands, it
would be a wonder if the dimensions were the same then as now. It
is likely that Cabeza de Vaca landed on a younger version of Galveston Island.

The shipwrecked men shortly discovered that they were on an island, and the Indians shortly discovered them. The meeting was
friendly. The white men gave the Indians bells and beads, and received food in return. Having recovered somewhat, the Europeans
tried to continue their journey. They stowed their clothing and
equipment on the barge, shoved away from the beach, and capsized a
hundred yards offshore. Three men drowned and the rest were cast
back on land "naked as they were born, with the loss of everything
we had." The Karankawas, understanding their plight, first sat down
and cried for thirty minutes in compassion. Then, after building four
large fires along the pathway to keep them warm, the Indians took
them to their village. The Spaniards thought that they would become sacrificial victims, but instead they received food, shelter,
and an all-night dance celebration.[95] The initial contact with
the Karankawas, therefore, was one of friendship, helpfulness, and
compassion.

Cold, malnutrition, and dysentery soon began to kill both natives
and Europeans. Five isolated Spaniards, in desperation, devoured
human flesh, and only the emaciated body of the last one was found
uneaten. This cannibalism shocked the Indians, and they blamed the
visitors for the dysentery and death. The Karankawas threatened to
kill the remaining sixteen Spaniards, but spared them to work as
medicine men and slaves. Later, after remaining among the Indians
of Texas for six years, Cabeza de Vaca and three other survivors of
the expedition walked into northern Mexico, thus regaining Spanish civilization.[96]

Cabeza de Vaca described two similar groups of Indians living on
the island. Both were tall and well-built. The men wore no clothing,
carried bows and arrows as their only weapons, and inserted large
pieces of cane through holes drilled in their nipples and lower lips.

The women covered themselves, in part, with Spanish moss, and maidens dressed in deerskin. The women worked incessantly in camp and in the mud flats gathering roots, while the men hunted and fished with cane weirs. They stayed on Galveston from October to February, and moved elsewhere during the rest of the year in order to harvest oysters and blackberries. They treated children kindly, readily shared their possessions, and observed elaborate marriage and death customs.[97]

Three centuries later the daughter of a ship captain, Alice Williams Oliver, studied the Karankawa language and customs. She recorded her findings shortly before her death in 1889. The Indians spoke, she noted, with repressed breath which gave a sighing sound to their speech, and they never looked at the person to whom they spoke. The men were tall, well-formed, and possessed good teeth. They had long, black hair which was sometimes braided and tipped with the rattle from a snake. It was rarely combed. Both sexes wore bracelets of untanned deer hide, and the women were short, stout, and disagreeable. Both sexes wore simple skirts, but children went naked until ten years of age. Everyone was dirty and smelled of shark's oil which was used to repel mosquitoes. They applied blue, curved tattoos to the face and possessed a reputation for cannibalism. They still used bows and arrows, but also clubs, tomahawks, and knives received from white traders. The arrows were a yard long, and the bows reached from the ground to a man's chin. They ate deer, fish, oysters, turtles, berries, nuts, persimmons, but had no corn and no agriculture. They waded across a shallow ford, Carancahua Reef, to reach Galveston, and also used crude dugout canoes with the bark left on them. By and large, Oliver found the Indians lazy, begging, dangerous when drunk, and generally "destitute of heroic traits."[98]

In 1962 while excavating the Jamaica Beach subdivision down the island near the location of Carancahua Reef, workers uncovered a Karankawa burial site. Rice University archeologists sifted the dirt and found no evidence of cannibalism or Spaniards.[99] Perhaps Malhado was elsewhere and the idea of cannibalism among the Karankawas was a bit of Spanish propaganda to hide their own indiscretions. There may have been some ritual eating of an enemy—other primitive people have done that—or the Indians may have learned cannibalism from the Spanish. There is not enough evidence. Karankawa technical knowledge, however, was slight. They possessed no agriculture and few tools; they lived uncomfortably at the mercy of nature. They had neither resources nor knowledge to challenge the environment in order to create a better life for themselves. The Indians of the area, moreover, could not withstand the powerful technology of the Western world. In the 1820's they fought the settlers and lost. As their numbers thinned, they joined other coastal tribes and slowly retreated into northern Mexico. After 1858 the Karankawas existed no more.[100]

One of the reasons for the Indians' hostility in the 1820's was their experience with the pirates of Galveston. At that time, the Spanish empire in the New World crumbled. Mexico, among others, struck for independence, and there were those who used this situation for their own profit. A priest, Don José Manuel de Herrera, represented the Mexican patriots in New Orleans. He appointed Don Louis Aury, the naval commander of the fleets of Venezuela, La Plata, and New Grenada, as the commodore of the navy of Mexico. Aury was instructed to go to Galveston Island to carry out offensive operations against Spain. Galveston Bay had been a rendezvous point for the former pirates of Barataria Bay (in Louisiana), led by Jean Laffite, and was well known.

On September 1, 1816, Aury arrived at Galveston with a dozen small vessels. He organized a government, declared Galveston a part of the Republic of Mexico, set up an admiralty court, and sent his privateers out to raid Spanish shipping. He was in business. Colonel Henry Perry soon joined him in this shadowy enterprise. In 1815 Perry had tried to assemble an army to invade Texas from Bolivar. Poor support and ill fortune defeated the effort. After the success of Aury, Perry returned with about one hundred followers and joined the men at Galveston. Another soldier of fortune with similar ambitions, Xavier Mina, brought in an additional two hundred troops which raised the total force at Galveston to around seven hundred.

They decided to attack the Spanish town of Soto La Marina as a start for the invasion of Mexico, destroyed the huts at Galveston, and left on April 5, 1817. The three commanders, however, would not cooperate, and after landing the soldiers, Aury decided to return to his profitable privateering business. Perry and Mina then split up. Perry tried to return overland, and Mina pushed on into the interior of Mexico seeking glory. The Spanish caught them and they found nothing but death. Aury, meanwhile, returned to his base, and met a surprise.[101]

During his brief absence a new set of buccaneers had taken over Galveston, and Aury, with smaller numbers, moved on to Amelia Island off the coast of Florida. The newcomers on Galveston pledged fealty to Mexico and organized a government under the leadership of Jean Laffite. After his expulsion from Barataria in 1814, the "Pirate of the Gulf" had searched for a new location. Armed with letters of marque from Venezuela, and serving as a double agent for Spain to spy on Mexican activities, Laffite set up his port to prey upon Spanish shipping. His affiliations meant little. It was pirate business as usual. Claimed by the United States, Mexico, and Spain, Galveston was located on an uncertain boundary, and, thus, was an ideal meeting place for freebooters to dispose of their contraband and take on fresh supplies. This was Laffite's role—a broker for pirates.[102]

From captured vessels Laffite sent jewelry, laces, calicos, silks, linens, seersuckers, and muslins by pack mules overland to New Orleans for sale in the black market. Other items—iron, rails, tallow, glassware, beef, crockery—he sent boldly to port aboard the prize ships to be sold openly. The population of the Mississippi port supported his efforts.[103] The pirates also captured slave ships. The slaves were sold to planters who went to Galveston to make a selection, or to dealers like the Bowie brothers. James, Resin, and John Bowie bought the Africans from Laffite for one dollar per pound, walked them down the Bolivar Peninsula and cross country to New Orleans, and turned them over to the customs officer. Since the slave trade was illegal, the Bowies received a reward of half the value of the slaves. The U.S. Marshall then sold the slaves and the Bowies bought them back again. These transactions made the slaves legitimate and the brothers then resold them legally in the United States. In two years the Bowies earned $65,000 with this trade.[104]

The U.S. Collector at New Orleans, Beverly Chew, wrote about this illegal traffic in his official correspondence. He stated that it started with Aury and continued with Laffite. It was practiced with impunity "by a motly mixture of freebooters and smugglers at Galveston under the Mexican flag." Chew reported one instance of a prize ship carrying three hundred slaves and a contagious fever which the pirates cut adrift in the Gulf to prevent the spread of the disease. The United States made an effort, then, to suppress the slave trade and close the base.[105]

The pirate camp at Campeachy on Snake Island, as the inhabitants called it, had grown rapidly to a mixed population of about one thousand. The most substantial structure in the town of crude huts was Laffite's two-story frame house. It had a ditch around it, four cannons, and red paint. The William H. Sandusky map of Galveston in 1845 places the house on the bay front at Avenue A and 14th Street. Others have located it variously between 11th and 15th on A.[106] There exists no explanation for the vivid color of the "Maison Rouge" except a story: Satan offered to build Laffite's house for him in return for the first living creature the Devil saw the next morning. Laffite agreed and Satan built the house. First thing the next morning, however, the pirate chief threw a mongrel dog into the Devil's tent. Outraged, the ruler of Hell took revenge by painting the house scarlet. It made a good target.[107]

The character and figure of Laffite are encrusted with legend, but there are several eyewitness accounts. Mrs. James Campbell was the wife of one of Laffite's captains. She lived at Campeachy for three years and provided the *Galveston Daily News* with her observation in 1879. She was born at the beginning of the century and lived with her stepfather on the Sabine River. In 1816 she married James Campbell who had been born near Baltimore, trained as a sailmaker, and served with Captain Oliver H. Perry at the Battle of Lake Erie during the War of 1812.

They moved to the buccaneer camp in 1817, when it had about one hundred houses. The mixed population of men of different nationalities with their wives and mistresses received supplies from New Orleans. Campeachy was located on the bay side on the ruins of Aury's camp. Laffite was then about forty years old, dark-complexioned, handsome, and over six feet tall. He was strongly built, had black hair, side-whiskers, and hazel eyes. He never wore a uniform, nor weapons except once when he expected an attack by a rebellious officer.[108]

Another witness was Colonel Warren D. C. Hall, who came to the area as part of the forces of James Long. Hall met Laffite in 1820, when Long was trying to obtain Laffite's assistance for an attempt to invade Mexico. Hall said that Laffite was six feet, two inches tall with remarkable symmetry except for small hands and feet. He wore no uniform, spoke English with a French accent, and closed one eye when conversing.[109]

The most remarkable description, however, resulted from an 1821 visit by the *U.S.S. Enterprise*. Because of piratical depredations, the United States ordered Laffite to leave Galveston and sent the *Enterprise* to enforce the order. A report of this visit was supplied by "T," presumably one of the ship's officers, to *United States Magazine and Democratic Review* in 1839. The ship arrived as Laffite was preparing to leave in his brig of sixteen guns. "T" said Laffite was five feet, ten inches tall, and simply dressed in a blue frock coat and foraging cap. He had an olive complexion and small, black eyes. The buccaneer was courteous and took the officers to see his red fort dismantled. "But I am not a pirate. You see there?" he gestured toward a gibbet on the beach where a dead man dangled. "This is my justice. That vaurien plundered an American schooner."

He invited them to dinner on his ship, and they ate turkey, dried fish, stew, yams, and wine. Laffite explained that he once had been a rich merchant in Santo Domingo, but had been captured and robbed by a Spanish man-of-war while en route to Europe. He was abandoned on a cay and rescued by an American schooner. He landed penniless in New Orleans, where his wife died. Joining with others he bought a ship and proceeded to wage war against Spain. That was why he hated the Spanish; he bothered no one else.

During the meal they were joined by a beautiful quadroon, but not introduced to her. According to "T" she was "the most glorious specimen of the brunett ever dreamed of. A full and voluptuous form of faultless outline—beautiful features and sleepy black eyes, with the blackest and most luxuriant hair that ever curled." She flirted with the guests, but a glance from Laffite resulted in her abrupt departure. The meal ended, and shortly after that Laffite vacated Galveston.[110]

On the island, Laffite ruled with an iron hand, and he was known to execute those who defied him. In 1819, for example, one of his captains against orders raided an American plantation, and a U.S. revenue schooner chased him back to Galveston. Laffite ordered the disobedient captain hanged and turned the crew over to the United States for punishment. The dead Captain Brown, suspended from the middle of a tripod, swung to face the settlement at dusk and turned away at night, so it was said. This was considered an evil omen.[111]

Following the visit of the *Enterprise*, Laffite burned Campeachy, departed on his ship, *Pride*, and disappeared into the mists and legends of history. There are various accounts of his later life and death, including a fake diary which says he died in East St. Louis in 1854.[112] Jean Laffite is one of those historical characters who attract collectors of documents and also forgers. The most reasonable conclusion is that Laffite died in Yucatan in the 1820's. An 1852 account by William Bollaert refers to a letter from Thomas M. Duke which claimed Laffite died in 1826. There is also a letter to Mirabeau B. Lamar from Rhoads Fisher dated 1838 which reported a meeting with a fisherman off the coast of Yucatan. The man told Fisher that he had sailed with the pirate chieftain and helped bury him about ten years before near Teljas, a village on the mainland. Laffite had died of a fever.[113]

In his wake Laffite also left tales about buried treasure, and the fortune hunters came immediately. Historian Joseph O. Dyer reported people looking in 1822 and 1823. Jesse A. Ziegler, who was born on the island in 1857, remembered searching for treasure as a boy, and often seeing men with sacks, lanterns, shovels, and picks go into the area of the three trees midway down the island. Only a few doubloons were ever found. A persistent tale, however, was that shortly before his departure Laffite paced the floor and was heard to mutter, "I have buried my treasure under the three trees." Some pirates who remained behind dug in the area and found a long, wooden box. They eagerly pried off the lid and found staring out at them in the moonlight the pale face and rigid form of the chieftain's dead wife.[114]

The legacy of buried treasure continues to the present and is a subject which fires the imagination. Government dredge boats in the Galveston channel in 1903 brought up six silver coins, two copper coins, large stones, and copper spikes and bolts. One of the silver coins carried an 1812 date. Reaction to divers who successfully plundered a sunken treasure galleon off Padre Island in 1967 resulted in a Texas Antiquities Law. Treasure seeking, nonetheless, goes on. Two people, one in 1970 and the other two years later, sought permission to dig on Pelican Island. Nothing came of it. Laffite's treasure, if such exists, and that of others have not been found.[115] What is left of the pirate's adventure at Galveston is a lurid memory. In the words of Stanley E. Babb whose poetry was inspired by Galveston:

A dead man's bones on a lonely beach,
A seagull's mocking cry;
The swelling lunge of long grey waves,
And a red moon in the sky.

A cutlass instead of a crucifix,
Splotched with blood and rust;
And a dead man's bones on a lonely beach,
Crumbling into dust.[116]

Shortly after Laffite's departure, General James Long moved to Galveston and rebuilt the fort. He had tried unsuccessfully to persuade the buccaneer to leave the base intact, and there is disagreement in the accounts about Laffite's promise to help Long in his enterprise.[117] Whatever the truth of the matter, in action, Laffite did nothing to help Long, and left the adventurer on his own.

Long sought the independence of Texas and in 1819 declared Texas a republic while raising a lone star flag over Nacogdoches. Long established a station at Bolivar and Galveston, and may have fought a battle with the Karankawas. According to one account, in February 1821 a French sloop loaded with wine went ashore on the beach. The Indians attacked, killed the crew, and drank the wine. In the midst of their revel Long crossed from Bolivar with one hundred men and surprised the Indians near the three trees. The Karankawas, numbering between one and two hundred, fought back, but lost thirty warriors. Long's force suffered seven wounded, none killed.[118]

Other accounts contend that it was Laffite who fought this battle at an earlier period. Some of his men, supposedly, captured an Indian maid, and the Karankawas struck back by eating two pirates. Laffite mustered two hundred men and two cannons and fought for three days against three hundred Indians. After losing thirty men, the natives fled.[119] The Laffite story seems more likely from the standpoint of circumstance, but the Long version has the authority of Warren D. C. Hall, who worked with Long and lived to relate the story. Be that as it may, the result afterward was a fateful and determined hostility on the part of the Karankawas. There was no one to tell their side of the episode.

Long, hearing of rebellion at La Bahia, rushed to the scene of the action, promising to return in three weeks. He left behind at Bolivar his wife and about fifty men. Long never returned and eventually met death in Mexico. After a month the men at Bolivar began to leave. Although she could have gone with them, Jane Wilkinson Long chose to wait for her husband to come back. The headstrong twenty-four-year-old pregnant woman was left alone at the fort with her daughter, Ann, her black servant girl, Kian, and a dog. Across the water at Galveston she could see Karankawa campfires, and when the Indians threatened she hoisted a red-flannel petticoat (or, perhaps, pantaloons) on the flagstaff and fired a cannon to keep them away.

During the winter, while Galveston Bay froze for one-fourth mile from the shore, she gave birth to another child. It was the first time American settlers had a child in this frontier, and Jane Long thus earned the sobriquet "the Mother of Texas." After losing her fishhooks, she used an old hammock as a seine and preserved the fish in a pickle barrel of brine. News came first of her husband's capture, and later of his death. With that information and near starvation, in the summer of 1822 she left with the first of the Austin settlers. She lived until 1880 and was known to wear a homespun dress with a palmetto-leaf hat, and smoke a pipe.[120] She was a tough woman suited for a hard land.

For the next decade and a half, developments on Galveston and Galveston Bay involved the struggle for Texas independence. What had proven an illusion for James Long became a reality for Stephen F. Austin and his followers. Settlers, moving by land and sea, poured into Texas seeking the cheap land and new opportunity offered through various colonization schemes. Grumblings against Mexican rule turned into full-throated protest and revolution in 1835. As the war progressed, Galveston with its natural harbor became increasingly important. The Mexican government designated it a port of entry in 1825 and built a small customshouse there in 1830. It was abandoned two years later, but during the revolution Galveston became the home of the Texas Navy and the last point of defense for the Texas government.[121] With Sam Houston and the Texan army retreating before the advance of Santa Anna, President David G. Burnet, other government officials, and refugee families took shelter there.

Lewis B. Harris, a young volunteer who arrived at Galveston on April 21, 1836, found people living in tents and drinking brackish water. The customhouse, a mere shell, still stood about a mile from the point of the island near Laffite's old fort. The ditches of the fort were still there, but the wood had been used for steamboat fuel. There were about one hundred men on the island, and they feared invasion from the west end. At one time freshly washed clothes flapping in the breeze were mistaken for the guidons of Mexican cavalry, and the camp went into a panic. Burnet, at the moment of Harris' arrival, was preparing to move the government to New Orleans.[122]

On that same day, however, General Sam Houston rallied the troops at San Jacinto and, to the music of a four-piece band playing the tune of a popular love song, "Will You Come to My Bower I Have Shaded for You?" the Texans won victory and everlasting glory in eighteen minutes. Surprised and routed, the Mexican army met defeat and carnage. The rebels took General Santa Anna captive, and the war ended.

Houston sent four men to carry the news to Galveston. One of them, Captain R. J. Calder, particularly wanted to go because of his interest in a young woman, Mary Walker Douglas, among the refugees on the island. The messengers left the battlefield on April 23 with no food, foraged through an abandoned farmhouse, found some cornmeal, and began to travel along the bay shore in a leaky skiff. They spent a night on a beach in a downpour with a rattlesnake for company, and then tried to cross the bay the next day. En route, a small Texas war vessel picked them up. The captain, William Brown, when he heard the news sailed his hat into the sea and fired his pivot gun three times. At Galveston the refugees crowded the rigging of the ships in the harbor while the commodore fired a thirteen-gun salute and fed the hungry couriers. Burnet, the last to know, was so angry he threatened to arrest the messengers. Commodore Charles Hawkins, however, intervened, and the anger passed. It is pleasant to note, moreover, that Captain Calder married Miss Douglas. They moved to a farm at Richmond, Texas, and reared five children.[123]

The government soon moved to Velasco because of the "entire want of accommodation at the Island."[124] Soldiers, meanwhile, gathered the scattered weapons from the battlefield, and Burnet ordered them sent to Harrisburg for storage to avoid the destructive "saline atmosphere" of Galveston. The island, temporarily, became a garrison of two thousand where the Mexican prisoners were taken. Santa Anna was there briefly, and Sam Houston passed through on his way to New Orleans for treatment of his injured ankle, shattered by a musket ball at San Jacinto.[125] At the moment, however, the future of the island remained uncertain.

THE NEW YORK OF TEXAS

Chapter Two

There is a man in town who can lift a schooner over a bar—a schooner of beer over a saloon counter.

—Galveston joke, 1878

The utility of the location of Galveston had been demonstrated once more, and Michel B. Menard decided to exploit it. Menard, the founder of the city, was born at La Prairie, north of Montreal, Canada, in 1805. Educated at a French school, he carried with him French manners and accent for the rest of his life. He worked as a voyageur for the Hudson Bay Company and later as an Indian trader for his uncle. Menard drifted westward with the Shawnee and in 1829 crossed into Texas at Nacogdoches. He later worked for Texas independence as a politician, as a representative to the Indians to forestall their alliance with Mexico, and as a funding agent in the United States.[1]

Menard's control of the Galveston city site came through a complicated process. In 1833 the land he wanted could only go to Mexican-born citizens, so Juan N. Seguin, an acquaintance, applied for a headright of one league and labor of land (4,605 acres). As attorney for Seguin, Menard directed the location of the headright to the eastern end of Galveston Island and obtained a survey by Isaac N. Moreland. The war intervened. Then, on October 3, 1836, Menard, again as Seguin's attorney, transferred the land to Thomas F. McKinney. McKinney resold it to Menard on December 10, 1836. Meanwhile, Menard and nine associates—Thomas F. McKinney, Samuel May Williams, Mosely Baker, John K. Allen, Augustus C. Allen, William H. Jack, William Hardin, A. J. Gates, and David White—petitioned the Republic of Texas for confirmation of the claim. This was granted on December 9, 1836, in exchange for $50,000 in cash or acceptable materials in New Orleans. The total amount had to be paid in four months.

Menard promised payment of the money to David White, one of the partners, out of the sale of lots. White would also receive 10 percent of the proceeds after the initial $50,000 payment. White, who was the Texas land agent in Mobile, then acknowledged receipt of payment and this was accepted as payment by the Republic. The transaction, therefore, was carried off without any real exchange of money or materials. The Republic later had trouble collecting from White. It was believed that he was often paid in land scrip (promissory notes based upon real estate), and that he extracted a commission of 7.5 percent.[2] Such was the state of finance in the frontier Republic of Texas.

Levi Jones, who bought half of White's interest in the enterprise, hired John D. Groesbeck to survey the site and divide the land into lots. Groesbeck, from New York, had come to Galveston in 1837 for health purposes. He laid out Galveston in a gridiron form patterned after Philadelphia, and set the configuration for the future. Avenues running parallel to the Bay and the Gulf he labeled in alphabetical order. The streets crossing at right angles were simply numbered in sequence. As time passed, letters and numbers changed. Avenue B, for example, became the "Strand," Avenue J became "Broadway," and Avenue E became "Postoffice." Half-numbers assigned to the alphabet, such as M½, had to be used as the city expanded toward the Gulf and the planners ran out of letters.[3] Groesbeck completed his map in 1838.

Menard and his associates, during this time, organized the Galveston City Company for the sale of land. The board of directors—Menard, Thomas F. McKinney, Samuel May Williams, Mosely Baker, and John K. Allen—appointed Levi Jones as the general agent and ordered the first sale of lots for April 20, 1838. Thus, the city was born. The Republic confirmed the company charter and it continued to operate until 1909, when Maco Stewart bought the remaining assets and it went out of existence. The stock of the company rapidly depreciated down to 10 percent of its face value, but lots could be purchased from the company with its own stock. In the first year Jones sold seven hundred lots at an average price of $400 each. There were sixty families and over one hundred buildings by the end of that year. Menard, the principal founder, lived in Galveston until his death in 1856.[4]

In 1839 the Texas Congress granted incorporation to the city with a charter which specified the election of a mayor, recorder, treasurer, and eight aldermen. White male property-owners could vote, and they selected a hero of San Jacinto, the liberal, democratic John M. Allen, as mayor. He was a threat to the conservative control of the Galveston City Company, and in 1840 Samuel May Williams pushed a new city charter through the Congress. It called for a new election based upon a franchise requiring real estate ownership of at least $500 value. This eliminated one-half of the electorate. The conservatives then selected John H. Walton mayor, with a new board of aldermen. Allen, however, refused to give up and argued that his term still had one year to run. He took the archives, retreated to his home, and fortified it with two small cannons. The district court agreed with Walton, and Thomas F. McKinney led a posse to force surrender of the archives. This was accomplished without bloodshed, and the "charter war" came to an end. Four years later the city again changed the charter to get rid of the property qualification and grant the franchise to all white male taxpayers who had resided in the city for one year.[5]

The new town was not much to brag about. Francis C. Sheridan, a young Irishman in the British diplomatic service, arrived in 1839 and recorded his impressions in a journal. "The appearance of Galveston from the Harbour is singularly dreary," he wrote. It was low, flat, sandy, and with few shrubs to be seen. "In short it looks like a piece of prairie that had quarelled with the main land and dissolved partnership." Nearby Pelican Island offered a "similar hideousness," and was occupied by nothing but pelicans. The beach, however, had "the whitest firmest, & most beautiful sand I ever saw."

The men wore boots, trousers, and frock coats made from blankets. They carried pen knives for cutting tobacco, trimming their nails, and picking their teeth. For more violent purposes they carried pistols, and Bowie knives manufactured in England and labeled "Arkansas Genuine tooth-pick." Business took place in the bars, and every new friendship had to be "wetted" as soon as possible. For those who bought drinks there was a luncheon of cold meat, pickles, bread and butter. There was also the benefit of the "spitting box." "No one who has not seen & suffered by this most disgusting custom of the Yankees can form the faintest idea how universal & incessant is the practice. High & low, rich & poor, young & old chew, chew, chew & spit, spit, spit all the blessed day & most of the night." Sheridan even observed a man teaching his two-year-old child to spit and praising the youngster's successful efforts. Where the spitting box was missing, floors and fireplaces suffered.

Outside on the irregular streets he found a mixed group of people— English, American, German, Dutch, Italian, Mexican, and African. They possessed exaggerated manners and stopped to shake hands even if they had met the person but ten minutes earlier. One hurried soul shortened it by simply raising his hand and stating, "Well Sir—Your most"—and left. They auctioned off trade goods in the middle of the street, recognized the song "Will You Come to the Bower" as the Texas national anthem, and hummed the tune "Old Rosin the Bow" on the streets and wharves. Sheridan met "old" Sam Houston, who was fifty at the time, and one of the founding fathers of the town, Thomas F. McKinney.[6]

McKinney, born in Kentucky in 1801, early had worked as a merchant in the Santa Fe trade, as a keelboat man, and as a supply agent for the Texas patriots. He was a man of action with strong loyalties and dislikes. When Sheridan met him he was wearing a scarlet blanket frock coat and cleaning his teeth with a Bowie knife. He was considered a generous, honest man who ate when he was hungry and drank when he was dry. Although it galled him, he bore the title "Colonel," which his old friend and partner Michel Menard stuck him with in jest.[7]

McKinney joined another "Colonel" in the merchant business. Samuel May Williams, who was born in Rhode Island in 1795, came to Texas to work for Stephen F. Austin. He became a Texas rebel and solicited funds for the Republic in the United States. In the early 1830's he set up a mercantile business with McKinney at the mouth of the Brazos River. In the summer of 1837 they built a store and warehouse in Galveston, only to have it swept away by the hurricane of October. They quickly rebuilt, however, and constructed a wharf and the Tremont Hotel. Henry H. Williams, Samuel's brother, bought the commission portion of the business in 1842. McKinney moved to Travis County, but Samuel May Williams continued in Galveston as a banker under the company title of McKinney and Williams.[8]

Sam Houston helped McKinney and Williams obtain the right to issue small denomination notes in 1841. On the basis of a charter approved by Texas in 1836, Williams with the aid of his brother opened the Commercial and Agricultural Bank in 1848. Shortly, Robert Mills, another Galveston merchant, endorsed and placed in circulation the notes from a wildcat bank in Mississippi. The anti-banking faction in Texas then began a ten-year campaign against "Williams paper" and "Mills paper." Williams' bank closed six months after his death in 1858. Mills lost his fortune in the Civil War and went bankrupt in 1867. Despite opposition and harrassment both men, in their time, provided responsible banking service to the state and to Texas business. The only valid complaint was that they charged a higher rate of interest than the bankers of New Orleans.[9]

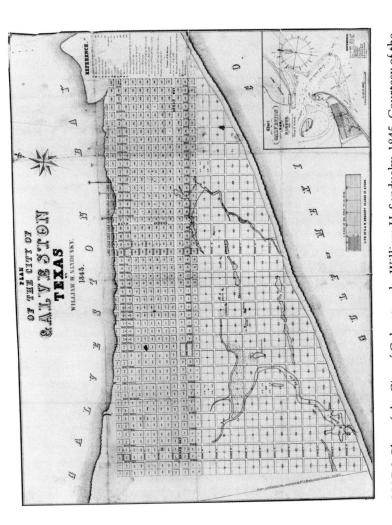

MAP 3. Plan of the City of Galveston, by William H. Sandusky, 1845. Courtesy of the Barker Texas History Center.

   Port activities provided the main thrust of Galveston's economy in the nineteenth century. The pattern formed early and remained unchanged. Galveston factors bought the produce of agricultural Texas and shipped it to other ports. Conversely, they imported supplies for the farmer and sent them to inland merchants. The city served as a storage and shipping point, with the Galveston merchants providing some services and arranging for transportation. River steamers brought the cotton of Southeast Texas to the island wharves. Before the Civil War 90 percent of this cotton came from the bay area; 80 percent came from Houston via Buffalo Bayou. The Bayou City was Galveston's door to Texas, where commerce shifted from water to land transportation. Houston had an immediate market around it which Galveston did not possess. In turn, Galveston served as Houston's ocean port, where cotton moved from river steamer to deepwater ships. The two cities needed one another, and traffic was constant. The steamboat trip from Houston to Galveston left in the late afternoon and crossed the bay at night. The boats sent a shower of sparks upward from their funnels "leaving a brilliantly lighted trail in the prevailing southern breeze somewhat akin to a playful comet."[10]

   Galveston factors sent their cotton to New York, New Orleans, and Great Britain, along with hides, sugar, molasses, cattle, pecans, and cottonseed. Before the Civil War exports were twenty times greater in value than the imports, which came in small quantities and in great variety. In the mid-1870's the main export still was cotton and the value of exports ten to eleven times greater than that of imports. To a large degree, then, the port of Galveston developed as a conduit whereby much more went out, in terms of value, than came in. The port was third in the nation for cotton exports in 1878, and fifth in 1882. Through the last half of the nineteenth century, excluding war years and bad crops, cotton receipts at the port gradually increased. In 1854 they amounted to 82,000 bales, and in 1900 they totaled 2,278,000 bales.[11] Galveston was able to remain one of the important cotton ports, but it lost almost everything else.

   Like other southern cities, Galveston continued dependent upon cotton while the northeastern United States industrialized. Manufacturing provided the future power and wealth of the nation, and agriculture diminished in comparison.[12] Galveston never made the transition to industry and consequently lessened in comparison to cities which were able to change. It was not that Galveston leaders did not see the problem. They did, and argued that water supply was the difficulty.[13] The analysis proved false, because the completion of the water system in the 1890's did not bring a rush of industrialists to the island. Even the wealthy people of Galveston invested their money elsewhere. Why?

Galveston lay in harm's way. People knew that it was subject to the onslaught of hurricanes. Why place expensive equipment, or a city for that matter, in such a place? O. P. Hurford, a newcomer to Galveston, explained in a letter to the editor in 1876 that he had heard in the commercial circles of Chicago, Cincinnati, Philadelphia, and New York that Galveston was unsafe for investment because of flooding. He advised, "There are to-day untold millions of Northern capital looking southward for investment, of which Galveston would receive her legitimate proportion if we could offer a reasonable argument that the island will not one day be washed away." [14]

Arthur E. Stilwell, the railroad magnate who built Port Arthur as a terminus in the 1890's, provided another example. He had a dream in which a voice said to him:

> Locate your terminal city on the north shore of Sabine Lake. Connect with deep water via canal from your terminal city. Build the canal the same width at the top, the same depth and the same width at the bottom as the Suez Canal. Dig it on the west shore of the lake and put the earth on the east bank to protect the canal from any storm, for Galveston will some day be destroyed. [15]

About the same time a New York capitalist asked William H. Sinclair, the builder of the streetcar system in Galveston, why the city should expect any investment when fifteen houses had just been washed into the Gulf. The capitalist based his statement on a false newspaper article which appeared in both New York and California. [16] This was but another example of the sort of reputation carried by the Island City.

Houston, meanwhile, surged ahead. In 1899, when Houston and Galveston were of comparable size, the Bayou City had 145 places of manufacturing to 100 for Galveston. Houston added twice as much value to the products it handled as Galveston did. In 1909 Houston had 249 places of manufacturing and Galveston 81. Houston added four times what Galveston did to the value of items handled. Oil exploitation brought industrialization to Texas in the early twentieth century. The pipelines led to Houston, Port Arthur, Beaumont, and Orange—but not to Galveston, which was still recovering from the devastation of 1900. [17] Why put vulnerable pipes, tanks, and refineries in such a hazardous location? No one did.

The dream of industry, and hence greatness, nonetheless haunted Galvestonians. Studies in 1959 and in 1965 dashed long-standing illusions and indicated little potential for manufacturing in Galveston.[18] Yet in the nineteenth century there were a few small factories. This gave some basis for the dream—what was once, might be again. Before the Civil War there were iron parts, soap, sash and door, furniture, and rope manufacturing. Gail Borden, Jr., briefly operated a meat biscuit plant, and there were cotton compresses. After the war small-scale factories produced flour, cottonseed oil, ice, and textiles, but not enough to engender an industrial "takeoff." The largest industry in 1880, oddly enough, was printing, which employed 107 people and listed an investment of $287,000. This capital was three times greater than that of the flour mill which was next in line.[19]

As might be expected from their interest in cotton commerce, Galveston leaders placed their greatest emphasis on improving commercial rather than industrial facilities. It was understandable, moreover, that they stressed improvement of water rather than land connections. After all, Galveston was surrounded by water. It was the harbor which gave the city its natural advantage and was its greatest asset. What the leaders accomplished with the harbor and port insured Galveston's continuance as a leading cotton point. What they were unable to do with railroad connections insured the success of Houston and other inland capitals. What should be kept in mind, however, is that Galveston did not control its destiny except in a limited way. Geography, weather, the technology of a nationwide system of railroads, and the shift in the national economy away from agriculture were much more important. It was fated that Galveston reach only the level of a mid-sized city. It was not destined by the dynamics that control urban growth to be anything more.

To promote commerce the businessmen established a Chamber of Commerce in 1845, reorganized in 1868, and founded a Cotton Exchange in 1873. The chamber gained a success in the mid-1870's with the promotion of grain trade through Galveston from Denver and Kansas City. The Wharf Company built an elevator, and the first shipments left port in July 1875. The handling of grain remained an important piece of port business from that point onward.[20] The Cotton Exchange began as a factors' association to coordinate the grading and handling of cotton; under the lead of William L. Moody it reorganized into an exchange. It was an effort to strengthen Galveston's position in the face of railroad development which threatened to carry cotton overland to the eastern ports. The exchange became part of the Chamber of Commerce in 1889.[21]

The history of railroad construction and control in Southeast Texas contrasted north-south direction versus east-west direction. Galveston and Houston, especially Galveston, wanted a north-south development which would bring commerce through them to the sea. The main national thrust of growth, however, was east-west—the transcontinental lines. Galveston was caught in a national trend, and lost.

Considering the muddy nature of the soil in the Houston-Galveston area, the difficulty of transport by ox wagon, and the expense of building roads, a railroad made good sense. It could run in all weather and in most directions, people were willing to invest, and the technology and equipment were available from the East. Although the Republic of Texas authorized four companies, and the citizens of Galveston and Houston talked about it, nothing was done until Sidney Sherman, allied with Boston capitalists, built the Buffalo Bayou, Brazos and Colorado Railway (BBB&C) in 1850–1856. Sherman offloaded the thirteen-ton engine for the line at Galveston in 1852. Fearing competition from Harrisburg, the eastern terminus, Houston entrepreneurs began railroad work, and by the time of the Civil War the Bayou City had become the railroad center of South Texas with lines reaching in all directions. After recovering from the war, Houston railways continued to grow, and in 1873 the Houston and Texas Central connected with the Missouri, Kansas and Texas near the Texas-Oklahoma border. Houston, and Galveston along with it, thus tapped into the vast intercontinental system. In 1876 Texas railroads converted to standard gauge and cars could roll from the Galveston docks to anywhere in the nation.[22]

Galveston, meanwhile, pursued its own schemes. One hundred and fifty citizens traveled by water on the *Neptune* and five miles over the new railroad at Harrisburg in 1853 to toast the new technology with champagne and claret. Galveston representatives promoted without success an idea of state-controlled railroads which would fan over the state and converge at Galveston. Before the war, at least, people on the island saw little to fear in Houston success. Since Galveston was the port for Houston, any commerce generated by the railroads would flow southward. There was a little nervousness about the eastern line toward New Orleans, but the Civil War halted that enterprise.[23]

The first railroad to reach the island was the Galveston, Houston and Henderson (GH&H). Backed by French loans and state land donations the promoters began construction in 1853. Because of the heat and severity of the work, the builders hired W. J. Kyle and B. F. Terry, the Brazos plantation owners who helped with the BBB&C, to use their slaves for digging embankments. Irish laborers, bolstered with whiskey as part of their wages, graded and laid the track imported from Great Britain. The citizens of Galveston voted $100,000 in bonds to finance a bridge across the bay, and in 1860 the boom of a cannon announced the first train from Houston.[24]

Despite the fact that it became a trunk line between Galveston and Houston and earned one-third more than other Texas railroads, the GH&H passed into receivership in 1867. It was sold in 1871 and controlled by Thomas W. Peirce of Boston. John Sealy took over as president in 1876 and saw to a change to standard gauge. In the early 1880's the railroad got into financial trouble again and shortly became part of Jay Gould's Missouri-Pacific system. Sealy told Gould that the cars leaked rainwater and the wet red-plushed cushions faded onto the ladies' dresses. Gould replied that the cars should run only in dry weather and that the passengers should carry umbrellas.[25] So much for the social responsibility of Jay Gould.

It was this railroad that first revealed urban rivalry between Galveston and Houston. When it built into the southern part of the Bayou City in 1858–1859, the Houston City Council refused it right-of-way to connect with the Houston and Texas Central. Merchants feared that the cars of cotton would roll straight through to Galveston without stopping in Houston. During the war, the Confederate commanding officer, General John B. Magruder, forced the connection for military efficiency, and in 1865 the connection became permanent.[26] The rivalry grew worse when a group of Houston merchants formed the Houston Direct Navigation Company in 1866 to transfer cotton from river barges directly to ships in Galveston Bay without touching at Galveston. Houstonians also moved to deepen Buffalo Bayou and dreamed of creating an inland port at Houston.[27]

Charles Morgan, the chief shipowner of the Gulf Coast, made the dream a partial reality in the mid-1870's when he took over the Houston Direct Navigation Company, dredged a twelve-foot deep channel with the help of Army engineers, founded the town of Clinton near Harrisburg on the bayou, and opened rail service to Houston. He did all of this to meet the competition of the east-west transcontinental rail lines, which had led to a 50 percent decline in his business.[28] In the process Morgan abandoned Galveston. It was a common interpretation at the time that he left the Island City because of monopolistic wharf charges. This idea arose at least in part due to the concurrent vendetta of the *Galveston Daily News* against the Wharf Company (see discussion below). It was a convenient event to exploit. Morgan probably did find the rates too high, but he never commented on the matter. The Wharf Company said that Morgan never asked for lower rates; the charge that monopoly control forced fees much higher than those at other ports has never been substantiated. Morgan left in order to compete with the railroads.

The shipowner died in 1878, and when the rail line between Houston and New Orleans opened in 1880, his successors abandoned Clinton.[29]

The Kansas City *Journal of Commerce* commented on the new situation of Galveston: "While the back door, so to speak, was closed, the trade was all forced to the Gulf to reach the markets of the world, and the interior was supplied from the same ports—cotton went to market that way, and bacon, flour and goods came in that way, for all the state." The opening of North Texas by railroads meant that cotton and trade goods could move to Kansas City and St. Louis more cheaply by other routes than through Galveston and Houston.[30] That was the problem—not Houston rivalry, not Charles Morgan, not a Wharf Company monopoly.

Galveston had no control over this fundamental change in transportation technology. Its leaders, however, did what they could. They tried to improve rail connections and deepen the harbor in order to remain as competitive as possible.[31] Led by Henry Rosenberg and Albert Somerville, Galveston businessmen formed the Gulf, Colorado and Santa Fe Railroad (GC&SF) in 1873. They collected $200,000 in subscriptions that year and persuaded the county to underwrite $500,000 for the enterprise. The county bonds were marketed at home. This is the largest amount raised by a city and county in Texas railroad history. It is a fact which offsets a common argument that Galvestonians refused to contribute to home railroad work. Another popular thought is that this line began in reaction to Houston quarantines for yellow fever. This is a good story, but there exists little evidence to support it. The businessmen were trying to build their own trade connections to compete with Houston and Charles Morgan.

Depression delayed the GC&SF, but in the spring of 1875 it pushed northwestward into the Brazos Valley. With only sixty miles of track and unable to purchase rolling stock, it had to be reorganized in 1879. George Sealy bought control of it and paid the county $10,000 for its $500,000 share. The company continued to build and reached Brenham in 1880, Belton and Fort Worth in 1881, and Lampasas in 1882. It had a price war with the Gould network in 1882 and experienced deep financial trouble in 1885. The stockholders authorized Sealy to negotiate with the Atchison, Topeka and Santa Fe. The AT&SF officials agreed to take over the road in 1886, but required it to build into the Indian Territory. After this enormous construction effort, through trains began to run to Galveston from Kansas City in June 1887.[32]

In 1884 there occurred one of the unsuccessful, but colorful attempts to build a narrow-gauge railroad down the island. This was the Galveston and Western, otherwise known as the "Little Susie." It accomplished no more than thirteen miles of track, never made a profit, frequently changed ownership, and served mainly to transport tourists.[33] More important was the coming of the Southern Pacific at the turn of the century. Through the effort of George Sealy in 1899 officials voted to allow Collis P. Huntington to use the west end flats owned by the city for the construction of a terminal. Huntington did not have the presentiment of Arthur Stilwell and determined to use Galveston as soon as it obtained deep water in its harbor. He worked with Congress to obtain funds for port improvement and began development of his site in 1900. He died before the great storm destroyed the half-constructed facility. Southern Pacific, nonetheless, picked up the pieces, finished the depot, and began operating in 1902.[34]

Railroad building had several secondary effects for Galvestonians. It created, for instance, a forty-two-year bitter argument with Houston over the "differential." In the 1880's interior shippers calculated their cost for Galveston by taking the rate to Houston and adding it to the water cost from Houston to the island. This added amount was usually less than a railroad would normally charge for hauling an item fifty miles. When created in 1891 the Texas Railroad Commission recognized the differential and permitted it to remain. Since steamship companies charged the same price from both places, Galveston agitated for elimination of the differential so that the two cities could compete evenly for the trade of Texas. It was a long fight filled with hearings, court battles, formal complaints, editorials, and election promises. By 1933 the differential had been eliminated on almost all items.[35]

Another secondary effect was the erection of bridges. Made of cedar and pine, the first railroad bridge was completed in 1860 and financed by the city for $130,000. It reached across the narrowest part of West Bay, 9,400 feet, from Eagle Grove on the island to Virginia Point on the mainland. Shipworms had already eaten much of it when the storm of 1867 carried away 5,200 feet of the trestle. The city had not regained any money from it, and now it had to be rebuilt. Trains, nonetheless, ran over a new bridge in June 1868. This time the span lasted until 1900. The Gulf, Colorado and Santa Fe put up a bridge in 1877, and the Galveston, La Porte and Houston constructed another in 1896.[36] The bridge which caused the most interest, however, was the one for wagons built in 1893.

During the Civil War the rebels put planks on the railroad bridge so that soldiers could walk on it. Afterward mainland farmers agitated for a bridge so they would not have to hire the sailboats of the "musquito" fleet to take produce to the Galveston market. They argued that a viaduct would result in lower food prices. Opponents pointed to the cost and to the useless land for thirty miles inland which was nothing but a "crawfish marsh." That meant expensive roads for the county, and the travel by wagon would be no cheaper than by rail. In response to a farmer in Hitchcock, "The only jackass in Galveston" wrote in 1889:

> Why should the taxpayers of Galveston city—which actually constitutes the whole county—be placed under a fresh load of taxation in order that Mr. S. can fetch in a load of onions occasionally without paying freight on them? The insular position of Galveston has been its protection from crime in the past and still remains its security. Why should this be destroyed to oblige Mr. S. at the expense of the city? [37]

The wagon bridge advocates won. The county financed the construction with $175,000 in bonds, and Major H. C. Ripley, an engineer who had worked on Galveston harbor, designed it. He used concrete piles to protect against the teredo and built the rest of cedar, pine, iron, and steel. The bridge featured ninety steel arches each spanning eighty feet with a drawbridge in the middle and a wooden plank roadbed. At 11,309.5 feet in length it was said to be the longest highway bridge in the world.[38] On the day it opened a Galveston reporter met the first wagon. It was eighteen feet long, pulled by eleven yoke of oxen, contained a horticultural display from Dickinson, and was driven by an animated black man with a long whip and "well-adjusted sentences."

> Whoa!
> You Red!
> What's de matter wid you, Ellick?
> Go on dar!
> You hear me, Bill?
> What I feed you fur, Jim?
> Gittup Red!
> Whoa, Bill!
> Hit you wid dis stick toreckly!
> Pull ur dar, John!
> You Red!
> You Bill! G——— d——— your soul to h———. I'll beat the G———
> d——— grass outen you if you don't go on dar! [39]

Judge W. B. Lockhart of the county court also made some interesting comments:

A great many people think that the bridge would pay for the building even if it accomplished no other purpose than to give confidence in the stability of the island and furnish a means of escape in case of a storm to those who are overtimid about the city's being washed away. Of course, we who live here have no fears of this kind, but it would surprise a great many of our citizens to know how many people in the interior are deterred from visiting us by fear that a storm will come up while they are here and they would never again be able to reach the mainland.[40]

Indeed. The wagon bridge blew away in the 1900 hurricane and was not replaced. Besides the differential and the bridges, the railroads had one other important secondary effect. They destroyed Galveston's cotton compress industry. It was as important to compact the cotton for shipment on rail cars as it was for overseas travel. By the 1880's the compresses moved inland, and interior cotton centers such as Denison, Dallas, and St. Louis emerged. Island factors sometimes squeezed the cotton again into a high-density bale, but this technology also moved inland by 1920.[41] Still, Galveston was able to remain a major shipping point for cotton while other Texas ports lost the trade. This was accomplished through harbor improvement.

The major trends of ocean transport in the nineteenth century involved a shift to steam power away from wind and sails, utilization of iron and steel to replace wood, and growth in size. Deeper drafts demanded deeper harbors, and the port was Galveston's only commercial advantage. It is difficult to imagine any development of the city on this sand barrier island without that asset. Deep water and harbor improvement, therefore, became an early and constant concern of city leaders. The attention to the port continues to the present.

The water outside the natural, tidal channels was shallow and dangerous. Charles Hooton, who visited Galveston in 1841, observed the bay area close by:

Sprinkled with wrecks of various appearances and sizes—all alike gloomy, however, in their looks and associations—it strikes the heart of a stranger as a sort of ocean cemetery, a sea churchyard, in which broken masts and shattered timbers, half-buried in quicksands, seem to remain above the surface of the treacherous waters only to remind the living, like dead camels on a level desert, of the destruction that has gone before.[42]

When Ferdinand Roemer arrived in Texas in late 1845 only eleven feet of water was reported over the outer bar, and the largest ships had to anchor outside.[43] Already depth was a problem. Such vessels had to be unloaded by lighter, a process which was slow and expensive. Also, there was shallow water at the bay shore of the city. Early visitors reached dry land by wading, riding the backs of sailors, or walking on unsteady planks. The Galveston City Company sold these flats as "wharf privileges" for the building of docks. Individuals and businesses, such as McKinney and Williams, built a series of wharves reaching across the flats to the channel, and in 1854 a consolidation of ownership began under the lead of Michel B. Menard, Ebenezer B. Nichols, and Henry H. Williams. The city challenged the right of this Galveston Wharf Company to take over the waterfront. The dispute began before the Civil War and continued afterward until 1869, when the city and the company reached a compromise. The city gained one-third partnership and representation, but not control, on the company board of directors. The Wharf Company took over city claims and completed the unification of the wharf area—thirty-one blocks along the bay front.[44]

Willard Richardson, the editor of the *Galveston Daily News*, in 1869 praised the consolidation as "the most important transaction as regards the future welfare of Galveston, that has ever taken place since the foundation of the city."[45] To the bewilderment of the company officials, the newspaper began an attack in 1871 and characterized the Wharf Company as a monopolistic octopus which said:

> Where the sea creeps there creep I,
> In the slimy 'Flats' I lie;
> For I'm the Vampire of the Deep—
>   Sucking in both ship and yawl,
>   Sparing neither great nor small—
> And all that I absorb I keep.
> On the good old rule, the simple plan,
> To keep all you get, and get all you can.[46]

The newspaper blamed high wharf charges for the loss of the Morgan business, and with a series of individual samples maintained the attack. "It is hard to conceive that a corporation of citizens, having the reputation for business forethought that the men have who compose the Galveston Wharf Company, would openly, willingly and flagrantly invite disaster and commercial ruin."[47] The company replied that the annual dividends rarely exceeded 6 percent and never went over 7 percent. In fact, from 1869 to 1926 the average dividend was 5.44 percent. That was not an excessive return on investment for that time, or for ours.

The company did not argue, however, that its wharfage was lower than others, and late in 1874 the company began to decrease the rates. Company income also declined, along with the amount of dividends—perhaps in part because of the depression of the time.

Dividends amounted to 1.75 percent in 1878. In 1881 the newspaper concluded, "The Wharf Company today is possibly in better condition than ever before in its history, while its tariff of charges, since first the *News* had occasion to direct attention thereto, has been scaled to an extent that leaves no room to grumble, by comparison with facilities afforded."[48] The paper, thereafter, complained about overloaded facilities, and about the increase in capital stock which reduced city ownership to one-fourth, but it defended and praised the rate structure.[49] What became more important to everyone was the quest for deep water.

Improvement upon nature for the benefit of commerce was not new. Human beings have been reshaping harbors and digging canals since the time of the ancient Greeks and Egyptians. For Galvestonians the first effort, other than clearing wrecks, came in 1850, when John Sydnor, Gail Borden, Jr., Samuel May Williams, and others put together the Galveston and Brazos Navigation Company to dredge a channel across West Bay to Quintana. Citizens subscribed $30,000 and the municipality borrowed $20,000 to start the project. David Bradbury, the contractor, completed the effort in 1855 at a cost of $340,000. The channel was fifty feet wide, three-and-a-half feet deep, and eight miles long. Its purpose was to reach the cotton trade of the Brazos and to provide a thoroughfare for emigrants to California. After the Civil War Bradbury deepened it to five feet, widened it to one hundred feet, and extended it seven miles. Stockholders considered cutting from the Brazos River into Matagorda Bay, which would give access to Corpus Christi, but this idea had to wait for the intracoastal canal of the twentieth century. For the moment railroads circumvented the need.[50]

Closer to home there was increasing concern about the sandbars obstructing the channels. Between Galveston Island and Bolivar Peninsula a tidal bore ran forty feet deep. Stretching across this natural channel in a semicircle pointing toward the Gulf was a sandbar twelve feet or so below the surface. A branch of this tidal bore coursed along the curving inner face of Galveston Island and formed Galveston harbor. Near the junction of the channels, pilots began to notice shoaling in 1843. This so-called inner bar continued to grow until it reached a depth of eight feet in 1869.[51] Shallow-draft Morgan steamships, built for the Galveston trade, began to have trouble crossing the inner bar in 1868 and often had to wait for high tide.[52]

"It is discreditable to our intelligence as well as enterprise, to allow so small an obstruction to subject our commerce to so heavy a burden," wrote the editor of the *Galveston Daily News* in 1868. Vessels which had to be serviced by lighters, the editor noted, gave opportunity for Houston barges to bypass Galveston. The Chamber of Commerce asked permission of the Reconstruction military authorities to allow a city tax for clearing the bar, but the federal officers refused. The city then set up a Board of Harbor Improvements. Led by Henry Rosenberg, the board raised $15,000 through the sale of city bonds, and adopted the plan of Captain Charles Fowler. The idea was to sink a series of piles to focus the current, rake the sandbar, and let the current wash it away. The goal was a twelve-foot depth.[53]

Eastward off the tip of the island toward Bolivar, Fowler drove three rows of cedar piles ten to twelve feet into the bottom. After appeal by the city government, the federal government began to help, and in 1873 the bar was twelve feet below the surface and sinking deeper. There was also an accumulation of sand on the Gulf side which restored five hundred acres to the end of the island.[54] Success, but it was not enough. "We might have the yellow fever every year for a century," said the newspaper in 1871. "We might persistently sit still and refuse to help railroads, and let our streets be hog-wallers—yet if we could put twenty feet of water on each of the two bars of our Harbor, we would prosper and become a great city."[55] The goal now was a twenty-foot depth.

What was successful on a small scale set the pattern for future improvement—use jetties to concentrate the current, and seek federal subsidy to pay for them. It made sense. Under the classification at the time, a first-class harbor could accommodate a ship drawing twenty-six feet of water at low tide. Second class meant twenty to twenty-six feet, and third class was less than twenty. On the Gulf Coast, Tampa and Pensacola ranked second class; Mobile and Galveston, third class. New Orleans was also a third-class port until jetty work by the federal government moved it into the first category. Galveston possessed the best harbor between New Orleans and Vera Cruz, and improvement at Galveston, according to Joseph Nimmo, the chief of the Bureau of Statistics, was "a work of great national importance."[56]

Beginning in 1874, the U.S. Army Corps of Engineers directed by Captain C. W. Howell launched a project to build two jetties parallel to each other reaching into the Gulf, one from the tip of Bolivar and the other from the tip of Galveston Island. The idea was to force the Bolivar tidal bore to scour the outer bar. The engineers used gabions—large wicker cylinders filled with sand—to build the jetties. They failed. Under a new director in 1880, the engineers tried to construct the jetties out of pine brush and cane mattresses weighted with stones. That did not work either, and the townspeople became restless.[57]

There was talk about the benefit of twenty-five- or thirty-foot water. Henry Seeligson, a Galveston banker, commented, "Deep water alone can solve the future of Galveston, and will invite to our port the deep water vessels of all nations, and cause the terminus of the railroads of our State to center at Galveston." He thought further that Galveston should appeal to Congress for the money to carry out the recommendations of Captain James B. Eads. Famous for his work on the St. Louis bridge and for the construction of the successful jetties at New Orleans, Eads, passing through Galveston on the way to Tehuantepec, had visited the Cotton Exchange and talked to local leaders. He later wrote to say that he had heard of the failure at Galveston and that he thought the harbor could obtain twenty-five-foot water at a cost of $5 million.[58]

Citizens in 1881 at the Cotton Exchange organized a "Committee on Deep Water" to direct the effort, and the city government asked Eads for specific recommendations. The engineer replied that he could guarantee thirty feet at a cost of $7,750,000 with Congress providing the funds. That was an enormous amount of money, but the Deep Water Committee, led by William L. Moody, went to work in Washington, D.C., to acquire appropriate legislation. Moody, born in Virginia in 1828, came to Texas in 1852. He fought for the South in the Civil War, became a colonel, and returned to Galveston in 1866. He built a strong cotton and banking business, helped establish the Cotton Exchange, and served in the Texas legislature.[59] Deep water was essential for his well-being.

To promote the Eads bill, the Galveston delegation and Eads tactlessly criticized the Army's effort in the harbor. "The jetty which is finished is wrongly located," said Eads. "The amount expended on it is wholly wasted, because of its mislocation." He pointed out that submerged jetties as designed by the Army would not work because of wave action and friction. Jetties had to extend above the surface, needed to be close together, and should be made of stone.[60] The Army engineers, embarrassed by the waste of $1,578,000 at Galveston, fought back. They did not want Eads in control of improvements at Galveston as designated in the bill. Fearing competition, representatives of New York, Philadelphia, and Chicago also opposed the work, and Galveston lost.[61]

Stung, the Deep Water Committee began over again, and looked for broader support. It sent representatives around Texas, first, to elicit help. To their surprise, committee members discovered a deep prejudice against the port. People believed that the wharf monopoly paid 70–100 percent dividends and that the merchants owned the company. The DWC offset that misinformation by pointing to the

1.5 – 5 percent dividends and the wide ownership of the Wharf Company.[62] It also worked hard for out-of-state support.

After returning from a ceremony to open the Fort Worth and Denver Railroad, the Texas representatives met in Dallas and passed a resolution to promote a deep-water convention in Denver. Meanwhile, at Fort Worth in July 1888, a Texas convention agreed to support the construction of a first-class port at "any point on the coast of Texas." In Colorado, where representatives of nine western states met in September 1888, the delegates adopted the Galveston resolution for a first-class harbor on the Texas coast at a site chosen by a panel of Army engineers. Despite competition from Aransas Pass and Sabine Pass, the Galveston group was self-confident. They had some special support. John Evans, governor of Colorado, wanted a transcontinental railroad for Denver. When that failed to come about, Evans turned to Texas and Galveston as the outlet for the Mile-High State. He helped organize the building of a railroad to Texas and worked to aid Galveston on the Eads bill. Evans was the temporary chairman of the convention in Denver, and better yet, he became the chairman of the panel of engineers to select the site.[63]

The Army chief of engineers appointed Lieutenant Colonel Henry M. Robert, Captain George L. Gillespie, and Colonel Jared A. Smith in 1889 to investigate the ports of Texas and make a recommendation. None of the men had ever been in the South. For Galveston it was fortunate that a new group of Army officers had taken over in 1885. They admitted that the work in Galveston had failed, and admitted similar failures at Charleston, South Carolina. They, moreover, adopted in large measure the suggestions of James B. Eads. For his part, Eads had died in 1887. That cleared the earlier difficulties.[64]

A second convention with Evans as chairman met at Topeka in 1889 and endorsed again the resolution for a first-class harbor on the northwestern part of the Gulf Coast. Two months later the engineers investigating the sites reported favorably for Galveston and said that $6,200,000 should be spent. This time Colonel Walter Gresham led the Deep Water Committee in Washington, D.C. Gresham, like Moody, was born in Virginia and fought for the South in the Civil War. He was a noted lawyer and railroad executive, and had worked for Galveston at the deep-water conventions in Fort Worth, Denver, and Topeka.[65]

The political salesmanship was thorough. Even President Grover Cleveland knew about Galveston and its quest. The editor of the *Galveston Daily News*, Alfred H. Belo, told him that Galveston was a great place to fish and Cleveland wanted to try it out. When the Senate approved the Galveston Harbor Bill in 1890, the Galveston

Artillery Company set up its cannons on the beach and boomed a one-hundred-gun salute. A month later, after Cleveland signed the bill, the mayor ordered a holiday, and the whistles of the city—on steamships, trains, and factories—blasted the air for thirty minutes in celebration.[66] Deep water had been won.

Work on the jetties, north and south, went on for the next few years. The engineers first built a railroad and trestle over the water. Then, from the cars they dropped five-ton blocks of sandstone to build a trapezoidal wall. When it reached the surface, they capped it with ten-ton granite squares so that it stood five feet above the water. The project cost $8,700,000. The engineers meant the jetties to do the job and endure.[67] They did.

After some dredging in the channel, in October 1896, the largest cargo ship in the world, the British steamer *Algoa*, drawing twenty-one feet, tied up at the Galveston wharves. The size of vessels using the port jumped by 24 percent. In the next few years Galveston exports increased by 55 percent, and imports by 37 percent. In 1885– 1886 the Island City shipped only 22 percent of the Texas cotton crop. In the 1897–1898 season it moved 64 percent and at the end of the century Galveston was the leading cotton port of the nation.[68] Deep water was a triumph which saved the vitality of the city at a time when railroad transformations threatened to destroy it.

Although commerce with its railroads, harbor activities, and cotton trade constituted the main current in the Galveston economy of the nineteenth century, an important minor stream of tourism also evolved. Within a month after the City Company began to sell lots in 1838, the President of the Republic, Sam Houston, with some of the members of Congress took an excursion ride to Galveston from the nation's capital on Buffalo Bayou. The seat of government at the time was none too comfortable and they probably needed a vacation. Littleton Fowler, a Methodist minister, accompanied them to his regret. On the boat he saw "*great* men in *high* life." They stripped to their underwear in view of the shocked preacher. "Their Bacchanalian revels and bloodcurdling profanity made the pleasure boat a floating hell," he recorded. It was too much for the delicate Fowler, and he physically collapsed after the trip.[69]

In December the same year Millie Gray passed through Galveston on the way to Houston. Behind a team of rough-looking but gentle horses she took the time to ride to the beach with her four children to gather seashells.[70] Sheridan, the British diplomat, saved sand dollars from the beach, and like others, found them brittle and easily broken.[71] Another traveler in 1875 thought the city expensive, but the beach a delight:

Couldn't get a cigar or a cocktail under twenty-five cents and there was very little "proof" in the whisky or "Spanish" in the cigar. But then the beach. This is superb! magnificent! (if a man don't care what he says). To the Galvestonian it is a joy forever. He gives his last five-dollar bill on a ride along that bare sand bank to hear what the wild waves are saying—though I did not learn that they ever communicated anything of importance.[72]

The tourist value of the beach began to be recognized toward the end of the century. People used it for swimming, driving their horses, courting, and gathering shells. Since swimming suits were not a common item of apparel and ladies were shocked easily in those days, there was a problem. As early as the Civil War the city had an ordinance against nude swimming between sunrise and sunset. There was a twenty-dollar fine for a violation. The city changed the ordinance in 1869, 1870, 1876, and 1877 as violations continued. The law of 1877 prohibited bathing in the Gulf between 16th and 27th Streets from 4:00 A.M. to 10:00 P.M. and anywhere else in the city between 6:00 A.M. and 8:00 P.M. unless "clothed in a costume sufficient to cover the body from neck to knee, arms excepted."[73]

The *Galveston Daily News* in 1869 described how to make a bathing suit. Male and female styles were the same. It was best, according to the newspaper, to use twilled flannel, moreen, or serge. Stiff wool was preferred because it did not cling as much as other fabrics when wet. Colors could be white, gray, blue, checked, or plaid. The blouse was made like a sack with separate trousers full over the hips and loose at the ankles. A full skirt could be worn if desired. An alternative style included a Zouave jacket and trousers loose at the knees. The hair could be protected with an oilskin cap—a large round bag with a pull string along the edge.[74]

Naked swimming, nonetheless, remained common in the nineteenth century. The newspaper reported two hundred nude people on the Gulf beach on a summer day in 1867, and twenty boys in a natural state in 1869 kept the ladies from the bayside wharves and off the decks of ships. Cavorting unclad boys drove some women from the surf in 1874, and a mixed group of nude men and women swimming near Lufkin's Wharf in 1879 shocked decent people. When Officer Williamson in 1881 could not force naked boys out of the water of the bay he gathered up their clothes and took them to the police station. In 1899 the police actually caught and fined a boy for swimming "au naturel."[75]

Of course, thieves sometimes made off with unprotected clothing and valuables. Returning from a moonlight dip in 1868, a man found all of his personal items stolen, including his shirt buttons. In 1872 two young men from a boarding house left the beach water at 11:00 P.M. to find all of their clothing gone. They made it home all right, but the ladies were sitting on the gallery and they could not reach their rooms without being seen. They waited in a vacant field where the mosquitoes feasted upon them like "carpetbaggers upon the unhappy South" until the women finally retired. Embarrassment prevented a report to the police. The next year a horse took off with the clothes of a mixed group of men and women. They had driven to the beach and left dry apparel in the dray to change into after swimming. Left alone, the horse decided to walk home. The clothes were still in the wagon—all except two "panniers" and a pair of "palpitators," which somehow were lost along the way.[76]

Despite such mishaps the beach became increasingly popular. Streetcars provided regular service to the Gulf shore in 1877, giving all classes of people access to the surf most of the time from early morning until midnight. Women and children visited the seashore in the morning, entire families in the evening. There was little undertow and it was relatively safe. A reporter in 1880 observed boys plunging into the surf with enthusiasm and ladies gathering up their skirts to wade and exclaiming "Ah" and "Oh." There were small bathhouses to rent, some mounted on wheels that could be rolled into the water. "Now and then," said the reporter, "there is a woman who shows to advantage in the prevailing style of bathing dress, but the majority of them when they leave the water look much the worse for wear as the wet garments hang closely to their forms."[77] Although he did not say so, the effect of the salt water was probably just as damaging to the appearance of the men.

Outside groups began to arrive at Galveston on excursion trips—a congressional delegation in 1873, the Missouri Valley Press Association in 1875, the state Democratic Convention in 1876, Kansas legislators in 1876, a trainload of tourists from St. Louis in 1877, and a fat man's convention in 1891. The Gulf assumed the condition of high tide, according to a reporter, when the "phorty phunny phat phellows" entered the surf for their annual wash.[78] Maggie Abercrombie, who prepared an article about Galveston County for *American Sketch Book* in 1881, wrote, "Galveston could be made the most delightful summer and winter resort if but half was known of its rare attractions." She saw Galveston as purely a commercial city.[79] Local businessmen, however, awakened to the opportunity.

The Galveston Surf Bathing Company took out a charter in 1881 to build bathhouses between 10th and 30th Streets, and the Galveston City Railway Company built the Galveston Pavilion at 21st

Street and Avenue Q the same year. The streetcar company hoped to increase patronage by placing this two-story resort on the beach. Designed by Nicholas J. Clayton, the most important architect of the Island City, the Pavilion boasted sixteen thousand square feet of unobstructed floor space made possible by four steel arches which carried the load of the wooden structure. It was the first building in Texas to have electric lights, and it could accommodate five thousand people for dances and performances. In 1883, however, it burned to the ground in a twenty-five-minute fire. The fire engines had a hard time reaching it because of deep sand on the beach, and a musician who had been sleeping in the south tower was killed when he jumped from a window and landed on his back.[80]

The Pavilion lasted only two years, but this did not halt beach development. In 1878 the *Galveston Daily News* suggested the construction of a hotel on the Gulf side with galleries to take advantage of the sea breezes. In 1882, led by Colonel William H. Sinclair, president of the streetcar company, a public subscription financed the erection of the $260,000 Beach Hotel. Nicholas Clayton, the architect, placed it upon three hundred cedar piles driven into the sand. It was three stories high with two hundred rooms and eighteen-foot verandas. It was colorful: the building was mauve, the eaves were trimmed in a golden green, and the roof had an octagonal dome painted in large red and white stripes. It gave the impression of three pavilions with gables and ornate grillwork pushed together to form an enormous E configuration. It had a dining room, gentlemen's parlor and reading room, saloon, grand staircase, electric and gas lighting, and water tanks in the dome. It opened July 4, 1883, after a grand celebration the night before.[81]

The Beach Hotel became the focal point for social activity. The front lawn provided a site for summer entertainment—fireworks, high-wire walkers, and bands.[82] It was unprofitable, however, except when the railroads offered special rates to the city. Sinclair commented that management had "shown a great deal more enterprise than sense in building it."[83] It was sold in 1889 and resold in 1894. In 1898 the city health officer blocked the seasonal opening because of an "absolutely disgusting and disgraceful" discovery. For at least a decade the hotel had collected the waste products of its sewers in cesspools. Each night around 3:00 A.M. it flushed these by steam pressure into the nearby Gulf. A broken pipe taken up for repair revealed the practice. The city forced the hotel to connect with the city sewer system. While this was being done, the hotel burned under mysterious circumstances.[84]

The wooden structure was a tinderbox. On July 3, 1898, the night watchman's dog disappeared. On July 4 the watchman discovered a fire in the boiler room, put it out, and bought a bull terrier. On July 22 the bull terrier disappeared and another fire started in the same place. This time the guard was too late and the Beach Hotel vanished in heat, flame, and smoke. The police arrested no arsonist, but the owner had taken out a $25,000 insurance policy on July 18.[85]

Across the city at his home the architect, Nicholas Clayton, anxiously watched the flames. It was terribly painful for this gentle, shy man, who was the first professional architect in the state, to witness the destruction of his art. He had come to Galveston in 1872 from Memphis to supervise the construction of the new Tremont Hotel. He stayed to design homes and buildings such as the Block-Oppenheimer Building on the Strand with its cast-iron balustrades; St. Mary's Infirmary, which was the oldest hospital in Texas; the Stewart Title Building (Kauffman & Runge Building); next door, the Trueheart-Adriance Building; the W. L. Moody Building on the Strand with cast-iron columns; the Galveston News Building; the University of Texas Medical School, now known as "Old Red"; Ursuline Academy, which survived until Hurricane Carla in 1961; and one of the most elaborate homes ever built in Texas, the Gresham House, also known as the Bishop's Palace.

Colonel Walter Gresham wanted the most elegant house in the state, and he got it. With eclectic abandon Clayton designed for the cramped site a stone mansion with four four-story towers topped with tiled cones, numerous chimneys, balconies, massive oak doors, sculpted stone facings, stained-glass windows, and delicate black iron grillwork. No one knows the exact cost, but it was great for the era—at least $250,000. In 1923 the Roman Catholic Diocese of Galveston bought it as a home for Bishop Christopher E. Byrne, and the Catholic prelate commented about his residence, "I never thought that a farm boy from Missouri would find a castle in the sky in far away Galveston."[86]

Clayton dominated Galveston architecture during the last two decades of the century. Although some of his work was lost in the great fire of 1885 and the storm of 1900, much of it remained. After his death in 1916 his widow worried about a monument. Rabbi Henry Cohen responded, "Oh, you don't need one, my dear Mary Lorena. He's got them all over town. Just go around and read some cornerstones."[87] Since the city grew but slowly after 1900, Galveston architecture became frozen in space and time. The cornerstones are still there, and the Victorian architecture for which Galveston is famous today is the legacy of Nicholas Clayton.

His accomplishment, also, is a tribute to the economic power of

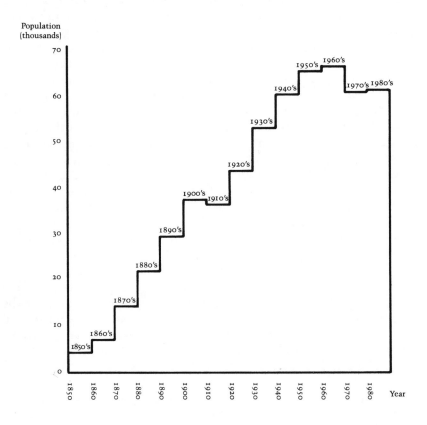

FIGURE 1. Galveston City Population, 1850–1980. *Source: Texas Almanac, 1982–1983* (Dallas: A. H. Belo, 1981), p. 189.

the city. Commerce, directly or indirectly, paid for his efforts. When Clayton arrived, Galveston was at its height of influence and prosperity. The moment was brief. With a population of almost fourteen thousand in 1870 and twenty-two thousand in 1880, Galveston ranked first in the state. The census of 1890, however, placed Dallas and San Antonio ahead, and in 1900 Houston, Galveston's archrival, eased past. Compared to that in other cities, Galveston's population

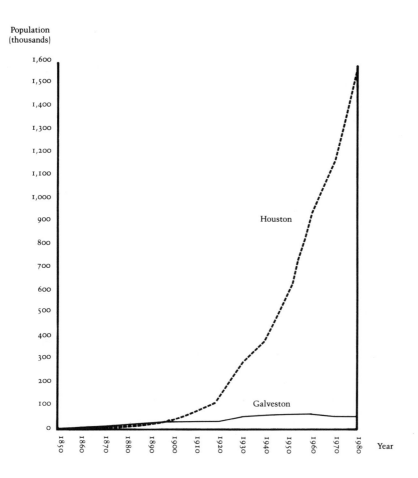

FIGURE 2. Galveston and Houston Populations, 1850–1980. *Source: Texas Almanac, 1982–1983* (Dallas: A. H. Belo, 1981), p. 189.

growth slowed dramatically after 1890. In the 1960's Galveston even lost 8 percent of its population and leveled off by 1970 at sixty-two thousand.[88] Its destiny was that of a medium-sized city, and the lack of growth has been a frustration to its citizens. In 1940, when Galveston ranked seventh in the state, an editor remarked, "There would be no point in trying to analyze the reasons for that condition, but it is no disloyalty to say that Galveston didn't make the progress it should. Discounting possible booms, this city has natural assets capable of supporting a considerably larger population."[89]

The reason for the frustration is the mistaken thought that Galveston could have been something more than it is now. It really could not have accomplished anything else. Galveston's fate was shaped by technology, location, and human reason. It was too risky, too reckless, and too uneconomic to place extensive businesses or population on an unstable edge of nature. It has been an error for islanders to measure importance according to population numbers. Greatness for Galveston came for reasons other than large size.

After the founding of the town, however, growth came rapidly. Galveston was a major gateway for the Republic, and the British consul reported in 1840 that it had grown from three houses to six hundred in three years. The population neared 4,000, and 228 ships of various sizes brought freight and 4,376 passengers to the docks in 1839.[90] The consul was more enthusiastic than Charles Hooton, who visited the island in 1841:

> From the sea, the appearance of Galveston is that of a fine city of great extent, built close upon the edge of the water; but its glory vanishes gradually in proportion to the nearness of the approach of the spectator, until on his arrival at the end of one of the long, rude, wood projections, called wharfs, which shoot out some quarter of a mile into the shallows of the bay, he finds nothing but a poor straggling collection of weatherboarded frame-houses, beautifully embellished with whitewash, (they may be mistaken for white marble from the Gulf), and extending, without measurable depth, about the length of two miles of string.[91]

On shore Hooton found wide, unpaved streets with ditches cut for drainage; a lack of fresh water; storekeepers who demanded 100 percent profit; pigs hunting snakes and cleaning garbage off the streets; and a hard-swearing, rough society where women were so scarce they had to marry in self-defense.[92] He would have agreed with Three-legged Willie (Robert M. Williamson, an early Texas lawyer) who said, "Galveston is a low island of sand somewhere floating on the bosom of the Mexican Gulf, peopled by the lordliest crew of fatherless bipeds that ever trembled between hanging and drowning."[93]

In the early 1840's the village of Saccarap, an enclave settled by immigrants from Saccarappa, Maine, failed. It occupied the high land of Laffite's camp near the bay shore and 9th, 10th, and 11th Streets. Amasa Turner, thinking it would be the center of town, built a wharf, hotel, and ice house there. It was too far from the deep water of the channel, however, and the center shifted to the Strand area.[94] An anonymous poet wrote in 1843:

The late proud modern town
Of Saccarap, like Birnam Wood
Has left the place where once it stood;
The wharf is down, the hotel gone,
And desolation, cold and lone
Has made here dark and dismal den
Within the haunts of vanished men
And wild weeds grow, and kidlings play
Where Deacon Bailey once held sway.[95]

Although a reporter for the *New York Sun* said in 1847, "The streets are wide and straight, but their cleanliness is about on a par with New York, which is no compliment," and a young man from Boston in 1859 found the town flat, rowdy, and drab with houses like "ugly Grecian boxes with pillars," after its first decades Galveston began to lose its rough edges.[96] Mrs. Isadore Dyer planted some imported oleander shrubs in her front yard in the 1840's, and they flourished with pink and white flowers. She gave cuttings to others, and they spread so that now there are over sixty varieties on the island—white, yellow, pink, salmon, and red. Known as the flower of Saint Joseph, the oleander, which grows twenty to thirty feet tall, gave its name to the city as a sobriquet in the nineteenth century.[97] It is ironic, however, that this plant, which adapted well to the saline soil and air and lent its beauty to the land, is toxic to human beings. Like Galveston itself, the oleander possesses an attraction that can be fatal.

Iron fronts imported from Philadelphia appeared on the new three-story business buildings downtown. Gas lighting, sidewalks, and shell pavement on the major streets also helped the appearance of the city. For the benefit and elevation of society, the town boasted a temperance group, dancing school, theatre, debating association, and newspapers.[98] The *Galveston Daily News*, Texas' oldest surviving newspaper, began in 1842. Willard Richardson bought it in 1844, and Alfred H. Belo joined him after the Civil War. Belo took over entirely in 1875 after Richardson's death. He started the *Dallas Morning News*, and the Belo Corporation continued to run the Galveston paper into the twentieth century.[99] Sharing the early period with the *News* were the *Civilian and Gazette*, the *Daily Advertiser*, *Die Union*, and *Flake's Bulletin*. These newspapers were the chief source of information for the people of the town and the surrounding counties. They printed not just editorial opinion, but also technical and commercial information.

The other major source of information was the mail system. Peter J. Menard, brother of Michel Menard, became the first postmaster in 1838. The mail came by packet from New Orleans. Galveston then sent it to the interior of Texas. After the Republic granted incorporation, it required mail delivery to Houston twice a week. There were no stamps until 1847, and it cost twenty-five cents to send a letter two hundred miles.[100] Telegraph service first came in 1854; information flow improved in 1859, when a telegraph wire was strung underneath the bridge built that year.[101]

Along with oleanders, new buildings, newspapers, and information sources, ministers also contributed to the transformation of early Galveston—at least to a degree. An early anecdote tells about three gamblers from New Orleans who found Galveston lacking in action. They turned virtuous and went to church. At the time for the collection the minister passed a hat, and the first gambler put in fifty cents. The second put in a dollar, and nudged the third man, who had fallen asleep. The sleepy gambler opened his eyes, saw the hat with money in the bottom, yawned, and said in a loud voice, "I pass."[102]

The Methodists, Baptists, and Presbyterians all organized in 1840, the Episcopalians in 1841, and the Roman Catholics in 1847.[103] When the Dublin-born Reverend Benjamin Eaton arrived in Galveston to establish Trinity Protestant Episcopal Church, he wrote to his bishop, "I know little about this town yet . . . but I have already seen and heard enough of the republic to cool my Texas fever, and to make me fear that I have left a most promising field (Wisconsin) for one where my exertions will not be half so useful . . . and where I shall experience almost every privation that a civilized man can endure."[104] He was close to being correct. After working for seventeen months to build a $4,500 church, this minister, who was once characterized as being "cold and so churchy that he made you feel as if religion was on ice from January to December and frozen stiff in Eternity," saw the building damaged three months after completion by the hurricane of 1842. Eaton escaped through a window, made it safely to a hotel, and exclaimed, "My God, my God has forsaken me this night." The congregation resurrected the building in six months, and after many changes the church endures to the present.[105]

Equally interesting is the early history of the First Baptist Church. When the Reverend James Huckins, a missionary agent of the American Baptist Home Mission Society, sailed into Galveston on a cold Friday evening in January 1840, he saw no need to leave the ship because he figured no Baptist would be found in such a dark, forlorn place. The next day he changed his mind, and organized a church within a week. This gaunt cleric with black eyes which moved independently of one another served as minister for First Baptist at various times.

The church records reveal the discipline of the congregation. People were taken off the rolls for gambling, intemperance, adultery, and joining the Methodists. Brother Jonathan Hughes failed to attend services. "Instead of letting his light so shine before him that they may see his good works, and glorify our Father which is in Heaven, he is a Stumbling Block to Sinners, and an injury to our church." Huckins too had to resign, apparently for owning slaves, or, perhaps, dealing in the slave trade:

> Bro. H. in settling in this country was obliged, for the comfort of his family, soon to be connected with the Institution of Slavery. This fact became known at the North, was used in Abolition papers, was employed in addresses, and became the cause of annoying enquiries in the form of epistolary correspondence—Even the Secretary of the Board wrote to him upon the subject.[106]

George Fellows, a neighbor in 1844, while on the way to Sunday school heard Huckins beating his female slave and spoke to the minister about it. The First Baptist Church, on the other hand, accepted black people on its membership rolls and supported them in a religious life. Huckins died administering to the wounded at Charleston during the Civil War, but while still in Galveston he baptized in the waters of the Gulf shore one of the fascinating characters of the town—Gail Borden, Jr.[107]

The great invention of condensed milk came after Borden's time in Galveston, but he had condensation on his mind. He reduced sleep to six hours per night, and condensed meat for the use of travelers. After boiling eleven pounds of meat he acquired one pound of extract. He mixed this with flour, baked it, and produced a meat biscuit. Borden won a patent for it in 1850 and a gold medal at an international exposition in London in 1851. He hoped to sell it to the U.S. Army, explorers, and sailors, and with the aid of Ashbel Smith built a factory in Galveston to produce it. Meat biscuit, however, was a failure. Its nutritional value was all right, but it had poor flavor. People just did not like to eat it.

In Galveston, meanwhile, Borden served as the collector of customs and later as an agent of the Galveston City Company. He built a house near 34th Street and Avenue P, and became the second-largest landholder in town. He was a member of the first city government, searched for a source of fresh water for the city, constructed a portable bathhouse so women could surf-bathe in private, and invented a "terraqueous machine." This was an amphibious vehicle powered by a sail which would turn wheels on land and a screw in the water. It failed on its maiden journey when frightened passengers panicked and dumped everyone overboard into the water. As his biographer, Joe B. Frantz, commented, "Some Galvestonians considered Gail Borden a genius; but more would have called him 'peculiar.' Almost all liked him."[108]

Even if he could not give good flavor to meat biscuit, Borden did give society the spice of his personality. Providing interest also to society were the voluntary military companies. During the period of the Republic a Mexican invasion was feared. Units formed for self-defense, with the men providing their own weapons and uniforms. They drilled, marched, and held dances. Most organizations lasted only a short time, but the Galveston Artillery Company has endured to the present. Formed by clerks and businessmen, the company started September 13, 1840. It merged with the Fusiliers in 1844, the City Guards in 1857, the Washington Guards in 1881, and the Light Infantry in 1884. The men acquired several cannons including "El Cruel" and "El Fuerte," salvaged from the wreck of the *Tom Toby*, which sank in the harbor during the 1837 storm. The company fired them for July 4, San Jacinto Day, and other momentous events.

After the Civil War, the Artillery Company reorganized in 1871 and in April of the following year paraded through the streets wearing blue coats, red pants, and red caps while carrying a white satin flag with the letters GAC formed in green, red, blue, and gold. The young ladies of the town had presented it to the unit, and that night the men repaid the generosity with a dance. The company became the elite social club of Galveston, and its annual ball marked the start of the debutante season.[109] The *Galveston Daily News* recorded in 1885, "As matrimony, each year, removes from the active circle of society many of its choicest ornaments, so, in a measure, does this annual ball of the Artillery Company replenish it, and in the number of accomplished and beautiful debutantes this ball was exceptional."[110]

The Civil War which interrupted the pleasant history of the Artillery Company was a major disruption for the Island City. It depopulated the city by at least 50 percent and demonstrated its vulnerability to invasion. The port was difficult to defend and militarily not worth the effort. It became a symbol, however, for both sides. For some islanders it became a test for survival, and they revealed a determination to remain regardless of consequences.

The state plunged into the maelstrom of secession early in 1861, and few stood against it. Ferdinand Flake, a spokesman for the German community and editor of *Die Union*, wrote a column criticizing the secession of South Carolina. Flake was not an abolitionist, and he was not disloyal. Yet a mob broke into his printing office, wrecked his press, and threw his type into an alley. Flake continued publication, nonetheless, with duplicate equipment which he had in his home.[111]

Another man of courage also spoke out. Sam Houston, governor of the state, opposed the action and after he lost went to Galveston to explain his position. Despite a threatening crowd the old man spoke from the balcony of the Tremont Hotel and pleaded, "Will you now reject these last counsels of your political father, and squander your political patrimony in riotous adventure, which I now tell you, and with something of prophetic ken, will land you in fire and rivers of blood?"[112] It was of no avail; the madness continued.

While most of the men hurried to join newly formed military units and the women rushed to make cartridges and tents, others, some 25 percent of the eligible young men, hastened to the foreign consulates to claim citizenship and avoid conscription.[113] Benjamin Theron, the French consul, particularly welcomed new citizens who wished to avoid Confederate service. He also complained to the United States about its bombardments of Galveston. As it turned out, both sides wanted to be rid of him.[114] Business had begun to decline, shortages to appear, and unemployment to rise when the *U.S.S. South Carolina* appeared off the coast in July to enforce Lincoln's blockade order. Captain James Alden issued a formal declaration and captured eleven vessels in five days. Business in Galveston collapsed, and the merchants did not have even enough money to pay their clerks.[115]

In preparation the Confederacy placed small forts at the extreme eastern point of the island, at Bolivar, and on Pelican Spit. An observation crew on top of the brick Hendley Building on the Strand watched ship movements with telescopes. Out of fun, and boredom, probably, the team at the Hendley created a club, the J.O.L.O., with elaborate titles for the club officers. It accepted pies from ladies, wrote elaborate resignations for members when they left for other duty, recorded club actions in the observation minutes, and never revealed the meaning of the initials.[116]

In early August the Confederate battery at San Luis Pass placed two cannon shots through the mainsail of the *Sam Houston*, a Union pilot boat captured by the blockade. In response the next day the *South Carolina* steamed toward the guns at Galveston and wildly exchanged a series of shots with them. One spectator, among the hundreds who rushed to the beach to witness the thirty-minute display, was killed. The Rebel gunners hit the hull of the Yankee ship three times with little damage, and the engagement ended when the *South Carolina* retired to sea.[117]

After the shelling the Confederate command determined that defense was useless. General Paul O. Hebert withdrew the cannons from the beaches and ordered an evacuation.[118] People were already leaving in wholesale numbers. Oscar M. Addison, a Methodist circuit rider, sent money to G. T. Maelling to move Addison's wife, child, and belongings to Houston. Maelling wrote to Addison, "Such a mooving as there is now a going on here, you never have seen in all your life; most every house is emtyed to Houston or Liberty."[119] Francis Lubbock, the governor of Texas, heard about the evacuation and wrote to Hebert that, if possible, Galveston and Galveston Bay should be defended. If impossible, then "Every cistern (wooden or brick) should be entirely destroyed, the water turned out, and the cisterns made wholly unfit for use again. The stock including horses, cattle, and sheep, to be driven from the island, and every spear of grass burned." It would be a humiliating loss for Texas, he thought, but "I would rather see the city one blackened ruin than that a miserable, fanatical, abolition horde should be permitted to occupy it." These words haunted Lubbock and later contributed to his defeat in a mayoral election at Galveston in 1875.[120]

Conditions in the city deteriorated. Charles Baker, a boardinghouse and saloon owner, ambushed and killed a soldier with whom he had quarreled. The soldier's companions took Baker from the guardhouse, beat him, and hanged him. They threatened to hang others too, and the local command had to place four guards at the door of every grog shop in town.[121] Commerce ceased for almost a year. There were destitute families of soldiers in Galveston, and almost three hundred aliens who claimed exemption from military service. Laboring people refused to help the Army in the evacuation, and martial law had to be proclaimed.[122] In June 1862 John Franklin Smith wrote to his cousin, Justina Rowzee:

> Two years ago this bay was almost covered with vessels of all shapes, sizes, colors and classes, with sails, steam and oars moving in every direction. Now but two or three are seen lying at the wharves or moving leisurely along. Now and then a steam boat moaningly whistles as if calling in dispair for its lost companions. . . .
>
> Now the wharves are vacant, and the streets almost deserted. . . .
> Little did I think two years ago, that I would walk the streets of Galves-

ton in my hickory shirt sleeves with a pipe in my mouth; and much
less, that I would sleep a dozen nights on the sidewalk in the most public part of town. Yet I have done both.[123]

It was difficult for the United States to maintain the blockade because of the long Texas coastline, so Rear Admiral David G. Farragut
decided to reduce the number of ports. The United States captured
Corpus Christi, Galveston, and Sabine City, and dominated Matagorda Bay. At Galveston, Commander W. B. Renshaw, after a preliminary attempt at contact, sailed into the harbor with his fleet and
white flags flying. The Confederate battery at Fort Point fired a
warning shot, and Renshaw reduced the guns to silence. On October 4, he demanded the surrender of the city and gave four days to
remove noncombatants. The Rebels took the opportunity to move
war materials and men across the railroad bridge to the mainland.
Renshaw was outraged at this breach of the truce, but there was
nothing he could do. The defenseless city then gave up.[124] William
Pitt Ballinger, a Galveston lawyer and Confederate supply agent,
wrote in his diary for October 4: "A bleek day in our history. Galveston is in the power of the enemy." About the talk of resisting the
enemy, he recorded, "But this I take it as all gas. For months it has
been a foregone conclusion not to defend the place. . . . I feel deeply
grieved and humiliated—and much of my pride and interest in the
place gone."[125]

Renshaw lacked troops to occupy the island, so he contented himself with 150 soldiers who raised the flag over the customshouse
during the day and retreated to Kuhn's Wharf at night. He allowed
the bridge to stand and trains to run to the mainland. He needed supplies and tried to purchase them locally, but the Confederates prevented that and captured one of his foraging parties at Bolivar. When
yellow fever began to appear on the coast, Renshaw wanted to pull
out of his weak position, but Farragut would not allow it. At this
point Renshaw should have blown up the bridge, but he did not. It
was a fatal error. In late December 1862, however, more northern
soldiers began to arrive from New Orleans to strengthen his hand.[126]

The situation was tense. Only 10 percent of the business places
remained open, people were starving and had to depend on rations
from the enemy, communication with the mainland was closed by
the Confederacy, and Confederate scouts roamed the city.[127] At night
while spying on the wharf, a scout carrying a shotgun refused to halt
at the command of a northern sentry. Worse, he told the soldier to
"go to hell." The Yankee fired, and the Rebel shot back. This created
a panic and the U.S. gunboats shelled the city for thirty minutes. No

one was injured.[128] Years later, a man who had been a boy at the time remembered that when this sort of event happened the old men, women, children, goats, pigs, and dogs would go running, crying and shouting, for the safety of the cemeteries. They would pause for breath, hear whistling cannonballs overhead, and stampede again.[129]

The condition soon reversed. A Union soldier stationed on Kuhn's Wharf recorded in his diary that on January 1, 1863, about 4:00 A.M. he was called up to the barricade with the first platoon. Shortly, "such a cannonading [as] I never heard" riddled the warehouse where he had been billeted.[130] The attack on the U.S. position was not a complete surprise, but it was a success. After the loss of the island in October, the Confederacy had replaced Hebert with John B. Magruder. The new general was six feet, four inches tall, rode a splendid horse, blustered a bit, talked with a lisp, cursed his boots because of corns on his toes, and possessed a reputation which said he could ride all day and dance all night.[131] Magruder was determined to recapture the lost ports of Texas. He settled an obstructive squabble between Army and Navy officers and planned an assault on Sabine Pass. When he heard of reinforcements at Galveston, he changed the point of attack and put together a coordinated land and sea campaign.

He ordered the small steamers *Bayou City* and *Neptune* armored with cotton bales and cottonseed sacks. Volunteers manned the ships under the command of Leon Smith. By moonlight the soldiers pushed a flatcar with an eight-inch Dahlgren cannon across the bridge to within a few hundred yards of the *U.S.S. Harriet Lane*. Magruder placed his five hundred men with their siege guns and field pieces in a two-and-a-half-mile line through the city and warned the citizens to move beyond range. After waiting for the moon to set, Magruder fired the first gun about 5:00 A.M. and said, "Now boys, I have done my part as a private, I will go and attend to that of General."[132]

The idea was to engage the enemy on the wharf from the city while the two cottonclads waged battle with the five U.S. ships anchored in the harbor. They were supposed to attack at the same time, but the Confederate ships came an hour late. Magruder knew that the northerners had removed part of the planking of the wharf, so he equipped his men with fifty scaling ladders. They waded through the water, only to find the ladders too short. The soldiers then retreated through withering gunfire. The *U.S.S. Owasco* steamed into position, began blasting canister into the C.S.A. position, and left the streets filled with shards of broken window glass.[133] One southern soldier forced from the shelter of a brick wall dashed across an open street. A cannonball plowed a furrow under his feet and sent him sprawling. Uninjured, he slowly got up, bowed to the U.S. ship, and casually walked the rest of the way to safety.[134] The fighting for the wharf failed, and Magruder considered a retreat.

Just as the Confederate troops were about to fall back, the cotton-clads arrived and attacked the *Harriet Lane*. The *Lane* sank the *Neptune* and tried to ram the *Bayou City*. While avoiding the maneuver the *Bayou City* took several point-blank broadsides and lost a side-paddle. Out of control, the Confederate ship swung around and rammed into the wheel of the *Lane*. With the two ships locked together, Leon Smith and his men raked the federal vessel with rifle and shotgun fire. Smith spotted the U.S. leader, Jonathan M. Wainwright, who had refused to surrender, and asked him if he was the captain. Wainwright said, "Yes," and Smith shot him in the head. Wainwright fell dead across the skylight. After this the Yankee sailors below decks came up with hands raised.[135]

Meanwhile Captain Renshaw (recently promoted), in the *U.S.S. Westfield*, ran aground. Another officer asked for a truce and it was granted, but Renshaw decided to blow up the *Westfield* and withdraw. He and his sailors took to the lifeboats, but something went wrong. The trail of powder to the magazine burned slowly, and the *Westfield* remained. Renshaw went back on board to see what was amiss, whereupon the ship exploded and killed the U.S. commander along with fourteen men. With that the other northern ships, in violation of the truce, retreated down the channel. The second in command gave the order and the ships fled all the way to New Orleans. The southerners, who also broke the truce, took prisoners, brought up more artillery, and towed the captured *Harriet Lane* to shore. The abandoned federal troops on Kuhn's Wharf, although not defeated, had no choice but to surrender.[136] Magruder had won the Battle of Galveston.

In the final accounting, the Confederates captured six ships, sank one, ran another aground, and took 300–400 prisoners. They lost one ship and 143 men, killed or wounded.[137] There was also, as always, an unmeasured emotional loss. Lieutenant-Commander Edward Lea of the U.S. Navy served on the *Harriet Lane* and fell mortally wounded during the fighting. His father, Major Albert M. Lea, was an engineer in the Confederate Army. He knew that his son was on the *Lane* and hastened aboard when it was brought to the wharf. He found the young man shot through the stomach, and the surgeon said he was close to death. "Good God!" exclaimed Magruder when he heard about it. "Lea, I had no idea of this. Take him to my quarters." The father searched for an ambulance, and when he returned he was told young Lea had just died while saying, "My father is here."[138]

The Rebels in victory placed cotton bolls at the mastheads, and, of course, Magruder was delighted. He sent a letter to the troops: "Your general is proud to command you; your State and country will honor you as long as patriotism and heroism are cherished among men."[139] Farragut, the northern officer in charge of the Gulf blockade, was disgusted and referred to the loss of the *Harriet Lane* as the "most unfortunate" and "most shameful" event that had happened to the U.S. Navy. He wanted to retake Galveston and planned an attack for January 11. The surprise arrival of the Confederate cruiser *Alabama* and its victory over the *U.S.S. Hatteras* in fifteen minutes upset the schedule. Then the Rebel victory at Sabine Pass ten days later, along with Magruder's fortification of Galveston, made the campaign impossible.[140]

The Confederates stripped the *Harriet Lane* of armaments and sold it to Thomas W. House, a commission merchant of Galveston and Houston, for use as a blockade-runner. The ship, built in 1859 as a revenue cutter, carried two masts, two side paddlewheels, and a low-pressure steam engine. With full sail and steam it could move at eleven knots. It was involved in the abortive attempt to take aid to Fort Sumter which provoked the start of the war. It was later part of the fleet which captured New Orleans, and it joined the Galveston blockade in 1862. The *Lane* was a beautiful copper-sheathed ship, 180 feet long, which could carry one hundred sailors. It was no wonder Farragut fretted over its loss.

House sent the skip through the blockade with a load of cotton to Havana. The *Lane* remained there for the rest of the war, went through a series of owners, and finally ended its existence as a lumber freighter with engine removed and rigged as a barque. During a storm in 1884 the crew abandoned the water-logged ship and it sank at sea.[141]

A snagboat finally removed the wreck of the *Westfield* from the shore of Pelican Island in 1906. Its engine shaft stood upright four feet under the surface of the water and obstructed navigation.[142] In 1893 a forty-four-pound conical gunshell was found protruding from the beach sand. It was thought to be left from the shelling of the *U.S.S. South Carolina*. A reporter wrapped it up and delivered it as a surprise to a businessman friend. The merchant tore off the wrapper, saw what it was, said, "Good Gawd!" and tried to climb the wall. After calming down, he rewrapped it and sent it on to another friend, who kept a lunch counter. The porter delivered it very gingerly.[143] Reminders of the war remained for a long time.

Although federal forces shortly re-established the blockade, they did not attempt another invasion. Magruder fortified Galveston with forty-one cannons and various installations—Fort Point, Fort Magruder, South Battery, Fort Bankhead, and Fort Scurry.[144] He maintained discipline with some difficulty. In July 1862 a soldier named Thomas "Nicaragua" Smith took a skiff and deserted to the Yankee ships. He had the misfortune to return on January 3, 1863, aboard a U.S. troop transport, *Cambria*, which came to Galveston without knowledge of the battle of January 1. The Confederates tried to lure it in by flying the U.S. flag on the *Harriet Lane*, but the cautious captain sent a yawl in first. The Rebels captured the small boat at the wharf, and the *Cambria* departed. Among the prisoners was "Nicaragua" Smith. He went through a court-martial and was hauled off in a cart to a firing squad. He tapped his foot on his coffin to the music of a band, and met death without covering his eyes.[145] For Magruder this was easy. It was not so easy in 1864 when five hundred armed soldiers with two artillery pieces surrounded the house where the ladies of Galveston entertained Magruder and his officers with a supper and dance. The rebellious soldiers threatened to level the house "instanter" if the partygoers did not leave. They told the general that it was no time for "feasting, fiddling, and dancing" while the soldiers and their families were suffering and the country was bleeding from every pore. Magruder cajoled them, promised them everything, called out a battalion and a regiment to disperse them, and went on with his fun.[146]

Poor rations, lack of pay, threat of disease, concern for families left at home, and boredom contributed to the low morale of the men. A group of them once marched through the town with a vile carcass of meat intended for their dinner and buried it with elaborate ceremony. Two officers barely escaped death when mutineers loaded a cannon not fifteen paces from their hut. The malcontents were preparing to fire when the officers rushed them with drawn swords. In 1864 there were 180 families drawing government rations, and children begged food at the camps. Soldiers refused to drill, deserted for Mexico, stole from merchants, and tore down fences for fuel. The citizens wished the Yankees would reoccupy the city, and welcomed the ultimate defeat of the Confederacy.[147]

The only excitement came from the exploits of the blockade-runners. The amount of traffic at Galveston was small compared to that of the eastern ports and, with the Mississippi River controlled by the North, of little consequence for the outcome of the war. The small ships loaded with cotton, with low hulls often painted a dirty white, slipped away from Galveston on dark, foggy, or rainy nights. There was no accounting, but it is estimated that three runners left and arrived each week and that only 10–15 percent were caught. By and large they carried cotton to Havana, Matamoros, Vera Cruz, or Nassau. They returned with trade goods, munitions, and Enfield rifles.[148] Runners made high profits and high adventure. William Watson, captain of the sailing ship *Rob Roy*, slipped into Galveston at night through a cordon of thirteen blockading vessels.

> We were now into the main channel, standing up before the wind with the last seen gunboat nearly astern, when suddenly a light flashed on our port bow, and we were hailed, "Schooner ahoy! heave to quick or we will sink you."
>
> I scarcely knew what to do. I thought it must be an armed boat from the blockading fleet.
>
> "No ship's boat comes in that far," said one of the men.
>
> "Who are you?" I cried.
>
> "Confederate guard boat," was the reply. "What vessel is that?"
>
> "The schooner *Rob Roy* from Havana," I replied.
>
> "All right, but heave to quick or you are sunk." . . .
>
> Explanations then followed.
>
> "Why did you threaten to sink us?"
>
> "To make you heave to quick as you were running upon certain destruction."
>
> "Why? are there torpedoes in the channel?"
>
> "Well, perhaps there are, but you were running right onto the wreck of the *Westfield*, and if you had struck that, you would have gone down right fast. Drop a little way astern and let go your anchor until daylight. It is here the boarding officer will visit you before you go up to town."
>
> We dropped astern and let go the anchor. Everyone breathed freely, and the general expression was, "In all right at last."[149]

Later, as the *Rob Roy* was on the way out with a load of cotton, the moon suddenly shone through a dark cloud bank and a federal gunboat spotted the ship. The gunboat drew alongside and held on with a hook, but due to the heavy swell and the movement of the schooner it was impossible to board. The federal officer demanded that Watson throw him a line.

> I got a rope, which I coiled up slowly; while unseen in the darkness I took the cook's hatchet from the galley door. I then cried to them to look out, and I stood near the man at the helm and threw the line to them. The main-boom, however, was in the way, and the rope fell short. This, I may say, was intended by me, as I wished to gain time and get farther away from the gunboat. . . .
>
> I passed forward of the main-boom, and threw the line again, which they caught.

"Let me make this end fast," I said, belaying the end to a belaying-pin under the quarter rail.

The officer then said, "Pass this line forward, and let the boat drop astern, and be ready to hold on."

Now was the time for the game I meant to play, but I nearly spoilt it by being too precipitate.

The boathook was cast off to let the boat drop astern, and the men began to haul in on the rope. Just then I seized the hatchet and severed the rope.

A volley of oaths came from those in the boat, but I had been rather too quick in cutting the rope; for before the boat fell astern, the man with the boathook made a sudden grab, and caught hold of our quarter rail, but with a heavy blow of the hatchet I knocked away the boathook, and the boat dropped astern, and at the same moment there was a shot from a revolver, and a ball whizzed past my head.

I threw myself quickly down, and crawled aft to where the man at the wheel stood protected by the dingey, which was crammed full of cotton.

They fired several more shots, but it was impossible for them to hit any of us.

The schooner, being freed from the weight of the boat, went off with a bound, and in a minute or two the boat was left out of sight in the darkness astern.[150]

In spite of such heroic efforts the end was inevitable. Captain Benjamin F. Sands, commander of the blockading squadron in 1865, heard the news of the fall of Richmond and the surrender of Robert E. Lee. He ordered a salute and sent the news to Galveston. Magruder agreed to give up and Sands landed at Galveston on June 5, 1865. His men hoisted the U.S. flag over the customshouse, and the war was over.[151]

The end had been foreseen. Four hundred Confederate soldiers had tried to desert with their weapons in May, but were turned back at the railroad bridge by a strong guard.[152] A New York reporter observed ransacked stores and houses at the time of surrender and said the "God-forsaken" port was a "city of dogs and desolation."[153] Within days, however, old Galveston people began to return, and by June 21 some two to three thousand federal soldiers arrived. The boarding houses filled up, and there was high demand for lumber, nails, and cement as people reversed the spoilage of war. The railroad began running three times a week to Houston, and three river steamers began bringing cotton to Galveston. General Gordon Granger, the federal officer in charge of Texas, arrived and paroled the Rebel soldiers. For a small fee the men could retain their swords and firearms.[154] Private individuals, such as William P. Ballinger, applied to President

Andrew Johnson for pardons. Ballinger received his by September 11, 1865.[155] The city recovered quickly, as Ferdinand Flake observed in August 1865:

> We cannot help observing how rapidly business is increasing in Galveston. The wharfs already, are crowded with steamers, ships, and other crafts, laden with merchandise of every description. Old stores are being refitted, and dwellings turned into stores. Hundreds of strangers pass through here every day, and all of our merchants seem busy. Galveston is rapidly regaining its former position as a commercial city, and the marks of war are being obliterated.[156]

With such a boom there were bound to be difficulties. Soldiers were accused of robbery, drunkenness, vandalism, and burning down the old Tremont Hotel. It had been severely damaged in the Battle of Galveston and parts of it had been stripped for fuel. While the relic burned, some soldiers fought the flames while others looted nearby saloons. The Army worked to suppress crime, as did the reorganized city police force.[157]

Throughout the period of federal occupation the civil government continued to operate, albeit somewhat uncertainly. An armed guard arrested Mayor Charles H. Leonard briefly over a misunderstanding about a freedmen's dance. An attempt by the governor to appoint a city government failed in October–November 1865, but General Charles Griffin removed Mayor James E. Haviland from office in 1867. Griffin, who was then in charge, had trouble with his black troops, and ordered Haviland to dismiss the entire police force in order to employ Army choices. Five of the new men were black, and only one of them was literate. Haviland took only those who met police standards and asked Griffin for more nominees. Agitated by prior public defiance in honoring the funeral of C.S.A. General Albert Sidney Johnston, Griffin replaced the mayor with Isaac G. Williams, who swore in the men Haviland had rejected.[158]

In 1870, when the federal soldiers left the island, the *Galveston Daily News*, nonetheless, graciously stated:

> In parting with the officers of the late garrison, we cannot but acknowledge that we have been peculiarly fortunate in having stationed at this post gentlemen of the strictest integrity of character, and who have on all occasions manifested a generous disposition to render any assistance in their power when occasion demanded it. The men were orderly and well behaved. The band is an excellent one, and will be missed sadly.[159]

The editor then added in another column, "While grateful for their mild exercise of authority, a sigh of relief at their departure is not to be restrained."[160] There was no despotism in Galveston during Reconstruction and no imposition of black rule, although Governor Edmund J. Davis replaced three aldermen in 1870. Galveston was not entirely free until the Democratic Party won the state and county elections late in 1873. The Galveston Artillery Company for that occasion fired a one-hundred-gun salute to "Coke and the Fourteenth Legislature to celebrate the triumph of the people."[161]

By this time the population, at 13,800, was almost double what it had been at the start of the war. The reopening of the port brought down prices, theatrical performances returned, gas-lighting came back, a streetcar line was built, and the city was linked to New York by telegraph.[162] Life returned to Galveston.

THE OLEANDER CITY

Chapter Three

"I say, landlord, that's a dirty towel for a man to wipe on."
"Well, you're mighty particular. Sixty or seventy of my boarders have wiped on that towel this morning, and you are the first one to find fault."

—Galveston joke, 1883

The greatest social change brought by the war and reconstruction concerned the status of black people. C.S.A. Major H. A. Wallace heard about it early. Messengers told him that troops had laid down their arms in Houston. He boarded the boat *Island City* and went to find out. It was true. Since there was neither Federal nor Confederate government at the moment, Wallace took over the boat as his own to set up a freight business between Houston and Galveston. When he reached the island on June 17 he found the blacks at the wharf throwing their hats in the air. "What is the matter?" Wallace asked.

"We's free now."
"What makes you free?"
"Yankees come down on ships on the outside to free us," was the reply.[1]

General Order No. 3 issued by Major-General Gordon Granger on June 19, 1865, at Galveston made the emancipation official.

The people of Texas are informed that in accordance with a proclamation from the Executive of the United States "all slaves are free." This involves an absolute equality of personal rights and rights of property between former masters and slaves, and the connection heretofore existing between them becomes that between employer and hired labor.
The freedmen are advised to remain quietly at their homes and work for wages. They are informed that they will not be allowed to collect at

military posts, and that they will not be supported in idleness either there or elsewhere.[2]

This order abolished slavery in Texas forever, and it destroyed, likewise, the legal and economic structure which supported it. "Juneteenth Day," consequently, became an annual celebration for the black community.

Black people had been part of the Galveston population since the days of Aury and Laffite, and even Cabeza de Vaca. According to the census reports there were 678 slaves and 30 free blacks in the city in 1850, 308 slaves and 2 free blacks in 1860, and 3,007 blacks in 1870.[3] This amounts to 16 percent of the total population in 1850, 4 percent in 1860, and 21 percent in 1870. The statistics are somewhat unreliable, but there was an antebellum effort to suppress free blacks in Galveston and Texas. Emigration into Texas was illegal, and the state required individual legislative approval for all free blacks. There were several in Galveston. The best known was "Major" Cary who had carried messages during the Texas Revolution and who had earned enough money to buy his freedom and that of his family. He ran a livery stable and was an expert rifleman.[4]

The law, however, was widely ignored, even though irritation with free blacks was constant. The chief justice of the county in 1848, for example, after numerous complaints by slave owners, gave notice to "free persons of color" against "harboring slaves, furnishing them with spiritous liquors and otherwise encouraging habits of idleness and dissipation." Unless in the county at the time of Texas independence, or born since then, free blacks were to leave within thirty days.[5] The order was not enforced. A city ordinance in 1851 required free blacks to give a bond for good conduct. "Free negroes and slaves do not do well together," said the editor of the *Civilian and Gazette* that year, "but the freest negroes in the county are nominal slaves, too much indulged in by their owners. Such are the worst pest of this community."[6] A housewife wrote to her sister in 1855 after a black servant girl almost burned down the house by leaving a candle lighted on a pine box, "She is terribly aggravating. And so are they all in one way or another. The descendants of Ham are a curse to his brothers. There is nothing in the world more worthless than a free negro."[7]

Pressure in the 1850's forced most of the free blacks to choose a master for protection. They gave the master a small sum in return for a promise of care in sickness and old age. In return, the master took responsibility for their good conduct before the law. In 1860 there were only two free blacks remaining in Galveston—the most fashionable barber in town, and the dancing instructor who taught the white children and played fiddle at social events.[8]

All blacks, slave or free, were subject to special laws. There were ordinances about drinking, gambling, disorderly conduct, carrying weapons, employment, and obeying the 8:00 P.M. curfew. A black who threatened to strike a white person received thirty-nine lashes.[9] Lucy, the slave of Joseph Daugherty, received more. She was an unhappy and rebellious house servant in a hotel. She was insolent, tried to run away, attempted to set the place on fire, and had to be confined to stocks at night. In anger, Lucy killed Mrs. Daugherty with a hatchet in the kitchen and dumped the body in the cistern. She confessed, and the jury found her guilty. On the second floor of the jail Lucy asked God for forgiveness, and the officials hanged her in front of twenty witnesses.[10]

Lucy was an extreme case. Anthony Hays, a free black from Boston, fought the system in his own way. He tried to hide a runaway slave on a ship for Boston, but was caught and fined $850 plus court costs. Since Hays could not pay the fine, the court sold him into slavery for life.[11] Most blacks did not go so far. They worked at their jobs and lived the best they could. Since there was not much farming around Galveston, the blacks worked in the homes, hotels, restaurants, wharves, and stores. According to the 1860 census, two black females worked in a bawdy house.[12]

Slaves were bought and sold in Galveston, but there exists little evidence of a regular slave market. Indeed, with the lack of nearby agricultural land and the illegality of overseas slave traffic, there was little need for a market. Colonel John S. Sydnor, a mayor and auctioneer, is often mentioned in secondary sources of Galveston history as a person who maintained a slave market. The *Galveston Weekly News* reported in 1863 that he sold sixty blacks of all ages at an average price of $1,774 each, and one man for $3,500.[13] The paper also noted the establishment of a depot for the sale of slaves in 1860.[14] There is no evidence, however, of the sale of slaves, year in and year out, on a regular basis.

There may have been some smuggling of slaves from abroad, but again, as might be expected, the proof is scanty. Aury and Laffite, of course, dealt in slaves, and at the time of the Texas Revolution Monroe Edwards engaged in the traffic. The Texas ship *Liberty* chased two of his suspected slave ships to Pelican Island, but the cargo was on land and gone before anything could be done.[15] In 1858 an American ship, *Thomas Watson*, with Mrs. M. J. Watson in charge, came to Galveston with a cargo of eighty-nine camels. On its way the ship lingered along the Gulf Coast, and to the British consul, Arthur T.

Lynn, it smelled like a slave ship. Watson turned the camels loose to wander and starve on Galveston Island, and Lynn thought the animals only a ruse for smuggling. She wanted a clean bill of health for Liverpool, and the consul refused. She did not need a certificate for Liverpool, but she did need one to get into Havana. The Cuban port was a slave center, and Lynn, with others, was very suspicious. Watson eventually weighed anchor and vanished.[16]

When the Civil War ended, young blacks flocked into Galveston despite the warnings of the military and established an enclave at the old location of Saccarap.[17] Emancipation, however, meant work, and the Army impressed unemployed blacks to cut wood and operate steamboats. City ordinances backed the requirement for employment, and the police shortly filled the jail with black vagrants. The sheriff discovered the prisoners trying to escape and decided to place them in chains. The blacks resisted, threw bricks, and the police opened fire. One prisoner who said that he "would not be ironed by any damned white man" was hit in the head, and another was struck in the body. Both died.[18]

There were complaints about drunken freedmen. Editor Ferdinand Flake explained, "In our walks about the city we notice many of our saloons make a practice of selling liquor to negroes. This should be stopped. Every one knows the effect of ardent spirits upon the black is very different to that upon the white man. The black, under its influence, is ready to make any engagement, to commit crime or mischief."[19] The newspaperman's statement is interesting because it not only reflects a local attitude about blacks and their capacity to drink, but also reveals that the saloons, at least, were integrated.

The freed slaves obtained civil rights through military enforcement. They could now vote and participate in the court processes. The unsympathetic editor of the *Galveston Daily News* went to register and met a crowd of 150 "sons of Ham," "the most loud-smelling that our nasal organs ever came in contact with." They registered, received papers, and remarked, "Here am a'noder citizen made."[20] The editor in his observations and his use of a stereotyped vernacular was patronizing, but this was typical of the white newspapers until well into the twentieth century. Consider the following "amusing incident" printed by the *News* in 1877: A judge was sitting on the Galveston to Houston train in the smoking car when a six-foot-three-inch black man came into the car. He had a large mouth with thick lips "like two monster Bologna sausages, wide open and curling upward and downward as if swollen almost to bursting." The judge sat upright and leaned over the seat in front of him to look. A conductor asked, "What do you think of it, Judge?" The magistrate continued to gaze, waved the conductor away, and said, "Hold still a minute, George, I'm waiting to see him finish turning wrong side out."[21]

There was little sympathy or sensitivity, moreover, expressed by whites about the difficulties of transition from slavery to freedom. One exception was another judge in 1865. In his court James Hall brought an adultery suit against his wife, Mary, and an alienation of affection suit against Cleyborne Dyer. James and Mary Hall had married with the permission of their masters six to seven years before. There was no legal status to the marriage. When emancipation came, Mary Hall took a new husband, Dyer, and the Provost Marshall married them. The Galveston judge dismissed the case. Under the old law free blacks were treated as slaves and punished with whipping, branding, or death. A white person in a similar circumstance would have been fined $100 to $1,000. The judge prudently decided to wait for new statutes which would bring the law into accordance with the new circumstances.[22]

Within the black family there could be some humor over the transition. Daniel Ransom recalled a situation to interviewers in the 1930's. His father, Henry Ransom, was a British citizen who worked on a whaling vessel. While in New Orleans before the Civil War he purchased his wife, Ellen, and later moved to Galveston, where he worked as a paperhanger. During family arguments, the son recalled, his father would say, "Don't you talk to me like that. I bought you and paid for you." Then, said the son, "She'd get riled up for sure."[23]

Two institutions—the black churches and the U.S. Army—helped to ease the birth pangs of freedom. Through the Freedmen's Bureau the Army assisted by establishing schools, taking care of the destitute, encouraging work, and adjudicating between the races. The whites generally disliked the bureau. On one occasion, the bureau took the side of a black in a dispute concerning a turkey, and sent a note to the Strand merchant. "That person, we suppose, not liking the tenor of the note," reported the *Galveston Daily News*, "said that he wished the Freedmen's Bureau was in ——, (never mind the word) a place much hotter than this gets to be, even in dog-days." The bureau, in response, sent a guard to arrest the merchant.[24]

It was the Freedmen's Bureau which brought George T. Ruby to Galveston from New Orleans in 1866. Born in New York in 1841 and reared in Maine, Ruby, a black man, acquired a liberal education and a lasting desire to win civil rights for his race. He promoted the immigration of blacks to Haiti, took heart from the war between North and South, and became a black educator in Louisiana at the end of hostilities. After being beaten almost to death by a white mob, he moved to Galveston as an agent of the Freedmen's Bureau, intending to continue his work in education. His path, however, led into politics. Ruby joined the Union League and became its Texas president in 1868. He was appointed Deputy Collector of Customs for Galveston for 1868–1872 and was elected state senator from 1869 to 1873. In the legislature he supported not only the rights of blacks, but also the economic enhancement of his adopted city. Through his influence in the Republican Party Ruby affected patronage, but with the return of the Democrats his political career waned. He refused to run for re-election, and, subsequently, in 1874, returned to New Orleans. This New England black man, a temporary Texan, left behind, however, a legacy of biracial politics in Galveston and an example of black achievement at a time when most white Texans doubted such capacity in the minority race.[25]

The greatest accomplishment of the Freedmen's Bureau was public education. Schools until this time were a private or parochial affair for white children. The bureau established public schools in churches and houses for whites and blacks and tried to make them self-sustaining. The schools had to be subsidized and met some public resistance, but the bureau, nonetheless, ran them for five years. In 1867 there were four schools by day and three at night. Unlike other places in Texas "Yankee teachers" could find a place to board in Galveston—mainly with German families.[26] Between three and four hundred blacks attended school, and the desire for education was impressive. "We saw fathers and mothers together with their grown up children, all anxiously engaged in the pursuit of knowledge," observed Ferdinand Flake.[27]

The *Galveston Daily News* generally supported the idea of education for all children, but had difficulty with the Freedmen's Bureau on the mixing of the races.

> Of the prime necessity of providing the means for the rising generation to acquire an ordinary education, there can be no difference of opinion, and in this State, if the matter was not mixed up with the eternal nigger, proper means for affording instruction would, doubtless, have been provided long ere this. . . . It will do no black child any good to be taught beside a white child, while the attempt would do the white child a good deal of injury, because the position is repugnant to its feelings, those of its parents, and of its associations, and all attempts at imparting an education under such circumstances would be worse than useless.[28]

For a decade after the end of Reconstruction and the Freedmen's Bureau, Galveston County ran the public schools, amidst criticism and uncertain funding. Racial separation was the policy for students. "Colored children are not sufficiently advanced in civilization to be the fit companions of white children," wrote the editor of the *Galveston Daily News*. "They are not as cleanly; they are not as well developed morally and intellectually."[29] In 1881 the citizens voted to take over the city schools, approved a tax levy, and elected trustees. The trustees hired a superintendent and in the fall opened a segregated system with one thousand white and four hundred black children.[30] This set the pattern for the next seventy years.

There was also an early attempt at segregation on the streetcars, but it failed because of the shortage of cars.[31] Separation of races on state railroads finally came in the 1880's and was confirmed by the state in 1891, but white society was ready for it earlier. Blum's Drug Store refused to sell soda water to blacks in 1872, and Henry Greenwall denied a seat to Mary Miller in the parquette circle of his theater because of race in 1875. The court held Greenwall guilty of deprivation of civil rights and assessed a minimum fine of $500. The judge commented that he wished it could be but one cent, and later dismissed the fine. In reaction, the black community met at the colored Methodist church and passed resolutions declaring the judge incompetent and prejudicial.[32] By 1881 there was de facto division of races in churches, theaters, hotels, saloons, and barbershops. In the 1880's blacks established their own fraternal organizations, sports teams, military drill units, and recreational facilities—in essence, the minority community put together a separate, parallel social structure.

The churches, a source of solace and inspiration, had always been segregated. Blacks sat in the gallery of white establishments or went to their own buildings. They held revival ceremonies, as did the whites, and developed their own style. One of the most popular black revivalists was the Reverend "Sin Killer" Griffin from Shreveport, Louisiana. Griffin, a large, brawny man with a voice that would put "seven steam calliopes to the blush" would leap, crawl, walk the aisles, and hoarsely shout, "Do you want to go to that golden city we have been talking about?" The audience would respond, "Yes, yes, yes! Hallelujah!" "You can go there brethren, but you must first be born again. Before you can write your name in the book of eternal life, you must be washed in the blood of the lamb. When you get there you will see your father and your mother and your brother and your sister. . . . Do you want to stay away from such a place and go to hell where the fiery demons are?" "No, no. Hallelujah! Amen!"[33]

A difference in style and a separation in social and economic matters were the pattern before the war and continued afterward, even though blacks possessed greater freedom to develop and more justice before the law. Prejudice, patronization, and stereotyping remained, and, as before, the flashpoint for the white majority was sex.

The newspaper complained in 1867 about a disorderly house kept by a black woman, Celia Miller, in the center of the city. Women of both races lived there and attracted all sorts of debased men at night. In another instance the editor reported a white woman living with a black drayman. She said she liked him and that others were doing the same. The paper bewailed the impudent, vulgar, audacious black prostitutes who used the alley behind the Episcopal Church as a place of assignation every night. "The hearts of the 'trooly loil' were made glad this morning by seeing one of the 'boys in blue' promenade market street holding in close embrace one of the most hideous negro wenches mortal eyes ever rested on," the editor observed in 1869. The *News* reported that the black Texas senator, George T. Ruby, married a blonde, white woman, to the rejection of black Galveston women. It recorded other biracial marriages as well with disapproval or sarcasm.[34]

In such circumstances you would expect lynchings, and there were a few. In 1843 a mob sentenced a slave to hang the following day for an attempted "outrage" on a white woman. A judge denounced mob rule and released him. The mob recaptured the hapless black, held him until the original time of execution, put a rope around his neck, dragged him to a tenpin alley, and suspended him from a beam. The mob then cut off his head and threw the body into the bay. It was later retrieved and buried.[35] Decent of them.

In 1865 a mob captured a black man and hanged him from a sign at the rear of a house on Winnie near 20th Street for a similar crime.[36] Then, there were several times when you would expect a lynching and it did not occur. Mose White, a large, belligerent mulatto, for example, exposed himself and insulted a lady on the street. He hit the policeman who arrested him and attracted an excited group of one hundred people. A sailor wanted to kill him, but was restrained by the citizens. There was no lynching. Five years later, in 1883, a teenage black without an "extra bright intellect" tried to rape a five-year-old white girl in a stable. He was arrested, taken to jail, and charged. There was no attempt at lynching.[37]

The community gave opportunity to the greatest of the Texas black leaders of the time—Norris Wright Cuney. He was the son of a white Brazos Valley planter and a black mistress who bore him eight children. She was able to gain manumission for herself and seven children, and an education for three sons. Not bad. Cuney went to Pittsburgh for schooling and would have attended Oberlin except for the interruption of the Civil War. He returned to Galveston in 1865 and may have been involved with a gambling ring for several years. The record is unclear about this. In 1872, however, he became a customs inspector. Cuney ran for mayor in 1875 and spoke out against the injustice of the Greenwall theater incident. The white twelfth ward elected him alderman from 1883 to 1887, and he became important to the Republican Party.[38]

When George Ball bequeathed $50,000 for a new high school, his heirs offered $10,000 more if it was reserved for white students. Cuney and another black member of the council wanted the school open to all, but he acquiesced and Ball became a white facility. When white dock hands struck in 1883, Cuney organized black laborers as strikebreakers and successfully moved them onto the wharves. The business elite wanted cheap labor and Cuney supplied it. He thus drove a wedge between the economic classes of the white majority. He was the only person in Galveston to raise the flag in honor of Benjamin Harrison's election, and a short time later received appointment as the chief collector of customs at the port of Galveston. It was a choice plum.[39]

During the last ten years of life the black leader suffered from tuberculosis, which finally killed him in 1898. This dapper man with his neat Prince Edward suits, constant cigars, friendly demeanor, and loping gait stood politically between the radicalism of W. E. B. DuBois and the conservatism of Booker T. Washington. He was no better nor worse than the other politicians of his day, and he offered an example of a competent black person.[40] "Negroes are human beings," he said, "and should be considered from that standpoint, if people would understand them as a race. In their actions and manner of life, they are prompted by very much the same motives actuating others of the human family."[41]

The entire human family of Galveston—black, white, yellow, brown—suffered together the frequent visitations of death. The rate was awesome, and similar to that in other port cities in the United States. The *Record of Interments, 1859–1872,* lists many causes—consumption, typhoid, dysentery, "bad whiskey," morphine, "shot," "hooping cough," "teething," and "hanged in jail."[42] The major causes of death listed by the health officer for 1875, a normal year without epidemic, were consumption, convulsions, general debility, enteritis, and stillbirth. In the nineteenth century the Grim Reaper was fond of children, for in this same normal year, 243 deaths out of a total of 682 were under one year of age. The National Board of Health in 1881 calculated the Galveston mortality rate at 25.8 per 1,000 people. The white rate was 18.2 and the black, 49.3. Death also was partial to blacks.[43]

The greatest epidemic killer was yellow fever. It was a virus transmitted from one person to another by mosquitoes. The etiology was unknown until Walter Reed's courageous experiments in Cuba in the early twentieth century. Before this, people understood that the disease came in the summer and disappeared with cold weather, especially after a heavy frost. They also knew that it spread through human contact, and that if it did not kill you, immunity was gained. Galveston, of course, always produced hordes of mosquitoes, rarely experienced frost, had a constant stream of unexposed immigrants, and carried on foreign commerce with Mexico and the Caribbean, where yellow fever was endemic. There were few window screens until the 1890's. Galveston, therefore, was extremely vulnerable.

The island suffered epidemics of yellow fever in 1839, 1844, 1847, 1853, 1854, 1858, 1859, 1864, 1866, 1867, 1870, and 1873. Symptoms included chills, fever, headache, muscle aches, nervousness, jaundice of the eyes and skin, coma, and regurgitation. Internal bleeding in the last stages caused discharges to turn the color of coffee. It was a fatal symptom. After the appearance of "black vomit," victims usually died. For those who survived, there was a long convalescence and a danger of relapse that could be as bad as the initial onslaught of the disease. Treatment varied with the physicians—none of them knew what they were doing—but consisted generally of confinement to bed, mustard baths for the feet and plasters on the stomach, cold compresses on the forehead, moderate food, warm tea, and no busybodies in the room. Of those who caught the disease one-fifth to one-fourth died. This often amounted to one-tenth of the population—a decimation.[44] It meant that as much as half the town—or, in the case of 1839, almost everyone—would be sick with fever. In that year a small ship came to the port from Vera Cruz and the captain asked Levi Jones to examine his sick son. Jones, a retired physician, diagnosed the illness as yellow fever. The boy was beyond aid and shortly died. The father as well succumbed in the next twenty-four hours, and the terror-stricken crew carrying the disease with them fled into the town.[45] Nicholas Labadie wrote his nephew shortly after Christmas:

> I was rejoiced to hear from you both, but could not but shed a tear on
> the little presents your kind wife sent to Mrs. Labadie: Alas! they are yet
> on my shelves and I feel not courage enough to taste or eat them as she
> is no more to this world and has gone to the land of spirits. The epi-
> demic which visited our infant city in October and November became a
> scourge to me, all my household became attacked at one time; my two
> little daughters recovered, my carpenter died on Sunday night, my clerk
> of the black vomit expired on Monday night, and my poor wife breathed
> her last about two hours after Nov 5th of the congestive fever [after] only
> six days of sickness.[46]

Another bad fever year came during Reconstruction in 1867. People returned to Galveston after the war, commerce recovered, and federal troops occupied the city. There were thousands of people who had never been exposed to "yellow jack," and there was heavy rainfall in the spring and summer. The newspaper registered complaints about stagnant water on the streets and underneath houses. There were so many mosquitoes that if you were exposed at night, as one poor man was after he chased a burglar, your face would be swollen with bites.[47] The stage was set for epidemic.

In late June, after reports of yellow fever in New Orleans and Indianola, the *Galveston Daily News* promised to give notice of any local appearance. It was already on the way. A young German traveler, George H. Moller, passed through Indianola and on to Galveston. He arrived June 28 and died July 3 with black vomit. The newspaper faithfully reported his death on July 5 and urged unacclimatized German immigrants to leave for the safety of the interior.[48]

Often there was reluctance to acknowledge the presence of illness—it was bad for business, and people did not like to face the facts. Greensville Dowell, a former C.S.A. Army doctor in Galveston, was in charge of the city hospital. He had diagnosed yellow fever in 1864 and was threatened with a court-martial for his effort. Still, he did not flinch in 1867. People were already calling him alarmist when he performed a post-morten exam on an early victim in the presence of the best private doctor in town. Dowell found black vomit in the stomach and held it up in his hand. "Mr. B.," the other physician, said, "Now Dowell, if yellow fever should break out here, don't you say that this is a case of yellow fever, and that is black vomit." Dowell retorted, "It is yellow fever; this is black vomit. I do not care who says to the contrary." With some justice "B." later caught the fever, but recovered.[49]

On July 30 the *Galveston Daily News* warned people that they should leave the city, although it was free of disease at the moment. On July 31, however, the equivocal newspaper noted five deaths in the past three days, and thought it nothing to become excited about. On August 2 the editor admitted, "We now tell the public candidly that yellow fever is epidemic." Some five thousand people fled, probably, one-third of the population, and spread the fever along the inland train and stage routes. Business came to a standstill. The banks refused to loan money; debtors refused to pay their bills. They waited to see who would die and would not have to be paid. Ice became scarce and high-priced. There were 22 deaths in July, 596 in August, and 482 in September. Probably, three-fourths of the population caught the disease. A total 1,150 died, and at a rate of 20 per day.[50]

Major-General Charles Griffin, the head of military affairs in Texas, perished, and a worker at the barracks observed:

> Every morning when the sun rose and the roll was called many familiar faces had disappeared forever. Merry, laughing and buoyant with life and spirits in the evening, silent and stiff in the arms of death in the morning. . . . Disease lurked in the sands, in the water, in the wind. The sun rose and set, the waters rose and fell, and the victims of the yellow fever scourge silently succumbed to their fate. It was a dreadful summer.[51]

Burning tar fumigated the air of the city, grass filled with small green frogs grew rank on the Strand, and ringing of church bells for the deceased was so constant that it irritated the sick and living. Amelia Barr, who had moved with her husband and family to Galveston in 1866, observed the beds of the dying drawn close to open windows—white faces with cracked ice to cool them, moaning, raving, shrieking, vomiting, and a strong, sickly smell of yellow fever mixed with the heavy, sweet odor of oleanders. She felt that the ghosts of Laffite's pirates haunted the house she lived in, and her own family fell ill. Her son Alexander while dying kept asking, "Who is that man waiting for me in the next room?" They all heard the heavy footfalls, but no one was there. The father held her other son while he died.

> "Papa, what is the matter with my brother?"
> "He is very ill, Calvin."
> "Is he dying?"
> "Yes."
> "Tell him to wait for me. I am dying, too, Papa. I cannot see you! I am blind! Kiss me, Papa."[52]

Her husband, Robert, after hearing his long-dead father calling him, also expired. Mrs. Barr survived, however, along with the three daughters. After suffering through the fever she gave birth to a son in December. He was born "yellow as gold" in color and died three months later. She thus lost all the male members of her family. She endured the hurricane of October and during the rebuilding period ran a boarding house. In 1868, leaving behind the four graves of her family, Amelia Barr departed for a new career in writing in New York.[53]

For Amelia Barr, Galveston was a "city of dreadful death."[54] There was little to do except help each other ease the pain, and await cold weather. It came in late November, but the number of victims already was declining. The fever had burned up the available fuel and had nowhere else to go. Volunteers, often people who had had the disease and were thus immune, joined a branch of the Howard Association, a national philanthropic organization. The group collected funds, disbursed money, nursed, and sent medical personnel to help other places. The association record book indicates a formal establishment in March 1854 with Reverend James Huckins acting as chairman and James W. Moore as president. The association may have existed as early as 1844 in Galveston, and it lasted at least until 1882.[55] In 1867 the Howard Association provided nurses and medicine, and sent people to the hospital. It spent $8,000, including $100 donated by Gail Borden, Jr., in New York, and provided nurses for Brenham and Alleyton. It ceased its work for this epidemic on October 11 and estimated that the disease covered 200 miles of coastline to a depth of 125 miles, from Galveston to Corpus Christi.[56] In the record book an anonymous member later recorded these verses:

I see him tall and gaunt and grim,
    As he stalks in the moonlight air.
He moves so fleet on his legs so slim,
    And halts and runs with a crazy whim
That he seems to touch everywhere.

He is pausing now, at a humble place,
    And waving his skeleton hand,
A father comes out, with a reddened face,
    And shudders to meet his hot embrace,
Then reels to the silent land.

A wail comes up, from the orphan group,
    As the hearse moves slowly away,
But the fiend will stifle their cries with a swoop,
    Tomorrow those flowers will wither and droop,
'Tis only the work of a day.[57]

The most powerful nineteenth-century weapon against "yellow jack" was quarantine, and the technique was responsible for the drop in yellow fever mortality after 1873. Twenty years earlier Ashbel Smith, the leading Texas medical authority, had written a letter to a Houston newspaper which claimed quarantine was an ineffective measure. He cited Galveston as an example. The difficulty, however, was not with the insufficiency of the idea, but with the poor enforcement of the barrier. In 1853 when Smith wrote, for instance, the captain of the *Mexico* from the infected port of New Orleans circumvented the quarantine by landing his passengers on the Gulf beach. They were into the city before Galveston authorities could stop them.[58] Despite the fact that quarantine did not work at this time, it was, nonetheless, Galveston's first concerted attempt.

As the debate over the efficacy of quarantine continued, there developed additional incentive—unmitigated fear. When yellow fever hit Galveston in 1870, widespread panic seized the coast. A militia armed with shotguns and bludgeons stopped a trainload of fleeing Galvestonians at the Houston city limit. The train returned to the island "butt end foremost," but not before most of the passengers scattered in all directions and walked into the Bayou City by different routes. Houston placed a quarantine on Galveston, turned other trains back with armed force, and threatened to tear up the track. Other towns followed Houston's lead, and Galveston closed off trade with New Orleans. Crescent City merchants accused Galveston of using quarantine for its own profit, but this was not true. The motive was well-justified fear, and traffic ceased all along the Texas coast. Only sixteen persons died that year in Galveston.[59] The lesson was plain.

The same thing happened in 1873—panic; sporadic, but tight quarantines; and complaints from merchants. Seven people died that year. In 1876 when yellow fever appeared in New Orleans, the state quarantine officer cut off the Louisiana port, and no appeal from Houston, Galveston, or New Orleans businessmen budged him.[60] There was no yellow fever in Galveston that year, no deaths. The lesson had been learned. Quarantine was used thereafter as a preventive technique. It was applied quickly, rigorously, and sometimes viciously. But quarantine halted the scourge of "yellow jack" until science in the twentieth century provided understanding and new technologies to fight the disease.

Ironically, it was the comparatively high incidence of disease in Galveston which brought to it the city's most prestigious institution, the University of Texas Medical Branch. Ashbel Smith played the key role. He was a small, ugly man with strong opinions and a feisty temper. Known as "Old Ashbarrel" behind his back, Smith never married, held women in low esteem, and yet exhibited courtly manners. Born in Connecticut in 1805, he studied medicine at Yale and in Paris. He arrived in Texas shortly after the revolution and became the first surgeon general of Texas. He served in the Texas legislature, fought in the War with Mexico, and suffered injury in the defense of the South at Shiloh. He owned a large plantation called "Evergreen" on Galveston Bay, accumulated a four-thousand-volume library, and wrote the first learned medical treatise in Texas. For this study of yellow fever in Galveston in 1839, Smith inspected bodies and tasted black vomit. He did not recognize the mosquito as the vector, but he did recommend cleaning and draining as preventive measures.[61]

His colleague, Greensville Dowell, helped start Galveston Medical College in 1865, but ran into trouble because of his equally contentious nature. Because of dissension between Dowell and the faculty, the college faltered, and a young man studying medicine at the city hospital thought the school a "humbug, a swindle in every sence [sic] of the word." The critic liked the hospital, though, where "any disease nearly that one wishes to study can be found." He treated "a very interesting case," of a sailor who had fallen from the top of a ship and whose broken thigh bone had stuck into the wooden deck.[62]

Smith helped Dowell reorganize the school into Texas Medical College in 1873, and worked for the location of the state institution in Galveston. At this crucial juncture Smith was both a trustee of the University of Texas and president of the Texas State Medical Association. Various cities competed for the colleges. Austin and Tyler wanted the whole system, including the medical school. Houston and Galveston wanted the medical branch and threatened to throw everything to Tyler unless Austin agreed to separate the medical and undergraduate campuses.[63]

Smith argued before the legislature in favor of Galveston because the Island City possessed size, wealth, opportunity to study diseases, noble citizens, and a school already in operation. Before the medical association he emphasized that students needed a practical education as well as a theoretical one and that such experience could be gained in Galveston as nowhere else. Opponents said, however, that Galveston was vulnerable to hurricanes and yellow fever, and that the so-called Texas Medical College really amounted to very little. In 1880, however, with Smith as the commencement speaker, the small, private college produced eight graduates. The *Galveston Daily News* boasted that fall, "No city in the south possesses better hospital accommodations or a greater diversity of diseases than Galveston."[64]

The decision for the location of the state schools was left to the people of Texas, and in October 1881 they voted for separate campuses with the medical division in Galveston.[65] In anticipation the Texas Medical College closed, but had to reopen when delays stalled the new facility. Finally, with a bequest of $50,000 from John Sealy, a local businessman, for a new hospital and the donation of a block of land by the city, the new state school began to move. Construction of "Old Red," the main building designed by Nicholas Clayton, started in 1890; John Sealy Hospital, aided by additional funds from George and Rebecca Sealy, opened the same year; and the medical institution with its new faculty started operation in 1891.[66] The school not only trained new doctors, but also contributed thereafter to the health, economy, and society of the island.

Public health and safety were critical issues at the time. The medical college helped, but the main difficulties had to be solved technically in the political arena. The problem was complex and demanded solution if the city was to advance. During periods of epidemic there was always a scurry to clean up the streets and alleys. One question was where to put the garbage and trash. From the earliest time Galveston used a four-footed answer—pigs. Swine have been used as urban scavengers worldwide from ancient times to the present. Hogs eat all sorts of garbage and develop a taste for human excrement. Until 1869, when they were declared a nuisance, pigs roamed free on the streets. An early visitor, Matilda Charlotte Fraser, noticed the work of Galveston hogs and the dogs which tormented them. The pigs lacked tails and ears, but otherwise flourished.[67]

Garbage was not well handled in the nineteenth century. Citizens were responsible for their own property and depended upon private collectors to haul the trash away. This was done irregularly. People dumped trash, offal, the refuse of outhouses, and slops in back alleys, and the dirt of stores into the front gutters. In 1879 the city provided a trench behind the dunes for garbage and the bodies of animals, and later allowed trash to be dropped in four-foot water off the eastern end of the island. By 1886 the municipality had established a regular dump at 33rd Street and Avenue A.[68]

The smell of Galveston, especially when the breeze stopped, must have been powerful. In 1868 an editor commented that people passing the fruit, vegetable, and chicken stand on Centre Street had to "grapple their noses" and move at a brisk trot. "Whoever owns the layout should clean it or bury it," was the conclusion. In 1875 the *Galveston Daily News* printed an estimate of 875 tons of fecal matter and 2,300,000 gallons of urine produced by the human inhabitants of the island each year. Much of this went into the soil.[69] Add to this the animal excrement dumped onto the streets. A normal city horse produced twenty pounds of manure and twenty gallons of urine per day.[70] Then there was the problem of the collectors. The product of the privies was placed in barrels, removed at night between 11:00 P.M. and 4:00 A.M., and dumped into the Gulf. The city physician reported in 1887:

The operation of the night carts has been a more difficult matter to control and has constituted one of the most annoying nuisances under the observation of the office. Drunken, careless and refractory scavengers have rendered the passage of these carts through the streets a curse to the residents along their line of march, filling the air with the vilest known stench and leaving an abiding reminder of their presence behind them in the form of a trail of their horrible freight, spilled and splashed from defective covers.[71]

So much for the good old days. Undoubtedly, the penetrating perfume of the oleander was a blessing.

There could not exist flush toilets in the city until the technical problems of water supply and sewerage were solved. Since Galveston was only a few feet above sea level, and because there was only a small tide, drainage and flushing were problems. Open ditches served the purpose, imperfectly, until the late 1860's. Then the city began to line some of the ditches with wood. They were supposed to carry away surface water, but they did not work well. Worse, some building owners began to connect toilets to them. When it rained, every street became a pond. "The water seems to run in streams in different directions, regardless of drainage, and when in one place it becomes of sufficient depth, a stream flows away from this as if to aid in filling up some other pond," wrote the editor of the *Galveston Daily News* in 1875.[72]

A system of drainage designed by Pierre G. T. Beauregard in 1873 was not carried out, and the city continued to have problems until the 1890's. In 1886 the city gave the Galveston Sewer Company the right to lay pipes and charge for connections. By the end of 1893 most of the area between 14th and 27th Streets, the bay and Broadway had been "sewered."[73]

There was still the problem of water supply. Water was necessary for drinking, business, and fire control; and the amount captured from rainfall was inadequate. In 1841, for fire protection, the city council appointed wardens for each of the five segments of the city to warn and watch. The first volunteer firefighting company, Hook and Ladder Company No. 1, was formed in 1843. It was followed in the next forty years by others such as the Island City Company No. 2; Old Ax Company; Mechanics No. 6; Young Eagles; Phoenix No. 2; and Protection Fire Company No. 8. They fought blazes, held dances, marched in parades, and raced each other. Part service and part social, they came and went. The city provided some street cisterns, engines, and hose. In 1872 the companies fought nineteen fires, and in 1873 there existed nine units, three steam engines, four hand pumpers, and 348 men. The municipality installed an electric alarm system in 1876 covering a twelve-mile circuit.[74]

The local board of insurance underwriters, nonetheless, raised the insurance rates 10 percent in 1880 because they thought Galveston only nominally protected. After a $707,000 conflagration on the Strand in 1882, the rate jumped 25 percent, raising a demand for a better water system, organization, and alarm system. The motive, of course, was to reduce insurance rates for business; greater safety was a side issue. The city contracted for a salt-water system which would draw from the bay and pump to 110 hydrants through eight miles of pipes. Although the project, completed in 1884, failed the test of throwing ten streams one hundred feet high at one time, it did wet the top of the seventy-foot Moody Building and scatter the watching crowd when a squirming hose writhed loose from the three men holding it. The city accepted the system.[75]

After another fire on the Strand, a small one, where "everyone seemed to be boss, and a dozen were calling out orders at one time," the aldermen in 1885 provided for a professional fire department. The elected chief of the volunteer companies, William Oldenberg, became the head of the new division. In his picture he appears proud of his long, sweeping black mustache, speaking trumpet, white helmet, badge, and vest which did not button easily over his ample stomach. With his new position he received a salary of $1,600. He bought a fancy buggy with striped wheels and an old fire horse released from service in the transition. Most of the time the aged horse moved no faster than a dogtrot, but at the note of a bell from church or railroad he pricked up his ears, lofted his "caudal appendage," and took off. He dragged the helpless chief along at breakneck speed, and yielded the right-of-way to no person or animal. He halted automatically, however, at every pile of burning trash.[76]

The department was barely a month and a half old when Galveston's worst fire struck. It began early in the morning of November 13, 1885, in the business section at a foundry near 17th Street and the Strand. The alarm was slow, and a stiff northeast wind sent a solid sheet of flame across the Strand to wooden frame buildings. A sea of sparks and glowing embers swirled on the high wind currents several blocks ahead and started new fires as they fell on wooden shingles. In five hours the conflagration cut a two-to-four-block charred swath from 16th and Strand to 19th and Avenue O, while thousands of geese, ducks, and seabirds floated high above the burning buildings with their wings illuminated by the red glow. The fire destroyed 568 homes in 42 blocks, and cost $1,500,000.[77]

Everyone turned out to save household goods. Furniture was moved to the streets, and then had to be moved again as the flames advanced. Much was lost. The population fought back with bucket brigades, wet quilts, and fire equipment, but the salt-water system failed to provide sufficient pressure and two steamers broke down when bits of shell clogged the nozzles. Some reports said that fire hydrants were left running and abandoned, and that hose was burned up. The fire eventually burned itself out, and fortunately no one died.[78] In defiance to the destruction, the *Galveston Daily News* stated:

> It is a great calamity. . . . But the driving wheel of Galveston's existence is unimpaired. The soul of the city is not disturbed. The busy marts of commerce go on as if nothing had happened; the great warehouses and counting-houses are open; the hundred rivulets of commerce and industry that throb and thrill and give life to the community are flowing on. . . .
> She will be as beautiful as ever in a few months, and is still doing business at the old stand.[79]

The city government provided $15,000 for relief, the Beach Hotel opened its doors to the homeless, and Mayor Robert L. Fulton confidently announced, "The affluent of Galveston can care for her poor." With outside donations the relief fund eventually reached $105,000. The city quickly rebuilt, and the officials dictated fireproof material for the business area. Elsewhere people reconstructed their Victorian homes with porches to catch Gulf breezes and intricate figures in black, white, red, blue, orange, and pink colors. The gable and mansard roofs were clothed in fireproof tin, slate, and galvanized shingles.[80] It was this phoenix with its ornate plumage which gave the city much of the architecture prized in the 1980's.

The fire underwriters raised their rates again after this disaster. They liked the fire department—the first professional group in Texas—but condemned the alarm and water systems.[81] The alarms could be easily fixed, but the supply of water did not come readily. Water was a major problem affecting not only fire protection, but also public health and the growth of business. The use of rainwater and cisterns did prevent the spread of water-borne cholera, but the amount was limited. There were no springs, nor streams to draw from. Some people used shallow brackish wells for bathing and there was some consideration of using a pond, Sweetwater Lake, down the island for urban supply. Cisterns went dry in 1870 and 1879, and water had to be purchased from peddlers with barrels.[82]

There was also some talk about using surface water from the

mainland, and condensing sea water, but the first serious attempt to solve the problem came with the drilling of deep wells. The technique of using a pointed steel bit attached to an iron rod for driving pipe down had been described by the newspapers in 1857. John P. Davie sank a one-and-one-half-inch pipe to eighty-one feet in 1873, and the C. B. Lee Foundry drove a two-inch pipe to 210 feet two years later. Both wells brought up brackish water. Charleston and Dallas, meanwhile, in the late 1870's found artesian water with wells.[83] Why not Galveston?

An attempt to pound a well 2,250 feet for the city in 1881 ended in "miserable failure" at 765 feet when the pipe telescoped underground. Using a revolving pipe with a toothed rim and water flushing through it, the Santa Fe Railroad six years later drilled to 759 feet and produced sixty-five to seventy thousand gallons per day. The water contained salt, lime, iron, soda, sulphur, and some natural gas. It was unsatisfactory for the railroad's boilers and later the company let it run into the bay. This deficiency was unclear at first. In the enthusiasm of the quest three other companies drilled and the city placed a contract for a system with thirteen artesian wells placed every 800 feet along Winnie Avenue. When the system was completed in May 1889, Galveston had spent $450,000 for the wells, 17,000 feet of mains, a pump house, and a standpipe.[84]

Initially, the cost of service to a six-room house with a bathtub and watercloset was $30 per year, plus $1.50 more per thousand feet of lawn. Water rates dropped after this, fire insurance cost declined 25 percent by 1889, and customers improved sanitation with flush toilets. It was a forward step, but the brackish water corroded pipes and produced pinhole leaks in industrial equipment. Water from a three-thousand-foot well proved no better.[85] Galveston still needed fresh water.

Across the bay in the late 1880's a Hitchcock rancher, Jacques Tacquard, drilled an artesian well which produced wholesome water. The Santa Fe Railroad also bored a well there in 1887. Following that hint, Galveston officials looked over the nearby mainland and in 1893 found a favorable site seventeen miles from the city at Alta Loma, west of Hitchcock. The civic authorities contracted for thirty wells and a thirty-inch main laid in a trench across the bay twelve feet below low tide. The main connected to the existing system, and pressure within the pipe kept out salt-water contamination. The cost was $780,000, but a large crowd celebrated the completion in 1895 at the Beach Hotel, which provided a fountain of fresh water.[86] The exhibition fulfilled a long-standing fantasy.

The basic problem of fresh water was solved. Over time Galveston added chlorine to the supply and began to look for additional surface sources. The water table at Alta Loma slowly dropped, and the water became more saline.[87] No city can exist without water, nor can it mature without sufficient supplies for business and sanitation. Galveston, with cost and effort, had solved the problem. It could go on.

In other ways the city progressed. Alfred H. Belo, owner of the *Galveston Daily News*, visited the Philadelphia Centennial Exposition in 1876 and viewed the exhibit of Alexander Graham Bell. He returned home and strung a telephone line between his home and office in 1878. A telephone exchange began service in 1881 and connected to Houston in 1893. A reporter testing the new double copper circuit asked the Houston operator about the weather in the Bayou City. The answer: "Horrid and warm." In 1899, long-distance lines reached St. Louis, Kansas City, and Chicago—and, through them, the rest of the nation.[88]

With a champagne toast, the Brush Electric Company in 1882 demonstrated a string of electric lights that turned the street corner at 26th and Postoffice "light as day." Businesses quickly installed the new technology, and the city established its own electric plant in 1889 for street illumination. Electricity, the new urban power source, was applied to the streetcars in 1891.[89]

Road conditions also improved. "While other cities complain of mud, Galveston mourns her sand," wrote the newspaper editor in 1870. "Pedestrianism is toilsome, and riding intolerable. Our citizens once off the business streets wade ankle deep in sand, and experience all the discomfort of ruined shoes, untidy hose, and uncleanliness generally."[90] As a remedy the city shared the cost of oyster shells with property owners. It did not work well, but much of the business area was shelled by 1871, when the city began using wooden blocks bound together with hot tar to pave the Strand. The wood offered a flexible, durable surface which was easy on the horses. It proved to be the pavement of choice for Galveston until the end of the century, even though officials experimented with bricks in the 1890's.[91]

Sidewalks before 1873 were much like the streets, and the condition none too good. "Half of the time it is found to be much easier to walk in the middle of a shelled street, despite the danger of life and limb, rather than the abominable sidewalks. We have hardly a decent one in the city," complained a newsman in 1872. The next year the city government required elevated sidewalks of brick, concrete, or asphalt with curbs of pressed brick. That helped—maybe too much, because the new sidewalks provided attractive pathways for bicycle riders, who developed into a menace for pedestrians.[92]

Life in the latter part of the nineteenth century in Galveston was rich, full, and varied. With its eastern and European connections, it became the most sophisticated city in Texas. The Island City was the largest for two decades, it was first with urban innovations, and it was the richest. In 1870 there were fifty-eight people in Texas with estates worth $100,000 or more. Eleven of these lived in Galveston County, more than anywhere else. They were all merchants from the city.[93]

The flow of immigrants through this Texas gateway provided cultural heterogeneity. Four thousand or so per year walked over the docks on their way to somewhere else. In one month, January 1871, 4,673 arrived. Jesse A. Ziegler, who lived in Galveston from 1857 to 1883, remembered standing and watching as the newcomers trudged up the middle of the road to the train depot—Russians in fur coats; Swiss in knee breeches; Scots with bagpipes; women and children burdened with pots, pans, and utensils.[94] Czechs on their way to farms in Fayette County began arriving in 1852 and continued to come until the turn of the century. Several poor Norwegian families passed through in 1869 and abandoned two dead children at the train station.[95]

The most important group were the Germans, who began their migration before the founding of the city and continued it throughout much of the century. They were mainly agricultural people looking to escape European poverty and politics. They influenced Texas culture, and some provided insight about their adopted country. After a forty-four-day passage Emma Altgelt, a twenty-year-old German immigrant on her way to Indianola and the interior of Texas, arrived in Galveston in 1854 and recorded her observations. To her the town looked like paper toys with the houses up on poles ready to be moved one place or another. More impressive, however, was the crowd of German men at the wharf who rushed on board looking for women to marry. She noted a middle-aged baker who spotted a pretty blonde peasant girl and first tried to hire her as a cook. She refused his high wages and said that she was going to her brother who had paid her travel expenses. Desperate, the baker blurted, "I want to marry you right now!" The girl coolly replied, "To be married is exactly what I do not want." Emma Altgelt liked that answer.[96]

The Germans who remained on the island founded a Turner Association and military unit, held an annual May Day celebration, and maintained a landscaped park and pavilion called the Garten Verein. It operated in the summer and offered music, food, bowling, and romance. Red-faced German waiters with flowing mustaches served platters of cold meat, salads, and ice cream with glasses of lemonade and steins of beer. "The Wednesday night concerts and picnics have been responsible for more changes of heart in the last twenty years than all the other agencies combined which Cupid has established in Galveston," remarked a reporter in 1897.[97] To honor his parents, Stanley Kempner bought the park in 1923 and presented it as a gift to the city.[98]

Among the outstanding immigrants was a Swiss named Henry Rosenberg. He arrived in Galveston before the Civil War at age nineteen and proceeded to make a fortune in dry goods and banking. He variously served as an alderman, vestryman for Trinity Episcopal Church, director of the Wharf Company, director of the Gulf, Colorado and Santa Fe Railroad, director of Galveston Orphan's Home, and consul for Switzerland in Galveston. He became one of the early philanthropists in 1888, when he gave $40,000 to the public schools. At his death in 1893, Rosenberg designated a number of bequests, the largest of which was $400,000 for a public library. The most interesting part of his will read, "I give thirty thousand dollars for the creation of not less than ten drinking fountains for man and beast in various portions of the city of Galveston, localities to be selected by my executors." This portly humanitarian whose statue sits solidly in front of the Rosenberg Library had sympathy for his fellow creatures and took advantage of the city's new-found water supply. A good man. Seventeen carved marble fountains of varying sizes were installed, but only four, in new locations, survive to the present.

Of greater endurance was his bequest for a statue to the Texas Revolution. It became the city's landmark. Created by sculptor Louis Amateis, the seventy-four-foot bronze and granite statue features the female form of Victory holding a laurel wreath in outstretched arm pointing toward the San Jacinto Battleground across the bay. Officials placed it in the middle of the intersection at 25th (Rosenberg) and Broadway.[99] The irreverent say that the statue gestures not toward the site of Texas independence, but to the location a few blocks away of Galveston's infamous red-light district. But that is a story from a later era, when Galveston achieved an independence of a different sort.

Enrichment of city life also came from other directions. The Galveston Lyceum presented debates—in March 1868 the debate subject was: which is more happy, an old bachelor or an old maid? The Galveston Historical Society started in 1871. Its purpose was to preserve materials about Texas history. Interest waxed and waned, and finally it ceased meeting in 1931. There was also the Galveston Chess and Whist Club, but most significant was the long success of theater in the city.[100]

There were theatrical presentations before and after the Civil War, but the man who dominated the latter part of the century was Henry Greenwall. He took over and remodeled the Tremont Opera House at Market and Tremont, and arranged for players to come from New York after the yellow fever epidemic of 1867. The troupe arrived in November, but by error their wardrobes went to Havana. Greenwall opened, nonetheless, on November 21. He scraped by for the next fifteen years or so, and explained to a critic in 1876 why he had to rely on second-rate talent. The top-flight people either would not come to Galveston or demanded three to five thousand dollars per week. That was a fee the city could not support. Interest soared in 1875, at least for five days, while Mme Rentze's Female Minstrels were in town. The male population from "banker to bootblack" jammed the Opera House to witness the variety show, which included the notorious Can-Can, "a lewd and voluptuous dance, in which a lot of depraved men and women throw themselves into all manner of lascivious motions." Feeling somewhat ashamed, men in the audience sat low in their seats with coat collars turned up, but the police refused to stop the show. After the group left town, the newspaper said, "It is understood that incense and olive oil will be burned in the Opera House throughout to-day to purify its atmosphere and make it a fit place once more for ladies."[101]

During the 1879–1880 season, which lasted from November to April, Galvestonians enjoyed opera, comic opera, troubadors, Buffalo Bill, a wizard, plays, and more minstrels. In 1882, with improved profits, a leading actor, Edwin Booth, presented the most brilliant engagement yet seen in the city. He was followed the next season by Fay Templeton. Booth returned in 1887, and in 1888, the "Jersey Lily," Lily Langtry, arrived by private railroad car for a performance. Sarah Bernhardt played *La Tosca* and *Camille* in 1892 with her fluffy auburn hair, delicate face, and teeth like "rows of pearls." A dazzled reporter found her handshake firm and her movements "poetry in motion." "She is rightly called 'divine,'" he concluded. One of the last plays in the Tremont Opera House was *Charley's Aunt*, a "hummer" of a comedy about college boys at Oxford.

Then, on January 3, 1895, Henry Greenwall opened a new theater, the Grand Opera House, a "thespian temple." It had a carved stone archway and marble tile in the lobby. It boasted a parquet floor, oak seats, boxes, yellow-pine wainscoting, gas and electric lighting, heat, air ventilators, a seventy-five-foot wide by sixty-eight-foot high by sixty-eight-foot deep stage, and a drop curtain featuring Sappho and her companions. Marie Wainwright, daughter of Commander Wainwright of the *Harriet Lane* and the Battle of Galveston, starred in *Daughters of Eve*. It was a gala evening in full dress; it was Galveston at its best.[102]

Galveston at its worst was found in the shadows of the underworld. In a port city with great numbers of transient people, the expectation, tolerance, and opportunity for vice and crime were greater than in other places. Aury and Laffite left that legacy, and a certain disrepute remained a characteristic of Galveston throughout its history. In the nineteenth century the police arrested two to three thousand people per year. Easily the most common crime was drunkenness, followed by fighting and disorderly conduct. A sure way to rouse a fight was to call someone a "damned Yankee." In the last quarter of the century, after Galveston gained continental railway connections, vagrancy became a popular charge.[103]

Vagrancy was a convenient reason for the arrest of tramps. These "knights of the road" arrived in the winter months seeking warmth. They were mainly a nuisance. "When they are seen lurking and skulking about places where they can have no possible object or business," explained a policeman in 1885, "they are hauled up short." The police herded them on a boxcar, sent them across the bridge, and dumped them out. It was illegal to send them to another town. Most of them followed the track right back to the island.[104]

The police also used arrests for vagrancy to harass prostitutes. In the boom recovery after the Civil War, with plenty of opportunity and demand, prostitution bloomed as never before. It was in this period that the area about Postoffice, Market, and 26th through 29th Streets developed as a vice district with bawdy houses, saloons, and "variety shows." The shows, according to the police, were "hotbeds of crime," but they were legal and given police protection. Captain J. M. Riley explained, "Bear in mind that by varieties shows I mean those places where beer is jerked by women, and the can-can and like performances are given on the stage." There, young men and boys developed a taste for beer and liquor, and the "nude adornments of the variety stage."[105] They were the nineteenth-century equivalent of a striptease club.

On occasion the activities of the demimonde broke into the newspapers and onto the police records. One man shot another in the mouth over a black harlot, Mollie Harris, in 1867. She had been arrested earlier that month for firing a pistol and using insulting language. Two years later she broke into the brothel of Caroline Riley and attacked another black prostitute, Jane Dickenson. The police arrested six black women in that squabble and charged them with street-walking and vagrancy. It cost them five dollars and court costs except for Riley. As the madam of the house she merited a ten dollar fine. Harris could not pay, so she went to jail for five days. Riley the same year started a three-year term in the penitentiary for accepting stolen goods, but she was back in business at Postoffice and 29th in 1872. The editor of the *News* shortly noted the numerous complaints of Riley's bawdy house, where black whores using obscene and profane language often appeared nude on the street. A raid two days later produced fourteen arrests, and a notice to the owner of the building to desist from such use in the future.[106]

Prostitution was illegal, along with drunkenness, gambling, and carrying dangerous weapons, but there was tolerance of these vices. "They flaunt their ribbons and wriggle their dresses with too much audacity, and ply their vocation with too much boldness," clucked the *Galveston Daily News*.[107] The police, however, reacted only when there was trouble, and brought "nymphs de pave" into the courts for periodic fines. Neither police nor courts closed the houses of ill fame. The women were simply fined, not too much, and turned loose to continue their business. The vagrancy law thus had the effect of an extralegal occupation tax for the benefit of the city treasury.[108]

The authorities and society had more important concerns, of course, than to be too upset over "the most ancient and agreeable of all professions," as a prominent Galvestonian characterized prostitution.[109] There were murder cases to be solved. In 1843 Charles Henniker, a German truck farmer, hit his partner with a mallet and dropped him into a well. When the victim tried to climb out, Henniker beat him back with a scantling and held him underwater until he drowned. He then robbed the man and burned his house. A woman exposed Henniker's guilt and a court condemned him to be hanged "dead as the devil." The German was a tough character. He rode to his gallows seated on his coffin while smoking a pipe. He threw his last dime into the crowd, rejected a hood, and dropped through the trap. Henniker's neck did not snap as it was supposed to and he looked out at the spectators with clear, calm eyes while he gently swayed and gradually strangled.[110]

The most sensational and grisly murder of the century occurred in 1884. According to the first reports, Emil Richard Fleschig, a young recent German immigrant, had committed an "outrage" on the wife of his employer. The husband, Charles Junemann, a dairyman who lived three and a half miles from town, organized a posse which searched without success for the young man. Two days later a farmer driving some hogs noticed flies buzzing in a clump of bushes. Upon looking he found Fleschig, dead, hanging from a low cedar branch with a rope around his neck. Henry Weyer, the local justice of the peace, held an inquest, found no violence, ordered the body buried, and opened a keg of beer for the people there. Fleschig had committed suicide.

That should have been the end of it, but it was not. Rumors circulated. Witnesses said the body appeared in strange condition. Fleschig stood five feet ten inches, or so, and the branch he used to hang himself was only five feet off the ground. The rope was carelessly wrapped around it and the body, on all fours, hung forward with the head only nine to ten inches off the ground. It was skinned up, and one eye protruded. Certainly, a strange suicide. The state forced a second inquest and examination of the corpse. The German society in Galveston offered $100 for information about lynchers.

Time passed, other witnesses spoke up, a trial occurred, and a new story emerged. Fleschig, who spoke little English, had worked for Junemann for about six months, and complained to his friends that he had a hard time obtaining his wages. In addition, Mrs. Junemann abused him, ordered him around, and struck him. Neighbors reported that she had commanded him to bring her water while he was chopping wood. Fleschig refused and she hit him with a billet. She also threw a hatchet at him. He threw it back and hit her in the head. She fell bleeding and young Fleschig, thinking that he had killed her, fled.

A neighbor, summoned by a boy, found Mrs. Junemann sitting in a rocking chair, bleeding from a one-inch head wound. "Emil struck me in the head with a hatchet," she said, "because I would not sleep with him." The hunt was on. Five men, including Charles Junemann and Judge Henry Weyer, found the fugitive hiding in a barn. Junemann stole a ten-dollar gold piece from Fleschig. Then, while two of them held the young man, the others choked him, "shoved a stick in his corruption," and kicked him to death. They tied Junemann's cow rope around his neck and left the body in the bushes tied to the cedar branch. As it turned out, one of the lynchers was already in jail in Kentucky. Three of them, including the judge, received five-year sentences, and Junemann a two-year term in prison. All were minimal penalties.[111]

To hold lawbreakers, the county maintained a jail from the start. The brig *Elba*, beached in the 1837 hurricane, became the first place of incarceration, and Henry Forbes, a black man charged with larceny, was one of the first inmates, in 1840. While the jury was deciding about him, Forbes escaped and was recaptured. Since breaking jail was a capital offense, he was hauled off to the gallows and hanged. En route, he sat on his coffin and sang a hymn at the top of his voice. Most citizens thought the punishment too harsh in this case.[112]

The county built new jailhouses periodically as the old ones fell apart. In 1866 the jail was so bad they put a twelve-foot wall around it with broken glass at the top. It was unfortunate that insane people often had to live there because of overcrowding in the state institutions. A disturbed woman who raged, cried, and broke everything stayed in the county jail for six months in 1874, to the great annoyance of the neighborhood, until there was room in the Austin asylum. "I don't mind watchin' murderers and burglars, but these crazy women are enough to drive a man wild," commented the keeper. Even in 1898 there were nine insane women and eleven insane men kept in the prison.[113] There was not much to be done about it, and it was not unkind. There was just nowhere to send these unfortunate people.

The city supported a paid police force from the beginning, and a saloon owner, Leander H. Westcott, was the first marshall. The department began a night watch in 1857, maintained a curfew over blacks, and offered to whip slaves at the owner's request for one dollar. During Reconstruction there was difficulty with the quality of appointments to the force, and one chief fraudulently placed extra names on the payroll. In 1869, on the other hand, the division improved by starting the use of photographs to identify criminals.[114] As was usual in the century, the main purpose of the police was to protect property by maintaining order.

Elsewhere in Texas the police sympathized with the laboring person and could not be relied upon during strikes. In Galveston this does not seem to have been the case, although in severe instances military units bolstered the police force. Galveston was a major center for union activity. Before the Civil War, lack of industry, sectionalism, ethnic loyalties, and the small number of workers all tended to discourage unionization. Printers on the island, nonetheless, formed the state's first labor organization, the Typographical Union, in 1857. The carpenters got together in 1860, and after the war they were followed by the brickmasons, black longshoremen, and hack drivers. By 1872 there existed over a dozen unions. The depression of 1873–1876 hurt, but the strikes of 1877 in Galveston and elsewhere heralded the birth of modern labor.[115]

In the ninety-nine-degree heat of July and August that year, the black wharf workers, followed by black women laundry workers, newspaperboys, and white street laborers struck for better wages. There were some rough encounters, but they were short-lived and little was gained. Draymen, black longshoremen, and streetcar drivers, however, successfully forced higher pay in 1881.[116] The Knights of Labor struck against the Santa Fe Railroad in 1885, and in Galveston the affiliated workingmen stopped the trains despite the efforts of police. "Don't do it, don't do it," the unionists chanted as the police-protected strikebreakers tried to fire up a locomotive. The scabs gave up, the engine remained dead, and the Santa Fe complained about the lack of protection.[117]

In response the county sheriff called out the local military units as a posse comitatus. The Galveston Artillery Company even arrived with two twelve-pound howitzers. "Probably never in the history of Texas has a posse been organized consisting of such wealthy and representative citizens," commented the paper. The labor crowd greeted them with hisses and jeers, and the good people of Galveston responded with the sound of cocking Winchesters, pistols, and shotguns. The sheriff stepped between the posse and the strikers and asked for peace. It worked, and shortly labor and management began to arbitrate.[118]

White and black union competition on the Mallory wharf attracted the Knights of Labor again in early November, and the trains stopped once more. This strike lasted but briefly, and again there was arbitration. The result was greater participation by blacks in the labor of the wharves.[119] The Pullman Strike of 1894 arrived in Galveston in July, but the mayor with the help of police and militia forces forced the trains through.[120] In 1898 the Mallory Company broke the strike of its black union by bringing in scab labor on barges from Houston. Even though the strikebreakers were protected by police and soldiers with Gatling guns, there were three deaths and several beatings.[121] Things were getting rougher.

A gentler effort to gain labor equity came from the women of the Galveston Cotton Mill. The mill, located at 40th and Winnie, employed 550 people, used thirty to thirty-five bales of cotton per day, and paid $150,000 in annual wages. Bertrand Adoue, "a monument to Galveston enterprise," was president, and the board of directors included business leaders such as Julius Runge, Morris Lasker, Leon Blum, and George Sealy. Although it represented a $500,000 investment, the mill was an anachronism. It was constructed in 1889, over a decade after cotton manufacturing in Texas declined.[122] It did not last long in Galveston either, but the Galveston Cotton Mill constituted one of the last major attempts to establish an industrial base for the city.

The women of the mill sent a delegation to appeal to the city officials in February 1895. They said that they were working thirteen hours per day with forty-five minutes off for lunch. They had previously worked eleven and a quarter hours per day, but the time had recently been extended. They earned ninety cents per day, but were docked for errors, thus losing five to fifteen cents per day. The mistakes came in the last hours when they were tired and it was dark. There was only one light bulb for every four looms. There were 150 children at work there, and they were slapped and hit by the foremen—Mrs. E. W. Ormond testified that her son bore scars from the ill treatment. The women did not protest the amount of pay, but they did object to the increase in hours. They asked the city fathers to investigate.

One alderman said that he would not work his horse that hard, and the city leaders agreed to arbitrate. The company explained that a sixty-six-hour week was normal—eleven and a quarter hours during the week and nine and a quarter on Saturday. There was a need for overtime, however, because they were testing new looms, and also because they had lost time to cold weather. It was necessary for the mill to work at a sixty-six-hour-per-week pace, and it was customary in the industry for the employees to work extra hours so the mill did not fall behind schedule. They also worked overtime so that they could have Christmas Day free. The city officers failed at arbitration, and the mill won the fight with the use of strikebreakers.

Forty to fifty women returned to the council and requested $1,000 so they could return home. They had been enticed to move to Galveston to work in the mill and now they wanted to leave. The aldermen refused the money, but took up a private collection among themselves amounting to $175.[123] There was obviously some sympathy for the women, but the power of government and the sanctity of law was on the side of business and private property. The cause of labor and unions gained but little in the nineteenth century in Galveston, or elsewhere in the United States.

The most interesting and successful union in Galveston history at the time was the Screwmen's Benevolent Association. It started in 1866, reorganized in 1868, and continued until 1924. The screwmen worked in five-man gangs with one man acting as foreman. Multiple teams, depending on need, labored together moving cotton bales from a warehouse to the deck of a ship and into the hold. Inside, the screwmen used two-hundred-pound jackscrews to compress the bales against the bulkheads in order to pack more cotton on the ship. It took several extra days to screw a transport, but the vessel could carry 15 percent more and earn about 4 percent more profit. When ships were small and moved slowly, this was important.

The screwmen, because of their skill, strength, and usefulness, became the elite workers of the wharves. The association formed a closed shop for white workers and obtained the highest wages on the dock. It did not last. Black competition through Norris Wright

Cuney's organization came in the 1880's, and the blacks formed their own screwman's union, the Cotton Jammer's Association. In addition, shipping technology eventually forced a decline. Faster, larger steel ships made screwing less important. Worst of all, high-density compresses squeezed the bales as much as the men could. After 1910 screwmen were obsolete and the unions declined rapidly.[124]

Even though economic miseries visited the laboring classes and others, there was the comfort of Galveston's buoyant climate and the entertainment in the city. Besides the saloons and the brothels, there were visiting circuses, tight-rope walkers, balloon ascensions and parachute jumps, high divers, freak shows, bell ringers, and sports.[125] Swimming—or, more accurately, surf bathing—and fishing were the two most popular sports for the island throughout its history. Everyone, regardless of age, race, or sex, could enjoy them. Roller-skating at the beach pavilion which opened in 1881 with electric lights and band music also attracted all ages and both sexes. The owner promoted the rink with contests and once with a greased-pig scramble. The object was to pick the pig up by the tail and put him in a barrel. The animal had the advantage of socks to give him traction on the slick floor, a well-greased tail, and unqualified fright. Boys chased him without success, and the event ended with an exhausted pig with a bent tail.[126]

Bicycle riding was another mass sport with broad appeal for those who could afford the equipment. A female "velocipedist" was an object of curiosity in 1875 as she tooled down Broadway, but in the 1890's women competed in bike races at the velodrome at P and 27th along with the men. One of the local favorites, Miss Frankie Nelson, advanced to speed biking in New York City. Bicycling was both a participant and a spectator sport. People, moreover, used bicycles for transportation then as now, with the same kinds of problems. In 1892 a wheelman rode to the beach for swimming. While he was there, a boy threw sand on him and he shook the lad until his teeth rattled. The youth took revenge by shoving tacks into the man's front tire, and the cyclist had to push his bike home "enveloped in a luminous, sulphurous haze."[127]

Although boating was generally an elite sport because of the time and cost involved, there was unusual interest in sailboat and rowing contests. Rowing began with a three-mile race in the Galveston channel in 1873. Two years later the Galveston Rowing Club met and began to sponsor annual regattas. Women were not excluded, and in 1875 there were two female teams, the Aquatics and the Dolly Vardens. John Crotty, however, emerged as the local star of the sculls, and with his companions won the senior four-oared race in New Orleans in 1885. In 1887 the club hosted an interstate regatta which brought teams from Moline, St. Louis, and Chicago. Interestingly, the local white longshoremen's association and the screwmen entered teams for the barge races. They were not excluded because of economic class. The high point was Crotty's victory over the Chicago champion in a match race of single sculls. The thousands of spectators along the wharf front roared approval, a young woman rushed up and kissed the hero, and then the participants retired to a convivial banquet.[128]

Crotty also entered the sailing contests on Galveston Bay. There were races as early as 1869, and they continued through the end of the century. The *White Wing* was a frequent victor. In 1894 the Galveston Yacht Club sponsored a race of working boats from the wharf to Red Fish Channel and back, and once in a while women on sailing parties were allowed to touch the tiller. That was unusual. Said an old tar about an enthusiastic female student, "They are all good seawomen [in the North]. But oh, what a difference down South. Why, this young lady here is the first southern girl I have ever seen who cared to learn anything about the handling of a boat, and here we live right on the sea."[129]

Other sports in Galveston tended to be the exclusive domain of the men. Males dominated wrestling, cockfighting, tennis, pedestrianism (walking races), horse racing, baseball, football, and boxing. Once in a while a woman raced a bicycle or a horse, but for the most part women were spectators. In 1874 at the opening of Oleander Park for horse racing, a reporter rhapsodized:

> The dark, cool green of the fields, striped with the "buff ribbon"
> of the course, and lit up with the gay silks of the riders; the grand stand
> swarming like an ant hill with the terraces of "ladyes fayre," combined
> in one picture, and set under a serene sky, made a total of beauty that
> our city has never excelled.[130]

Northern soldiers playing on a field north of the Ursuline Convent introduced baseball to Galveston, and Texas, at the end of the Civil War. The men organized a club in 1867, and the women established one for croquet in retaliation. Merchants objected to clerks taking time off for the game, but the newspaper argued that exercise would do them good. Once started, there was no stopping. Various amateur clubs formed, played one another, and challenged Houston. In 1887 a Texas League included two Galveston teams, but the big rival was the Houston Mud Cats. In 1889 at a game in the Bayou City the Galveston Sand Crabs led 9−4 in the fifth inning. In the eighth the Mud

Cats pulled within one run and the referee called the game because of darkness. There was an hour of daylight left, and the crowd shouted, "Mob him!" The umpire ran into the Houston dressing room and could be heard weeping inside as the best citizens of the Bayou City looked for a rail to give him a ride. A local attorney dissuaded them, but the rumor circulated that the referee had bet on the Galveston team. Maybe not. The Sand Crabs beat the Mud Cats again the next day.[131]

Since the game had to be played in daylight when many people worked, baseball might be considered a middle- and upper-class sport. Yet the Chinese of the city played a game in 1876, and the blacks joined a colored state league in 1888. White fans attended their games, and at least once, in 1888, the black Flyaways played an amateur white team. The black athletes lost 2–1 and said they were nervous because it was their first encounter with a white team.[132] Football came to the island in 1890. Clubs from the high schools, YMCA, and city played one another, and the Santa Fe Rugbys from the mainland played Ball High School in 1892. The Ball fans met them with a cheer set to music: "Brekekekex, coax, coax. Bredededex, coax, coax. Ball high school! Ball high school! Yellow and blue, rah! rah! Boom!!!" The Rugbys listened in amazement, and then beat Ball 14–0. Central High, the black school, also formed a team in order to participate in the excitement. They offered to play any team, but apparently no one responded to their attempt to be a part of the larger community.[133]

In the brutal sport of boxing, however, the races did mix. The Reconstruction era which brought baseball to Galveston also brought prizefighting. It flourished in the "Smokey Row" area west of Strand and 25th in the vicinity of the brothels. There were a series of "sporting houses"—Jim Burn's, Mike Harrington's, Mrs. Baker's, Tom Garrigan's—where bets were placed and fights arranged. The "Gulf Verandah" on the beach had a twenty-four-foot ring and charged fifty cents to a dollar for the Sunday bouts.[134]

Texas taxed prizefights at first, but banned them entirely in 1891. In spite of a city ordinance to the same effect, there was confusion about the law, sporadic enforcement, and studied avoidance of the statutes. Exhibitions were legal, and so a fighter would be paid for that purpose.[135] Prizefighting, thus, persisted. In 1889 on the New Wharf a fighter named Raynor knocked his opponent down in the fifth, sixth, seventh, eighth, and ninth rounds. For the tenth the handlers carried the victim "to scratch" and stood him up. Raynor walked up and pushed him down and out with an open hand. Everyone walked away and left the fighter lying on the dock. "He is badly used up and presents a horrible appearance," commented an observer.[136]

In 1890 a sellout crowd at the Galveston Athletic Club saw the Texas lightweight champion, Tom Manyhan, close his opponent's eyes in the fifth round, knock him down in the seventh, and hit him through the ropes for a knockout in the eighth. In 1891 the police raided and caused a stampede from a prizefight staged at the new engine house. Two years later a hundred men and boys watched a fight between a German and a black man in the glow of a smoky kerosene lamp. The German won in two rounds, and the restless crowd induced two black youths to fight. They scrapped for five rounds and a draw. One of them brought a laugh when he turned to the referee and said, "Look yah, man, when you going to call time? I'se gettin' tired." The same kid sparred again three nights later before a crowd of three hundred in the hall over Pitcher's Saloon at the corner of Market and 25th. He was involved in one of five bouts, and the police were on hand to be certain that it was an exhibition and not a prizefight.[137]

John L. Sullivan, the heavyweight champion, gave a presentation at the Tremont Opera House in 1884. His volunteer opponent went down three times in fifty-five seconds and quit. He said that Sullivan's blows felt like a piledriver encased in a football. Another champion, James Corbett, visited the island ten years later. A large crowd greeted him at the depot and followed the genial boxer around town. There was an initial mixup at the station when the Episcopal Bishop George H. Kinsolving alighted from the same train. He was there to lay the cornerstone of Grace Episcopal Church, and since he was a "stalwart specimen of manhood" the crowd gave him a rousing cheer. "What does it mean?" the surprised bishop asked a friend. "Hush," was the reply, "they think you are Jim Corbett."[138]

Fighting continued through the 1890's, sometimes in fancy places like the Tremont Opera House, often elsewhere, such as the beach. In 1899 a ring on the sand was erected with three posts and a buggy. The carriage was held in place by two skinny men and a fat one. In the excitement the fat man rolled backward off the buggy and shoved it five feet forward, thus collapsing the ring. The referee declared the fight a draw.[139] In such conditions, with boxing matches on the docks, beach, back streets, and in smoky saloons and sporting houses, Galveston's black community produced a heavyweight champion, Jack Johnson.

The history of Johnson's early years is hazy. His recent biographer, Randy Roberts, says that he was born in Galveston in 1878 to poor and pious parents. He was the oldest son in a family of six children, and, according to Johnson, he grew up like other kids, "a happy-go-lucky little pickaninny." He was among the first generation of blacks born free, and he learned early that he was quicker and could hit harder than most youngsters. By his late teens he was a professional fighter, acquiring his skill through ring experience. In 1899 Johnson left Galveston for Chicago to advance his career, but he returned in 1901 to fight Joe Choynski at the Galveston Athletic Club.

Choynski was one of the better pugilists of the time, and he flattened Johnson in the third round. At that juncture, Texas Rangers arrested both men for illegal boxing and put them in jail. They were held for twenty-four days and never brought to trial. Johnson used his incarceration as a training camp to learn from his wiser companion. Upon their release they both left town. Johnson won the world's championship in Australia in 1908. He became a hero to the black race of the nation, and an embarrassment to the white.[140]

Sports provided a unique dimension to life in Galveston. Fishing, surf swimming, and biking gave enjoyment to thousands on a constant basis. Jack Johnson found economic opportunity, and John Crotty acquired local fame. Small-scale businesses—skating rinks, velodromes, sporting houses, tennis facilities, baseball fields, a racecourse, bathhouses—emerged. Sports provided a distraction from the worries of life, created moments of excitement, and gave the fans a common experience. They were a point of identity for the community, and therefore a bond to link one citizen with another. The actions of the sports arena generated conversation and newsprint, and consequently gave Galveston a facet of character it otherwise would not have had.

By the end of the century the Island City was the most advanced and sophisticated in Texas. True, it had begun to slip. The faults in its economic structure and the limits of its location were starting to show as other places developed in contrast. With a population of thirty-seven thousand in 1900, Galveston trailed Houston, Dallas, and San Antonio. It would never catch up, but at the time this fact was but dimly grasped. Galveston still was the most important port, it was the first to have telephones and electricity, it had the best newspapers and theater, it had the greatest variety of sports, it had the most individual wealth and the most advanced architecture, and it was a place of unique, sensual beauty which every visitor could feel.

Galveston had learned to accommodate a diversity of people and views—as a mature city should do. The whole town paused at the death of Robert E. Lee in 1870. Businesses closed, ships lowered flags to half-mast, and churches held memorial services. The buildings displayed banners—"Texas Weeps For Lee," "He Was Worthy of all Honor," "Lee." Yet, ten years later Ulysses S. Grant visited the island and the officials held a fine dinner for him at the Tremont complete with toasts and speeches. "General Grant, our honored guest— greater armies than Napoleon's have marched at his command, and greater glories than a crown have been his."[141]

The population, in part or in whole, celebrated Washington's Birthday, San Jacinto Day, July Fourth, Juneteenth, New Year's Day, Christmas, Labor Day, Thanksgiving, May Day, Cinco de Mayo, St. Patrick's Day, and Mardi Gras.[142] The people enjoyed April Fool's Day by nailing watches or coins to the sidewalk and watching others trying to pick them up. Youngsters, for a joke, placed dressed-up dummies on the streetcar tracks and threw firecrackers under dozing horses.[143] The town enjoyed stories such as the one told by a Galveston real estate agent about a spectator at the Labor Day parade who stepped on the toes of the person behind him:

If you do that again, I'll punch yer jaw.
Do what again?
Step on my foot!
Did I step on your foot?
You did.
I beg your pardon.
That's all right, but don't do it again.
Why not?
I'll punch your jaw.
Who are you, anyhow?
That's all right.
I want to know who's going to punch my jaw.
My name's Smith, sir.
Occupation, Mr. Smith?
I'm a butcher, if it's any of your business.
Make sausages, do you?
Sometimes.
Then do your wurst.[144]

Also, people liked anecdotes such as the one about a young man in Galveston who went shopping with "his darling." Bored with her endless looking, he retired to another part of the store while she continued her searches. He rested his arm on the display dummy of a woman and gave way to daydreaming. He was aroused from his reverie by a sharp push, while the dummy received a vigorous whack from his lady's parasol. The reporter concluded, "We have no language in our vocabulary to describe the scene which followed."[145]

The newspaper recorded also an old joke, well played anew. An anxious neighbor in 1870 woke a local bachelor to say that a stranger had come to his house the previous evening. The stranger did not make much sense, was weak, and stark naked. Out of sympathy the neighbor had clothed, fed, and cared for the stranger, but this morning the person absolutely refused to leave. The bachelor promised to help pitch the intruder "neck and heels" into the street and hurried, half-dressed, over to his friend's home. There he found that the stranger was his neighbor's firstborn child, less than one day old. They all celebrated with champagne.[146]

Life in Galveston at the end of the century was full, human, pleasant, and varied. The city possessed unusual charm, humor, maturity, and personality. Its climate and hazy sunshine produced a narcotic effect. Living was good. But Galveston existed on an edge, where nature's two worlds met. It was unsafe. This fragile, beautiful city on the border was caught and crushed as once more the sea, with its voice howling and its heavy, rolling power unleashed, rose again to challenge its old adversary, the land.

The 1900 hurricane destroyed one-third of the city and killed 6,000 people.
This is the remainder of the Sacred Heart Church. Photograph courtesy of
Rosenberg Library, Galveston, Texas.

Top: This was said to be the longest highway bridge in the world when it opened in 1893. It was destroyed in the 1900 hurricane. *Bottom:* The concrete seawall, cast in sections and completed in 1904, provided the city its main defense against the sea. Later additions extended the work from 3 to 10.4 miles. *At right:* Governor Colquitt led a line of 1,500 cars across the new arched concrete causeway in 1912. This bridge provided another line of defense against storms. Photographs courtesy of Rosenberg Library, Galveston, Texas.

Top: Using the materials of the city, the hurricane created its own break-water six blocks from the Gulf shore. *Bottom:* The completed seawall, shown here during the 1909 hurricane, diverted the force of the waves upward, rather than across the land. Photographs courtesy of Rosenberg Library, Galveston, Texas.

The Texas Heroes Monument, a symbol of the city, erected in 1900. The outstretched hand of "Victory" points to the San Jacinto Battleground on the mainland, and also to the location of the old red light district. Photograph by David McComb.

Top left: The Gulf beaches were a major tourist attraction from the beginning of the city. Bathing suits have changed from these of the early twentieth century to current styles which give a greater opportunity for sunburn. *Bottom left:* Bathhouses like this on the Gulf shore provided a place to rent bathing suits and to change clothes. *Above:* During the 1950's the "Free State of Galveston" ended with the destruction of gambling equipment by Texas Rangers and local policemen. Photographs courtesy of Rosenberg Library, Galveston, Texas.

Top left: Throughout the nineteenth century and much of the twentieth, Galveston was a major U.S. cotton exporting point. *Bottom left:* The Strand, shown here in 1894, was the financial and commercial heart of the city. Photographs courtesy of Rosenberg Library, Galveston, Texas. *Above:* The channel between Pelican Island on the left and Galveston Island on the right formed the port of Galveston. Photograph by Carl Schuh, courtesy of the Port of Galveston.

Above: The Trueheart-Adriance Building, 1882, designed by Nicholas Clayton, was restored by the Junior League in the 1960's. Photograph by David McComb. *Top right:* A "Tall Ship for Texas," the *Elissa*, restored as a project of the Galveston Historical Foundation. Photograph courtesy of the Galveston Historical Foundation. *Bottom right:* "Old Red," the Ashbel Smith Building at the University of Texas Medical Branch. It was designed by Nicholas Clayton in 1890. Photograph by David McComb.

Above: A souvenir shop in the seawall. Photograph by Susan McComb. *Top right:* Supposedly, this apartment was once a whorehouse. It is the last remaining building of its kind on the once notorious Postoffice Street. Photograph by David McComb. *Bottom right:* Fishing piers provide all-year sport for all peoples. Photograph by Susan McComb.

Top left: The "Mosquito Fleet" at Pier 19. *Bottom left:* The modern "Strand," a historic preservation project featuring restored buildings with shops and restaurants. *Above:* Ashton Villa, 1859, one of the earliest brick mansions in Texas, was saved by the Galveston Historical Foundation. Photographs by David McComb.

"The Bishop's Palace," designed by Nicholas Clayton in 1888 for Colonel Walter Gresham. Photograph by David McComb.

THE GREAT STORM AND THE TECHNOLOGICAL RESPONSE

Chapter Four

When he opened the fourth seal, I heard the voice of the fourth living creature say, "Come!" And I saw, and behold, a pale horse, and its rider's name was Death . . .

—Revelation 6:7–8 (Holy Bible)

The hurricane which swept in from the Gulf and devastated Galveston on Saturday, September 8, 1900, killed more people than any other natural disaster in the history of the United States. It was the most profound event in the lifetime of the city, and the reaction of the citizens provided one of the strongest statements by American people about humanity's relationship to the environment. It has been the technological quest of Western civilization to conquer and shape nature for the benefit and comfort of human beings. This basic principle of the culture, heritage of the civilizations of Europe, carried to our shores by immigrants, asserted itself in Galveston in response to the unforgiving devastation of the storm. There, on one of nature's frontiers, on an edge of time, the survivors utilized their technical ability to pronounce mastery over their hostile surroundings. It is a story of valor.

During its first week of life, the tempest crossed south of Puerto Rico, through the Windward Islands of the West Indies, curved northward over Cuba, and reached the western side of Florida. It returned to the sea and gathered strength as it moved parallel to the coast until it reached Galveston. There it turned northward on September 8. Between noon and 8:30 P.M., when the center passed about thirty miles to the west, the barometer dropped from 29.48 to 28.48 inches. The wind shifted from north to northeast in this time. The anemometer registered 84 miles per hour before it blew down—there were probably gusts of 120 miles per hour. As the hurricane passed, the wind direction changed to east, then southeast, and finally south by midnight. The storm tide pushed inland by the cyclone reached a height of fifteen feet between 8:00 and 9:00 P.M. Waves and spray, of course, bounded much higher. The 125 thirsty refugees in the 130-foot-high Bolivar lighthouse placed a bucket at the top to catch rainwater. They found the captured water salty.[1]

The wind blew against the tide, which meant that bay water flooded in from the north and storm water from the south. As the wind changed to the south and the surge ended, the bay water was blown back. The flood tide, therefore, fell rapidly after midnight as the storm moved inland across Texas and was gone by morning. The hurricane blustered with reduced strength through Oklahoma and eastern Kansas, reaching Iowa on September 11. It crossed the Great Lakes and Montreal the next day, traveled through the St. Lawrence region, and went back to sea off eastern Canada by September 22. The storm charted a four-thousand-mile path and had enough punch at the end to cause havoc to a French squadron in the Atlantic near Newfoundland.[2]

No one knows for certain how many people died on Galveston Island and the mainland—probably, 10,000–12,000. The best estimate for Galveston alone is 6,000 deaths. Every year the Morrison and Fourmy Company published a directory of the city. They guessed that twice the number of people listed was an accurate count. In 1900, therefore, they placed the population at 42,210. The U.S. Census figure for that year was 37,789, but Morrison and Fourmy argued that the census was taken in the summer when a lot of people were out of town. In 1901 when the company canvassed the city they calculated a population of 34,086, which meant a loss of 8,124. Considering the estimate that 2,000 had moved away from the city, they concluded that the figure of 6,000 dead was accurate. The *Galveston Daily News*, on October 7, 1900, listed 4,263 identified dead. The destruction of 3,600 homes, plus commercial damage, meant a $30 million loss.[3]

Modern sociologists have worked out a model for the study of disasters which includes the following stages: preparation, warning, impact, emergency rescue, short-term recovery, and long-term recovery. They have discovered that in disaster most people do not panic or become hysterical; there is little looting; there is an unusually high level of cooperation; victims often form "emergent" groups to deal with unforeseen problems; and people often do not respond to initial warnings of danger.[4] Although developed seventy years later, many of these conclusions apply to the 1900 storm.

After almost a century of experience with hurricanes, it is surprising how little preparation had been made. The city had planted a line of salt cedars on top of the dunes to stabilize them, and had built a wagon bridge as well as three railroad bridges to the mainland. Sand had been hauled into the city to elevate it and promote drainage, but even then the highest point in 1900 was slightly less than nine feet above sea level. Entranced by the "lotus-eater charm" of the island, natives took the presence of hurricanes casually.[5]

The seafaring community, of course, assimilated traditional folk warnings of bad weather. "Mackerel skies and mare's tails / Makes lofty ships lower her sails," and "Red sun in the morning, sailors take warning, / Red sun at night, sailor's delight." A halo around the moon, high circling gulls, or a storm bird flying low across the water toward land were all bad signs.[6] "Crab Jack" took warning from the crustaceans he tried to catch.

Crabs is mighty queer critters, and the best barometers ye ever seen. When there's a storm coming crabs goes for deep water and buries 'emselves in the mud, an' they don't come back afore the storm's over, neither. Why, just 'fore the big storm in '75 I din't get no crabs, only one er two, and them was all black with mud. I knowed right away there was goin' ter be a storm, and jest pulled up my nets an' took my things all ashore. . . . That storm didn't catch Crab Jack, though—not much. The crabs told him it was comin', an' he got out of the way.[7]

By 1900 there were more scientific methods of prediction. The United States established one of the earliest weather stations in Galveston in 1871. It provided careful barometer readings and wind measurements. The day before the 1900 storm the barometer showed little change, but the resident climatologist, Isaac M. Cline, was suspicious. He had been in Galveston for eleven years and was fascinated by hurricanes. He knew about cyclones in India which pushed huge storm tides ashore and killed thousands of people. He thought such a storm could move right over Galveston Island with equally destructive results.

The weather service informed Cline by telegraph that a hurricane had smashed across Florida and was at sea somewhere between the Galveston and New Orleans weather stations. At midnight September 7 the moon was bright and there was no sign. Perhaps the storm had spent its force in the Gulf? There was only slight wind. The weatherman noticed, however, long swells breaking on the beach with an ominous roar, and a tide rising above normal height. "The storm swells were increasing in magnitude and frequency and were building up a storm tide which told me as plainly as though it was a written message that a great danger was approaching." By dawn the high tide, some two feet over normal, began creeping over the lower parts of the island. The barometer slowly dropped, and Cline, contrary to department procedures, harnessed a horse to his two-wheeled cart and headed down the beach to warn people to seek high ground. The hurricane flags—two red squares with black squares in the center flown in tandem—were sent whipping in the freshening wind to the top of the flagstaffs. Sometime before the storm reached full fury, men tried to raise the warning atop the Cotton Exchange Building, but the wind had already carried away the pole.[8]

The warning time was adequate. The fearsome flags were flying all along the Texas Coast and in Galveston. John D. Blagden of the local weather service stuck by the telephone all day to warn the people who called. Even with that, many people went to work and hundreds of others toured the beach to watch the excitement. The city had been through storms before. "Everybody 'round here got so used to de storms dat dey don' mean nothing," said Ella Belle Ramsey, a black woman who survived. But this one was different. " 'Bout time we got settled de wind come up an' den de water come," she continued. "Chile, I can't tell you how dat water come. It jes come pouring in. Dere wasn' nothing to stop it den. We wen' on upstairs 'cause de water come in de downstairs. I was praying to de Lord an' I never think 'bout nothing else."[9]

Even the chief climatologist was fooled. Cline warned the inhabitants within three blocks of the beach to evacuate, but that was not enough. With the storm tide still rising, at mid-afternoon he sent his brother to inform the weather headquarters in Washington, D.C., that Galveston was going under and to request aid. Joseph Cline waded through the streets to the telephone exchange. The wooden block pavement was afloat "like a carpet of corks," but he was able to get the message through to Houston shortly before the line went dead. With that, the Cline brothers waded to Isaac's house to wait out the storm.

About fifty people were there, including Isaac Cline's pregnant wife and children. His home, located four blocks from the beach, had been specially braced to withstand hurricanes, and even the builders took refuge there. The whole town was awash, but the houses on their stilted foundations stood above the waves. Debris, however, piled up around the structures and dammed the water. It poured into Cline's first floor, and the occupants retreated upstairs. The construction was stout and might have withstood the onslaught, but there was another hazard for which there had been no planning.

The storm uprooted the trestle of the beach streetcar line together with ties, cross pieces, and fifty-foot rails. It moved, lashed, floated, and rolled like Death's scythe in the fury of the storm. The trestle battered the Cline house, turned it over, and beat it to pieces. Joseph Cline felt the home move, grabbed two of his nieces by the hand, turned his back to a windward window, and smashed through the glass and wooden shutters into the howling wind and rain. They were alone on the side of the overturned house and he shouted back through the window, "Come here! Come here!" There was no response, and as the house disintegrated into the swirling water the three of them moved to the trestle.

Isaac Cline, his wife, and their youngest daughter were in the center of the room when it turned over. They were pinned by wreckage and carried under. Helpless, Cline thought, "I have done all that could have been done in this disaster, the world will know that I did my duty to the last, it is useless to fight for life. I will let the water enter my lungs and pass on." He lost consciousness. Shortly, however, the timbers lifted him above the surface and he woke up. A flash of lightning revealed his daughter next to him, and he could see his brother with his two other children one hundred feet away. His wife was gone.

They gathered the youngsters in front of them, turned their backs to the wind, and put planks behind them to protect them from flying debris. The slate shingles, so practical against fire, proved lethal while sailing and skimming at a hundred miles per hour in the hurricane wind. At times the brothers were struck so hard they tumbled into the water. They clung to the trestle, listened to the crunch of shattered houses and the screams of the dying, and rescued a seven-year-old girl from the waves. They moved to various pieces of flotsam as necessary and finally grounded on a long line of debris at 28th Street and Avenue P. In its grinding fashion the storm constructed a breakwater of wreckage stretching roughly from the eastern end of the city to 45th Street and parallel to the Gulf about six blocks from the beach. The hurricane destroyed everything outside of this— about one-third of the city, 1,500 acres.

From the debris wall the brothers and four children clambered through the upstairs window of a house and stayed there, huddled with others, for the remainder of the nightmare. They were among the few who escaped the Cline house. Two weeks later searchers working in the planks and timbers at 28th and P found the body of Mrs. Cline. Entangled in the wreckage of her home, underwater, she had traveled with her family to the point where the living found safety. The seven-year-old, Cora Goldbeck, whom the brothers pulled from the water had been visiting her grandparents with her mother. They were all dead, and the Clines promised to care for her. Several weeks after the event, in a drugstore, Joseph Cline met a grief-stricken man from San Antonio who was looking for his lost family. He asked their name, and, happily, Cora was reunited with her father.[10]

Others experienced their own adventures and tragedies. St. Mary's Orphanage washed away, and rescue workers found ninety corpses nearby, including a nun with nine children tied to her. The bodies of two sisters showed up at Texas City across the bay, and three boys survived by drifting about on a tree for three days. Henry Ostermeyer, who farmed down the island, survived by clinging to a salt cedar while waves washed over him. The next morning he made a stew from sea gulls and potatoes before walking into town. He lost everything from his farm, but the following May a cow with his brand and a new-born calf were found on one of the small islands in Galveston Bay. They were returned to him.[11]

John Newman had no place to go for shelter, so he went to a bar. The water rose neck deep and the bartender stood on the counter while serving the customers. "Talk about devotion to duty!" thought Newman. He bought a flask, left, floated about a bit, and arrived at the second-story veranda of a house protected by a brick building. He knocked on a door, and a woman came and asked him what he wanted. "What do I want? What do I look like being in need of?" he retorted. She rented him a bed for thirty cents and he slept for the remainder of the night. The next morning he discovered part of the house missing and the occupants gone. Undisturbed, he found the remains of a store, opened a bottle of beer and a can of sardines, and ate breakfast.[12]

Sunday morning, the day after the disaster, began with the sound of bells from the ruined Ursuline Convent calling people to worship. There was a brilliant sunrise, clear sky, and calm sea—it was as if nature were embarrassed by what had happened. To Joseph Cline as he climbed from his shelter, "dreadful sights met our gaze on all sides."[13] There was a thirty-block-long line of debris, head high and four to ten feet deep, packed with pieces of houses, branches, sand, household items—the broken remnants of urban life. The previous high-water mark from 1875 was 8.2 feet; in 1900 it was 15.7 feet. Everything—trade goods, household items, machinery—not eight feet above the first floor was water damaged, and the salt water was insidious. Later, startled riders found their bicycles collapsing beneath them, the frames rusted from the inside.[14]

There had been sixteen ships in the harbor, and they were now scattered and aground. The hurricane stranded the British ship *Taunton* twenty-two miles away at Cedar Point in Trinity Bay and blew the British steamer *Roma* sideways down the channel. It took out three bridges. The lightship, moored between the jetties with a 1,500-pound anchor and sixty fathoms of two-inch chain, was pushed four miles across the bay. The telegraph, telephone, and electric lines were down, along with the water pumping station, streetcar line and the trains. Worst of all, bodies, human and animal, everywhere were beginning to rot in the warm, moist sunlight.[15]

There were a few positive points. The water main under the bay and the Alta Loma facilities survived. Most of the brick buildings, including the hospitals, endured, and injuries were not extensive. It seems that people were either alive and all right, or dead. A railroad bridge, although damaged, remained and could be repaired. The grain elevator was all right and the wharves not too torn up. The jetties suffered a 720-foot breech, but the harbor suffered only minor shoaling on the inner bar. Above all there was a fierce determination by most of the citizens to stay and fight back.[16]

When Colonel William G. Sterett, one of the most celebrated journalists of the time, came to Galveston for the *Dallas Morning News* to inquire about the condition of the sister newspaper, he came ashore at the wharf. As he walked across a plank, he looked into the water and saw four or five naked, swollen bodies, floating face up, open-eyed, looking at him. He found the newspaper with its doors broken, flooded, engines and press damaged. He met Major Robert Lowe, the general manager of the *Galveston Daily News*, and remarked that if he were Lowe he would print the paper in Houston. Lowe exploded, "You would, would you? Well, I won't," he exclaimed as he shook his fist and stamped the floor. "You never lived here. You don't know—and you would ask me to desert? No, no, no! This paper lives or dies with this town. We'll build it again and *The News* will help."[17] The newspaper did not miss an issue.

To be sure, people moved from Galveston never to return. Some left later, like Julius Stockfleth, a marine and landscape artist, who lived in Galveston from 1885 to 1907. He was a bachelor who enjoyed his fourteen relatives. Twelve of the family perished in 1900. He retired to his native island of Fohr in the North Sea, where, haunted, he was often observed pacing the seawall when storms approached.[18] Most of the population, however, refused to give up. "I shall return to Galveston as soon as the City is in sanitary condition,

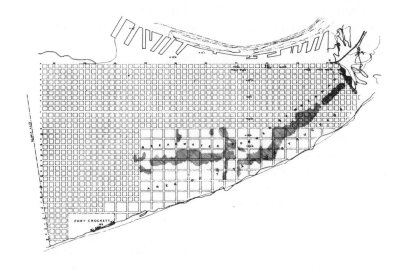

MAP 4. Hurricane Damage, 1900. From Henry M. Robert, "Effect of Storm on Jetties and Main Ship Channel at Galveston, Tex.," *House Documents,* 56th Congress, 2d Session, Document 134.

for to go in its present condition, I would be in the way," wrote a friend to Rabbi Henry Cohen. "I have not lost faith in Galveston, and am willing to stay with her through thick and thin, for with all her faults and calamities, I love her still, and am anxiously awaiting the time when I can return there."[19]

For the immediate future, however, there were immediate problems. What was to be done about restoring the city—water, lights, trash, caring for the injured and destitute, food, clothing, burial, control of sightseers, finance, looting? In many disasters where local officials are incompetent, or nonexistent, an organization emerges to handle the crises. In Galveston the designated leader, Mayor Walter C. Jones, did his job properly and organized the short-run recovery. He called a council meeting at 10:00 A.M. and another at 2:00 P.M. on September 9. He appointed a Central Relief Committee made up of leading citizens and assigned them specific tasks. John Sealy was placed in charge of finances; Ben Levy, burials; W. A. McVitie, relief; Daniel Ripley, hospitals; and Morris Lasker, correspondence. McVitie formed subcommittees for work in each of the twelve wards.[20] The government remained in charge of traditional political matters; the new committee took care of the emergency.

The Central Relief Committee decided that every able-bodied man should work on the clean-up squads and that those who did not would not be fed. It also decided that women and children should have preference on outgoing transportation, and that visitors would be restricted unless they were coming to help the city. The committee set up a pass system with guards to check the passes. The isolation of the island helped control the convergence problem, a phenomenon of disasters in which sightseers try to get into the area and victims try to get out. Levy shortly discovered the magnitude of the burial problem and asked Jones for permission to forego formal inquests. The aldermen approved. The bodies were taken care of as quickly as possible and with minimal attempt at identification.[21]

Six volunteers, meanwhile, crossed the bay on William Moody's yacht, and reached Texas City. The storm had flooded inland about ten miles, and the couriers walked through a prairie littered with debris and corpses. At the railway they found a handcar and pumped fifteen miles until they met a train to carry them to Houston. The Bayou City and others responded quickly and began sending supplies and volunteer workers by boat and train; the first relief party of 250 men arrived on Monday, September 10.[22]

Rumors of looting brought out an armed guard of Galvestonians on Monday and Tuesday with permission to shoot on sight. The current story, which was roundly exploited in the national media, held that seventy-five "ghouls" were shot. Clarence Ousley, who was there at the time and later edited a book about the disaster, doubted the figure—there were no records nor proof—and reasoned there were no more than six killed. The *Galveston Daily News* on September 11 reported eight black looters killed, but two days later verified only seven. The police record for September listed only one arrest for robbing a body and five for looting. The October report noted only one ghoul and one looter.[23]

There was one dramatic, but questionable, eyewitness. Albert E. Smith went to Galveston to make a film for the Edison Company. He lied to the officials in Houston in order to obtain a pass and also lied to the guard who questioned him on the island. He bribed workers with whiskey to arrange body scenes for the camera and later wrote:

> On the following day I was preparing to leave the area when I saw militiamen seize a man as he was hacking off a finger from a cadaver. His pockets were full of fingers, each bearing a ring. I saw the soldiers slip a sugar sack over his head, stand him against one of the funeral pyres, shoot him, then throw his body into the fire.[24]

Maybe so. On November 30 the newspaper reported forty-five bodies found in a swamp down the island with the pockets turned inside out. In mid-December forty-four more were found with the pockets slit open and no jewelry. On September 30 the police had arrested a man and woman picking up loose items. Their house was filled with all sorts of household furnishings and they claimed that they were going into the second-hand furniture business.[25] So, what can be concluded from this evidence? Ousley is probably correct about the executions, and there was probably some looting. People in disaster, however, generally do not act in such a manner; there is a moratorium on crime. By September 13, furthermore, there were two thousand armed police, soldiers, and deputy sheriffs on duty in Galveston. Adjutant-General Thomas Scurry of the Texas militia took over police duties at the request of the mayor on September 13, declared martial law, established a curfew, and closed all the saloons.[26] There just was not much opportunity for crime even if there had been the inclination.

The task of body disposal was enough preoccupation for everyone. There is no odor more powerful nor more repulsive than that of a decaying body. The crews worked with handkerchiefs soaked in camphor over their noses, and were given whiskey to ease the gruesome task. Father James M. Kirwin, the local Roman Catholic leader, commented, "It soon became so that men could not handle those bodies without stimulants. I am a strong temperance man . . . but I went to the men who were handling those bodies, and I gave them whisky. It had to be done."[27]

Kirwin, who helped direct this task, had trouble getting volunteers, but the police and military units rounded up workers at bayonet point and forced them. At first, the burial details tried to dig trenches for mass disposals, but the ground was so saturated that the holes filled with water. Next, they decided on burial at sea. By Monday evening the crews had collected seven hundred bodies, mostly naked, enough for three barges. A gang of fifty black men were forced on board at gunpoint, and the barges were towed eighteen miles into the Gulf. The corpses had to be weighted and dumped; the next day the barge workers returned, ashen in color. Two days later the body of a woman buried at sea with a two-hundred-pound rock attached to her was discovered on the beach. Others shortly began to float ashore on the west end of the island. Following that grisly episode, workmen burned the bodies where they found them.[28]

The dead were uncovered at a rate of about seventy per day for at least a month after the storm. A Red Cross woman held the following conversation with a man attending one of the fires:

"Have you burned any bodies here?" I enquired. The custodian regarded me with a stare that plainly said, "Do you think I am doing this for amusement?" and shifted his quid from cheek to cheek before replying.

"Ma'am," said he. "This 'ere fire's been goin' on more'n a month. To my knowledge, upwards of sixty bodies have been burned in it—to say nothin' of dogs cats, hens, and three cows."

"What is in there now?" I asked.

"Wa'al," said he meditatively, "it takes a corpse several days to burn all up. I reckon thar's a couple of dozen of 'em—just bones, you know—down near the bottom. Yesterday we put seven on top of this 'ere pile, and by now they are only what you might call baked. To-day we have been working over there (pointing to other fires a quarter of mile distant), where we found a lot of 'em, 'leven under one house. We have put only two in here to-day. Found 'em just now, right in that puddle."

"Could you tell me who they are?" I asked.

"Lord! No," was the answer. "We don't look at 'em any more'n we have to, else we'd been dead ourselves before to-day. One of these was a colored man. They are all pretty black now; but you can tell 'em by the kinky hair. He had on nothin' but an undershirt and one shoe. The other was a woman; young, I reckon. 'Tenny rate she was tall and slim and had lots of long brown hair. She wore a blue silk skirt and there was a rope tied around her waist, as if somebody had tried to save her."

Taking a long pole he prodded an air-hole near the centre of the smouldering heap, from which now issued a frightful smell, that caused a hasty retreat to the windward side. The withdrawal of the pole was followed by a shower of charred bits of bone and singed hair. I picked up a curling yellow lock and wondered, with tears, what mother's hand had lately caressed it.

"That's nothin'," remarked the fireman. "The other day we found part of a brass chandelier, and wound all around it was a perfect mop of long, silky hair—with a piece of skin, big as your two hands, at the end of it. Some woman got tangled up that way in the flood and jest na'cherly scalped."[29]

It was a hard situation, but the human fortitude was remarkable. In mid-September, for instance, a gang of black laborers uncovered the body of a small negro. One of the crew identified the body as his own child and broke down in tears. The men shared his grief and offered to bury the body rather than cremate it. The father refused to violate the orders and walked along as his fellows carried it to the bier on a plank. He then turned and went back to work.[30]

You would think that people would go crazy under such stress, but they did not. There is only one example. A man went insane the day after the storm and had to be lodged in jail. Most persons responded in a rational manner, as people have in other disasters. One man explained to a reporter how he reacted when his house washed away: "How did I feel? I was not excited. I was not in fear of my life. There was a restless, uneasy feeling among us all, but actually no fear."[31] At the Ursuline Convent, where a thousand people, black and white, took refuge, the blacks began singing in camp-meeting fashion after the north wall fell. The mother superior rang the chapel bell to quiet them and announced that the convent was no place for such scenes. If they wished to pray, she said, they should do so silently, from the heart. She then offered baptism to all who desired it. People there did not panic. They rescued others floating by, and one woman gave birth in a nun's cell.[32]

The days passed, and at night observers on the mainland could see the long line of cremation fires glowing in the darkness across the water. There were no vultures in Galveston, and the pyres burned into November. By mid-December only skeletons turned up. They found the last one on February 10, 1901, ten miles down the island, a fourteen-year-old girl.[33] Meanwhile, the city had begun to recover. In the first week the telegraph and water supply were restored. During the second week workmen cleared most of the streets and alleys, began to lay underground telephone lines, and restored the Gulf, Colorado and Santa Fe Railroad bridge. All the rail companies shared the bridge, and the first train arrived September 22. That was the same day General Scurry revoked martial law. In the third week the Houston relief groups returned home, the saloons reopened, the electric trolley began operating, and freight started moving through the harbor. On October 14 one of the largest shipments of cotton, 30,300 bales, cleared the port.[34]

During a sidewalk conversation about the future of Galveston, Joseph Cline commented, "Commerce always takes precedence over life,"[35] and, indeed, business quickly reasserted itself. Henry M. Trueheart, who ran a real estate firm and managed property, sent the following form letter to his customers:

> Many thanks for your sympathy. All of us and our families safe, except our Mr. Minor [Lucian Minor, an employee], lost in endeavoring to save others. We are all cleaning up and repairing buildings fast as possible. We are cast down, but not destroyed, nor discouraged. Loss of life and property not exaggerated. Your papers safe.[36]

Trueheart explained to a client in Colorado Springs that Galveston property had devalued by one-third, and that Trueheart intended to operate on that basis even though the tax assessor wanted to keep last year's rates.[37] To D. C. Jenkins of Los Angeles, Trueheart wrote about the house he had been trying to sell:

Until yesterday we were unable to examine your house, and we found it in the following condition: forty-two panes of glass out, back stairs in dangerous condition, plastering in very bad condition, many of the shingles off the roof, kitchen down and card posted on it condemning it; stable all to pieces and some of the fences.[38]

Before the hurricane the top offer had been $3,000; afterward the best was $1,000. That news must have made the Los Angeles man rather unhappy with the turn of events.

For much of the population there was nothing left, and no insurance. Outside aid was necessary, and initially stores and restaurants fed people from their supplies free of charge. The city organized relief stations in the wards, and hundreds, mainly women and children, traveled to Houston for emergency shelter and aid. For several months the railroads gave victims free passage anywhere in the nation, and there was no lack of employment.[39] The city paid $1.50 to $2.00 per day plus food and housing. The commissaries gave free supplies to those with no money for ten days, and afterward to those who could not work.[40] Clara Barton and the Red Cross appeared somewhat late, September 17, expecting to find a large number of orphans. There were not that many, and they had been absorbed already by other institutions in Texas. Barton, nonetheless, appealed nationwide for donations: ". . . if you can believe me, your country woman, I am here and my fingers are in the wound, and I assure you that the side was pierced and the nails did go through."[41]

The Red Cross competed with the ward commissaries, so the city simply turned relief work over to Barton and her retinue. She organized a subsidiary group for the black community, dispersed $17,341 in contributions, and gave away piles of clothing. People were generous in some instances, such as the seventeen-year-old New England girl who sent a satchel with three good suits and all accessories for someone her age. Others sent bedraggled finery, crushed bonnets, soiled work clothing, 144 left shoes, ragged shirts and towels from a city laundry. The Red Cross women sifted through the assorted boxes, gave away the good items, and placed the trash in barrels outside on the street. They did not want the bad publicity of burning clothes. In the morning the containers were empty. The organization tactfully bought some items from local merchants and left Galveston on November 14.[42]

The Central Relief Committee continued to operate a commissary at the turn of the year, and the editor of the *News* warned about creating a permanent pauper class. Some 450 families, 1,700 people, were drawing supplies. The commissary closed the second week in February with a rush of 150 uncontrolled people who helped themselves and cleaned out the shelves.[43] The committee also dispersed money directly to institutions and individuals, built 1,432 water closets and cesspools, gave away 222 Singer sewing machines, provided money for 1,114 building repairs at an average of $106 each, and constructed 483 three-room cottages at a cost of $300 each.[44]

The committee received $1,258,000 in donations from around the world. New York State with $94,000 gave the most—a bazaar at the Waldorf-Astoria netted $50,000.[45] After six months no one depended upon relief, commerce had revived, and the stricken population possessed the necessities for living. It was a remarkable recovery carried out with efficiency. On Sepember 8, 1901, seven thousand people attended a memorial service at Lucas Terrace near the beach, where two hundred had sought shelter from the great storm and twenty-three survived. They planted salt cedars and oleanders, and the following day threw garlands into the placid waters of the Gulf.[46]

It was well to remember, and grieve, but what of the future, the long run? The vulnerability of the island was now plain to almost everyone. No one could forget. What could be done to make it safe? Who would pay for it? After the hurricanes of 1886 there had been discussion about building a seawall and raising the elevation of the city to prevent flooding. There was insufficient interest to carry out the ideas then, but at least the thought was there. Shortly after the great storm in 1900 the ideas revived. In late October Henry M. Robert, one of the Army engineers who had recommended Galveston as a deep-water port, met with civic leaders and discussed the future. The subject of a seawall came up, but there were no definite plans expressed. Robert was of the opinion that the storm was unique and that Galveston should go forward.[47]

Then a surprise occurred. The Fort Worth Board of Trade called a convention in late November to discuss the needs of Galveston. There, representatives from the old Deep Water Committee presented a program: replace the current city government with a commission appointed by the governor, exempt the city from state and county taxes for two years, refinance the bonded debt at a lower rate, and pass a local tax to raise the grade level.[48] This was the opening salvo in an attempt by the power elite to take over the municipal government.

The Deep Water Committee had not disbanded after obtaining federal support for the building of the jetties, but had continued as an ad hoc group promoting the commerce of the island. It was in their self-interest to do so. Members of the committee and their associates directed the eight local banks, dominated 62 percent of the corporate capital, and controlled 75 percent of the valuable real estate. Morris Lasker, John Sealy, Isaac H. Kempner, and Bertrand Adoue provided a link between the DWC and the Central Relief Committee. Kempner was also the city treasurer.[49] The DWC accused the city government of incompetence and used the hurricane as a mask to take over. The motive is not entirely clear. Mayor Jones and the aldermen, however, came from a lower class, and the committee did not trust them with the fate of Galveston. After the take-over, members of the DWC rarely ran for office, but they continued to control Galveston's direction until 1917.[50]

Within days after the storm, R. Waverly Smith, Walter Gresham, and Farrell D. Minor of the Deep Water Committee began working on a new form of government. They were aware of the commissions used in Washington, D.C., in Memphis in 1878 during a yellow fever epidemic, and for ruling subsidiary divisions of government such as police and fire departments. The Central Relief Committee, moreover, gave them a local example of elites appointed to positions of political power. What they developed was a plan by which the governor of the state would appoint a mayor-president and four commissioners—for finance and revenue, police and fire, waterworks and sewerage, streets and public improvements.[51]

The plan was obviously undemocratic, and had to be modified later so that the commissioners were subject to election. It also turned out to be rather inefficient. Each commissioner was selected in his own right, with a combination of legislative and executive authority in his own area, and with little inclination to cooperate with others. In America the commission plan flourished during the progressive period before World War I, but then gave way to the city-manager plan. In Galveston it placed the elite in temporary control to carry out their plans for long-range recovery of the city and protection of their economic base.

In order to discredit the old government, the Deep Water Committee claimed that "past extravagance and carelessness" had brought the city to bankruptcy. Change was a matter of "civic life and death," they said. Every two years the municipality had to pay off its floating debt with a bond issue, because it was impossible to pay the debt with current taxes. Governor Joseph D. Sayers said he would refuse state aid to such a place, and, therefore, something had to be done.[52] It was basically an argument of fiscal irresponsibility.

The propaganda was largely false and opportunistic, but with a blush of truth. An independent audit of the city books in 1895 revealed that no trial balance had been taken since 1891. The official accountant did not know how to keep books, and there were many irregularities. Wealthy citizens, and some aldermen, chose to ignore their taxes in these circumstances. There was no fraud, just procrastination, laxity, and error. Mayor Ashley W. Fly had to ask the legislature to permit a bond issue of $200,000 to pay off the floating debt in 1895. He then discovered that it was not enough and asked for another $200,000 in 1897. Walter C. Jones, who had been chief of police, then defeated Fly in 1899.[53]

Jones reduced the city budget both in 1899 and in 1900, sold city securities above par value, and avoided default on bond payments or salaries in spite of the crises created by the hurricane.[54] In December 1900, however, after the fight opened with the Deep Water Committee, he had a problem collecting taxes. The city auditor considered it a "combination, or conspiracy of certain parties who refuse to pay" in order to embarrass the government.[55] The auditor did not accuse anyone directly, but the DWC possessed that kind of power.

There were public meetings about the proposed change in government, but the members of the DWC appealed directly to the legislature for a charter change without a vote of the citizens. The newspapers took the side of the committee, and Jones ceased talking to reporters. In his annual address to the city council, however, he said:

> While conceding to everyone honesty of purpose and patriotic motives, it is a matter of sincere regret to all lovers of a republican form of government that among our citizens are a number, who boldly organized into a committee for that purpose, seek before the Legislature to discredit our citizenship and submit to the world that we are incapable of self government without the consent of the governed in the form of a commission, in the selection of which not a citizen of this city would have a voice. . . .
>
> By a concert of action they have withheld their just obligations to the government at a time when patriotism would seem to have indicated an opposite course and attempted to place the city in an attitude of a bankrupt municipality until at last, forced by public opinion and the strong arm of the law, a majority have become conscience-stricken, to use a mild term, and paid their taxes.[56]

The *Galveston Daily News* labeled Jones' statement "demagogism" and said he was appealing to class differences.[57] It is more likely that the mayor and the city auditor spoke the truth. There is little evidence of fiscal incompetence. Considering the crisis of the hurricane, his defense of democracy, the success of the short-run recovery, and the fact that the newspapers were against him, Mayor Walter C. Jones was one of the unsung heroes of the great storm. Galveston was fortunate to have him, even if he was not one of the elite.

The Deep Water Committee, of course, won. The legislature approved the new charter after amending it to require the election of two commissioners. In the September 1901 election the two candidates of the City Club, a political party backed by the elite, won overwhelmingly. There was no class antagonism, no split in society.

The DWC had chosen its time well. During emergencies such as that of the great storm, communities pull together and differences between groups diminish in the face of the common peril. Kempner called it the "Galveston spirit." This commonality helped gain approval of the commission government, and Galvestonians pioneered a new form of municipal rule which lasted, for them, until 1960.[58]

The governor designated Judge William T. Austin, one of the elected commissioners, as the mayor-president. The other commissioners were Isaac H. Kempner, finance and revenue; A. P. Norman, police and fire; Herman C. Lange, waterworks and sewerage; and Valery Austin, streets and public improvements. Facing court questions over constitutionality, the legislature amended the charter in 1903 to require election of all commissioners. Mayor Jones took the transition in good grace. At his last meeting he said to Judge Austin, "In presenting you this gavel, I want to express my best wishes for your administration and hope that it will lead to the upbuilding of Galveston."[59]

One of the earliest actions of the new government was to appoint a committee to select engineers to devise a plan for protecting the city. The commissioners were thinking about a simple breakwater, but their action was significant. Throughout the country at this time, civic leaders turned to technology to solve problems. Few communities had the severe difficulties of Galveston, but most reacted the same way—they turned to engineers. This professional group stayed in close contact across international borders through journals and organizations. There was a free flow of information, and engineers were among the chief purveyors of technology. The commissioners also broke the old attitude of government strictly as an agent for business. In Galveston as elsewhere there emerged concern for the greater welfare of the populace. In the face of hurricane destruction there was little choice but to act for the benefit of all if the city were to survive. Social concern, however, was a part of massive change in the United States wrought by the progressive movement, the social gospel, and the rise of unions.[60]

It is interesting that not all Galveston leaders made this transition. In one of the often repeated stories about Colonel William L. Moody and the 1900 storm, his son asked him what they would do about their business if people abandoned the city. "We both like to fish and hunt," the old man replied. "If they do abandon the city, remember the fewer the people, the better the fishing."[61] There is wit in the reply, but also cynicism. When Galveston could not market its bonds to pay for storm protection, all the local banks responded generously, except the Moody bank, which subscribed for only a nominal amount after the bonds were almost gone.[62] The Moody family did not make the transition to social responsibility until the end of the second generation.

Upon the recommendation of the special committee, the commissioners appointed three engineers: Henry M. Robert, Alfred Noble, and H. C. Ripley. Robert, who became the spokesman of the group, had recently retired from the Army Corps of Engineers, had been instrumental in the deepening of the Galveston harbor, and was famous as the author of *Robert's Rules of Order*. Twenty-five years before, while a young soldier in California, he had witnessed the tyranny of a presiding officer in public discussion. "I made the rules for the people, rather than for officers. The people have their rights if this is a self-government, and should not be subject to the whim or caprice of any chairman or presiding officer," he related.[63] This famous book became the law for the running of democratic bodies throughout the world. Robert also knew something about ruling nature.

Alfred Noble, an engineer from Chicago, had been in charge of the harbor and locks at Sault Ste. Marie, built a bridge across the Mississippi at Memphis, constructed a breakwater at Chicago, helped in the grade raising of the Windy City, and worked on the problem of a canal across Nicaragua. H. C. Ripley had been a member of the Corp of Engineers at Galveston and designed the wagon bridge for the city. They were paid $1,500 each plus expenses, and they reported in two months.[64]

In an hour-long presentation the engineers recommended a three-mile wall of solid concrete, paved on top, from the south jetty, across the eastern edge of the city, and down the beach. To prevent flooding in the city, the elevation of the land would be raised to eighteen feet at the wall and then decrease at an angle of one foot every 1,500 feet to the bay. The engineers estimated a total cost of $3,505,040.[65]

The city leaders accepted the recommendation without question. Their problem was financing. In December 1901 the new commissioners allowed a $17,500 default on 1881 forty-year bonds. This may have been a ploy to convince New York bondholders to lower the interest rate. The nonpayment was not too much—the old government after the storm had paid out $160,000 in interest and retired another $40,000 of debt. Negotiations in New York resulted in lowering the interest rate from 5 percent to 2.5 for five years. This saved the city $100,000.[66]

The default, however, made it impossible to sell additional Galveston bonds, necessary for the seawall and grade elevation. Isaac Kempner suggested a meeting with the county officials to ask the county to issue the bonds. After all, the city paid 85–90 percent of the county taxes. The county agreed to construct the seawall and called for a vote to authorize for a $1,500,000 issue. Before the vote, individuals, banks, unions, companies, and other groups came forward to pledge purchase. Eighty-four percent was subscribed before the county electorate went to the polls. The count was 3,119 in favor, 22 against, and 98 percent of the voters responded.[67]

For grade raising, the city turned to the state for help. There was initial resistance to a relief bill based upon past dislike of Galveston, and Isaac Kempner related how he learned to lobby during this period. He and other Galvestonians made rational but self-seeking appeals for support before the State Democratic Executive Committee with no response. Jens Moller, another lobbyist, then set up a special room to entertain the SDEC and found the politicians susceptible to champagne. There, one of the upstate members of the committee explained to Kempner that Galveston tactics reminded him of two girls sitting on a river bank with their fishing poles dipped in the water. Two boys passed by and one asked, "What luck?" A girl responded, "We have caught no fish, no men." The boy replied in explanation, "You are sitting on your bait." After that Kempner argued before the legislative people that the whole state would benefit from the recovery of Galveston.[68]

The legislature at first provided aid by permitting the city to keep its state taxes for two years. In 1903 the state passed a bill allowing Galveston to sell $2 million in 5 percent bonds, and retain the state ad valorem tax, 75 percent of the occupation taxes, and all of the poll taxes from the county to help pay for them. The law ran for fifteen years, but later the legislature extended it to forty years. The tax allowances paid about one-third the cost of the bonds.[69]

With the financing arranged, the county contracted with J. M. O'Rourke and Company of Denver to build the seawall. It was the first job for O'Rourke with his new partner, George Steinmetz, but both had prior construction experience. They moved to the island, bought machinery in Chicago, and laid a cornerstone in February 1903. Along the site they excavated three feet deep and sixteen feet wide and drove pine piles forty to fifty feet deep. These were protected from undermining with sheet piling—one foot planking—driven down twenty-four feet. Using forty men, the contractors built the wall in sixty-foot sections by pouring concrete into molds over the top ends of the piling with steel reinforcement rods every three feet. Since it took seven days for the cement to set, the workers put down seven alternate sections. They then returned, poured the sections in the gaps, and linked them together with tongue-in-groove joints. The wall was fifteen feet thick at the base, five feet thick at the top, seventeen feet high, and weighed forty thousand pounds per foot. Toward the sea it presented a concave face so that the force of the waves was driven upward, and in front, to protect the toe from washing, it had twenty-seven feet of four-foot-square granite blocks.[70]

The U.S. Army, which had established a post along the beach front in 1897, Fort Crockett, also planned a protective wall. Since there would be a six-block gap between the county segment and the fort, the county bought the land and gave it to the Army, thereby expanding the base by twenty-five acres. In return, the Army agreed to fill in the gap and extend the wall to 53rd Street. When completed, the seawall connected with the south jetty at 8th Street and Avenue A, angled to 6th and Market, followed 6th to Broadway, angled again from Broadway to the beach, and then out the beach to 53rd.[71]

In conjunction with the county, the federal government in the 1920's extended the wall from the curve at Broadway out the beach to the south jetty in order to protect another military installation. This permitted filling the land on the eastern portion of the island beyond the old wall. In 1927 the county lengthened the western end to 61st Street, and in 1951 began a further extension. It took eleven years to complete the new effort due to problems in funding. When finished in July 1962, the wall was 10.4 miles long, one-third of the Gulf coastline. The total cost was $14,479,000.[72]

During construction in the early part of the century it became popular to "promenade" atop the unfinished seawall, especially on Sunday. Boys set up ladders and charged five cents to use them. One opportunistic group of men and women used a ladder while the owner's back was turned, but the boy charged them to get down. A reporter commented that this form of enterprise would give Galveston a reputation for "bleeding its excursionists."[73]

Women and girls, for the most part, would not go onto the wall because they would have had to climb a ladder. In a day when ladies wore full skirts and the glimpse of an ankle was a thrill for men, ladders were a risqué business. Yet thousands of females wished to inspect "their" wall, and not all were forestalled. A reporter observed an intrepid "Miss Girl" who scrambled up a short ladder and hoisted herself three more feet to the top of the wall while she thought no one was looking. Then a band of boys saw "Miss Girl" at the same time she saw them. They all rushed for the ladder, but the boys reached it first and offered to hold it steady while she came down. "There is one thing a girl will not do. She will not climb a ladder while a boy is down below holding it." Undaunted, she raced along the wall for three hundred feet and jumped off into a pile of sand. None of the boys would have jumped from that height. She landed on her feet, "kissed her hand" to the disappointed gang, and disappeared down a side street.[74]

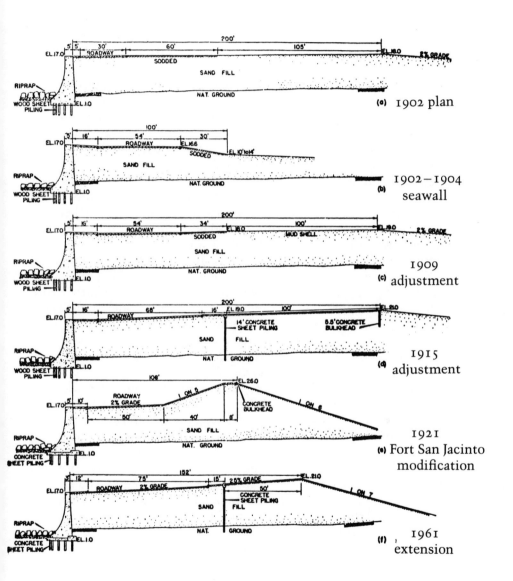

FIGURE 3: Seawall Construction Plans. *Source*: Albert B. Davis, *Galveston's Bulwark against the Sea* (Galveston: U.S. Army Engineering Department, 1961).

In 1904, when the contractors completed the city portion, ten thousand persons attended a dedication of granite monuments to the effort. The work was done on schedule and within $326 of the contract amount. Among others, J. M. O'Rourke, one of the partners who built the $1,250,000 project, was asked to speak. He commented simply, "I will not say anything for the wall, for if it ever has an opportunity you will find it well able to talk for itself."[75] And so it did, in 1915.

The original plan called for paving the top. During construction it became obvious that a walkway should be there also. With a 150-foot right-of-way there was plenty of room. In 1911 Governor Oscar B. Colquitt led in the first car to travel the entire Seawall Boulevard from the south jetty to 53rd Street.[76] Thus opened one of the most impressive marine drives in the world.

It took longer to raise the grade of the city, and the technology needed for this task was less known. Engineers knew how to lift houses and buildings. You could do that with hundreds of jackscrews moving a quarter-inch at a time. It had been done in Chicago; Alfred Noble knew about that. The problem was finding and transporting sufficient fill material, and P. C. Goedhart, a Dusseldorf engineer, had the answer. He joined with a New York engineer, Lindon W. Bates, and proposed to take sand from the channel in the harbor with self-loading hopper dredges, move the dredges through a canal cut into the city, and discharge the fluid sand through pipes onto the land. The water would drain away and the sand would remain. The elevation would increase and the channel would be deeper.

It was a unique solution and Goedhart and Bates received a contract to supply 11 million cubic yards of fill in three years. The city agreed to pay $1,938,000, and the county added another $142,000.[77] Filling was accomplished in quarter-mile-square sections. Each area was enclosed in a dike, and then all structures, sewers, water mains, and gas lines were lifted. Owners had to arrange for jacking up their houses, but the city paid for the grade raising. While the company pumped in the sand, people learned to walk on planks and trestles eight to ten feet in the air. Individuals even jacked up gravestones and tried to save the trees. Most of the trees perished, however, and fresh landscaping with topsoil from the mainland was necessary. Workers raised 2,156 structures of various kinds, including the three-thousand-ton St. Patrick's Church, which they uplifted five feet with seven hundred jackscrews without interrupting services.[78]

The grade raising took longer than expected because of unpredicted problems. The canal, two hundred feet wide, twenty feet deep, and two miles long, shoaled periodically and was too small for the largest dredges. It ran parallel to the seawall from the jetty to

21st, then along P-½ to 33rd, where there was a turning basin. Homes along the way had to be removed, and then returned when the filling was complete. There was difficulty between Goedhart and his partner, and toward the end, in 1910, the North American Dredging Company took over the contract and pumped sand from Offatt's Bayou. Goedhart and Bates lost $400,000 on the contract, but won the praise of the Grade Raising Board. When the work was over in 1911, five hundred blocks had been filled with 16,300,000 cubic yards of sand spread as thin as a few inches to as thick as eleven feet. In later years further filling occurred.[79]

Although it was not mentioned at first in conjunction with the seawall and grade raising, Galveston required a third major piece of engineering technology for storm protection—a weatherproof bridge to the mainland. In addition to trains and wagons, two new kinds of transportation, automobiles and the electric interurban railroad, demanded attention. Seth Mabry Morris of the medical school reputedly owned the first automobile in Galveston, a 1902 Olds, and the first advertisements appeared in 1903. Despite the fact that drivers were limited to the island, cars became popular. Said Moritz O. Kopperl, the leading enthusiast, "This makes no difference to me, because I can find plenty of sport driving in town and on the beach with my car."[80] Excursions to San Luis, racing over the sand, and a maiden trip to Houston in 1909 enhanced the growing love affair with the automobile. By the end of 1909 Galveston had three garages and 145 cars on the streets.[81]

The city imposed driving on the right hand side of the road in 1907, license plates in 1908, a ten-mile-per-hour speed limit in 1910, and head and tail lights in 1911.[82] Regulations helped, but the impact of the new upon the old was not always pleasant. The newspaper recorded the adventure of a man driving a pony and gig into town on 51st Street in 1915. The pony had never met a car, but he did this day—an automobile without a muffler, snorting and puffing. The pony jumped, jerked loose one rein, dumped the gig over, bolted, dragged and destroyed the equipment, escaped, and left for home on fast-flying, stumpy legs. The driver of the car went over to the driver of the gig as he was getting up unhurt and dusting himself off. "What's the matter, your horse afraid of the car?" "Oh, no," was the reply, "not in the least. He's a circus horse and I've taught him to do that." Then he charged the auto driver fifty dollars for admission to the circus. The amount was paid.[83]

In 1917 the county replaced its mules and wagons with motor trucks, which were cheaper to maintain, and as the cars replaced horses, a new folklore emerged. Judge O. B. Wigley remarked that a speedometer was unnecessary for the Model T. At ten miles per hour the lamps rattled, at twenty miles per hour the fenders rattled, at thirty miles per hour the windshield rattled, and faster than that, your bones rattled. There was also the story around Galveston about a man who had torn a piece of leaky tin from his roof and sent it to the Ford Motor Company. He shortly received a letter: "Your car is one of the worst wrecks that we have ever seen, but we'll fix it for you in a week or two."[84]

Just as people had sometimes accidentally driven their horses and wagons off the end of a wharf, similar incidents happened with cars and the seawall. In 1918 Mrs. Frank Briggs steered her one-month-old auto to the seawall with her two children and nursemaid and tried to park. She could not find neutral, and the car eased forward at slow speed. The occupants leaped free while the car nosed over the edge, rolled down the concave face of the wall, and turned over with its wheels spinning in the air. In the future others, usually at higher speeds, were to imitate Mrs. Briggs' unfortunate example. In her case the outcome was not too bad. Bystanders turned the car upright, and it was driven off under its own power.[85]

Other artifacts of auto culture began to appear: the first traffic signal, at 23rd Street and Seawall Boulevard, in 1924; a bus system in 1936; parking meters in 1939; one-way streets in 1951; and police radar in 1955.[86] Throughout this automotive popularity there was a demand for better roads in city and county, and, of course, a bridge to the mainland.

There was talk of restoring the wagon bridge shortly after its destruction in 1900. The railroads, which were sharing the restored Santa Fe bridge, resisted in order to avoid competition from automobiles and the proposed interurban railway to Houston. The Texas Railroad Commission condemned the wooden trestle and ordered the railroads to construct a causeway within reasonable time. The county voters approved a tax levy to help pay for construction and officials called upon Henry M. Robert to review the plans. Fires on the trestle and delays of passenger trains, meanwhile, caused increasing irritation, while the railroad representatives bickered over construction details. A blaze in June 1906 burned 357 feet of the bridge and required a bucket brigade from the city to extinguish it. Fifteen months later, in September 1907, an oil line broke on an engine and soaked the track and ties. Fire burst out under the dead locomotive and moved toward the oil tender. There were two hundred passengers on board, and there might have occurred a disaster. Another train, however, came up from behind and pulled the stranded cars out of harm's way.[87]

It was finally agreed that the rail companies would pay 50 percent of the bridge's construction cost, the county 25 percent, and the interurban line 25 percent. Santa Fe tore down the old trestle as part of the agreement. The causeway, following the example of a viaduct along the Florida Keys, utilized twenty-eight concrete arches with seventy-foot spans. In the center a rolling lift gave a one-hundred-foot stretch for boats to pass through. In order to save money, the roadway approaches on the ends, foolishly, were made from earth.[88]

The bridge accommodated two railroads, the interurban rails, a thirty-inch water main for Galveston, and a nineteen-foot roadbed for cars. It stood seventeen feet above the water, cost $1,329,000, and was designed to "bid defiance to wind, wave and fire."[89] The Galveston-Houston Electric Railway, the interurban, offered service to the Bayou City every hour from 6:00 A.M. to 11:00 P.M. for $2.00 round trip or $1.25 one way. Travel time was one hour and nineteen minutes, which made it the fastest interurban in the United States in the 1920's. Stone and Webster Engineering Corporation of Boston built it and operated it throughout its lifetime from 1911 to 1936.[90] For twenty-five years the interurban brought the two cities closer together and promoted Galveston as a tourist area for Houston.

When the causeway opened in 1912, Governor Colquitt led a line of 1,500 cars and broke a ribbon at the drawbridge. It was a great day celebrated with blowing whistles, fireworks, speeches, and a dance at the Galvez Hotel.[91] Federal money financed another causeway just for automobiles in 1935. It opened in 1938, but a three-and-a-half-fold increase in traffic made a third causeway necessary by 1956. Arched seventy-two feet above the water to avoid the need for a drawbridge, the new one opened in 1961. The old auto causeway was then remodeled and raised to match the new one. It reopened in 1964.[92]

Thus, twelve years after the great storm, the people of Galveston had completed a massive seawall, raised the level of the city, and strengthened transportation links with the mainland. They had used engineering technology and great amounts of money to accomplish security from the onslaughts of nature. They were confident in what had been done, and it was time for a test.

A preliminary review came in 1909. Although the weather service received advisories from the central office in Washington, D.C., starting on July 18, these were not passed on to the people of Galveston until the storm flags went up at 7:15 A.M. July 21. At 9:00 A.M. the halyards parted, and by 10:40 A.M. the wind was blowing at sixty-eight miles per hour. For the most part, the city was unwarned. On the north jetty thirty-eight people, thinking to get an early start on fishing, had spent the night at Bettison's Fishing Pier. They woke at 4:30 A.M. with twenty-foot waves and a boiling sea rocking the pier. The sailors of the pilot boat *Texas* spotted a distress flag and came within two hundred feet of the swaying resort. Two deckhands launched a yawl and rowed through the waves five times. They rescued thirty-two people, and then the pier collapsed, throwing the remaining six into the water. The yawl picked up four of them and the *Texas* reached the other two. The deckhands, Charles W. Hansen and Klaus L. Larsen, later received the Carnegie Medal for Heroism for their bravery. The pilot ship was not so lucky at the Tarpon Fishing Pier. It could not get close enough and four people drowned, including the circulation manager of the *Galveston Tribune*.[93]

At Galveston, men and women went to the seawall to watch the storm and to witness the performance of their handiwork. It was a success. Altogether, only five people died, and the tempest inflicted $99,000 in damages. Galveston sent out the news that it was all right, and there was a feeling that the seawall had proven its mettle.[94] A greater test was yet to come.

There was ample warning for the hurricane of 1915. It was first noticed by the weathermen 2,500 miles southeast of Galveston on August 10, and the local weather officer began informing shippers at that time. On August 14 the barometer began to fall and the sea started to flow in long, heavy swells counter to the prevailing wind. Mare's tails streaked the sky and the wind rose with a dull whir. White pockets of rain splattered the houses as the storm came ashore on the evening of August 16, with its center fifty miles to the west. The barometer dropped to 28.63 inches, compared to 28.48 inches in 1900, but the tide was three inches higher and the wind velocity about the same. Although it lasted twice as long, the 1915 hurricane was comparable in severity to the one of 1900.[95]

By August 15 it was clear that it would strike the island, and people were told to stay behind the seawall. Hundreds left by train, and there was plenty of time to reach shelter. The last interurban train to leave was crammed with people and their pets, including chickens. Since he was loaded to capacity, the conductor did not intend to take on any more, but at Texas City the passengers opened the windows and a crowd of refugees scrambled aboard. The conductor did not bother to collect fares, but headed for Houston and noticed another interurban train moving in the opposite direction across the ill-fated causeway.[96]

The cyclone caught the three-masted schooner *Allison Doura* 137 miles from Mobile and hurled it across the Gulf. Captain Evans Wood ran before the storm with a full staysail until the wind ripped it away. He then left the masts bare, set out drag anchors, and scudded along among waves higher than the ship. He and the crew had no idea where they were when the vessel hurtled over the top of the Galveston seawall at Fort Crockett. The anchors caught in the toe of the wall and, held by the lines, the ship was battered to pieces by the wind and waves on the land side of the seawall. Tangled in the wreckage, his right leg broken and his neck caught on the top part of a shed, Wood began to strangle. Luckily, soldiers stationed at Fort Crockett saw the wreck and rushed to the rescue. All hands, including the captain, escaped death. The storm scattered the cargo, 709 bales of sisal for Mexico, for three hundred yards, and left the broken bow of the ship at 31st Street and the seawall.[97]

Others were not so fortunate. Falling wires cut the power and halted the interurban car from Houston with sixteen passengers aboard at the drawbridge in the middle of the causeway. They got out and walked back to the Causeway Inn at Virginia Point, where sixty people took refuge. When water threatened the inn some of them, groping in the water for the rails, crawled back to the railroad blockhouse. The inn washed away at 2:00 A.M. and fifteen people there died in the water. The two-story concrete house of the bridge tender protected the ten persons who sought its shelter, even though waves broke into the second story, twenty-seven feet above the normal surface of the bay. In the bay the U.S. dredge boat *Houston* sank two miles from Texas City, and as it settled the forty-two crew members clambered into the wet rigging. The dredge turned over, and only seven men survived.[98]

At the Galvez Hotel on the beach behind the seawall the orchestra played for twelve hours, and the assistant manager claimed that "many women were prevented from growing almost hysterical by incessant dancing."[99] Nellie Watson, a nurse in training at John Sealy Hospital, wrote to her friend Golda Willis, a nurse who was away at the time, about the evening in the nurses' quarters:

From the very first poor Bing was scared witless. Her poor little eyes stared out of her head in a way that made one believe she was going blank wild any minute . . . I felt very uncomfortable myself.

I did let Bing sleep that night as long as she could. She woke in about two hours and got up too. Everybody on the first floor except Wag and Collie sat up, but they slept on. Excitement is simply not in Collie's bones. While everybody was perfectly frantic, she was lanking around in her usual manner, talking about hot water being in the cold water faucet.

The wind was so strong we couldn't stand up. We could see that the water was rising and great sheets and clouds of spray were blowing inland. The Gulf was beginning to sound so angry and the wind seemed to be getting worse. We went in and sat still and waited.[100]

The hurricane which continued into the following day blew out the windows at the nurses' building and flooded the first floor. When the wind abated the nurses waded to work and spent their time dipping and mopping.[101] The storm demolished 90 percent of the buildings outside the seawall and at Bolivar. The bathhouses were gone and riprap boulders had been lofted on top of the seawall. The fifteen-ton granite monument dedicating the wall had tumbled across the boulevard, and at Fort Crockett there was a two-foot nick at the top of the wall where the *Allison Doura* came ashore. Water washing over the wall took out the pavement from 11th to 19th Streets, and there was minor scouring under the toe. The seawall, otherwise, withstood the test in superb fashion, and protected the city from the battering of the waves. As engineer O'Rourke had predicted, the wall spoke for itself when the time came.[102]

Water, however, covered the downtown section five to six feet deep, and the wind took out the telephone and telegraph service. Worse, the hurricane washed away the earthen approaches to the causeway and broke the water main. The concrete arches endured well, however, and pointed the way for reconstruction. Every ship in the harbor suffered damage, but the jetties were intact. At Galveston 8 people died, but elsewhere in the storm 304 lost their lives.[103]

In ten days the streetcars were running, electricity was back, and a temporary water supply line had been put together on the damaged causeway. The city hauled off more than a thousand wagonloads of debris, but there was almost no crime, no cases of looting, and only a few arrests for vagrancy. Business recovered, but the Galveston Pirates of the Texas League had to give up their winning baseball season because the team lost its stadium. Trains began running again in early September, and five ships badly aground were refloated early the next month. Two of them were lodged over four miles from deep water, and workers had to dig a canal to free them. Salt spray and flooding severely damaged foliage, and replanting was necessary. Estimated total property loss was between $4 million and $5 million.[104]

Compared to the horrendous loss of life in 1900, the injury of 1915 was minimal. Engineers repaired the causeway by adding more concrete arches for the approaches, and the legislature extended the tax-rebate support used earlier to help Galveston in its task.[105] The protective devices were a success. Flooding, to be sure, caused damage, but the grade raising and seawall kept the storm loss at a bearable level. As an editor wrote, "If the seawall had not stood, it would have been folly to have urged the expenditure of more money in the effort to make the city proof against damage from storm."[106] The effort, in other words, gave to Galveston the chance to continue as a city.

In the years to come the engineering accomplishments of the early century—seawall, grade raising, causeway—insured the city's survival. Other hurricanes came to Galveston: in 1919, 1932, 1941, 1943, 1949, 1957, 1961 (Carla), and 1983 (Alicia). There was plenty of warning for Carla, which hit with eighty-mile-per-hour winds and a nine-foot tide. It was not as severe as the storms of 1900 and 1915, but it did contain a surprise. A man on the fifth floor of the Jean Lafitte Hotel called the radio station in the midst of the storm to say that something with the noise of a train and spraying gravel on his window had just gone by. This was one of four tornadoes spawned by the hurricane. It touched first at the seawall at the location of the Pleasure Pier, skipped, and then ripped through twenty blocks along 23rd Street. It destroyed 120 buildings and killed six people. The Courthouse, Ursuline Academy, and City Auditorium suffered severe damage. Estimated total loss from Carla was $15 million to $18 million.[107]

Hurricane Alicia in 1983 killed no one at Galveston, but left an estimated $300 million in property damages. It will be, after all is settled, one of the most expensive hurricanes in history. Down the island where Alicia's twelve-foot tides and 102-mile-per-hour winds washed away fifty to two hundred feet of beach, private property holders suddenly found their damaged houses standing on public land. The beach belongs to the people, and now the beach had moved to their front door. The storm, thus, left a legal question in its wake that remains, as of 1985, unresolved.[108] There can be only one outcome, however, if freedom of the beaches is to remain. For private property holders this is part of the risk of building in an area where nature is still at work deciding the dominance of land and water.

Human technology made it possible, however, for the city of Galveston to remain on such unstable land. The city did not flourish. Houston, the nemesis to the north, left the Island City far behind in the race for population, wealth, and power. Galveston simply survived. The public defenses against nature came at high cost, but they succeeded for the most part. Hurricanes still caused damage, but Galveston was not quite so dangerous for human existence. Its struggle for survival against nature through the application of technology represents the strongest tradition of Western civilization. Galveston's response to the great storm of 1900 was its finest hour, and demonstrated that rationality and determination can prevail. This is the lesson that Galveston teaches all visitors who come to the edge of time, stand on the seawall, and gaze in wonder upon the vastness of the sea.

THE FREE STATE
OF GALVESTON

Chapter Five

My candle burns at both ends;
It will not last the night;
But ah, my foes, and oh, my friends—
It gives a lovely light!

Edna St. Vincent Millay, 1920

While Galveston put its urban energy into erecting defensive structures, Houston used its resources to construct a port. In 1896 Congress approved the idea of digging a channel up Buffalo Bayou, like that at Manchester, England. There were delays, but dredging began in 1902. In 1908 the engineers achieved a depth of eighteen-and-a-half feet and built a turning basin at Harrisburg. Houston leaders created a navigation district which sold bonds to the local banks in order to match federal funds and hasten the work. During 1914 the water course reached a depth of twenty-five feet, and the daughter of the mayor, while dropping white rose petals into the water, pronounced, "I christen thee Port Houston; hither the boats of all nations may come and receive hearty welcome."[1]

This was no surprise to Galvestonians. They had watched Houston's deep-water ambitions for half a century, and when a blue-water vessel traversed the ship channel in 1915, the Galveston newspaper grudgingly admitted, "Well, one thing about that ship—it did turn around in the ship channel; they didn't have to unhinge it to get it through."[2] By using engineering technology, as Galveston had done, the Bayou City canceled Galveston's age-old natural advantage. Others did the same thing. Texas City, across the bridge from Galveston, dredged a passage in the bay and received its first ocean-going vessel in 1904. Houston passed Galveston's tonnage in the 1920's, and by 1937 the island port had been left behind by Corpus Christi,

Beaumont, Texas City, Port Aransas, and Port Arthur. In the 1960's Freeport joined the Texas ports ranking ahead of Galveston.[3]

Oil was an important factor. The gusher at Spindletop, near Beaumont, opened the rush to Southeast Texas in January 1901. Houston, because of its railroads, became the jumping-off place for Beaumont and a center for speculation in oil stocks. In 1905, with oil discoveries around the Bayou City, pipelines began to snake toward the Houston rail terminals. Oil companies in the next two decades established offices and facilities in the Houston area, and the Houston ship channel was made to order. The young Texas Company (Texaco), for example, required for its refinery large acreage, fresh water, protection from storms, and deep water. It rejected Galveston and Texas City because of the hurricane potential. World War II provided a catalyst for the industry, and afterward a wide-ranging petrochemical complex bloomed in a "golden triangle" between Houston, Beaumont, and Orange.[4] Galveston shared little in this industrial boom.

At first, advertisements for speculative stocks in the Beaumont field listed leading Galvestonians as directors—Walter C. Jones, J. S. Lobit, Isaac H. Kempner, William L. Moody, Jr., Leon Blum. A count of oil company charters filed by mid-April 1901, furthermore, gave Galveston twelve, Houston five, and Beaumont fifty.[5] But this situation did not last. Capital in Galveston was already tied up in commerce, or absorbed in the cost of building defenses against the sea. The Galveston economy, consequently, stagnated, and the city changed in a surprising way.

It became the sin city of the Gulf Coast, based upon a triad of prostitution, gambling, and drinking. All of these activities were illegal in Texas, yet they flourished in Galveston under the benign eye of the local authorities. There is no simple explanation for this phenomenon, but vice in Galveston was the chief feature of its history in the first fifty years of the twentieth century.

To be sure, Galveston as a port city had always had a rough side. There were saloons, "soiled doves," and gambling from the beginning. The first settlers, after all, were pirates. A vice area began after the Civil War and continued as a mixture of bars, bordellos, and sporting houses. With sailors, businessmen, and soldiers passing through, there was always a vigorous, transient population with an appetite for illicit pleasure. Old-timers have stated that Galveston never changed into an open city; it had always been that way. The morality of others shifted, and Galveston stayed the same.[6] Maybe so.

The Confederate States of America established forts on Galveston, and the federal forces took them over after the war. The impact of modern military activity, however, started in 1897 with the authorization of Fort Crockett for the coast artillery and the placement of a Coast Guard station on Pelican Spit. In the excitement of the Spanish-American War the Army put mortars and cannons at old Fort Point on the eastern tip and assigned soldiers to protect the island. About a thousand men stayed for five months camped in tents along the beach and at the bicycle park. The old social-military units of Galveston refused the required two-year enlistment and returned their arms to the state. A Galveston regiment called the Immunes (immune to yellow fever), nonetheless, formed, but got no closer to Cuba than New Orleans before the fighting ended.[7] It was a short war.

In 1903 the federal government began to rebuild Fort Crockett, which had been damaged by the 1900 storm, and also to work on Fort Travis at Bolivar and Fort San Jacinto beyond the seawall in the east end flats. The Army built a seawall at Fort Travis, thirty buildings at Fort Crockett, and brought in a garrison. Because of trouble along the Mexican border, Galveston became a mobilization point with about four thousand soldiers and sailors present in March 1911.[8] The men played baseball, football, and soccer; welcomed visitors to camp; fought with Hispanics and blacks in the red-light district; and rattled windows by firing the ten-inch guns of Fort Crockett. "With a clang the breech is closed and slowly the big gun rises with its muzzle pointing out to sea. A blinding flash and a deafening roar and the projectile is on its way, its passage marked by a loud rumbling noise ending with a thud as it strikes the water."[9]

By March 1913 there were seven thousand soldiers in Galveston and another eight thousand at Texas City. This meant a $450,000 monthly payroll. In April 1914 they embarked from Pier 14 for Vera Cruz on large white transport ships, but returned in November when the Mexican imbroglio ended.[10] Symbolic of Galveston's decline, is the fact that the Army selected the upstart town seven miles across the bay as the headquarters for this mobilization.

Texas City was the project of a Great Lakes shipmaster from Duluth, August B. Wolvin. With others, he bought seven thousand acres on the edge of the mainland across from Galveston in the 1890's. He was attracted to a ten-to-twelve-foot ridge which extended from the shore back into the prairie. It was well drained and protected from storms by its height. In addition, there was a natural channel, six to eight feet deep, that coursed along the shoreline to Virginia Point. To the surprise of the Galveston representative to Congress, a Cleveland, Ohio, lawyer persuaded the chairman of the Rivers and Harbors Commitee to insert $250,000 for the dredging and survey of the Texas City channel. The reason given was that the port of Galveston was congested and high priced. Even Mark Hanna, the confidant of President William McKinley and a national political boss, expressed concern about the matter.[11] Wolvin, obviously, possessed friends in high places.

Colonel Henry M. Robert laid out plans, and dredging commenced in 1899 for a channel twenty-five feet deep, one hundred feet wide, and seven miles long to connect with the main channel at Bolivar Roads. In six years, starting in 1904, Wolvin opened harbor facilities, railroads, a grain elevator, an oil refinery, and steamship service to Mexico and New York. He also planned and constructed a townsite. In 1904 the "Port of Opportunity" handled cargoes worth $998,000; in 1910 it was $47,114,000. Galveston, with its own deep-water port and its problems with nature, took the development of Texas City calmly. "It should mean a greater Galveston," said the *News*, "a New York of the gulf with a Brooklyn and a Jersey City."[12] Texas City would be Galveston's industrial arm according to this reasoning, and to a certain degree, that is what happened.

Wolvin, meanwhile, put one past Galveston. He called upon the War Department while it was planning the mobilization against Mexico, told the officials about the advantages of Texas City, and offered three thousand acres for a campsite. The Army agreed, placed its headquarters at Texas City, and sent six thousand men in three days. Shortly thereafter, Congress appropriated $1,400,000 to deepen the Texas City channel to thirty feet and widen it to three hundred. Later, Congress added a 28,200-foot dike to protect the work from shoaling. The Galveston Commercial Association tried to discredit the site in a telegram sent to Washington, D.C., but Chief of Staff Leonard Wood said, "The Texas City camp, from a military standpoint is fine. The work that has been done is wonderful . . . I can see no necessity for removing the camp to any other location."[13]

It was, however, a temporary installation, fragile, and the hurricane of 1915 destroyed it. Twenty-five people died at Texas City, and under martial law the town with the help of the soldiers cleaned up the wreckage. Because of the storm, however, the secretary of war refused to re-establish the camp, and in two weeks ordered the troops to Florida.[14] The soldiers never returned to Texas City, but a small number remained at Galveston.

During World War I the military men continued to scrap with blacks in the "segregated district" of whorehouses and saloons from 25th to 30th and A to Broadway. In April 1917 fifteen blacks and twenty-five soldiers from Fort Crockett exchanged gunfire. Police tried to stop it without much success, but the rioters stopped using guns and resorted to fists. One black and one doughboy had been shot; the black died.[15] Marines and blacks fought the next year and scattered glass along the 400 block of 25th Street.[16] Galveston, however, experienced nothing like the riot of black servicemen in Houston in August 1917, when forty people died. Troops from Galveston helped suppress that outbreak.[17]

The soldiers also drilled and trained. Once, by error so it was claimed, artillerymen from Fort San Jacinto shelled the Bolivar lighthouse with twenty-five dummy projectiles. One of them tore a hole twenty-five feet up, but no one was injured. The citizens for their part of the war effort bought Liberty bonds, registered for the draft, marched off to fight, and installed engines in wooden steamships built at Orange. In 1927 the Army built an airstrip at Fort Crockett and the Third Attack Group under the command of Major Frank D. Lackland came to stay until 1935. Then, in 1940, with the rumbles of World War II in the distance, the fort began to receive more men for training in coastal defense. Most of the soldiers who came to the area, however, as many as 10,000 at a time, stayed at Camp Wallace on the mainland near Hitchcock. Although Galveston did have a 2,500-man Army airfield, the island was still considered vulnerable to bad weather and to enemy attack. German U-boats roamed the Gulf and during the course of the hostilities sank thirty-three ships.[18] In the folklore of the island there is a story that German submariners landed secretly on the beach and walked to town to enjoy the illicit pleasures of the red-light district. There is no proof that this actually happened.

As in the previous world war, Galvestonians were as patriotic as everyone else. They bought war bonds, built transport ships at Gray's Iron Works, joined the military services, practiced blackouts, set up receptions at the U.S.O., rationed food and gasoline, sacrificed the metal light-poles to the scrap drives, respected price controls, and mourned the dead. They did not take too seriously the 650 German prisoners of war at Fort Crockett, and they broke out in spontaneous celebration of V-J Day. People honked their horns, rang bells, shook hands on the street, and approved as a small Hispanic boy ran down the street shouting, "My brother's coming home!" Gas stations proclaimed, "No Coupons," and drivers who pulled up to the pumps said, "Hallelujah, fill 'er up!"[19]

Fort Crockett was used as an Army recreation center for a while following the war, but it was finally dismantled and sold at public auction in 1957. Fort Point endured as a Coast Guard Station of 150 people with access to an array of cutters, patrol boats, and helicopters. It became the main installation between New Orleans and the Rio Grande.[20] The long presence of military personnel in and around

Galveston not only helped the economy, but also provided customers for the bawdy houses. This created a major problem for the military health officials.

A venereal infection took a soldier out of action for thirty days,
and the Army had to pay the cost of treatment. In August 1917 national law banned houses of prostitution within five miles of a military base. This officially closed the brothels in Galveston, although
the inmates were permitted to stay in the houses if they wished. The
law, of course, did not stop sex, and the next year the War Department complained that Galveston was the worst city in Texas for venereal disease, that penalties rarely exceeded one dollar plus court
costs, and that prostitutes were not given medical exams. The Galveston Ministerial Association investigated the charges and found
no basis for judging their city any worse than others. The police did
admit, however, that they readily released offenders because it cost
too much to keep them in jail, and promised to require treatment of
infected whores in the future.[21]

In June 1918 Texas law required free curative measures for VD, and
city officials wondered where to get the money. The Army, however,
threatened to place the entire city "off limits," and the local government quickly opened a clinic in October. It serviced 116 patients in
the first five months, and 721 in the first year. The most common
ailment was gonorrhea, and second was syphilis. After the war the
clinic continued to operate on a limited basis, and the houses of ill
repute continued wide open.[22]

Before the modern Army arrived in 1897, Fat Alley in the block of
Market, Postoffice, 28th, and 29th was notorious. Ten years earlier
the police arrested twenty-five to thirty women of "disreputable
character" in the vicinity and charged them with vagrancy. In 1899
the police found the body of a man, never identified, who had been
murdered with an overdose of drugs, robbed, and dumped in the
alley. Jewish prostitutes in 1905 made the area of 28th and Church a
"Port Said in miniture [sic]." A police raid at 2610, 2701, and 2727
Postoffice netted seventy people, including three madams who were
accused of running whorehouses.[23] By the time of World War I, the
several blocks of Postoffice, Market, Church, and Mechanic between
26th and 27th had evolved into the red-light district, although there
were still some higher-class houses elsewhere. The most exclusive
bordello was adjacent and to the rear of the Artillery Company club-
house.[24] By the late 1920's no one could recall a time when the district
had not been there; it was an established part of the community.

In 1930 Granville Price, a student at the University of Texas and a
former police reporter for the *Galveston Daily News*, presented for

his master's thesis "A Sociological Study of a Segregated District." It provided a close look at Galveston prostitution in the late 1920's and is one of the most remarkable documents on the subject in the history of the state. Price visited the bawdy houses, asked fundamental questions, interviewed people, and reported it all in a straightforward manner.

The red-light district ("red light" is used here in a generic sense; in Galveston they used plain, clear light bulbs) was a former residential area with two-story, narrow-front, box-like frame houses that had front porches and lattices to screen the customer from the street. The structures lacked paint, and there were shacks scattered about. In the area, which was near the docks, YMCA, churches, and Ball High School, there were fifty-four brothels with an average of six prostitutes per house. Counting casual whores, Price estimated that there were between eight hundred and nine hundred prostitutes in Galveston in 1929. For comparison, Rhoads Murphey in a study of Shanghai listed the ratio of prostitutes per population for the following cities in 1934: London, 1:960; Berlin, 1:580; Paris, 1:481; Chicago, 1:430; Tokyo 1:250; Shanghai, 1:130.[25] For Galveston the ratio was 1:62. As loose as these statistics may be, it is certain that the number of prostitutes on the island was extraordinarily high. In this respect, Galveston was world-class.

The property was owned by a variety of people including widows, a fireman, a barber, a manufacturer, a policeman, the wife of a butcher, a grocer, the manager of a piano company, the owner of a black mortuary, and a guard in the U.S. Customs service. To enter a house a man would go behind the lattice and knock at the front door, which would be answered by a maid, or by the madam. The interiors showed signs of hard wear, but the parlors would have settees, bare floors for dancing, papered walls, maybe some obscene pictures, subdued lighting, and the strong odor of perfume. A customer would be asked to buy drinks, dance, and play the electric phonograph or piano. In due course, he would be urged to go upstairs with one of the women to a private bedroom, and after an indecent interval, encouraged to leave.

The standard price in the late 1920's was three dollars for a younger woman, one dollar for an older one. In the 1950's the usual price in a better white whorehouse was five dollars; somewhat less in black places. The "ladies," according to Price, were mainly Americans, and they followed their free will. The causes of their choice of profession were desertion, family problems, bad company, and desire for money or pleasure. They had poor educations and spoke mainly in obscenities about the weather and solicitations. The men who visited were of various classes: sailors, longshoremen, soldiers, clerks, gamblers, bootleggers, conventioneers, waiters, students from the medical school, policemen, and young men on a toot. When business was slow, the women solicited by telephone or called out to passersby from an upstairs window.

The red-light district was not a political issue and was seldom discussed in public, or in the newspapers. The police kept order, informed parents of wayward sons, and responded to the madam if she called for help. About the only law consistently enforced was that against miscegenation, and the houses were accordingly segregated by race. It was a female business, female run. The madams owned the enterprises, and there is no indication of organized vice lords in the profession. The whores had to pay for room and board, medical inspections, bribes to the doctor when they failed, dresses, boyfriends, new cars, and periodic fines. It was an expensive life, but some managed to save money. One madam, for example, bought a $50,000 hotel and remodeled it. Hundreds of prostitutes, however, simply drifted, their lives impossible to trace.

While other cities eliminated their vice districts during World War I and before, Galveston floated on, seemingly with little concern except for a few crusaders. Mrs. Ardie Smith, proprietor and madam of the "Brick House," said, "I have something that men want and are willing to pay for. It's my property, so why shouldn't I sell it? Your goody-goody wives that try to drive us out make me tired. Why can't they see that Galveston's better off because of us?" The police, politicians, and ministers said that it was realistic to expect prostitution and better to keep it segregated than to try to suppress it. Bishop Byrne commented, "We segregate mental and physical diseases. Let us do the same for moral sickness, for soul sickness. . . . As long as man has free will some of us will fall into impurity."[26] So it was. Citizens were willing to let it be, but the Army still had its problem of disease.

Concerned with the same difficulty, the city in 1936 required VD inspections for prostitutes every two weeks and set up a card file to keep track of them. The police imposed a charge of vagrancy for violators, and periodically raided to check the cards. In the spring of 1941, for example, they arrested thirty-two black women who had not secured health certificates after being warned to do so. "The arrests were a precautionary measure," said the police chief, "preparatory to the movement of some 2,000 negro soldiers to Camp Wallace."[27]

Authorities at Fort Crockett and Camp Wallace warned Galveston in April 1941 that "commercial prostitution is a detriment to national defense" and that unless it ended the city would be off limits to the soldiers. A nervous city commission met and declared the red-light district closed for the duration of the war. This did not end prostitution, of course, but drove it underground and scattered it across the city. In a May 1942 roundup of harlots the police discovered that 53 of 206 were infected with syphilis, gonorrhea, or both. The commander of Camp Wallace complained of the high VD rate at the camp, and both municipal and military police concentrated on arresting and treating the whores. There were eleven houses operating in 1943, and an estimate of 800 prostitutes working the city along with countless amateur "victory girls." Bishop Byrne protested the sale of prophylactics and the distribution of "impure" literature at the bases, while the U.S. Public Health Service pointed to the high VD rate in the civilian population. At the time of induction Galveston draftees revealed an incidence of syphilis at 148 per 1,000. The normal rate elsewhere was 48 per 1,000.[28] Galveston was a moral mess.

The police forces maintained the pressure, John Sealy Hospital opened a VD clinic, and penicillin became available in May 1944. The disease rate dropped to acceptable levels for the Army, but still one in ten Galveston draftees carried syphilis.[29] Following the war the madams reestablished the district and again ran wide open. There were sporadic, small-scale forays by the police, rumors and some court testimony about payoffs, and protests by the churches. State Representative William H. Kugle counted forty-two brothels in the district, but a madam said there were only fifteen. Under pressure from the Galveston County Citizens Committee for Law Enforcement led by Kugle, the police commissioner, Walter L. Johnston, reluctantly closed the area in 1953. This did not end prostitution, and Johnston warned, "I therefore ask the people of Galveston to remember that when they suddenly discover vice conditions next door to them, they have the members of the citizens committee for law enforcement to blame for it."[30]

The issue of prostitution reached a high point, or low point depending on one's view, in 1955 when George Roy Clough first became mayor. He felt that prostitution was a biological necessity for a seaport, publicly declared his support for a wide-open town, reinstituted the district, and initiated a systematic raid program in order to collect fines. "I am keeping my eyes on city payrolls and with raises granted recently it is more important than ever that these people pay their share of the cost of municipal operation," he said.[31] Time, however, was short for open prostitution in Galveston, and it ended along with widespread illegal drinking and gambling in the late 1950's through the determined efforts of the state.

The other parts of the triad of vice in Galveston—drinking and gambling—developed together, with many of the same persons involved. Like prostitution, drinking and gambling had always been present in Galveston, but they had not always been illegal. There had been minor sentiment against liquor since the Reverend W. Y. Allen gave the first temperance lecture in Galveston in 1839.[32] Much later, the country's most flamboyant anti-liquor crusader, Carrie Nation, paid a visit to the isle. She pushed open the door to a Strand saloon and said to the barkeeper:

> This is a mighty bad business you are in, an awful business. . . . Do you suppose your mother raised you to stand behind that bar and sell whisky? I see behind you there a picture of a woman half naked. When I see such pictures as that around I know it is a very bad place. There you go pouring out some of that slop. Men, you ought not to drink that stuff; it will ruin your liver and damn your souls.[33]

It was World War I, however, not lectures, that gave the movement against liquor the push it needed. Everywhere through the country there was a strong urge to protect the youthful servicemen, and Texas adopted a law forbidding saloons within ten miles of a military base. At the same time the state endorsed the Prohibition amendment, and in April 1918 Galveston became legally dry.[34]

As it turned out, Galveston became very illegally wet. It was geographically in the correct spot to develop as a major entry point for smuggled liquor, and the contraband flowed like water through a sieve. Federal agents, for instance, discovered one stream when they opened a railroad car labeled "junk" in Cleveland. It was filled with liquor from Galveston. The shipment originated in Canada, went by ship to British Honduras, and then traveled aboard a large freighter to "rum row," forty miles at sea off Galveston Island. Here, the liquor ships waiting outside American jurisdictional waters met the small, fast boats of the bootleggers. The racketeers slipped the alcohol into the city in small quantities and loaded it on railroad cars outside the yards where the cars moved to pick up junk. The smugglers sent the rail cars off to Cleveland, Detroit, and Pontiac. Officials estimated that $500,000 worth of liquor had been transported that way in six months before being stopped.[35]

The Galveston bootleggers operated as wholesalers, and two major groups emerged—the downtown gang and the beach gang. Although facts and figures are understandably shadowy, the federal agents figured they formed the major smuggling ring on the western Gulf Coast. The beach gang, led by O. E. "Dutch" Voight, acquired its name by using Galveston's western beach for its landing point. At one time the Coast Guard, on foot, captured two trucks, an automobile, three men, and a shipment worth $25,000. The boat lay three hundred yards offshore and loaded the cargo on dories. The men rowed to shore, put the dory on a trailer, used the car to haul the trailer out of the water, and transferred the cases to one of the trucks. In this instance the boat escaped in a hail of gunfire.[36]

The downtown gang was led by George Musey and John L. "Johnny Jack" Nounes. "Johnny Jack," also known as the "Beau Brummel of Galveston," wore a diamond stickpin, gave toys to children at Christmas, supposedly had a bank account of $1 million, and spent money quickly. He started with a keg of expensive liquor found on the beach, and was caught in 1924 taking delivery from a two-masted British schooner loaded with 4,200 cases of assorted liquor. Nounes was sentenced to two years in Leavenworth and given a $5,000 fine. Caught again in 1928 with Musey while smuggling into Seabrook on Galveston Bay, he commented while leaving for prison in Atlanta, "It's in again, out again, caught again. Just the same old story. It's too tough a racket to continue." Perhaps—in 1940 he was arrested for robbery.[37]

George Musey, convicted at the same time in 1928, chose to skip his $10,000 bail and flee to Canada. His contact there was Marvin J. "Big Jim" Clark, and with Musey and Nounes restricted, Clark took over the operation. According to the stories, Clark and Musey, who was in Montreal, argued over money, or perhaps a woman. Clark, in anger, tipped off the rival beach gang about a $210,000 shipment belonging to Musey. The beach gang hijacked it at Beeville in February 1931. Supposedly, the crooks made peace and settled the matter, but three weeks later, four of the gang members, two from each side, got into a blazing gun battle in downtown Galveston.

It started in Kid Backenstoe's cigar stand at 413 Tremont and moved onto the sidewalk. Kye Gregory, with an old-fashioned six-gun in his hand, hit three times, fell mortally wounded to the pavement. Mitchell Frankovich, with a slug in his chest, crouched between parked cars and exchanged shots with Theodore "Fatty" Owens, who was in a nearby alley. Pedestrians scattered in panic, and an errant bullet shattered the glass window of the Mainland Motor Company. When the police arrived and ordered the gangsters to stop shooting, however, they did. Frankovich staggered out and asked to go to the hospital. At the subsequent hearing a reporter observed that the approach of the court was to avoid hurting anybody's feelings. "In fact," he wrote, "the general attitude seemed to be that it was all a regrettable incident, troublesome, of course, but best forgotten."[38]

Owens came to trial for murder. "I don't even like to kill a bird," he testified before an audience of racketeers. He just pointed his .45 automatic, he said, closed his eyes, and pulled the trigger. The police chief and one of the city commissioners confirmed that Owens was a law-abiding man, but he drew a two-year sentence anyway.[39] Federal agents, meanwhile, arrested Voight, Musey, and Clark. This left the Galveston gangs without direction, but the remaining members merged and followed a new, dynamic leadership.[40]

The Maceo family immigrated to the United States from Palermo, Italy, in 1901 and settled in the lumber town of Leesville, Louisiana. Rosario (Rose) Maceo and his younger brother Sam, who attended barber school in New Orleans, moved to Galveston in the years shortly before World War I. They established a barbershop and after the war began giving some "Dago Red" (cheap red wine) to their customers at Christmastime. Their friends wanted more, and the brothers drifted into bootlegging. According to one version, Rose Maceo agreed to hide a load of liquor at his house for a dollar per case. He was nervous about the deal, but when the smuggler moved it out and offered to pay, Maceo said, "I don't want the money. When you buy the next load of booze, you put my "$1,500 in it and let me go with you." His action was understandable; he was making twenty-five cents per haircut at the time.[41]

In 1921 the Galveston city directory listed the brothers as barbers, but not after that date. Shortly, they became bootleggers allied with the beach gang and Dutch Voight. Sam Maceo opened a "cold drink place" in 1921 to sell liquor, and Ollie J. Quinn, one of the older leaders, agreed to share his downtown gambling territory. Rose Maceo was one of the cosigners of Quinn's $10,000 jail bond in 1928, after Quinn shot and killed a gangster who had given him a bad check. At the trial, where he was acquitted on grounds of self-defense, Quinn was asked his occupation. "Well, judge, nothing in particular. I deal in a little real estate once in a while." His attorney prompted him. "Be fair with the jury. Is that all?" Quinn replied, "I gamble a little bit."[42]

For the Maceos, gambling was most important, and they brought genius to its functioning in Galveston. Gambling, of course, was illegal; the city council had passed an anti-gambling ordinance in 1884. It was also illegal throughout Texas, so, like prostitution and drinking, gambling could find no comfort in the law. It went on, anyway, at Galveston in many forms. There were lotteries, poker games, crap shooting, slot machines, policy tickets, keno, monte, bingo, and horse betting. Policy tickets, or "numbers" gaming, was a home industry, primarily for local consumption. A person bought a ticket for a nickel and then designated a "gig" (three numbers between one and seventy-eight) or a "saddle" (two numbers). At a designated time and place the players gathered and twelve numbers on wooden discs were drawn out of a "wheel" which looked like a bushel basket. A winning "gig" paid nine dollars, a "saddle" less.[43]

It has been a long-standing myth that the Maceos and others protected the local people from too much gambling. The numbers racket, however, drained $300,000, mainly from blacks, in 1939. It was estimated at the time that 60–70 percent of the numbers players were on some kind of relief. Organized gaming penetrated to the level of the junior high schools, and when gambling finally ended on the island, there was an immediate and sharp drop in the numbers of neglected and dependent children on the relief rolls.[44] It is simply not true that gambling did not hurt the local population; the gambling establishment was not that altruistic. Except for entertainment and employment for people in the business, gambling produces nothing of economic value. It builds nothing, and adds nothing to the strength of the community. Gambling is like a diet soft drink—filled with fizz and excitement, and no nutrition. This was the world of the Maceos.

In 1926 Rose and Sam Maceo, with the backing of Dutch Voight and Ollie J. Quinn, opened the Hollywood Dinner Club, which became one of the famous nightclubs on the Gulf Coast. They built it on the western edge of town at 61st Street and Avenue S, and marked it with a searchlight beacon. It had Spanish architecture, a hardwood dance floor for five hundred, crystal chandeliers, rattan furnishings, an elegant menu, and gaming tables. The affable Sam Maceo greeted his customers at the door and brought to the club the top entertainment of the day—Guy Lombardo; Ray Noble with his first trombone player, Glenn Miller; Sophie Tucker; Joe E. Lewis; and Harry James.[45]

In his first appearance outside of California, Phil Harris arrived in 1933 for a one-month engagement at the Maceo club. He enjoyed it so much and became such good friends with Sam Maceo that he adopted Galveston as a second home. One of his band members wrote "My Galveston Gal," which he played over the KPRC radio broadcasts.

> You can have your shuffle off to Buffalo,
> Picture me beside the Gulf of Mexico,
> With the only one who really gets me,
> My Galveston Gal.

This song helped identify Galveston to the nation, as did a later song, "Galveston" by James Webb, popularized by Glen Campbell in the late 1960's.

Harris returned repeatedly to the island and once played a free concert to twelve thousand people at Murdoch's Bath House. Taking off his coat in the August heat, the man with "a mouthful of the South" sang to the crowd "My Galveston Gal," "Three Little Fishes," "Sleepy Time Down South," and his trademark song, "That's What I Like about the South." In 1941, after marrying Alice Faye, a former singer with the Rudy Vallee band, in Mexico, he came to Galveston to marry her again in Sam Maceo's suite at the Galvez Hotel. Maceo served as best man, and the reception guests included the mayor and the police chief.[46]

Harris also testified for Sam Maceo in a narcotics trial. Federal agents in a 1937 roundup of suspects in New York, New Orleans, Houston, and elsewhere picked up Maceo and accused him of being involved in drug traffic. He claimed innocence and said, "I believe there is nothing lower in the scale than handling dope." Dressed in a dark blue suit, white shirt, blue tie with small white dots, white handkerchief, and white carnation, Maceo with sixteen others pleaded not guilty. He gained freedom with a $10,000 bond and fought extradition to New York, where the trial took place five years later. The case for the government consisted of the testimony of a criminal and a prostitute. The U.S. attorney said, "We didn't pick the witnesses. They had their dope runners, their prostitutes, their thugs and their gangsters. We hold no brief for them. We took our witnesses where we found them, in the gutters and in the sewers."[47]

The case was too weak, and Sam Maceo sobbed with both hands over his eyes at his acquittal. "There could have been no other verdict, because Maceo is an innocent man," said his attorney. "Thank God, the jury saw the truth."[48] The judgment seems just; there is no evidence in the historical materials to indicate that the Maceo brothers were involved with drugs. They had enough problems, in any case, with illegal gaming and drinking, and protecting their territory.

Between 1929 and 1937 there were a series of gangland slayings, and although some of the events are murky, the Maceos were in the middle of what was happening. At midnight, October 10–11, 1929, gunmen in a light-colored sedan killed James Clinch with a shotgun blast in the back. The killers left Clinch sprawled face down on the sidewalk with his car still running and its lights off. In the prior year there had been four attempts to kill him, and he had told his mother that the Musey gang was after him. Police Chief Tony Messina said, "This is not the type of crime that can be solved in twenty-four hours time." It never was solved.[49]

Two years later, in 1931, Sam Lachinsky's bullet-riddled body was found, still warm, dumped from a car on West Beach. No solution; the Galveston underworld remained silent.[50] In 1933 Lee Hausinger, a young aviator, apparently robbed Frank Fertitta, an employee of the Sui Jen nightclub, of $900. This was a Maceo enterprise, and two hours later Hausinger died on the operating table at Sealy Hospital with a bullet in his heart. Before death, he whispered the name of his assailant—Rose Maceo. The police arrested Maceo, but a Galveston jury acquitted him.[51]

In 1935 George Musey, the former leader of the downtown gang, met death, supposedly through Maceo orders. Musey, after release from prison for bootlegging, had returned to Galveston, where he began operating a successful marble machine business. He was moving in on Maceo territory, and early in the morning at a saloon at 24th and Church, O. J. "Windy" Goss called Musey to a side door. Goss was an underling in the Maceo operation and connected with the pistol-whipping death of another shady character, Pee Wee Ellzey, who had been caught stealing money from slot machines. Goss had talked to Musey earlier, and Musey went to the door. There, Goss shot him five times.

Musey fell in the doorway and said to a friend, "Ed, they got me." The police arrested Goss one block away with a .38 caliber pistol. At the trial a Houston ballistics expert said that a bullet taken from Musey's neck matched another fired from Goss's gun. Goss confessed, but said that Musey had threatened him earlier and that he thought Musey was reaching for a handgun. There were no eyewitnesses, and Musey had no pistol in his possession. After sixteen hours' deliberation the jury declared Goss not guilty.[52]

Early in 1937 witnesses heard Theodore G. Kirchem, who had been associated with "Johnny Jack" Nounes, beg for his life before being shot in front of his house. He staggered to his door, rang the doorbell, and fell dead at the feet of his wife and daughter. The murder went unsolved, as did the killing of Maxie Parsutte several months later. The rumor was that Parsutte had ejected an influential man from a beer parlor. Be that as it may, assassins awaited him as he returned to his rooming house. As he approached, car doors silently opened and gunmen fired three blasts from shotguns as Parsutte unsuccessfully tried to flee. The cars raced away, and the case remained a mystery. An old man who had been sitting outside said he could not see what was happening; he was busy lighting his pipe.[53]

The most important incident occurred in 1938. On Christmas Eve, Harry T. Phillips, a decent young man who was the assistant chief engineer for the Galveston Ice and Cold Storage Company, took his fiancee, a student nurse, to a bar on the seawall to celebrate their engagement. After a period he took her to the nurses' residence and returned to his friends at the bar. Phillips was leaning on a chair when a man, Mike Calandra, came up and said, "This is my chair, Buddy. Do you mind?" Phillips released the chair and replied, "I am sorry about that." Calandra then hit Phillips in the face with his fist. Phillips' friend, John Miranda, rushed in and grabbed Calandra. Leo Lera, Calandra's friend, then pulled out a .45 caliber gun with a hair trigger, shoved Calandra aside, and fired four times. Three of the shots went into the ceiling, but the fourth struck Phillips below the left ear and went out the top of his skull.

Lera worked for one of the Maceo enterprises, the Little Turf, and that night was driving a car which belonged to Dutch Voight. Vic Maceo, a cousin of Sam and Rose Maceo, was there at the time, and the police asked him to deliver Calandra and Lera to the police station. He did. Before the hearing, barmaids received telephone threats, "Pack your clothes and get out of town." The police laid in an extra supply of tear gas in anticipation of mob violence, and looked for witnesses. Lera's comely girlfriend said she was there "reaching for a pickle from a dish on the bar, heard a noise like firecrackers and looked around to see a boy lying on the floor." She then left because she "didn't think it was any place for a lady."[54]

Enough was enough. The city roused in protest, and friends of Phillips visited the ministers to gain support for an anti-vice crusade in Galveston. They urged people to vote for reform in an upcoming election, and a leader of the group, Herbert Y. Cartwright, Jr.—ironically, a defender of the vice system later when he became mayor—said, "We felt that the death of Harry Phillips was a challenge to the good people of Galveston from the underworld." Of more importance, George Sealy, R. Lee Kempner, and Walter Kelso, three leaders of the elite of the city met as "private citizens to discuss local matters with the municipal heads." The session was secret, but Police Chief Tony Messina, who had been the head of the department for a decade, immediately resigned "for the best interests of the police department and of the city."[55]

At the trial Lera, accused of murder, said that it was an accident and that he was not guilty. There was a question of malice, but on January 26, five days before the election, to the cheering of the courtroom the jury pronounced Lera guilty. Through appeals Lera received two more trials, one of them in Richmond, and each time he was sentenced to death. He even attained two stays of execution, but at last time ran out. "God bless each and every one of you," he said as he died in the electric chair at Huntsville four years and two months after the killing.[56] There was no anti-vice reform. Messina and Lera had been sacrificed, and the power structure remained in place.

Following recovery from the great storm, the Galveston elite remained active in politics, usually one step removed from the hustings. Isaac Kempner, however, was a long-time commissioner and served as mayor from 1917 to 1919. George Sealy, too, was a commissioner from 1915 to 1919. The Kempner and Sealy families supported the City Club, a political party formed at the time of the first commission government, and following its demise they backed the City Party in the late 1920's and 1930's. With a few exceptions their side dominated Galveston politics through World War II.[57]

The Kempners and Sealys constituted two of the three dynastic families which composed the power elite of the city. John Sealy, one patriarch, was born in Pennsylvania in 1822, moved to Texas before the Civil War, and made a fortune in commerce, banking, railroads, and the port. When he died in 1884, he designated $50,000 of his $1 million estate to build a hospital for the new medical school of the University of Texas. His younger brother, George Sealy, who followed him to Texas and who continued to expand the estate, was distinguished for his work with the Deep Water Committee, grade raising, and seawall. He died in 1901 on a train to New York to negotiate lower bond rates for his city. Other family members remained active after this, including R. Waverly Smith, who married into the second generation and helped write the charter for the commission form of government. George Sealy, Jr., a city commissioner of the second generation, formed the Cotton Concentration Company in 1910 which set up vast warehouses and provided services for the efficient handling and storing of cotton. It helped maintain the vitality of the port. This generation also created the Sealy and Smith Foundation for the philanthropic use of family monies; most of the donations were given for the building of the University of Texas medical center.[58] The members of the second generation lived into the 1930's and 1940's. By then the family money was bound legally into the foundation, or had been dispersed among the third and fourth generations.

The port and the Wharf Company were the special province of the Sealy family. Upon the death of the older George Sealy in 1901, the presidency of the Wharf Company passed to his nephew, John Sealy, Jr., who, in turn, died in Europe in 1926. George Sealy, Jr., then became president and went on to form the Galveston Corporation, which was a holding company for the Wharf Company, Cotton Concentration Company, Bay Cotton Bagging Company, and Gulf Transfer Company. Moody interests had been reduced along the way, and Sealy thus established nearly complete control of the cotton business and waterfront. When the city finally took control of the docks in 1947, the largest owner among a widely spread bondholder group was the Sealy and Smith Foundation.[59] Before this final dissolution, however, several notable events in the history of the port occurred.

A longshoremen's strike which began in New York City reached Galveston in March 1920. The basic issues were demands for a wage increase from sixty to eighty cents per hour and recognition of the bargaining authority of the International Longshoremen's Association. The Morgan Lines responded with scab labor, and the Mallory Company diverted traffic to Port Arthur. The Morgan management contacted the Texas Chamber of Commerce in Dallas and threatened to leave the Port of Galveston. The Dallas organization queried the Galveston Commercial Association, which responded that there was plenty of labor in Galveston, but that workers were afraid to challenge the union. Business complaints to the Dallas organization indicated that seasonal goods were not moving and that the banks could not carry the loans. Along with island businesses, the Texas Chamber of Commerce asked Governor William P. Hobby to use troops to open the port.[60]

The Galveston police in this instance were sympathetic to the strikers and often did not interfere with union acts of intimidation, so Governor Hobby declared martial law, suspended the municipal government, and sent in soldiers to break the strike. The city commission formally protested this "insult to the citizenship of this city," but the takeover was cordial. The military spent $50,000 per month, the ladies organized dances for the soldiers, the ships were serviced, and at the end of September martial law ended. The city presented the commander a twelve-inch loving cup at a farewell banquet, where the toastmaster declared: "And though we are unable to compensate them [Texas National Guard] in full for the valuable service rendered, the fact that not one of them is leaving us without taking from ten to fifteen pounds more of flesh back home than he brought down here seems in slight degree to bespeak the fact that their stay with us was not without its results to each of them."[61]

Texas Rangers remained in charge of the police force until January 19, 1921, and the workers went back to tasks at a wage of sixty-seven cents per hour, but with the union shattered.[62] It was a temporary setback for organized labor, but the I.L.A. and other unions reasserted themselves by the mid-1930's. Labor trouble, as in 1920, usually started elsewhere, often on the East Coast, and the port was caught in tides beyond its control.

During this year of turmoil the harbor acquired one of its curious landmarks, the ship *Selma*. It was built in 1919 by the U.S. Shipping Board at Mobile as an experiment—421 feet long, 54 feet wide, 34 feet deep, two decks, two masts, a round stern, and constructed of reinforced concrete. After it hit the jetty at Tampico, tugboats towed the odd vessel to Galveston, in August 1920, for repairs at a recently established dry dock. Iron bars protruding from the damaged hull made it impossible to restore, so the government gave up and, after a few mishaps while moving, sank the *Selma* near Pelican Island and the entrance to the Galveston channel. It rested at an angle in three-to-seventeen-foot water and became a favorite fishing site. It had a succession of owners, the most colorful being "Frenchy" LeBlanc, who bought the grounded vessel for $100 in 1946. He retreated from the world, lived on board, and caught most of his food. He later left for health reasons, but the *Selma* remains as an enduring curiosity.[63]

The port continued its preeminence as a cotton and grain shipping point, and in the 1920's became the main place for sulphur cargo as well. The Intracoastal Canal, which opened in 1933, and the removal of the railroad differential (see page 53) the same year aided exports and helped the city ease through the Depression. Todd Shipyards of New York bought the Galveston Dry Dock Company in 1933 and acquired land on Pelican Spit for expansion. The firm repaired ships in World War II and took control of Gray's Iron Works, which built tankers under government contract in Galveston. At its peak during the war 4,500 people worked there. Todd maintained its facility afterward and became the main repair station for the western Gulf of Mexico.[64]

The most important event in the history of the port in this period, however, was the transfer of ownership and control to the city. Private ownership of the facility had long been a point of contention, a smolder that periodically broke into flame. The Moody-directed newspaper said in 1928: "Galveston has been a fief of the Galveston Wharf Company since 1869. We now see this port lagging behind the march of progress, while competing ports appropriate an increasingly larger share of the business which Galveston must depend upon for sustenance. The Wharf Company should be called to account before the bar of public opinion for its laggard and selfish administration of the trust imposed upon it by its monopolistic control of the waterfront."[65]

There is little evidence that the Wharf Company was inefficient or slow to improve. It caught the blame, however, for the success of Houston and other rival ports.[66] Enmity, moreover, existed between the family which controlled the newspaper and the one which ruled the wharves. Early in 1939 the Galveston Chamber of Commerce began to investigate and promote the idea of municipal ownership of the wharves. The thought gained momentum, the voters approved, and in 1940 the city bought the Wharf Company for $6,250,000 in bonds. Under the agreement the wharves would be directed by a board consisting of the mayor, a member of the city commission, and three representatives of the Galveston Corporation. The municipality would not gain command until all the bonds were redeemed, and although the Wharf Company dissolved, the leader of the Galveston Corporation, George Sealy, remained in control.[67]

Sealy died in 1944, but trouble continued, aggravated by disagreements and the refusal of the corporation's board of trustees for three years to authorize the annual payment of $160,000 to the city in lieu of taxes. A court finally ordered the board to pay the city. The directors also received criticism for holding $3 million in the Hutchings-Sealy Bank as a reserve without collecting interest. The president of the bank was a vice president of the Galveston Corporation and a member of the board that controlled the wharf. This was too much. The voters in 1947 approved another $2,500,000 in city bonds to redeem the remaining wharf bonds, and William L. Moody, Jr., probably with great satisfaction, bought the bonds at par to provide the money. The newly selected municipal board then utilized the surplus to pay back the $2,500,000, and, at last, the waterfront belonged to Galveston.[68]

The other two dynastic families—Kempner and Moody—followed much the same pattern as the Sealy family. The founder earned the initial fortune, the second generation expanded the estate, and the third dispersed the money among its members and to charitable foundations.[69] The patriarch of the Kempner family, Harris Kempner, was born in Poland in 1837 and sailed to the United States in 1854 to escape service in the Czar's army. He lived near Cold Springs, Texas, worked as an itinerant peddler, fought for the South in the Civil War, and moved to Galveston in 1870. He opened a wholesale grocery business, dealt in cotton, and invested in country banks, railroads, and real estate. His financial connections reached to New York, Paris, London, and Basel. Kempner and his wife had eleven children, three of whom died in infancy.[70]

The second generation continued the businesses and spread into life insurance and sugar refining. Four of the brothers ran the enterprises and administered the profits through an unincorporated association called a "Massachusetts trust" under Texas law. The leader, informally selected, was Isaac H. Kempner. He was deeply involved in the municipal recovery from the 1900 hurricane and the formation of the commission government. He possessed an interest in the welfare of his community and expressed socialistic leanings in his youth, which prompted his father to comment, "If at twenty you are not socialistic, you have no heart. If at forty you are still socialistic, you have no mind."[71]

The Kempners began as a strong Jewish family, but became diverse. As Isaac Kempner stated: "Oh, I've got one child married to a Jew, one child married to a Baptist, one child married to an Episcopalian, and one child married to a Catholic, and I am president of the Synagogue."[72] It is of interest that in their long association with Galveston there was little antisemitism directed toward them. There was never a ghetto in Galveston, and Jews were active on all levels of society and politics. A major reason for this lack of prejudice was the community concern of the Kempners and the presence of leaders like Rabbi Henry Cohen.

This remarkable rabbi was born in London in 1863, and arrived in Galveston in 1888 to lead Temple B'nai Israel after several other assignments elsewhere in the world. During his career he worked to gain aid for the destitute, reform Texas prisons, and facilitate immigration to the United States. Woodrow Wilson called him the "foremost citizen of Texas," but he was best known around Galveston for visiting the hospitals. "I never ask what religion each patient professes or whether he has any religion at all," Cohen said. "To me, there is no such thing as Episcopalian scarlet fever, Catholic arthritis, or Jewish mumps."[73]

The rabbi once traveled to Washington, D.C., to gain freedom from deportation for a Greek Orthodox who faced a firing squad at home in Russia. On another occasion he charged—all five feet of him—into a Galveston brothel to free a young woman held against her will. He found her naked in a room, wrapped a blanket around her, marched up the street with her and his bicycle, stormed into a store, and commanded in a stuttering voice, "Fit her out from head to foot!" Cohen then took her to his home and found her a job in town. He labored with Father James M. Kirwin to aid in the recovery from the great storm and stood beside him before the city commissioners to block a parade permit for the Ku Klux Klan. He was a force for righteousness and beloved in his community. A granddaughter recalled walking with him through the dark streets to a Saturday night movie when a shriveled stranger stepped out of the shadows. "Rabbi Cohen?" he asked. "Yes." "God bless you," the man said and disappeared.[74] Cohen was a man who touched the heart.

There was little love, however, extended between the Kempners and the Moodys. In 1903–1904 Isaac H. Kempner and William L.

Moody, Jr., took over the American National Insurance Company (ANICO), but, according to Kempner, "trickery and deception, which I should have anticipated, gradually but definitely permeated the policies of [my] associate." Moody told him that the Texas insurance commissioner had recommended that one family or the other own ANICO to avoid the split in responsibility. Kempner sold his part of the successful company to Moody, but later found out that the commissioner had said nothing of that nature. Moody had tricked him. Kempner reacted in 1910 by starting the Texas Prudential Insurance Company, but it was not nearly so prosperous as ANICO.[75]

When the Galvez Hotel was built, Isaac Kempner led the effort, and the Moody name was not to be seen. There had been a long-standing idea to replace the Beach Hotel, and in 1907 Isaac's brother, D. W. Kempner, offered $100,000 for construction if the city would match with $500,000. Nothing happened, but in 1910 four business leaders—Isaac H. Kempner, Bertrand Adoue, John Sealy, and H. S. Cooper of the Galveston Electric Company—subscribed $50,000 each as a nucleus. The rest of the money came from small purchases of stock in the Galvez Hotel Company, and Kempner became the president.

The $750,000 landmark hotel opened its 250 rooms in 1911 with all places reserved. It had a specially designed silver service, waiters imported from New York, a view of the Gulf from behind the seawall, and a character that won the affection of the citizens as a symbol of the "Galveston spirit." Hyman Block, an employee of Isaac Kempner, remembered the Galvez for its dances. The bands played one-step, two-step, and waltz music. There were selections called "Paul Jones dances" during which the band stopped and everyone changed partners. "I'm telling you," said Block, "it was gorgeous. You would be with your date and the more you danced, the closer you got, and the closer you got, the warmer it got. And finally you'd say, 'Whee, it's hot in here. We'd better go outside.' Then on the Galvez' south lawn you could look at the tropical moon, listen to the roar of the Gulf and sit on their wonderful wooden swings . . . and yes, there was some courting that went on there, even in those days."[76]

After Isaac Kempner died in 1967, the last of the second generation, the Kempner trust left the cotton business and developed mainly into an investment operation for the benefit of numerous, scattered family members, and for the support of the Harris and Eliza Kempner Fund for philanthropic purposes.

In a monetary sense, no one else in Galveston history was as successful as Colonel William L. Moody and his son, William L. Moody, Jr. Colonel Moody made his fortune after the Civil War in cotton and banking. He founded the Cotton Exchange in 1873. In the 1880's he sought, without success, a deeper harbor for Galveston, but he did little for his home town during its recovery from the great storm of 1900. Colonel Moody died in 1920, but meanwhile his son, who had become his junior partner in 1886 and who displayed considerable financial ability, had expanded the family activities into insurance, hotels, and ranching. In 1923 he bought the *Galveston Daily News* and consolidated it in 1926 with the *Galveston Tribune*, although they continued as before—the *News* in the morning, the *Tribune* in the afternoon. In 1932 the "Moody Interests" published a public New Year's greeting which listed: City National Bank; American National Insurance Company; W. L. Moody and Company, Bankers; W. L. Moody Cotton Company; Galveston Compress and Warehouse Company; Buccaneer Hotel; *News; Tribune;* and radio station KFUL.[77]

The Moodys, father and son, were hard-driving, self-seeking capitalists with a reputation for parsimony. Colonel Moody placed his desk by the door of the office and checked the clock as people came to work. When hiring, he asked people to recite the Lord's Prayer, spell "Tuesday," and explain one-eighth and one-thirty-second of a dollar. This was in 1908.[78] His son was equally punctual, and once left the governor of Texas standing behind on the dock when he was a few minutes late for a fishing trip. To his grandson, W. L. Moody, Jr., wrote in 1945 his philosophy of business: be truthful, honest, fair in dealings; do not take unfair advantage of your fellow man; do not gamble, especially in the stockmarket; do not smoke or drink. "They are vulgar and expensive habits that lead you nowhere," he stated.[79] Even Colonel Moody's wife, who lived ninety-three years, had a reputation for tightness. According to a story told among the Kempners, she owned a car but did not like to drive it because she had to buy gasoline. It was a cruel dilemma for her, however, because if she did not drive, the tires would rot and that was just as bad.[80]

The Moodys built the first ANICO building in 1913, and opened the second in 1971 as a statement of faith in Galveston. They built the Buccaneer Hotel in 1929, established a school for children with cerebral palsy in 1950, and constructed a convention hall in 1957.[81] W. L. Moody, Jr., opposed the Kempner and Sealy factions in local politics, particularly in the mid-1930's. He was unsuccessful, but his son-in-law, Clark W. Thompson, became the congressman from the Galveston district in 1933.[82] Moody's son, Shearn Moody, led in the political fights of the 1930's and was taken into the business. At age forty, however, Shearn Moody died of pneumonia and the family lost its heir apparent. Shearn Moody's brother, William L. Moody III, lost favor by going into bankruptcy after the 1929 stock-market crash. His ranch was put up for sale on the courthouse steps of Kimball County, and W. L. Moody, Jr., bought it so his son would have a place to live. He placed the ranch in trust so that W. L. Moody III, would have an income but no control for the rest of his life. W. L. Moody, Jr., was embarrassed; no family member had ever chosen bankruptcy before.[83]

Before his death in 1954, William L. Moody, Jr., worried about the effect of taxes on his estate and arranged for the bulk of the fortune to go to the Moody Foundation for the support of religious, educational, scientific, and health institutions in the state of Texas. The amount of money involved, estimated at $440 million, ranked the new foundation among the top fifteen in the nation. The will cut off William L. Moody III with one dollar, and placed direction of the empire in the hands of his dutiful sister, Mary Moody Northen. She was a widow of seven weeks at this juncture, and had never spent a day at the office. She commented later, "Up until my father died, I had never been farther than Houston by myself. The next day I was head of all Moody interests."[84] She proved tougher, however, than anyone suspected.

William L. Moody III, who felt that he did not receive enough from the estate, sought to break the will on the basis that the old man was insane. If he won, the foundation's share would have shrunk to $73 million, but Mary Moody Northen opposed him, and he settled for $3,640,000. She also beat off suits from other family members in 1959 and 1970, weathered a state investigation in 1970, and blocked attempts to transfer funds to family members by special state law in 1965, 1967, and 1969. Behind much of this turmoil was Shearn Moody, Jr., whose business, W. L. Moody Bank, was closed by the Securities and Exchange Commission and fell into receivership in 1972. Even though all depositors eventually recovered their funds, the old man must have rotated in his grave.[85]

After six years of litigation, the foundation began functioning in 1960, and it was like opening a floodgate. The foundation, for example, gave the Buccaneer Hotel to the Methodists for an old folks' home; the convention center plus money to operate it for three years to the city; $1 million for the establishment of the Texas Maritime Academy in 1965; $500,000 for a new wing of the Rosenberg Library in 1968; various amounts for planning, building, and equipping Galveston Community College; a basic sciences building at the medical school; and much of the money for historic preservation work in the city. From its beginning until 1976, the foundation gave 750 grants throughout Texas amounting to $75 million; it had donated $40 million to Galveston projects by the end of 1981.[86] The philanthropy of the Moody Foundation provided a satisfying conclusion to the lifetime work of two generations of hard-working capitalists.

The Sealys, Kempners, and Moodys ran the economy, ruled society, and directed politics until after World War II. They reigned because the economy was stagnant and the population grew but slowly. There was no new blood, no one to rock the boat, and people of vitality went to Houston. Only the Maceos provided a dynamic element, and they ran an illegal empire. The patricians tolerated the vice and the criminal leadership of the Maceos. Why?

There is no easy answer, but a feeling existed of "live and let live," within limits. The elite rose to action over the Phillips murder, but generally allowed vice to operate until it caused a problem or threatened their own domain. There is a story that Sam Maceo once began to build twenty nice apartments at 23rd Street and Avenue Q. W. L. Moody, Jr., sent for Rose Maceo, the older brother who ran the family, and said, "I stayed out of the gambling business, and I expect you to stay out of the hotel business." The Maceos tore down the apartments.[87]

There is little evidence of joint investment between the Maceos and the others, and no intermarriage. During an investigation of ANICO in 1970–1971 it was revealed that the company had loaned money to Las Vegas casinos, but there was nothing illegal about that.[88] Both Moody and Maceo invested in the Galveston Pleasure Pier, but to say that they were business associates would be incorrect. The Maceos, furthermore, were not welcome at the country club. Johnny Mitchell, an oil millionaire who grew up poor in Galveston, said about Sam Maceo, "He did more for Galveston than anybody I ever knew. But that's the kind of town Galveston is. It's a two-class town, all poor and a half-dozen snobs. They're still wearing high button shoes down there. The old-timers, they never had a bit of fun; they never been nowhere; they ain't going nowhere."[89]

The elite, however, enjoyed the pleasures offered by the Maceos. Their own investments, often off the island, were uninvolved, and socially it was a one-way street. They could live in a city of vice and not be a part of it. Isaac Kempner wrote to his daughter, Cecile Kempner, in 1942 after a visit to Maceo's Balinese Room:

> Crowded as usual but very few people that we knew. They have two orchestras so there is no lull in the music realm—one of the orchestras is a Mexican or Cuban Rhumba band, and when they play, conversation is a futile proceeding. I never encountered so much noise condensed in

one evening. Besides that, the food was poor, though when I got out of the dim and darkened light, I found I had carried away quite a portion of it (in a spotted inventory of each dish) on my shirt front.[90]

He also noted the decorations of the remodeled Turf Club, operated by the Maceos: "Nowhere this side of Hollywood has there been more lavish or lurid decor. It is on the whole in good taste—but I imagine it would be rather trying to live with night after night."[91] Isaac Kempner once held a debutante party at Maceo's Hollywood nightclub. On another occasion, Isaac's son, Harris L. Kempner, smuggled several cases of champagne needed for his sister's wedding. He sailed a small boat out to Bolivar Roads, picked up the cases, landed at the Beach Club, carried the cases down the jetty and a block or two into town to a car in plain sight, and took them home.[92] The Kempners saw that gambling was a problem, but took an easy-going attitude toward it, and drinking, and the Maceos.

It was easy to tolerate the gangland family. They brought excitement to the city and provided it with a naughty reputation. During Prohibition days in the United States it was considered "smart" to know a bootlegger and thumb your nose at authority, at least in a small way. People, great and small, continued to drink during Prohibition, and it was the same with gambling. It did not appear that anyone was getting hurt. It was fun, slightly risqué, and no one in Galveston seemed to mind. If you did not like it, you could leave. In addition, the people of Galveston had beaten Mother Nature with a seawall. They had been through hell and high water, and survived. Galveston, and the people who lived there—better, those who were born there—were different from others, so they thought. They broke the laws, natural and human, and got away with it. The island, therefore, was unlike the rest of Texas or the United States. It was insular. In a country increasingly regulated and bureaucratic, the general attitude of the island was one of independence—the free state of Galveston.

Sam Maceo made this myth easy to believe. He was a nice guy, and even the minister of the First Presbyterian Church characterized him as "a very lovable sort of fellow." It was hard to see that he was a crook, or that the Maceos had anything to do with gangland slayings. In 1933 Sam Maceo paid for a large Christmas party at the city auditorium for needy children; he sponsored swimming contests in the Gulf to prove the water was free of sharks; he gave $1,500 to the building fund of the First Methodist Church; he was chairman of entertainment for the Franklin Delano Roosevelt birthday celebration to fight infantile paralysis; he worked with the Beach Association of businessmen to contract big-name entertainment for the annual opening of the beaches; he was a committeeman to fight pollution in Galveston waters; he brought in Edgar Bergen and Charlie McCarthy to make Mardi Gras a success; he organized a benefit for the aid of Texas City disaster victims; and he personally cooked spaghetti dinners for his friends. How could anyone not like Sam Maceo? Even his rough, taciturn older brother, Rose, who was the boss of the operations, once outbid Glenn McCarthy, the famous oil magnate of Houston, and paid $5,300 for a feathered hat designed by Hedda Hopper at a benefit for the Houston Boys' Club.[93]

The Maceos successfully courted the heart of the people, made a lot of money, and retained most of it in Galveston County. The termination of Prohibition in 1933 also ended bootlegging, but it remained unlawful to gamble and to sell liquor by the drink in Texas. The brothers provided these illegal services at the Hollywood Dinner Club into the 1930's, and at the Grotto, a restaurant on a pier off the seawall which they bought with Dutch Voight in 1926. It was closed for gaming violations in 1928 and damaged by a storm in 1932. They remodeled it, however, and opened it as the Sui Jen (pronounced Swee Rin) in 1932 with a Chinese menu and a small pagoda for a bandstand. Along with these enterprises the Maceos operated a bathhouse, amusement park, nightclubs and casinos on the mainland, the Turf Club in their headquarters building in downtown Galveston, and a rental service for slot, pinball, and phonograph machines. Three hundred places rented these machines, usually with an agreement to split the income in half. The organization also distributed policy cards and took bets on horse races.[94]

In 1942 the Sui Jen was remodeled and renamed the Balinese Room, which became the premier nightclub of Texas. "The atmosphere attempts to be extremely El Morocco," wrote an observer, "but came up extremely rococo." After earlier experiences in which open clubs were closed by injunctions, the Maceos and others began to operate on a private basis with easy access to membership. They posted a guard at the front of the two-hundred-foot Balinese pier to screen patrons, issue memberships, and warn of unwanted visitors. By the time law enforcement officers reached the restaurant and gaming room at the end of the long pier, the illegal paraphernalia had been hidden. It is possible that, especially after World War II, the Maceos developed a warning network which tipped them off about raids of the Texas Rangers. According to stories, the townspeople would spot the big hats of the Rangers and tell the Maceos before anything could happen. There were also rumors of inside sources in Austin. Be that as it may, a successful raid on the Balinese Room or other Maceo operations was rare. On one occasion, according to legends, as the unwelcome state officers charged down the pier and into the nightclub, the band struck up "The Eyes of Texas," and the leader announced, "And now, ladies and gentlemen, we give you, in person, the Texas Rangers!"[95]

The local police, city and county, adopted a complacent attitude. They enforced the law on the basis of complaints, and very few people complained. The police maintained general order and were not corrupt. Since enforcement was lax enough, there was no reason for the criminals to bribe them.[96] Typical were the words and actions of Frank L. Biaggne, who served as county sheriff from 1933 to 1957. He was born in Louisiana in 1894, went to war in 1917, worked as a Galveston fireman for two years, and became a patrolman in 1921. He was considered a "lovable character" by the underworld, and early learned to discriminate when he made raids.

In 1930, while still with the Galveston police department, Sergeant Biaggne and Sergeant Tom Lyons staged a series of attacks on slot-machine operators. Lyons revealed initiative, found violators on his own, and made arrests independent of orders. Police Chief Tony Messina suspended Lyons, cited him for insubordination, and ordered the baseball gambling books seized by Lyons returned to the owners. A maverick commissioner, Jacob Singer, asked embarrassing questions about the case, said Lyons should be commended for doing his duty, and explained that the problem arose because the sergeant had struck "protected places." Nothing came of it. Lyons was reinstated with back pay, and the police actions ceased. In all of this Biaggne received no word of criticism; he had played the game correctly.[97]

Sporadically, raids occurred on gambling and drinking places. If staged by the city or county, the actions usually meant very little, and were often a response to ministers or occasional crusaders seeking reform. The slot machines disappeared for awhile as the "lid" clamped down, and then quietly re-emerged later after the pressure had decreased. More serious were the attacks of the Texas Rangers. They, also, were sporadic and inconsistent, mainly because of lack of manpower and the resistance of the community. "We can't raid them all," explained State Director of Public Safety Homer Garrison in 1951. "We've only got fifty Rangers. When we raid we have to raid all places simultaneously. You've got an extraordinary communication system here. We can't raid one place and then go to another place down the street, because all evidence of violations disappears." He later added, "There is no use in raiding Galveston County as long as juries there won't convict on gambling charges."[98] That was another aspect of the problem.

Biaggne, the county sheriff, was a master of innocence through all of this. In 1937, after Rangers confiscated dice tables from two clubs and could not find the sheriff to take custody of them, Biaggne commented, "I was by the Little Club about 11:00 or 11:30 o'clock and nothing was going on. I didn't know the Little Club had a dice game. I'm surprised at them out at Del Mar!"[99] With marble and slot machines operating all over the county in 1940, Biaggne said, "I haven't seen any marble machines paying off, and I haven't seen anyone paying off a machine."[100] Reacting to an ultimatum from the county attorney to clean up vice in 1948, Biaggne arrested four people and said that he knew of no houses of ill fame in the county.[101] In 1951, during an investigation by a committee of the Texas legislature, the sheriff gave a classic response to the question about why he never raided the Balinese Room. "I go to the man at the desk and say, 'How about getting in?' He says, 'Nothing doing.' You see . . . I'm not a member."[102]

Sheriff Biaggne, obviously, was not a man to look very far for trouble. Ironically, he was elected president of the National Sheriffs' Association in 1952. Long before, in 1938, Dr. W. F. Bryan, pastor of the First Methodist Church, had said in a sermon that the underworld had Galveston "buffaloed."

> Why, I could take a bird dog, not a good one, but just an ordinary bird dog and smear beeswax over his nose, and he could still flush more quail in an hour than the police officers of Galveston have flushed gamblers in a week. Slot machines, marble machines and gambling devices of all sorts litter the city of Galveston and a few men, men whose names we can hardly pronounce, are getting fatly rich off these machines.[103]

The police should not be blamed too much for their inaction. As William J. Burns, a policeman in the 1930's and long-term police chief, commented in 1949, "You know as well as I know and all of Galveston knows that there are liquor and gambling violations here." He tried to keep places decent. "That is about all we can do unless we close the town." Even Biaggne, after being needled by editor Clyde B. Ragsdale of the *Texas City Sun*, said in a burst of reality, "That Ragsdale is an s.o.b. If I closed down all the joints, they'd have to close all the hotels in Galveston." Burns thoughtfully reflected years later, "People get the kind of government they want."[104]

After 1941 the City Party—the political organization of the Sealy and Kempner families—offered no candidates for election, and the political influence of the old elites waned. In 1947 Herbert Y. Cartwright, Jr., with no particular political affiliation, scored an upset victory over the incumbent mayor, George W. Fraser. The chubby, friendly Cartwright personally handed out nine thousand cards during the campaign with his trademark phrase, "Thanks a million." He was young, thirty-two, with a definite political stance concerning vice. "I don't believe in prostitution or kids gambling and drinking, but when a man or woman gets to be 21 years of age I don't worry about them. Where we should do most of our teaching is in the homes, churches and schools." He commented during an investigation that he had refused bribes to let outside gamblers into the city. When it was pointed out that this meant a closed shop for the Maceos, Cartwright retorted, "Do you want us to let them all come in?" Later, he said to a Dallas audience, "We don't butt into the affairs of our sister cities and we don't want them to butt into ours." The mayor was for a "regulated open town," and there was a block of five thousand votes from the gambling establishment to support him.[105]

In 1955 George Roy Clough, owner of the local radio station, KLUF, defeated Cartwright for mayor. He remained in office for two terms. Clough had much the same views about Galveston as Cartwright, but Clough was erratic and irascible. He had a knack for attracting unfavorable national publicity to the city and a tendency to squabble with his commission members.[106] Clough advocated a "clean and open city," and told the Junior Chamber of Commerce of Houston, "Gambling and prostitution will keep Galveston an 'isle of enchantment' as long as there are people around to spend money on them and as long as I am around to see it."[107] He arrested former commissioners and forced them to pay overdue parking tickets—Cartwright had sixty-two—but in 1959 Cartwright returned to office.[108] By then everything had changed. Galveston had burned the candle from both ends, and its world went up in smoke.

Before the denouement Galveston promoted a number of activities to make it an "isle of enchantment" in addition to gambling, drinking, and prostitution. In the first half of the twentieth century there were a series of all-city celebrations designed to entertain tourists and citizens. Colonel William L. Moody, in a sweat about his diminishing cotton business, started the Cotton Carnival in 1909. He led a list of men supporting the idea with a thousand-dollar donation, made a rare public appearance, and gave a speech at an open meeting of the Business League.

> Capital is not coming in as it should. We are losing ground in cotton factorage. . . . We are now admitted to be the second port in the United States. It is wonderful. But, gentlemen, hasn't the port run away from the

city? Let us think much of our port, but let us also build our city. We have lost much of our factorage business. Shipping got ahead and became of paramount importance. It is time that a change were effected.[109]

The goal of the carnival was to attract cotton growers to Galveston to acquaint them with local facilities, but the idea was anachronistic. Factorage had shifted to the interior of the state, but Galveston hosted the carnival for eight years. It included parades, balls, exhibits, and sporting events, particularly automobile racing on the beach. As many as sixty thousand people attended the two-week affair, but the Cotton Carnival ceased with the coming of World War I because of high costs.[110]

A secret boosters' club called the KKK (Kotton Karnival Kids) promoted the fest until its demise, and then shifted its efforts to the Mardi Gras in 1917. Several years later the group changed its name to MMM (Mystic Merry Makers) to avoid confusion with the Ku Klux Klan.[111] The club sponsored the crowning of King Frivolous, debutante balls, parades, receptions for visiting U.S. Navy ships, and general fun. A Mardi Gras revel had occurred irregularly since 1867, but it was held annually from 1902 until 1952 except during World War II. A similar city festivity, the Oleander Fete, sporadically occurred in late May from 1921 until 1977.[112]

Splash Day, the most famous Galveston celebration, began in 1916 at the suggestion of the manager of the Galvez Hotel, to mark the opening of the beaches for the summer season. The idea found wide approval, and there were parades, exhibitions, fireworks, dances, and the coronation of King Neptune. In 1946 Johnny Weissmuller, the movie Tarzan, came ashore from a World War II landing craft as the king. He was supposed to be accompanied by forty bathing beauties with combat helmets and rifles to establish a beachhead. The water, however, was rough, and the photographers delayed the boat. As a result, seasickness wiped out half the landing force. Splash Day continued until 1965, when it had to be stopped because of crowd-control problems. The police could not handle it. Thereafter, the Easter weekend became the unofficial Splash Day for thousands of teenagers from Texas and the Southwest.[113]

On this occasion, naturally, beach apparel became an object of comment and observation. The general trends after 1900 were a change from a costume which was essentially a modification of everyday dress to a specific garment designed for swimming and sunning, and a gradual diminution exposing an ever greater amount of skin to a point approaching nudity. In 1914 colors and plaids with caps, stockings, and shoes were in fashion, and in 1916 the California one-piece suit with stripes and colored trim for men and women appeared. It reached to mid-thigh, was sleeveless with a scoop neck, was made of mohair or silk, and had a skirt attached for women. The problem was that girls began wearing boys' suits without the skirt and without stockings.

People rented these garments at the bathhouses, and the police worried about violation of the old city ordinance that required bathers to be covered from knee to elbow. "The biggest thing that we want to put a stop to on the beach," said the chief of police, "is the wearing of men's bathing suits by women. If the women will not ask for and wear men's bathing suits there will be but little trouble in the matter of enforcing the regulations."[114] But there was no stopping the trend in a day and place where women reached for equality and people liked to tweak the nose of authority. Female competitive swimmers with pictures in the paper, moreover, set the style with sleeveless, scoop-necked, clinging suits cut across the top of the thigh.[115] The briefer costumes, which daringly revealed the feminine figure, also helped women swim faster.

Men shed their tops and women tried two-piece suits in the 1940's. In 1948 the newspaper called attention to the Riviera, or Bikini, style for women, but it was not common at Galveston until the mid-1960's. In 1964 some topless women's suits appeared in Galveston shops, although the style did not catch on.[116] Nudity was still against the law, and no one seemed willing to go that far. As they were, the styles left ample opportunity for sunburn.

As might be expected there were bathing beauty contests. The Bathing Girl Review, which evolved as part of Splash Day, began in 1920 and changed into the International Pageant of Pulchritude in 1926. At its height it attracted close to forty entries from around the world and crowds of 250,000 people. First place won publicity and a cash prize of $2,500. The most famous entrant, due to later success, was Dorothy Lamour, but she did not win the 1931 contest and later said that the pageant had nothing to do with her movie achievements. Women's church groups, the WCTU, the YWCA, and the PTA protested the event because it was a "destruction to all sense of modesty," and in 1927 Bishop Byrne wrote to a potential entrant from Vienna:

The pageant is an uncouth, vulgar display for the purpose of advertising. If you come here you will be asked to parade in only a bathing suit before a motley crowd who will scrutinize you at close range as they would a beautiful animal. I cannot see how any self respecting or decent young lady would enter such a contest.[117]

Criticism and protests did not stop the pageant; high costs and the Great Depression did. It ceased after 1931. The Depression struck Galveston much as it did Houston—a glancing blow. Tourism, port activity, Fort Crockett, insurance companies, the University of Texas Medical Branch, and the New Texas State Psychopathic Hospital buoyed the Island City economy. Tax delinquency was half that of other places, and the county continued to redeem seawall bonds. The city benefited from a high level of philanthropy, orphan and aged care was good, and the Community Chest continued to function, although at a diminished level. Still, city employees took a 10 percent pay cut, the schools experienced budget problems, and transients increased three times. The Salvation Army became the clearinghouse for meal tickets and care of vagrants, while the YMCA and the Adoue Seamen's Bethel, a refuge for sailors aided by Bertrand Adoue in 1913, ran at full capacity. In 1938 the WPA in Galveston County employed 438 men and 235 women at a basic wage of $33 per month. The agency spent $858,872 that year on such items as road repair, drainage, sewers, tree planting, malaria control, water mains, school repair, and planting oleanders along the streets.[118] The Depression was no lark, even in Galveston.

Housing was a problem even before the 1930's. The Women's Health Protective Association first brought slums to the attention of city officials in 1914. The WHPA was a white women's organization formed in 1901. It worked to plant trees and shrubs, improve the cleanliness of milk, gain proper health inspection of restaurants and markets, clear debris, and give decent burial to victims of the 1900 storm. It gathered 350 to 400 members in the first two decades of the century and then evolved into the Women's Civic League. The WHPA in 1914 pointed out slum houses on West Mechanic where derelicts lived in places with bare floors, no glass in the windows, and no care except through private charity.[119]

A special committee looking into a mixed racial area from 36th to 46th Streets and Avenue I north to the railroad in 1940 found that among the 516 houses, 305 used outhouses, 145 had no sewer connections, 182 had no inside water, 274 heated with wood, and 343 had no baths. Most were in bad repair.[120] Low-cost public housing did not come to the island until the opening of Oleander Homes for whites and Palm Terrace for blacks in 1943. The demand for wartime shelter quickly filled these places, and they did not fulfill their function as public housing until after the hostilities ceased. A survey of housing units in 1945 revealed that 46 percent were substandard. Thirty-six percent of the white population and 75 percent of the black population lived in these places, which were scattered across the city. When asked if Galveston had plans to do anything about the poor housing, an official responded, "Do you want us to tear down the whole city?"[121]

By 1961, with additional construction, almost 7 percent of housing in the city was public and operated by the Galveston Housing Authority. At this point 21 percent of all private homes in the city were substandard, but this was average for the United States. The percentage of people living in public housing, however, was among the highest in the nation. An effort to sell part of this public housing in 1982 met effective protests, and an editor commented, "Successive generations have now grown up in poverty-laden Magnolia Homes. The residents are enveloped by the public housing lifestyle and mentality which entraps them. The lifestyle unfortunately perpetuates itself."[122] Poverty has always been a problem, in Galveston and elsewhere, and seems destined to remain.

In the various festivals and celebrations, and the organizations designed to advertise the city and entertain the population, sports played an important role. Both poor and rich, in economic depression or not, enjoyed these events. Galveston continued to field professional baseball teams in various leagues and with various names—Sand Crabs, Pirates, Buccaneers, and White Caps. The storm of 1915 destroyed the ball park, and Shearn Moody's death in 1936 interrupted financial support. Galveston won the Texas League Championship in 1934, and there was always someone around to sponsor the team even though it was a long-term financial loss. Even in bad seasons there were bright moments, as sportswriter Ed Angly wrote in 1919:

> When a team goes on the road and loses twelve out of sixteen games and then on its way home gets stuck behind a train wreck, so that the choo-choo reaches town just two hours before it's time to play again, and the players find that owing to the lateness of the hour all their favorite dishes have been sold out at the restaurants, and after that they go out to the ball yard and knock the old horsehide to all corners of the lot and make up for most of their weak hitting on the road—oh boy! ain't it a gr-r-r-and and gl-l-orious feeling?[123]

With fewer than four hundred people attending games, the last Galveston team folded in 1955. The president of the Big State League, Howard Green, commented bitterly, "Galveston dropped out because it was the world's worst baseball town, a resort city of the rankest type. Baseball was too wholesome for a population more interested in gaming, night clubs and that which goes with both." It was an unfair statement; three other league teams had quit, and amateur baseball with high local participation took away the fans.[124] Five years later, when Major League baseball arrived in Houston, there was no hope for a revival in Galveston.

During the early years of the century, drivers raced their automobiles on the beach, often as part of the Cotton Carnival. Much later, after World War II, the airport became the site of sports-car races sponsored by the Junior Chamber of Commerce. These began in 1957 and lasted through the 1960's. The Greater Galveston Beach Association, in which the Maceos played a big role, sponsored football, starting with the Oleander Bowl from 1948 to 1951. The games were played at the high-school stadium and featured outstanding junior-college and small four-year-school teams. Galveston paid only room and board and "one hell of a party afterwards." Other groups took over the project, changed the name to Shrimp Bowl in 1952, and invited military service teams in 1954–1959. At the last game the Quantico Marines scored almost every time they touched the ball and beat McClellan Air Force Base 90–0. The bowl games did not endure because of small crowds, poor facilities, non-interest by the media, bad weather, and a decline of military service teams.[125] But there was more to it than that. The "Free State of Galveston" was under attack, and the old leaders were not around to hold it together.

George Sealy, Jr., died of pneumonia in New York in 1944. William L. Moody, Jr., succumbed at age eighty-nine after a short illness in 1954. Isaac Kempner lived on into the 1960's, but he was an old man by this time. Sam Maceo, at fifty-seven years, died of cancer in 1951, and Rose Maceo passed on in 1953 at age sixty-six after being in ill health with heart disease and clinical depression for two years. Herbert Y. Cartwright, Jr., the mayor since 1947, met defeat in 1955, and Sheriff Frank L. Biaggne lost his office in 1957. What this meant was a change in leadership and control. In the dynastic families—Moody, Sealy, Kempner—the money and power went into foundations or was dispersed among numerous relatives. The younger men who inherited the Maceo empire did not have the ability of the founders, and Cartwright's successor lacked political adroitness. The web of relationships which held Galveston together, consequently, was ripped by death and the ballot box. The city became vulnerable to outside forces, as it once had been to the hurricane power of nature.

In 1951 the Internal Revenue Service began to apply pressure on gamblers and required them to purchase $50 licenses. The IRS filed income-tax-evasion suits against Maceo family members, and eventually won a $600,000 judgment against the estate of Sam Maceo in

1964. The case revealed that total income from Maceo operations was $3,239,000 in 1948, $3,433,000 in 1949, and $3,835,000 in 1950. About half this income came from gambling. The syndicate kept excellent books, but the IRS pointed to unstated income. Rose Maceo, for example, according to Sam Serio, the Maceo accountant, in the summer of 1947 brought a small safe into the Turf Building headquarters, opened it, revealed twelve bundles of money, and said to Sam Maceo, "Here's $600,000. Three hundred of that is yours and three hundred is mine." The safe and its contents did not show up in the record books. Neither did Sam Maceo's personal betting. He shared with six others a gambling pool containing $670,000, and he won $49,000 on the election of Harry S. Truman. The federal suit diminished the Maceo fortune considerably. How much is not known, but according to newspaper reports, Rose Maceo left an estate of $357,000.[126] More important, the family lost its gaming equipment and the freedom to operate.

The Maceo enterprises owned about 80 percent of the 1,300 slot machines in Galveston, which cost $250 to $300 each. In 1951 the Texas legislature made it prima facie evidence of felony gambling to display, possess, or even have the parts of a slot machine. The federal government made it illegal to transport machines across state lines, and the Maceos were stuck. To make it worse, four of them were called before the "Little Kefauver Committee" of the legislature to testify on crime in Texas. They sat "tight-lipped" while the state examined their well-kept books. The lawmakers found no evidence of bribery, no attempt to hide evidence, and a lot of contributions to charity.[127]

While this was going on, the state attorney general, Price Daniel, obtained a court injunction forbidding Southwestern Bell Telephone Company to allow use of its lines to transmit horse-racing information to the Turf Athletic Club and other Maceo establishments. The data were coming by phone from New Orleans via a cafe at East Orange, Louisiana, to the Turf Club. The circuits were open four to seven hours per day, and as the service was cut, the loudspeaker at the Turf said, "They're off and running in the fifth at Lincoln [Chicago] . . . close everything on the post." That meant that all bets were off; horse betting in Galveston was shut down.[128]

For several months during the Austin investigation, "the tightest lid ever slammed down on Galveston" kept the casinos dark. Isaac Kempner wrote to his daughter that he was surprised at the revealed amount of money the Maceos took in, and that the crackdown had put a thousand people out of work. An indirect loss, he noted, was the donations to charity and civic causes "by an element that has always been liberal." Kempner thought that in the long run the eradication of gaming would be good, but that at the moment the tourists found time heavy on their hands.[129] This did not last long. The clubs reopened, but without the slot machines.

A Galveston grand jury returned twenty-two felony indictments against Maceo partners late in 1951. The judges postponed the trials five times, and finally the county attorney dismissed the cases for lack of evidence. Slot machines returned in 1954, and the 1956 grand jury reported, "It is commonly known that open gambling, sale of intoxicants to minors, illegal sale of liquor, and prostitution exist in Galveston county, but no charges were presented to the grand jury by law enforcement officers."[130] It was business "at the old stand" for Galveston.

In 1956, however, another knight errant appeared, and this one possessed unusual talent. Will Wilson ran for state attorney general and won. Galveston County did not vote for him, but there was little in the newspapers, or in his inauguration speech, to indicate what was coming. Shortly Wilson warned, however, that he would rid the town of crime, and announced that "gambling is the hub upon which the wheel of lawlessness spins." To the new attorney general Galveston was a symbol of vice in the state. The island was notorious, and had the only mayor who openly supported gambling. Wilson prepared a surprise raid with sixty Rangers and held a secret meeting in Houston with twenty-three assistant lawyers. Before anything happened, however, gambling spots in five counties mysteriously began to close, including the Balinese Room. The plans had obviously been leaked, and the Rangers were dispersed for other duties.[131] Wilson needed a better tactic to crack Galveston's defenses, and he knew what to do.

Earlier, while county attorney in Dallas, Wilson had learned to use undercover agents to gather proof of gaming in order to provide evidence in the courts. With his secret support, two men from Texas City and their wives visited the gambling and drinking places in Galveston, played the slot machines, and talked to prostitutes to see if they were "available." They worked for three to four months and went to the same establishments three to four times each. As attorney general, Wilson could not file criminal complaints, but he could obtain injunctions to halt public nuisances.[132] This was what he was after.

Wilson arrived in Galveston in June 1957 demanding injunctions to close forty-seven clubs, bingo places, and brothels for "openly and flagrantly violating the laws of Texas." He blanketed the town. "From the plush Balinese Room to West Market street upstairs bawdy houses to West Broadway bingo parlors, such runs the range of drinking and gambling establishments caught in the attorney general's dragnet," reported the newspaper. State police officers on the causeway intercepted gambling equipment being sent off the island, while Texas Rangers systematically searched for hidden paraphernalia.

They found 375 slot machines in three warehouses and a gun bunker at old Fort Travis on Bolivar, and another 1,500 to 2,000 at the closed Hollywood Club. The Rangers smashed the slot machines with ten-pound sledgehammers, burned them, and dumped them into Galveston Bay. They confiscated 200 boxes of Maceo tip books, found another 250 to 300 slot machines in a Dickinson warehouse, and successfully raided the night spots. A tavern owner who was caught said, "I couldn't believe my eyes when they walked in. We weren't expecting it and I guess it was sort of a shock."[133] The warning system had broken down, and the city closed.

The state maintained pressure for a year, the district attorney pressed felony gambling charges, and the Rangers relentlessly smashed gambling machines and tables. "Closed. Will Wilson's boys was here!" announced a sign on a padlocked door of a club on 24th Street. There were a few trials, but most of the indictments were not pursued. In 1969 the courts dropped 164 cases.[134] They had hung like an ax over the necks of gamblers for a decade and were no longer necessary. The criminal element scattered, traveled to Hot Springs or Las Vegas, and became legitimate. Anthony J. Fertitta, a Maceo lieutenant who ran the Balinese Room, for example, came to trial in 1959 and was found guilty. He received a two-year suspended sentence, went to Las Vegas for a while, then moved to Houston to work at Glenn McCarthy's Cork Club, and finally entered home construction work with his brother in Leesville, Louisiana.[135]

Gambling, prostitution, and illegal drinking were not completely eliminated. They never are in any city, but in Galveston vice diminished to normal limits. The Maceo empire had been crushed, and the dynastic families had little power except in areas of benevolence. The "Free State of Galveston" existed no more except in memory and nostalgia. When a rumor said the town would open again to vice, Ruth Levy Kempner, a councilwoman, said, "We'll obey the law. Galveston is not a place apart."[136]

Still, Galveston was different from the rest of Texas in climate and architecture. In the recent period of time an interest in history emerged as the force which shaped the city. At the National Archives Building in Washington, D.C., there is an inscription, "What is past is prologue." For Galveston the past was not only prologue; it also became the present and the future.

GALVESTON ISLAND: ITS TIME HAS COME ... AGAIN

Chapter Six

The residents say the beach is honky-tonk and the tourists are lower
class. The tourists say the honky-tonks are too expensive and the beach
is dirty. The upper crust says the offshore element is composed of criminals. The offshore element says it's only trying to make an honest buck.
The natives say Galveston isn't what it was in the old days. The politicians and the entrepreneurs and the promoters say the time has come
again. I suppose that there may be truth on all sides, but all I know for
certain is that it's an evening sky again, that intermingled pink and blue,
no, lavender, but yet there's all that gold . . . and if I could find a name
for that color my own name would shine.
                                    —Kate Cambridge, *InBetween*, August 1982

In 1960 the city population was 67,200; in 1970 it was 61,800; and in
1980 it was 61,900. The numbers declined and then stabilized. Galveston was not dying, but it was not growing either. Houston, meanwhile, jumped from 938,200 to 1,594,100 in the same twenty years.
Galveston County moved from 140,400 to 195,900, and Texas City,
Galveston's nearest neighbor, grew from 32,100 to 41,400 during the
same period. The population of the Texas coastal area increased, but
the island did not share the development. It was limited by its exposure to storms, lack of industrial water, and nearness to Houston.
The city had a reputation of being "an old lady by the sea," or as one
observer said, "an old lady frowning at a bikini."[1]

There were losses. The central business district deteriorated, despite the building of an open mall along two blocks of Postoffice Avenue in 1970. The E. S. Levy and Company store, for example, could

no longer make a profit there and closed in 1979 after four generations of business. The Coca-Cola bottling plant stopped in 1981
after seventy-six years. The downtown movie theaters shut down,
and the Broadway movie house went through a transition from
showing popular films to Spanish-language films to pornography.
There was a joke toward the last that if you wanted your shoes
shined, you could go to a downtown theater and the rats would do
the job as they ran across your feet. Three Roman Catholic schools
consolidated because of fewer students, and the U.S. Public Health
Service terminated the Marine Hospital in 1982 after a long political
effort in the 1970's to keep it open. The Santa Fe Railroad moved its
offices from Galveston in 1965, and the last passenger train left the
island for Houston in 1967. Major airline service to Scholes Field
ceased in the 1970's, and the commuter airline filed to abandon service in 1982. The airport thus declined to a place for private planes,
helicopters, and sports cars.[2]

Boosters of Galveston, nonetheless, dreamed of glory. In 1937
there was talk of building a bridge for vehicular traffic between Galveston and Bolivar, but shippers objected. The War Department and
the Public Works Administration turned down the plan, so, city officials began talking about a tunnel. Discussion of this project continued from 1939 to 1957, but various investigators found it to be
unnecessary and too expensive. In 1946 Galveston lost a bid to
Houston for a Veterans Hospital. The grandest illusion of all was
"Magic Harbor." This was an idea for a $20 million theme park like
Disneyland to be built near Sydnor's Bayou on the bay side of the island. After several years of negotiations, the company promoting the
project went bankrupt and the sheriff sold the land. Almost as exciting, in 1966 representatives of several Gulf ports including Galveston
began to talk to oil companies about construction of a superport for
large oil tankers. Galveston planned to build offshore terminals fifty
miles out in the Gulf. With the rise in the cost of oil, however, the
petroleum companies lost interest. It was economical for them
to continue lightering, and to revert to smaller tankers.[3] The idea
flickered out like the other dreams.

Not all of the schemes, however, were unsuccessful. Galveston
won part of the time, and the gains and losses balanced each other.
After a twenty-year effort the county built a toll bridge across San
Luis Pass on the western end of the island. It opened in 1966. In the
same decade two new shopping malls were planned and constructed.
Sears moved into the Galvez Plaza Shopping Center near the island
side of the causeway along with a variety of other stores and a new
movie theater. R. E. "Bob" Smith, meanwhile, built a yacht basin

and a shopping mall near the medical center. Down the island, Sea Isle and Jamaica Beach, beginning in 1957, led the way for construction of vacation communities located on marinas. Others followed, including Tiki Island on the mainland side of the causeway, which bragged, "You can get a boat into salt water faster from Houston at Tiki Island than any other place in the Gulf Coast area." Condominiums also appeared, such as Islander East, a major project built in 1975 on the beach in front of the seawall. This was not a good location for safety, but the $3 million ten-story building, with concrete piles sunk 120 feet into the sand, was designed for 250-mile-per-hour winds. Its first floor is 24 feet above sea level, and it has endured the storms which have come its way.[4]

A project which began as a loss and turned into a success was the Pleasure Pier. The idea went back to 1912, when civic promoters thought Galveston should have a large amusement pier like the one in Atlantic City. The thought lived, and plans were drawn in 1931 for a seven-hundred-foot pier with an auditorium. Construction actually began shortly before World War II with a $1,100,000 loan from the Reconstruction Finance Corporation. The city added another $350,000. The war delayed completion until 1944, but even then the pier was not fully open until 1948. The four-block long pier had a ballroom, an outdoor theater, a snack bar, and a T-head fishing area at the end. It was never profitable, and the city defaulted on the payments to the RFC. It became Galveston's "white elephant."

In 1963 negotiations opened with Houston financier James E. Lyon. As it worked out, he paid the U.S. government $179,000 for the defaulted bonds, which with accumulated interest had a value of $2,300,000. Galveston then gave Lyon $2,000,000 in new bonds in exchange for the RFC bonds and issued an additional $1,800,000 in bonds which Lyon bought. After all this swapping Lyon was ahead by $21,000 plus possession of $1,800,000 in bonds. He used this to build the Flagship Hotel, 240 luxury rooms on the pier, which opened in 1965. Lyon agreed to pay the city $185,000 annual rent for forty years, an amount sufficient to pay off the bonds. It was tricky, but when the bonds were paid, Galveston would own the hotel.[5]

Another story with a happy ending involves Sea-Arama. The idea of an oceanarium had been around for a time. Nothing happened, however, until an Austin venetian-blind builder, Jack Dismukes, led a group of fellow businessmen from the state capital to construct the $2 million facility. The huge marine aquarium with its thousand seat stadium and porpoise show modeled after Marineland of Florida opened in 1965. The organization brought in personnel from around the country, including a trainer named Ken Beggs. While working in

California, Beggs had made friends with a shark-scarred female dolphin named Zza-Zza. She had been stubborn in training, and was in a tank with four or five killer whales. "One day she just turned and looked at me," Beggs related. "I blew the whistle and sent her a fish. She made the connection so quickly." Thereafter, she tried to outperform the whales and became a spectacular performer.

Beggs, however, took the job in Galveston. Zza-Zza, left behind, refused to eat. The veterinarians shook their heads, transferred her to a tank on the back lot, and left her to die. After being gone six months, Beggs happened to be in town and stopped by to see his old friend. No one knew where she was, but the trainer wandered into the back lot and up to a tank. There she was, almost dead. The weak dolphin moved slowly over to his side in recognition. Beggs persuaded Sea-Arama to buy her, and he nursed her back to health. In a year she was a star again. "We're very close, Zza-Zza and me," Beggs said. "She's my pet and I'm hers, you know. We've come through a lot together."[6]

Another triumph for the city which helped offset its losses elsewhere involved higher education. The University of Texas Medical Branch, as it was called after 1919, weathered the 1900 hurricane, beat off threats to change the location, and became the state's chief medical college. By 1982 it ranked eleventh in the nation in terms of enrollment. Counting admissions in the schools of nursing, biomedicine, and allied health, UTMB had 2,000 students working in fifty buildings on an eighty-acre site. In the years following World War II it became the most important industry on the island, and by 1955 provided 20 percent of the island's income. In 1983 UTMB supported 7,314 people, more than five times as many as ANICO or the Galveston Independent School District, which were the second and third largest employers.[7]

The development would not have been possible without the benevolence of the Sealy family. John Sealy's estate provided the money for the first hospital, which enabled the school to begin operation. In the years which followed, the Sealy and Smith Foundation provided timely and well-placed funds. It donated the money for a new wing on the hospital in 1913, an out-patient clinic in 1930, the R. Waverly Smith Memorial Pavilion in 1954, a new John Sealy Hospital in 1954, the Jennie Sealy Hospital in 1968, and another John Sealy Hospital in 1978. The foundation gave money for expansion and paid the annual deficits of the budget from 1927 to 1942. Altogether the foundation provided about $150 million for the medical complex. Others also granted funds—the Houston Endowment, the Moody

Foundation, the Borden Company, the Kempner Fund, the University of Texas, the M. D. Anderson Foundation, and the Shriners, who built a children's burn institute.[8]

As a result of the facilities and the work which went on there, UTMB won a reputation—"If you can't be cured at the medical branch, you're already dead." The faculty in research worked on such diverse subjects as muscle transplants for knee surgery, electroshock therapy, open-air treatment for burns, measurement of fat in the blood, measles vaccine, and a cure for salmonellosis. Surgeons separated Siamese twins, and once transferred a left foot to the right leg of a woman who had been dragged and mangled by a train. She at least had one good leg.[9] Seth Mabry Morris, a member of the first faculty, became the leading rediologist in Texas. He read about X-rays, ordered a Crookes tube from Boston, hooked it up to an induction coil, and exposed his hand to a photographic plate for ten minutes. He must have fried his hand, but he obtained a picture. Known as "Old Test Tube" among the students, he would write equations on the blackboard with his right hand and, to the frustration of his class, erase simultaneously with his left.[10]

Early students were treated the same as soldiers by Galveston society—as temporary visitors to tolerate, but not to befriend. Black parents told their children to be home at night lest the medical students capture them for experiments. Adolescent street kids tormented them as they trudged home from classes carrying skulls and pieces of skeleton to study. "Yeah, bone jugglers, bone jugglers!" they yelled and hoped to be chased. If successful, the kids scattered with wild whoops and yelps. At school, first-year students became part of the small scholastic community through an initiation of eating with dissecting instruments a meal designated as autopsy meat and boils in pus (actually beef and creamed onions). During the interwar period students became more acceptable in Galveston society. After World War II, however, the wives of married students filled the teacher ranks of Galveston public schools, and town physicians were denied part-time teaching positions at UTMB.[11] This created a town-versus-gown split that has never been healed.

A terrific internal fight between the faculty and an autocratic dean in 1940–1942 resulted in a threat to move the school to Austin, probation by the American Medical Association, several investigations, the dismissal of all department chairmen, and the appointment of Chauncey D. Leake as the new head of the school. The warm, hospitable Leake moved easily among the warring factions and brought about the necessary reforms to restore harmony. He objected, however, to the vice-ridden larger community. "Except for the Sealy

Family and the Sealy and Smith Foundation, the people of Galveston have done little for the medical branch. The least they can do is to assure a wholesome community situation, so as to obtain the backing of the people of the state for the work of the medical branch."[12]

Even so, the medical school complex served its purpose of protecting the health of the island and providing a refuge in time of trouble. Historically, with the coming of hurricanes, people rushed to John Sealy Hospital even though it was not a designated shelter. During Hurricane Carla in 1961 a refugee exclaimed, "They are trying to make me move out of my corner. Why, this is where I was in the 1915 hurricane and every big storm since then. This is *my* corner— and I'm going to stay right here." And he did.[13]

The quality of the facility and its staff had also been demonstrated during another kind of disaster in 1947. The shock wave of an enormous explosion rumbled across the city a little after 9:00 A.M. on April 16 of that year. Windows rattled and shattered, buildings vibrated, surgical instruments at the hospital skittered on the table, and people rushed into the streets to see what had occurred. The chairman of the medical and nursing committee of the Galveston Red Cross happened to be standing at a window looking across the bay. Before he felt the shock wave he saw a large bloom of orange smoke rising ten miles away over Texas City. He picked up the phone and alerted John Sealy Hospital, and the staff, which included veterans from World War II, acted instinctively. Within minutes two teams of surgeons and nurses were en route to establish emergency field stations. The hospital converted the outpatient clinic into a large emergency ward, local merchants sent supplies without being asked, volunteer doctors and nurses appeared, level-headed citizens blocked traffic on Broadway to provide a one-way conduit to the hospital, and the victims in great numbers and frightful condition began to arrive.[14]

Texas City, "the Port of Opportunity," with a population of eighteen thousand, had developed as Galveston's industrial arm. It contained oil refineries, chemical companies, a tin smelter, various small businesses, residential areas, rail connections, and a fine port. On this fateful day longshoremen were loading a French cargo vessel with one-hundred-pound sacks of ammonium nitrate fertilizer. This brown crystalline powder will burn, fume, and smolder if ignited. So long as there is plenty of open space to carry off heat, such as in a warehouse fire, there is no further difficulty. If confined, however, the heat builds up like boiling water in a covered pot. When it exceeds 292 degrees, it explodes. The method of fighting an ammonium nitrate fire, therefore, is with plenty of water and air circulation.[15]

When the crew opened up the number four hatch of the *S.S. Grandcamp* to load more fertilizer, they noticed smoke in the cargo. After removing a tier of bags, a stevedore found fire—probably from a misplaced cigarette—and tried to extinguish it with two buckets of water and a fire extinguisher. This did not work and a hose was ordered. The first mate canceled the hose, however, in fear of damaging the cargo with water. He ordered the hatch closed and turned hot steam into the hold. It was a fatal error, and the fire heat blew the hatch cover off. The mate then turned in a fire alarm and ordered the crew to abandon ship.

The Texas City Volunteer Fire Department responded with its entire force of twenty-five men and four trucks, while Monsanto Chemical Company and Republic Oil Company sent Foamite to combat the blaze. Reddish-orange smoke boiled from the hatch, and the deck was so hot the water from the hoses vaporized into steam. Burning paper bags floated in the heated air toward nearby ships, where the crews hastily wet the decks and closed the hatches. Spectators wandered onto the dock, but were warned away in fear that a small quantity of small-arms ammunition on board might blow up.

Then came an enormous blast followed seconds later by another as the *Grandcamp* disintegrated in a double explosion. An orange ball mixed with black smoke rolled upward and blotted out the sun. Two light aircraft circling overhead fell like shot ducks, and a fifteen-foot wave surging across the harbor dropped a 150-foot barge 200 feet onto dry land. Debris scattered for as much as 13,000 feet; a twenty-ton piece of decking fell 2,000 feet away; red-hot missiles pierced the natural gas tanks of nearby refineries and caused secondary explosions and fires; every house within a one-mile radius collapsed; every window in a two-mile radius broke. From the sky over the city drifted down strands of burning sisal twine and cotton, part of the cargo of the disintegrated vessel. Fires were everywhere, but the town no longer had a fire department. The men and equipment had been destroyed on the dock in the explosion.

Rescue workers of all sorts poured into the beleaguered city from the surrounding area to fight the fires, remove the dead, and aid the wounded. Men in asbestos suits searched the burning wreckage of the Monsanto plant for victims while tugboats tried to free the flaming *S.S. High Flyer* from an ensnared anchor chain. It carried the same cargo as the *Grandcamp*. At 1:12 A.M. on April 17, the *High Flyer* also blew apart in a double explosion. From a far distance the detonation produced an appearance of a gently rising rainbow disappearing into dark, smoky skies. The four-ton turbine of the ship landed 4,000 feet away.

The death toll reached 512—399 identified and 113 missing. Counted among the missing were 63 unidentified bodies which were buried in a mass grave. Of the injured, 852 went to hospitals and 932 to doctors' offices for treatment. Those who went to St. Mary's Infirmary and John Sealy Hospital in Galveston suffered mainly lacerations, broken bones, and ruptured eardrums. There was a curious lack of burns among the survivors. Thirty percent of the bodies, however, were charred. At the hospitals, where employees mixed gallons of dry plasma and tetanus antitoxin, the emergency lasted forty-eight hours. The hospital staff placed mattresses and cots in the hallways, and priests moved about giving last rites. In the final count, with a loss of 539 structures, the Texas City disaster cost $200,000,000 in property damage, and $15,500,000 in personal injury and death claims.[16] In general, Galveston with its medical resources responded generously and efficiently to the need of its neighbor.

In less dramatic fashion other Galveston educational institutions also contributed to the quality of life on the island. In 1958 people in Texas City began to promote the idea of establishing a junior college, but county voters disapproved. In 1965, however, after much promotion by the *Galveston Daily News* voters approved and elected a seven-member board of trustees. They agreed with a consultant from Austin who suggested two campuses, one on the island and one on the mainland. The electorate, however, defeated an $11,500,000 bond issue, and there was rivalry between the Galveston Independent School District and the Union Junior College District. The end result was that in 1967 the Union District founded the College of the Mainland at a site near Hitchcock and Texas City, and the Galveston School District established Galveston College at the location of the old St. Mary's Orphanage.[17]

The Moody Foundation aided in the purchsae of facilities for Galveston College and also for the Texas Maritime Academy founded by Texas A&M University. Galveston was a logical place to study the sea, and the idea of a maritime school to train people for careers on marine transport began in 1958 after a meeting between the head of the U.S. Maritime Commission, Walter C. Ford, and Robert K. Hutchings of Galveston. A local committee thereupon promoted it, Texas A&M provided the academic structure and personnel, the Moody Foundation donated buildings, and George Mitchell along with the city gave the land on Pelican Island for its current site.[18]

According to one account, Mitchell had to be persuaded to give the space. "I can't do that," he said at first. "That's my best land.

That's a million dollars' worth of land." But he was a graduate of Texas A&M, with the strong loyalties typical of Aggies, and in addition his deal over possession of Pelican Island might have fallen through without the donation.[19] This small isle, which forms the north shore of the Galveston channel, had long inspired a dream of industrial development. The Texas legislature gave it to the city in 1856, and the Confederacy built a small fort there in 1861. Through the years there was located on Pelican Island, at least for awhile, a fish and oyster business, an immigrant station, a boat club, a life-saving station, and the Todd Shipyards. It was a good place to hunt, but to the frustration of city boosters, Pelican Island had never blossomed as an industrial area.[20] In 1952 the city officials made plans to develop the island with a syndicate of New York financiers. As part of the scheme the citizens created a navigation district and voted $6 million in bonds to build a bridge. The viaduct opened in 1958, and in the meantime, the city established a park on the island in 1955–1956. The bold plans for industry, residential areas, and an amusement park—"Galveston's New Frontier"—never became reality. George Mitchell terminated an imbroglio with the Pelican Island Development Company and the city in 1965, when he bought 2,750 acres for $1,868,000. He donated the site for the marine college and promised long-range use for homes and business.[21]

George P. Mitchell, one of the new elite of Galveston, was one of four children born to Savva and Katina Pareskivopoulis. His father came to the United States as a poor Greek immigrant and changed his name to Mike Mitchell because the Irish timekeeper of the Arkansas railroad where he worked thought the Greek name too difficult. He moved to Galveston in 1911 to open a shoeshine parlor and dry-cleaning shop. The family was poor, but the children went to college. In the process Mike Mitchell wrote some bad checks, but the judge said, "We will let this man go and someday perhaps his children will do something for Galveston."[22]

Of the four children, Maria married and moved to San Antonio; Christie with his Panama hat and cigar remained on the island to write a newspaper column, "The Beachcomber"; while George and his brother Johnny moved to Houston and plunged into oil exploration. R. E. "Bob" Smith became a role model when he employed George Mitchell as a petroleum geologist, and after World War II Johnny Mitchell borrowed capital from Sam Maceo. The boss of Galveston gambling visited the wildcat wells to cook spaghetti for the men, and Mitchell claimed, "He was the nicest partner I ever had." The Mitchell brothers organized drilling ventures and struck oil and gas repeatedly. They became wealthy—among the richest in the nation—and branched into real estate. George Mitchell, with the aid of $50 million in federal grants, developed The Woodlands, a "new town" for 150,000 people, north of Houston.[23]

The brothers also took an interest in their old hometown. In the mid-1960's they helped reopen the Balinese Room and began drilling for oil and gas on Galveston Island. Their offshore rigs, clearly visible one and one-half miles from the beach, worried environmentalists, but no harm occurred to the sea or the beach. The Sierra Club, however, blocked George Mitchell's effort to dredge a marina through the salt marsh off Eckert's Bayou for the Pirate's Cove subdivision down the island. The club said the excavation would ruin the ecosystem, and complained that Mitchell did not consider the surroundings as he had done at The Woodlands. The club spokesman, Peter Bowman, consequently, referred to the developer as a "second-rate environmentalist," who considered the ecology only when it did not interfere with profits. For his part, Mitchell found the environmentalists equally hard to work with.[24]

In 1972 George Mitchell bought twenty-two acres of old Fort Crockett, where he began construction ten years later of a $36 million hotel, "The San Luis on Galveston Isle." He chose the name "to help perpetuate a grain of island history," and said, "I have a lot of confidence in Galveston."[25] Indeed, Mitchell became one of the major forces in the preservation of Galveston history. He and his wife, Cynthia, bought six buildings in the Strand National Historic Landmark District to restore former glory and thus help rehabilitate the downtown. They started a gourmet restaurant, The Wentletrap, and began work to convert the Blum Building into a 120-room luxury hotel. It was Mitchell's thought that Galveston needed to extend the tourist season, and that these projects would help. "Now Galveston is not Savannah," he explained, "but Galveston is the most historic city in the Southwest. There is a lot of beauty in Galveston that Dallas doesn't have, San Antonio doesn't have and Houston doesn't have."[26]

Interest in historic structures began to surface as the "Free State of Galveston" crumbled. History was something to attract tourists after gambling, prostitution, and illegal drinking were gone. But there was more to it than that. Curiosity about the past is innate with human beings. People want to know where they come from, and how they got where they are at the moment. Like old persons reflecting upon their lives in order to understand them, Galvestonians began to consider and value history. There was something to be learned, and outsiders—foundations, wealthy people from Houston, federal agencies—sensed the unique quality of Galveston's past. History, consequently, became the driving force in modern Galveston, and the past became prologue.

Anne A. Brindley rallied the Galveston Historical Foundation in 1957 in order to save the Williams-Tucker House at 3601 Avenue P. This home, constructed by Samuel May Williams in 1839 from pre-cut timber framed in Maine, was one of the earliest extant structures on the island. It might have been lost except that the foundation took it over, restored it, and opened it for tourists in 1959.[27] In the early 1960's, Texas State Historical Survey medallions began to be affixed to the sides of various historic structures, and in 1966 James C. Massey of the National Park Service, at a luncheon with the Galveston Historical Foundation, Chamber of Commerce, and City Council, pointed out that people traveled thousands of miles just to see historic buildings. Historic preservation was good business for a city, and he urged a careful survey of old structures. An additional boost came in the same year with the publication of Howard Barnstone's *The Galveston That Was*, a book filled with fine photographs and commentary about the nineteenth-century architectural treasures on the island.[28]

A resulting two-year study pointed to the importance of the Strand, Ashton Villa, Old Red at the medical school, and the George Sealy House. With the aid of the Moody Foundation and the Kempner Fund, the Historical Foundation took over six Strand buildings with the thought of selling them to people who would agree to restore the "Wall Street of the South." Membership of the foundation jumped from two hundred to eight hundred, and Peter H. Brink, who came from a Washington, D.C., law firm to head the group, accepted the immediate challenge to save Ashton Villa.[29]

The James M. Brown House, or Ashton Villa, built in 1858–1859, was one of the first brick mansions in Texas. Fashioned in the style of an Italian villa, the house retained through time its plaster work, frescoes, French panel mirrors, and cast-iron grillwork. It was even reputed to have a ghost—Miss Rebecca Brown, the daughter of the builder, who long after death still played the piano in the gold room. She was known to have had a chronic bronchial cough loud enough to startle the streetcar mules on the street. Amused contemporaries had gathered to witness the plodding animals awaken with a surprised "hee haw!" and bolt for the turntable two blocks away.[30] In 1968 El Mina Shrine Temple, which owned the villa, offered it for sale for $200,000. The Shriners had outgrown the house and wanted to sell or destroy the structure within ninety days.

The Galveston Historical Foundation rose to the cause and offered $100,000. That was not enough, and the Shrine began taking bids for demolition. After urging by the GHF, the city council passed an ordinance prohibiting the defacing or destruction of historic structures over one hundred years old. The Shrine objected, but the city denied a demolition permit. Finally, in 1971 the city bought Ashton Villa for $125,000—the Department of Housing and Urban Development gave $50,000, the Moody Foundation donated $60,000, and the GHF raised $15,000. The GHF assumed management of the property, and the Sid Richardson Foundation of Fort Worth gave $25,000 for renovation.[31] It was a happy ending, except, perhaps, for the Shriners. About this event the Institute for Environmental Action, a national organization dedicated to the improvement of urban life, commented:

> In addition to protecting an outstanding piece of Texas history, the Ashton Villa episode offered some important lessons. It demonstrated how Galveston could effectively employ the expertise and judgment of outside specialists to help win support locally. It also demonstrated how new and effective coalitions could be formed to unite traditional island families, newcomers and city government. And it underscored that private and federal funding sources could reinforce one another, provided there was enough vision and determination. All these lessons would be valuable for Galveston in its subsequent preservation struggles.[32]

The historic preservation movement also resulted in the creation of the East End Historical District and the Silk Stocking Historic Precinct; the restoration of the Grand Opera House and the 1861 Customs House; the purchase of the Santa Fe Building by the Moody Foundation for a railroad museum; a sit-in to preserve the Ufford Building, which was later destroyed by fire; the establishment of a county museum in the old City National Bank Building; a restoration of the Garten Verein Pavilion, which had been damaged by fire; and the designation of the Strand as a National Historic Landmark District. Individuals such as Marjorie Trentham, who restored the Sonnentheil House at 19th and Sealy, became part of the movement, as well as organizations such as the Galveston County Cultural Arts Council.[33]

The Cultural Arts Council, responding to the national bicentennial and through the leadership of Emily Whiteside, organized among other things an enormous festival of the arts on the Strand, a performing arts series, and renovation of the Grand Opera House. Whiteside drove herself ten to twelve hours per day to keep some forty-seven projects going, because she saw Galveston as a place that "cheers the eye, satisfies the senses, and replenishes the soul." She eventually burned herself out, but she left a legacy of community consciousness. Evangeline Whorton, GHF vice-president for programs, perpetuated this in 1974 with the first annual "Dickens Evening on the Strand," a city-wide celebration in nineteenth-century costume featuring oysters, beer, hot cider, banana bread, and street entertainment. The event has attracted as many as eighty thousand people and has become a focal point of community spirit.[34]

The most expensive historical project, and one that probably would not have been started if anyone had known how much it would eventually cost, was the *Elissa*. A suggestion to the GHF that a replica of a sailing vessel might provide a link between the harbor and the Strand turned into a search for a real ship to restore. In 1961 Peter Throckmorton, a marine archeologist, spotted an old sailing vessel being used to smuggle cigarettes between Italy and Yugoslavia. It had been much altered, but Throckmorton went on board and found a plaque which identified the vessel as the *Elissa*, an iron-hulled, square-sailed barque built in 1877 by Alexander Hall and Son of Aberdeen, Scotland. The masts had been shifted, the bow configuration changed, an engine added, its rails cut off, and a false bulwark plate welded on. It was genuine, nonetheless, and the oldest ship registered with Lloyds of London. Better yet, according to the log, it had visited Galveston in 1883 and 1886. The *Elissa*, therefore, had the potential to be a "Tall Ship for Texas."

The GHF bought the ship for $40,000 in 1975 and sent a team to Piraeus, Greece, to bring it home. It had been nine years at anchor and was in poor condition. Greek welders had to replace 25 percent of the hull and remove tons of rust, rotten planks, and junk. The *Elissa* was impossible to sail, as originally planned, so it was towed to Galveston. Little remained intact on the ship. There were no blueprints, very few people in the world remembered what went into such a vessel, and much had to be handcrafted. It was decided, nonetheless, to make the *Elissa* operational and to recruit volunteers to make it sail. Walter Rybka, one of the principals, explained, "The only way you can keep a ship from deteriorating is by the constant attention of hands. But if the boat never sails, you will not attract the caliber of people you need, the kind of people who will care about the ship."[35]

The GHF divided the labor into categories of steel, rigging, carpentry, and miscellaneous, and located experts in Europe, Africa, and the United States. Volunteers gathered from around Texas to varnish the woodwork and coat the rigging with tar. They were sent aloft to wipe the galvanized parts and in the process gave themselves a coating as well. In the old days sailors were called "Jack Tars" because of this occupation, and in the 1980's at Pier 22 in Galveston, the Jack Tars lived once more. The two-hundred-foot ship required an investment of $3,600,000 to restore, but in 1982 its time had come . . . again. A fresh wind filled the new sails, and the proud *Elissa* coursed through the Gulf waters as it had one hundred years ago.[36] Texas had won its "Tall Ship."

In an interesting way the port of Galveston felt the impact of this rising interest in history. The port like the city had not changed much in recent years, although it did try to remain competitive. It still exported cotton, sulphur, and grains, and imported some crude petroleum, sugar, and fruit. Galveston ranked seventh in total tonnage among Texas ports in 1979, and the old deficiencies remained— location, storms, closeness to the port of Houston. Thinking to promote manufacturing, the city officials built facilities on the wharves and leased them to the Lipton Tea Company in 1951. The tea came to Texas, however, in small lots. It was shipped into Houston and trucked back to Galveston, and the port did not even have the chance to collect wharfage fees. Cotton exports, the old standby, shifted via rail to the California coast for shipment to the Orient, and the port was unable to establish an adequate traffic in petroleum.[37]

The most successful harbor enterprise was Todd Shipyards, which contained the foremost dry dock on the Gulf Coast. Todd, the fourth-largest employer in Galveston, also had facilities in Seattle, San Francisco, Los Angeles, Houston, New Orleans, and Brooklyn. The Galveston branch gained a certain fame in the 1960's as the fueling station for the *Nuclear Ship Savannah*, an unsuccessful attempt to demonstrate the feasibility of nuclear transports. In 1972 the federal government took the *N.S. Savannah* out of service and towed it to its namesake city for storage.[38]

Demonstrative of the port's sliding prestige and power in the city was the struggle over the "mosquito fleet"—the small shrimp boats which hoisted their green and white nets to dry in the air after a day's work. For a hundred years the fleet had docked at Pier 19, but in 1974 there were only forty-six boats at the slips, a decline of 75 percent since the early years of the century. The colorful shrimp boats were nonetheless significant to the town. Growing out of the Splash Day celebration, the first Blessing of the Fleet occurred in 1962. Three clergymen—Episcopal, Greek Orthodox, and Roman Catholic—gave a benediction at the channel as the decorated boats cruised past them. Although the surrounding celebrations changed, the annual blessings continued, indicating the deeper meaning of the event. It was not simply another tourist attraction; it was important to the sailors and to the community. The seamen felt it was important for the luck of the season, and townsfolk saw it as symbolic of their seafaring heritage.[39]

Contrary to plans announced ten years before, in 1974 Galveston Wharves wanted Pier 19 for other uses and proposed to move the fleet across the channel to new docks on Pelican Island. The wharves, the International Longshoremen's Association (ILA), the *Galveston Daily News*, and the Chamber of Commerce thought it a good idea, but ten thousand people signed a petition objecting to the move. The shrimpers did not care to change, and neither did Charles R. Hill, who owned a restaurant at Pier 19. The wharves board, nonetheless, sent out eviction notices to the mosquito fleet, while the Galveston County Historical Commission at the head of the protesting groups obtained an injunction to block the transfer.

The injunction inadvertently impaired the ability of the wharves to issue revenue bonds, and this, in turn, obstructed other plans and threatened the proposed installation of a grain elevator on Pelican Island. Seeking peace, the wharves agreed to a public referendum on the issue. The various historical groups thought this was fair and withdrew their suits. After almost three years of controversy the electorate settled the fight in 1977 by voting 6,189 to 3,342 in favor of keeping the mosquito fleet at Pier 19. "We were soundly defeated, and it's tough," admitted C. S. "Chuck" Devoy, the manager of the port.[40] The people supporting historic preservation had won a symbolic and substantive victory. In this case, as elsewhere in contemporary Galveston, the "dead hand of history" proved to be alive, well, and powerful.

The need for preservation of a different sort arose as pollution of the air, water, and land became a threat. Galveston was lucky most of the time, since its constant offshore breeze carried pollutants away and gave it clean air from the sea. Nearby oil refineries and chemical plants in Texas City, however, caused enough trouble. When a sulphuric odor settled over the east end of the island in 1965, for example, oil-based paint on houses discolored. The speculation was that the pollutant came from Texas City, but no one knew for certain.[41]

The air at Texas City and La Marque hovered almost all the time near the maximum safety limits for pollution, and in a five-year study physicians at UTMB discovered that particulates from Texas City air caused almost half the mice injected to develop cancer. Air difficulties continued at Texas City through the 1970's, and in 1980 an unusual number of deaths by brain cancer among workers turned up. Physicians suspected vinyl chloride fumes as the cause, and a former plant official at Union Carbide commented that workers had been routinely exposed in the 1940's and 1950's. "We used to get drunk on vinyl chloride fumes just walking around," he said. The plant, and others, however, had later taken steps to protect workers, and when brain cancer showed up in 1980, investigations proved inconclusive.[42]

Galveston itself contributed to dirty air by burning trash at the city dump. In 1942 the city bought an incinerator, but it never worked well. The dampers clogged with molten glass, and it was expensive to operate. The city shut it down in 1953 and proceeded to get rid of garbage through a combination of open burning and burying. This created a black "airmark" over the dump which greeted tourists as they traveled the causeway. In 1968 the Texas Air Control Board ordered burning to cease, and three years later it closed the dump as a public nuisance. Galveston, thereafter, trucked its garbage to the mainland for burial.[43]

Another problem of urban metabolism was water pollution. Sporadically since the 1930's, mysterious fish kills fouled the shores of Offatt's Bayou, Texas City, and Galveston Bay. A county survey in 1950 revealed that most of the coastal cities dumped raw sewage into the sea, and Offatt's Bayou became so bad in 1963 that the city health director posted a ban on swimming. A few cases of infectious hepatitis turned up, and sometimes people complained of "Galveston Crud," a looseness of the bowels, but nothing definite could be traced to the water even though it contained coliform bacteria.[44]

The major polluter of Galveston Bay in the 1960's was Houston, a source of 68 percent of the contaminants. The only large supply of fresh water came from the Trinity River, and this declined with the construction of Livingston Reservoir in the 1960's to provide water for Houston. The ship channel to the Bayou City was one of the top ten polluted water courses in the world at the time, and when it rained a large plug of industrial pollution flushed into Galveston Bay. In September 1968 such an event killed thirty thousand fish. Under pressure from the Texas Water Quality Control Board Harris and Galveston counties began discussions in 1967 to correct the condition.[45]

Early in 1970 Governor Preston Smith invited a federal panel dealing with water pollution to meet in Houston in order to witness the fine accomplishments of Texas. The plan backfired because the panel discovered that Galveston dumped raw sewage into the bay and provided no sanitary facilities for ships. In dry weather the city normally passed seven million gallons of sewage per day, and in wet weather, twenty-five million gallons per day. Only 40 percent of this waste was processed adequately in the treatment plants. The executive director of the Federal Water Pollution Control Administration, Gordon E. Kerr, commented in a letter to the Secretary of the Interior, "Our visit to Galveston demonstrated an amazing situation— an island city polluting itself into extinction by threatening its tourist industry and its own beaches. And, while federal funds gave this city a plan for its needed water pollution control, action has not followed study."[46]

After threatening the city with a daily fine, the Texas Water Quality Board approved a plan to chlorinate the effluent and build separate storm sewers to prevent rainwater from overburdening the system. The program took time to complete, and Gus Herzik of the board said the city "notoriously failed to fulfill its obligations in the realm of water pollution for years."[47] In 1974 Galveston received a fine of $30,450 for dumping raw sewage in Offatt's Bayou, and meanwhile, due to the pollutants and the dredging of shell reefs, the oysters, once among the best in the world, died in the bayou. Conflict between oystermen and polluters as well as dredgers also occurred in the bay. Shell was used for the subsurface of highways, chicken feed, the production of lime, and the paving of streets and parking lots. Dredging was a $25 million a year business which ended only in recent years, after major reefs had been destroyed. Ironically, the state replaced eight hundred feet of reef in the bay to help the oysters recover.[48]

Once in a while a special pollution incident happened. In 1979, for example, the freighter *Mimosa*, traveling at excessive speed through the anchorage area four and one-half miles off Galveston, rammed and gouged a hole into the side of the *Burmah Agate*. The *Burmah Agate* caught fire and sank in forty feet of water with the loss of thirty-two crew members. The officers and crew of the *Mimosa*, meanwhile, abandoned their ship and left it running at full throttle. Narrowly missing oil platforms and ships, it circled for hours until tugs ensnared its propeller with steel cables. The flaming *Burmah Agate* carried 400,000 barrels of oil, which slowly leaked into the sea. The ship burned for sixty-nine days and lost 250,000 barrels, part of which floated onto Galveston beaches. The oil left an odor and dark stain lines on the sand. Booms in the water were used to collect drifting oil, crews cleaned the shore, and the owner of the *Burmah Agate* accepted responsibility for the environmental damage. The incident, however, gave pause to those promoting a superport for the island.[49]

The city needed to protect its beaches. They provided the chief attraction for the tourist, and they deserved preservation as much as the old buildings of town. The issue of the beach, however, was multifaceted. Once in a while nature threw excessive seaweed or Portuguese men-of-war onto the shore, which then required clean-ups. Periodic summertime red tides caused by an offshore algae bloom during periods of hot temperature, high salinity, and calm weather deposited dead fish which municipal crews had to remove.[50] These were minor grievances. More important was a threat of losing the beach entirely.

Shorelines are inherently unstable, and human beings who place structures along them and expect permanence are doomed to frustration. Affected by storms, currents, wind, dams which retard river sediment, subsidence due to groundwater removal, and even the melting of polar icecaps, the beach changes and moves. Generally, on the sand barrier islands of Texas, the shift is toward the mainland, and any attempt to block the migration, in the long run, is an exercise in futility. Stabilization attempts cost more than moving buildings. The National Park Service, for example, has spent $15 million trying to save the Cape Hatteras lighthouse, and Miami expended $64 million in the early 1980's hauling sand to its eroding beaches.[51]

Seawalls are notorious for speeding up beach damage. In most cases the sea moves up to the wall—it almost seems, in order to challenge the obstruction. The waves crash against the wall, churn up the sand, and wash it out. In Galveston beyond 61st Street, Gulf waters lap at the riprap in front of the seawall. Where the barrier ends on the west, there used to be a ramp to the beach. Now, the ramp leads into the water. A study in 1977 indicated that the western portion was losing 200,000 cubic yards of sand per year due to overgrazing, development of subdivisions, and the influence of the jetties on the littoral currents. Sand accumulates on the east end of the island and is lost on the west.[52]

Across the Gulf face of Galveston in the middle, from 12th to 61st Streets, however, there is a narrow beach maintained by the presence of groins. Civic leaders began to worry about the loss of the beach in the 1880's, and an examination of maps by Henry M. Robert in 1897 revealed a loss of three hundred feet since 1838. An engineers' convention in London in 1898 suggested the use of narrow, solid walls extended finger-like into the sea. These groins, standing at right angles to the shore, intercept the offshore currents and force them to drop their sand. The groins thus help build up the beach. Robert in 1909 recommended such structures, and the county built thirty-six short ones the following year. They failed, but in 1922 as an experiment the city workers drove a five-hundred-foot double row of piles knee-high into the surf. It seemed to work, and in the 1930's the Army Engineers built thirteen more between 12th Street and the western end of Fort Crockett. In the late 1960's the corps removed five of the wooden pile groins and covered the others with granite. They are only a partial success, but without them there would be no beach at all in front of the seawall.[53]

Removal of sand from the beach for fill purposes also has been a factor over the years. Before the storm of 1875 the sand dunes had been fairly well leveled, but afterward the city passed an ordinance against sand removal. Despite laws and conservation measures, however, people still took sand from the beach under the assumption that the sea would restore it. The county even allowed commercial operators to take it in the 1960's, and the city council permitted a private company to take "surplus" accumulations in 1970. County Judge Ray Holbrook exploded over the city action, "Damn it, that's where I run on the beach and they're interfering with it." He considered removal "illegal and immoral." At the moment beach depredations have ceased.[54]

Other rules had to be set up and enforced. In the late 1950's and afterward, particularly with the growth of subdivisions, private individuals and companies tried to fence off parts of the beach for their own use and control. The argument was that the fencing was necessary in order to keep the beach clean, and also that the highway down the middle of the island made it unnecessary for cars to use the beach. It was in reality a move for exclusion. In 1959 the legislature passed a law to guarantee public access, and after suits, cases, and protests the private barricades came down. The shore from mean low tide to the vegetation line belonged to the public. Ironically, the city had to put up its own barriers in 1978–1980. Automotive traffic became so heavy on summer weekends that it became a hazard to people going into the water. The solution was to provide roads of access and small parking areas down the island, and to block through driving on the sand.[55]

Restriction with greater intensity had already started at Stewart Beach, established by the city in 1941, at Galveston Island State Park, begun in 1970, and at the county's Beach Pocket Park, built in 1979. The city zoned the beach in 1963 to prevent building, banned the use of glass containers in 1968, and set up regulations for surfers beginning in 1965. Although surfboard riding is anything but spectacular with such small tides, young people with short boards found the waves around the Flagship Hotel satisfactory. So did the people who fished at the end of the pier, and the two groups became entangled over the right to enjoy this portion of the sea. The municipality did its best to compromise and establish regulations about time and place. Even so, no one was happy, and it was difficult for a police officer in a squad car on the seawall to arrest a surfer on a board three hundred feet away on the waves of the Gulf.[56]

Safety has always been a concern at the beach. Drownings in the turgid waters of Galveston have long been a common phenomenon, and "floaters" turn up with shocking regularity. As examples, in 1886 down the island officials examined the body of a working man which had drifted ashore. He wore a brown frock coat, a red and blue checked vest, cotton shirt, brown jean pants, and lace gaiters. In his pockets were a towel from a Pullman Palace Car, a piece of soap wrapped in a handkerchief, a comb, a package of tobacco, and a number of cigar stumps. There was no identification, and his face had been eaten by crabs. The authorities held their inquest and buried him on the spot. In 1891 two surprised blacks fishing with a seine twenty yards offshore near Fort Point hauled in a body which was still limber. The person was well clothed, but the pockets were inside out and there was no identification.[57]

The Chamber of Commerce and the federal government took an interest in lifeboat stations for the rescue of sailors in the 1870's, but the beach had no regular protection by lifeguards until 1945. Even then, the local Red Cross chapter urged greater security and stated in 1964, "By advertising our beach we are attracting people to use it, and we are thereby morally obligated to provide safety services for their protection." Particularly dangerous were the rip currents which swirled around the groins.

Although Franklin D. Roosevelt cited Charles Bertolino, Sr., a local fisherman, for saving over 500 people, LeRoy Colombo, one of the first official lifeguards, established a place in the *Guinness Book of Records* with 907 rescues. He lost his hearing through illness at age seven, learned to swim to recover from leg paralysis, and saved his first life at age twelve. At fifteen he joined a group of volunteer guards and developed a sixth sense about danger. He once rescued nineteen people in one day, and never received a reward. Colombo, reputedly, saved over a thousand lives, but ended his own in 1974 as a beach bum housed in a battered car, penniless and embittered.[58]

In 1980 the city turned over the organization of lifeguards to the county, which enforced a higher degree of professionalism. In recent years there have been an average ten drownings per summer season with twenty near ones and a hundred assists. Throughout the year about twenty drownings occur, 80 percent of them drug- or alcohol-related.[59] There are some beach problems, however, which the life-guards cannot handle—those involving crime.

The Gulf shore area has developed into a deceptively dangerous place. The people who live on the island know that and are cautious. Outsiders, tourists with their families, blithely stroll the seawall and beach at night unaware of the lurking violence. Drunkenness is still the most common offense, but the city is high in burglaries, assaults, auto thefts, and armed robberies. It is above the state average in eight of ten FBI categories and the highest in violent crimes and aggravated assaults.[60] At times, crowds on the beach have erupted in riot.

In 1966, for example, police with tear gas and clubs had to clear the east beach of a cursing, drunken, bottle-throwing mob of three to four thousand people. In 1971, on Independence Day, an unruly crowd twice that size broke out in racial obscenities and random violence. A crowd of blacks attacked five white youths in a van near a beach tavern called the Down Beat. One boy escaped in the badly damaged van; an injured boy and girl broke loose on foot; four black men pulled another girl into a car and protected her; and a gang dragged the last girl, fourteen years old, under the tavern for multiple rape. When the police cleared the area they interrupted the last rapist, shouted for the man to come out, and shot him in the foot when he tried to run. Altogether the riot injured thirteen people.[61]

A week later the police recovered the bound and gagged body of a fourteen-year-old black girl floating in the harbor. She had been strangled, and the coincidence was very strong. The publisher of the *Galveston Daily News* wrote about the murder and riot together, but no one broached the suggestion of racial warfare, and there was widespread condemnation of both events. The city had to budget several million dollars each year for crowd control, and continued to have trouble. At Apffel Park on the east beach in 1982, for instance, eight young women took off their bikini tops and drew a crowd. When they stripped off the bottoms as well and began dancing, the spectators almost went berserk and the police were called to break up the crowd.[62]

Part of the difficulty with Apffel Park was its use for illegal drug traffic. Mandrax, a popular "downer," was sold there in 1982, and police recognized users by the "Mandrax shuffle." The new vice was drug usage and sale. Gambling, illegal liquor, and prostitution were still around, but not in epidemic proportions. Illegal distribution through small dealers of marijuana, barbiturates, and amphetamines, in the 1960's—followed by opiates in the 1970's—became pervasive. The head of the vice and narcotic division of the Galveston police,

Paul De La Rosa, Jr., commented that before 1967 drugs were a downtown problem and the police knew who was involved. After that summer the problem spread like an unchecked cancer throughout the city to all classes and groups.[63]

Not only Galveston, but the whole Texas coast became an entry point for the new smugglers. Cargo ships, sailboats, small aircraft, and fishing boats were used. The Coast Guard, for example, caught the *Texas Star*, a converted Galveston shrimp boat, off the coast of Yucatan with twenty thousand pounds of marijuana, a $7 million value. They caught another Galveston boat, *Agnes Pauline*, with twenty-two tons of marijuana on board at Port Arthur. The Coast Guard became suspicious of this fishing vessel when it left port with neither ice nor fishing gear, but loaded with sophisticated radio equipment. Since the crime carried a maximum sentence of five years and a $15,000 fine with a possibility of parole in two years, the possibilities for profit outweighed the risk involved. In 1978 and 1979 agents seized $250 million in marijuana along the Texas coastline, and it was estimated that this was only 10 percent of the traffic.[64]

On the island marijuana could be home grown and was found on occasion by police. People also searched through the dunes down the island for a psilocybe mushroom which grew in cow manure. When ingested, the mushroom produced hallucinations. The problem was that it was easy to pick the wrong mushroom and become sick rather than high. UTMB treated about twenty cases of such poisoning per year in the mid-1970's.[65]

The old red-light district, now known as the "Bottoms," stretched north of Broadway from 25th to 29th, and became the worst area for theft, assault, muggings, and prostitution. Neither victims nor residents cooperated with police, and human derelicts infested the section and nearby downtown blocks. They came to Galveston to escape the cold and programs for rehabilitation. The Supreme Court in the late 1970's held that vagrancy laws were unconstitutional, so the police stopped trying to control the drifters and alcoholics. If arrested, they could not pay fines, and they created a health hazard in the jails. The county would not shelter them, the city could not afford them, the federal government withdrew social services, and the winos did not care. So, begging on the street, sleeping behind bushes, sitting in the sunshine, they were allowed to stay. "What's the word? Thunderbird! What's the price? A quarter twice!"[66]

The city produced its share of bizarre crimes—a nude twenty-one-year-old woman from California found on the east beach with her throat slashed to the bone; an eight-year-old girl abducted, buried alive under the rocks on the Gulf shore, and later rescued; a twelve-year-old girl who disappeared while walking to her grandmother's house and whose body was found in a field at Alta Loma two years later; thirty-nine homosexual men arrested in the steambath and rooms for indecent exposure at the Kon Tiki Club.[67] One of the worst episodes was a rash of rapes in the early 1980's. They increased from one every six days to one every other day. A man, for example, held a dance class at gunpoint while he raped a twelve-year-old. A former city councilman, Paul Quintero, heard his daughter scream from his front yard and rushed out. He thought, "My God, it's either him or me, or he'll rape my daughter." He struggled with the assailant, received a gunshot in the leg, and drove off the attacker. In the trial of Henry S. Hegwood, the so-called towel rapist, a courageous senior medical student at UTMB told how he broke into her room, held a knife to her throat, hit her when she tried to escape, pulled her to the bed, and fell on top of her. She refused to cooperate and called, "Jesus, help me!" There was pain and she thought it would last forever. Finally, he finished, pulled her to her feet, and left. She felt the blood running down her leg as she called the emergency police number. Hegwood received sixty-five years in prison for this, but it was no wonder that there was an undercurrent of fear among women who lived and worked on the island.[68]

Fear based upon racial differences has, by and large, declined through efforts of desegregation. In the twentieth century until after World War II, the community continued the separation of social, religious, and educational institutions which had been there from the beginning. Residential areas, however, despite an effort to drive blacks north of Broadway, remained integrated even after the separation of races in public housing in the postwar period. For residential areas discrimination was more a question of economics than race. Segregation, however, came on local public transportation by ordinance in 1906, and at the beach about the same time. White groups wanted blacks pushed beyond Fort Crockett. The Business League stated in 1907: "This objection is made through no prejudice nor ill-feeling toward our fellow colored citizens, but to do otherwise than above suggested would tend to jeopardize the good terms at present existing between the two races, and at the same time in a large degree diminish the revenues which would otherwise be derived from our surf bathing."[69] The catch was that such a location was beyond easy reach by public transportation, and despite such feelings, a black bathhouse opened at 28th Street and Seawall Boulevard in the early 1920's.[70]

In another dispute, city officials got into trouble about the location of a park for black citizens. John H. Clouser, a black school-teacher, in one of the first clear protests against segregation, stood before the city commission in 1928 and demanded that the signs in Menard Park which read "For White People Only" be removed. He argued that black taxpayers had the right to walk through the park and listen to city band concerts, and added, "You spent $26,622 last year for recreational purposes and not one cent for the negro children. . . . Unfortunately, our children live in alleys and there is no place for the children to play."[71]

The signs came down, and the commissioners designated the block of P, Q, 42nd, and 43rd as a park for black people. Protests by nearby white landholders led by H. H. Treaccar flooded city hall and forced the first referendum vote in Galveston history. By a two-to-one ratio the action of the commission met a veto, and the site became Lasker Park for white children, while the former Lasker Park became Cuney Park for blacks.[72] Although two white crosses bearing the brand of the Ku Klux Klan appeared at the controversial block during the protests, the Klan never gained a foothold on the island. Klansmen had appeared in 1922, solemnly interrupted a revival at the First Baptist Church in order to donate $100, held an initiation ceremony under a large cross decorated with red electric lights, and found themselves denied the right to march in the streets. There was too much local resistance from people like Rabbi Cohen and Father Kirwin for the Klan to find growing room.[73]

For the most part, however, there was little challenge like Clouser's to white authority and dominance. The black editor of the *City Times* said in 1904, "The talk of the Negro seeking social equality is all rot and politics. The Negro is well satisfied of the right to labor." At a trial held in Galveston of a black man who shot and killed his wife and white lover, the all-white jury acquitted the man for killing his unfaithful wife and condemned him to hang for the murder of a white person. This was later changed to ninety-nine years in prison, but the *City Times* editor wrote, "So far all the verdicts in this case point in the direction that any colored man who kills a white man down this way is going to have a mighty hard road, it matters not whether in self defense or for other just causes of protection, etc."[74]

In 1921 the editor explained that blacks had a loving spirit for the whites: ". . . the colored people of Galveston are not trying to run the city in her commercial, financial, labor, or political progress, but instead are honestly doing their humble part to help keep things going right." It was understandable, moreover, to the editor in 1931 that blacks were dismissed from service at the Owens gangster trial because there was no way to feed a black on jury duty at a white restaurant. In addition, during the Depression blacks could not be hired as case workers because it was socially impossible for a black to deal with white clients. The reverse, of course, was not true, and the black reporter who inquired about the situation agreed.[75] This world of segregation, intimidation, and dominance, however, cracked apart in the 1950's and 1960's.

During World War II black men and women served the nation in responsible and patriotic ways. Their horizons expanded and there could be no return to subservience. In Galveston, furthermore, the black population increased from 22 percent of the total in 1920 to 29 percent in 1980. In 1943 the Negro City Teachers' Association sued for equal pay with white teachers and won. In 1950 for the first time a county judge appointed a black person to the grand jury because, shortly before, the Texas Court of Criminal Appeals had overturned a death penalty because there were no blacks on the grand jury. In 1952 the Galveston Bar Association admitted its first black lawyer, but Sheriff Biaggne in 1955 refused to appoint a black deputy upon the appeal of thirty citizens. "Communists have entered the South-land by accusing sheriffs and constables of not appointing negro deputies," he blurted. But after the county commissioners gave him the money to do it, the flexible sheriff said, "I feel that the appointment of this deputy would be beneficial to the county as a whole and furnish a peace officer for the protection of our colored citizens."[76]

In 1954 the Negro Chamber of Commerce and the Galveston Chamber of Commerce merged. In 1955 Mayor Clough appointed a black to a city board, and in 1957 three blacks were hired by the fire department. In 1958 the minority won the right to use the municipal golf course. Blacks had requested permission in 1951, 1954, and 1956, only to be given a run-around by city officials. Finally, a group simply went out, placed their balls on a tee, and began to play. After a while someone came along to collect green fees, and that was it. The course was open.[77]

The major thrust for desegregation, however, came in the schools. In 1954 the U.S. Supreme Court destroyed the separate-but-equal doctrine in the famous case of *Brown versus Board of Education of Topeka*, and in August that year, 267 people signed a petition calling for an immediate end to segregation in the Galveston schools. There were delays, and the next year the school board received a petition from four hundred parents backed by the NAACP. In 1956 a biracial committee urged desegregation while the school board still hesitated. In 1957 the NAACP filed suit on behalf of black students, and in 1961, finally, Judge Ben Connally ordered integration to begin. Both the Catholic schools and the Galveston Independent School District integrated the first grades in the fall term of 1961. Total desegregation came for the public schools in 1964, and in 1967 the district received the praise of the U.S. Office of Education for its efforts. To achieve greater balance, the GISD tried busing in 1969 and magnet schools in 1981.[78]

Symbolic of racial equality was the publication for the first time in 1962 of the name of high-ranking black students in the *Galveston Daily News*, and the election of Teri Simmons, a black girl, as homecoming queen at Ball High School in 1977.[79] The students, moreover, picked up the tempo of equality from what was happening at home and across the land. They started a series of sit-ins to integrate Galveston stores in 1960. Chanting, "We'll take a seat and sit for a week," they struck at Woolworth's, McCrory's, Kress, and Walgreen's in downtown Galveston.[80]

The confused merchants closed the snack counters, and Walgreen's even removed the seats. The police stood by, and there was no violence. Kelton Sams, who had grown up in the rough area of Palm Terrace, was the spokesman for the students. He felt inarticulate at first, and slipped away from the crowds to go to a nearby bookstore to scan for something appropriate to say. He soon began a self-improvement program and continued to pressure the merchants. The more liberal whites—Ruth and Harris Kempner and Griffith D. Lambdin, for example—worked behind the scenes to insure a peaceful transition. Lambdin, an attorney, met Sams over the phone. The young black said to him, "My name is Kelton Sams and I'm going to jail next Monday. Will you get me out?"[81]

At one of the meetings on the issue, Lambdin recalled that George Clampett, a partner with Grady Dickinson at the Star Drugstore, stood up and said to his fellow businessmen, "I was born in the South, my parents were born in the South . . ." Lambdin thought, "Oh, my Lord," but Clampett continued. "You know, Grady and I got together and discussed this business about losing business, causing trouble, and we finally got around to the ultimate question—what is right? What is right?" He and his partner concluded that trade should be total, not just toothpaste and Kleenex, but also food and Cokes. Their stand was persuasive, Sams restrained the students, the media kept it quiet, and the lunch counters reopened without fanfare to all people regardless of color. George Clampett lost one indignant white customer, but she came back a week later.[82]

Under pressure from the student group led by Sams, outlying stores such as the Dairy Queen on Broadway and 26th desegregated, and the city opened up all parks, including Stewart Beach. Other barriers, at restaurants and theaters, fell in time. Virginia Stull became the first black graduate of UTMB in 1966; the state dropped the miscegenation law in 1967; and in 1971 the Supreme Court ordered all

ILA local unions to merge.[83] A major accomplishment for human dignity had been achieved in Galveston as in the nation.

In the midst of this social revolution the National Municipal League selected Galveston as one of eleven "All American Cities" in 1962. It was recognition for reform in city government, a change from the commission to the city-manager structure. This shift began as a study by the League of Women Voters under Frances K. Harris in 1954, and was part of the breakdown of the sin city. It was a way to end the control of government by the vice bloc, and to administer the city in a more professional manner. Under the proposal the elected city council would function as a policy-making body. The departments would be run, however, by a city manager, a nonpartisan professional, hired by the city.[84]

In 1958 the league opened a campaign for the city-manager plan which involved fifty-five public forums; twenty-two thousand phone calls, distribution of flyers and pamphlets, and meetings with unions, churches, social groups, civic organizations, and school gatherings. Despite opposition from incumbent politicians, the electorate approved the plan in a special election in April 1960—one month after the sit-ins started. It may well be that the social upheaval was a factor in persuading people that change was needed in government. Some of the women leaders wanted the students rather than the mayor to accept the All American City Award in 1962.[85]

In the election of the new council, six out of seven "charter" candidates won, including Ruth L. Kempner, the first woman elected to the city government, and T. D. Armstrong, a black civil-rights leader. The successful candidates selected Edward Schreiber, the chairman of the charter commission, as mayor, and appointed Robert E. Layton the first city manager. Quickly, the council moved to set up a new accounting system, eliminate racial discrimination from the ordinances, and formulate long-term goals.[86]

By annexing a ten-foot strip down the island, the municipality extended its jurisdiction to three-quarters of the island and three miles offshore. Such annexations were commonplace in Texas at the time, and this action was considered necessary to protect the future of the city. Not so easy to solve, however, was the question of tax revenues. About half the urban land was tax exempt, so that property assessments provided only 37 percent of municipal funds in 1966. Elsewhere in the nation property yielded 70 percent on the average. Worse, in 1979 a group called the Association of Concerned Taxpayers (ACT), led by Walter Teachworth and Nat Pepper and inspired by Howard Jarvis of California, who visited Galveston at the time, forced a referendum which reduced the property tax rate from eighty-seven cents to seventy cents per $100 valuation and limited budget increases to 7 percent per year.

Inflation at the time was running at 12 percent. The city lost about $500,000 in revenue, and its credit rating in the bond market dropped. This meant increased interest payments of $500,000 to $1 million when borrowing money. The government responded by eliminating 5 percent of the municipal jobs, the health department, the lifeguards, summer bands, school crossing guards, and a fire station. It also reduced bus routes, turned off the gaslights on the Strand, and switched off the lights on the causeway for several months. After a fatal accident on the viaduct, Teachworth, the ACT president, blamed the city manager for making "visible" cuts, but what else could be expected under such stringent conditions? [87]

To an extent the county assumed the burden. It raised taxes three cents and took over, for example, the lifeguard duty on the beach. The Texas legislature, in addition, provided a hotel tax in 1981 for support of the beaches and maintenance of the convention center. [88] A decline in the inflation rate also helped, but the cramp in the budget has remained a major factor. The whole episode reflected a nationwide "taxpayers' revolt" and distrust of government spending. It represented on a local level what the election of President Ronald Reagan represented on the national level.

Conservatism is often an attribute of old age. If you accept an organic theory of development, such as espoused by Arnold Toynbee, then Galveston is in its old age, and conservatism should not be a surprise. The economy and population are stationary, there is fear of crime, taxes are thought to be too high, and Galveston is looking backward to its past for identity and justification. These characteristics of old age are not necessarily bad, and may well be the fate of all cities at one time or another. Galveston history, furthermore, offers worthwhile lessons and experiences: there is the story of ambitious men and a city on the make in the nineteenth century; there is the monumental struggle of people against nature seen in the seawall, grade raising, and causeway; there is a demonstration of the dark side of human character in the era of the sin city; and there is the reflective nature of historic preservation which underscores the best achievements of the past. Finally, at the shoreline a pilgrim can still feel the heartbeat of nature. It is a primordial rhythm which all visitors have felt—Karankawa Indian, soldier, pirate, poet, sailor, settler, tourist—when they stood in the surf at Galveston, on the edge of time.

NOTES

PREFACE

1. See Theodore Herschberg, "The New Urban History: Toward an Inter-disciplinary History of the City," *Journal of Urban History* 5 (November 1978): 3–40; Deborah S. Gardner, "American Urban History: Power, Society and Artifact," *Urban History: Reviews of Recent Research* 2 (Fall 1981): 49–78; "Technology and the City," a series of articles in *Journal of Urban History* 5 (May 1977).
2. Herschberg, "The New Urban History," p. 7; see also p. 11.
3. *Galveston Daily News*, June 15, 1907; May 13, 27, 1962.

CHAPTER ONE. THE EDGE OF TIME

1. Cyclone Covey, ed., *Cabeza de Vaca's Adventures in the Unknown Interior of America* (New York: Collier, 1961), pp. 59–60.
2. Josef Evia, *alférez de fragata*, "Map of Galveston and San Bernardo Bays," Philip C. Tucker Collection, Barker Texas History Center, University of Texas at Austin; Henry Taliaferro, "Cartographic Guide to Maps in the Rosenberg Library" (manuscript), p. 121; "Evia, José de," *The Handbook of Texas*, vol. 3 (Austin: Texas State Historical Association, 1976), p. 287; "La Harpe, Bénard de," *The Handbook of Texas*, vol. 2 (Austin: Texas State Historical Association, 1952), p. 8.
3. Alexandre de Humboldt, "A Map of New Spain," 1804; Stephen F. Austin, "Mapa Geografico de la Provincia de Texas," 1822; David H. Burr, "Texas," 1833; all at Barker Texas History Center.
4. Virginia Eisenhour, *Galveston: A Different Place* (Galveston, 1983), p. 1.
5. Texas Writers' Project, American Guide Series (WPA), "Galveston: A History and Guide" (manuscript, Barker Texas History Center), p. 13; Samuel C. Griffin, *History of Galveston, Texas: Narrative and Biographical* (Galveston: Cawston, 1931), introduction (no pagination); Charles W. Hays, *Galveston: History of the Island and the City* (Austin: Jenkins Garrett, 1974), 1:251.
6. Frank P. Slingluff, "Sedimentation and Shore Processes in Southwestern Galveston Island, Galveston City, Texas" (Master's thesis, University of Texas at Austin, 1948), pp. 6, 19, 22, 25; Miles O. Hayes, "Sedimentation on a Semiarid, Wave Dominated Coast (South Texas) with Emphasis on

Hurricane Effects" (Ph.D. dissertation, University of Texas at Austin, 1965), pp. 3–5; Thomas W. Stern, "Sedimentation and Shore Processes on the Northeastern Portion of Galveston Island, Texas" (Master's thesis, University of Texas at Austin, 1948), pp. 1, 22, 24, 32–33, 41, 52–53; Jean Andrews, *Shells and Shores of Texas* (Austin: University of Texas Press, 1977), pp. 14–15; *Galveston Daily News*, November 11, 1934.

7. *Galveston Daily News*, June 28, 1891.
8. Zera C. Foster, *Soil Survey of Galveston County, Texas* (Washington, D.C.: Government Printing Office, 1935), p. 13; *Galveston Daily News*, April 22, 1955.
9. U.S. Board of Engineers, *The Ports of Galveston, Houston and Texas City, Texas* (Washington, D.C.: Government Printing Office, 1924), pp. 1–2.
10. Edward Lovelace to Judge Austin, June 26, 1822, in *The Austin Papers*, ed. Eugene C. Barker (Washington, D.C.: Government Printing Office, 1924), 1:526.
11. Joseph L. Clark and Elton M. Scott, *The Texas Gulf Coast: Its History and Development* (New York: Lewis, 1955), 1:54–67; Clark Seibert, "Two Million Years of History on the Texas City Dike," *InBetween* 91 (December 1980): 7.
12. Clark and Scott, *Texas Gulf Coast*, 1:69, 2:25. Foster, *Soil Survey*, p. 2.
13. Foster, *Soil Survey*, pp. 2, 4.
14. *Galveston Daily News*, June 22, 1941; October 16, 1943; April 30, 1944; December 10, 1944; August 17, 1945; November 14, 1946; September 10, 1960; December 24, 1972.
15. David G. McComb, *Houston: A History* (Austin: University of Texas Press, 1981), pp. 21–30.
16. John Tveten, *Coastal Texas: Water, Land and Wildlife* (College Station: Texas A&M Press, 1982), pp. 88–103.
17. Frank M. Fisher, Jr., "The Wetlands," *Rice University Review* 7 (Fall 1972): 16.
18. *Galveston Daily News*, November 2, 1875; September 2, 1877; April 27, 1948; December 13, 1958; November 20, 1961.
19. Joel Barna, "Danger in the Dunes," *InBetween* 102 (June 1981): 6; *Galveston Daily News*, May 17, 1964; September 12, 1982.
20. W. Richard Ferguson, "Fighting Inflation (The Karankawa Way)," *InBetween* 118 (January 1982): 21.
21. *Galveston Daily News*, December 2, 1974.
22. Ibid., November 14, 1912.
23. Ibid., December 2, 1974.
24. Ibid.
25. Linda Snyder, *Birds of Galveston Island State Park* (Austin: Texas Parks and Wildlife Department, 1976), pp. 2–10; *Galveston Daily News*, July 22, 1962.
26. "Sea-Arama Marineworld Begins Project to Re-Establish Brown Pelican in This Area," *Port Galveston* 30 (February 1977): 14–15; *Galveston Daily News*, December 1, 1955; March 10, 1966; December 17, 1976.

27. "Gulls of Galveston," *Port Galveston* 27, no. 8 (1974): 3–5; *Galveston Daily News*, May 15, 1904; June 14, 1953.
28. Tveten, *Coastal Texas*, pp. 23–29.
29. Ibid., pp. 30–32, 39; Andrews, *Shells and Shores of Texas*, p. 39; *Galveston Daily News*, September 3, 1922.
30. Tveten, *Coastal Texas*, pp. 43–44; *Galveston Daily News*, June 5, 1869.
31. Andrews, *Shells and Shores of Texas*, p. 310; *Galveston Daily News*, May 16, 19, 1970; July 11, 1970.
32. *Galveston Daily News*, August 12, 13, 1977.
33. Ibid., May 29, 1909.
34. Ibid., April 14, 1872; May 15, 1880; April 5, 1951; July 29, 1978; September 13, 1981; Nicky DeLange, "Headstarting the Heartbreak Turtle," *In-Between* 135 (September 1982): 26, 28.
35. *Galveston Daily News*, July 6, 8, 14, 16, 1875; August 21, 1916; September 10, 1916; December 12, 1937; February 22, 23, 24, 1951.
36. Tveten, *Coastal Texas*, pp. 52, 55, 58, 59, 61, 63–65, 66, 68; Ephraim Douglas Adams, ed., "Correspondence from the British Archives Concerning Texas, 1837–1846," *Southwestern Historical Quarterly* 18 (July 1914): 93.
37. *Galveston Daily News*, June 1, 1875; October 14, 1964.
38. Oscar M. Addison to Mrs. Sarah Addison, May 2, 1845, Oscar M. Addison Papers, Barker Texas History Center.
39. Andrews, *Shells and Shores of Texas*, pp. 24, 25; Stephen P. Leatherman, Michael S. Kearney, and Beach Clow, "Assessment of Coastal Responses to Projected Sea Level Rise: Galveston Island and Bay, Texas" (prepared for the U.S. Environmental Protection Agency, February 1983), p. 7.
40. *Galveston Daily News*, December 30, 1876; Henry Beston, *The Outermost House: A Year of Life on the Great Beach of Cape Cod* (New York: Rinehart and Company, 1928, 1949), p. 43.
41. Clark and Scott, *Texas Gulf Coast*, 2:13; *Galveston Daily News*, October 22, 1922 (article by J. O. Dyer); January 19, 1964.
42. *Galveston Daily News*, September 4, 1885; November 18, 1910; March 3, 1912; June 19, 1949; January 19, 1964; February 22, 1970.
43. Ibid., December 1, 1958; Alan W. Moffett, *The Shrimp Fishery in Texas* (Austin: Texas Parks and Wildlife Department, 1974), pp. 9–14. See also Robert L. Maril, *Texas Shrimpers: Community, Capitalism, and the Sea* (College Station: Texas A&M University Press, 1983), pp. 9–52.
44. *Galveston Daily News*, March 25, 1882.
45. Ibid., July 24, 1910 (article by Ben Stuart); August 31, 1961; August 15, 1982.
46. Ibid., August 15, 1939; August 15, 1982.
47. Ibid., August 12, 1982.
48. Ibid., October 24, 1887; November 30, 1887.
49. Ibid., September 26, 1963; October 2, 1964; September 22, 1967.
50. Ibid., May 28, 1885; July 28, 1887; July 24, 1910 (article by Ben Stuart); September 10, 1951; September 8, 1957; August 31, 1962; *Civilian and Gazette*, September 4, 1860.

51. *Galveston Daily News*, July 14, 31, 1885; August 1, 1885; August 21, 1910.

52. Ibid., June 17, 1856; July 28, 1868; August 19, 1873; August 29, 1877; July 2, 1890; April 30, 1932; July 17, 1947.

53. Ibid., November 17, 1907 (article by Ben Stuart).

54. Ibid., April 17, 1951; September 17, 1964; July 2, 1978.

55. Ibid., April 9, 1905 (letter to editor from G. W. Baylor); June 16, 1937; *Texas City Times*, June 16, 1911.

56. *Galveston Daily News*, April 29, 30, 1976; May 1, 1983.

57. Ibid., July 31, 1868; September 24, 1887; July 24, 1910 (article by Ben Stuart).

58. Ibid., June 23, 1875; July 4, 1880; January 25, 1914; March 18, 1915.

59. Ibid., July 23, 1961.

60. U.S. Board of Engineers, *Ports of Galveston, Houston, and Texas City*, pp. 3–4; *Texas Almanac, 1982–1983* (Dallas: A. H. Belo, 1981), p. 280; Clark and Scott, *Texas Gulf Coast*, p. 26.

61. Robert Hancock Hunter Diary (typescript copy, Barker Texas History Center), p. 4.

62. *Galveston Daily News*, November 8, 1886; February 20, 1955.

63. Ibid., November 15, 1876.

64. Ibid., January 9, 11–13, 1886; Anne A. Brindley, "Jane Long," reprint from *Southwestern Historical Quarterly* 56 (October 1952): 16.

65. Ibid., January 13, 1886.

66. Ibid., February 9, 17, 1895; March 11, 1932; February 14, 1933; January 24, 1935; February 3–5, 1951; January 11, 12, 1962.

67. Ibid., June 4, 1950; April 18, 1973; Christian Friedrich Duerr Diary (typescript, Barker Texas History Center), pp. 94–95.

68. *Galveston Daily News*, September 1, 1857; August 1, 15, 16, 1872; October 5, 12, 14, 19, 1876.

69. Two versions of this story have been collected by Patrick B. Mullen, *I Heard the Old Fishermen Say: Folklore of the Texas Gulf Coast* (Austin: University of Texas Press, 1978), pp. 139–140.

70. James S. Hanna, *What Life Was Like When I Was a Kid* (San Antonio: Naylor, 1973), p. 58; *Galveston Daily News*, August 8, 1890; August 20, 1937; June 5, 1962; October 30, 1969. See also Patrick B. Mullen, "The Function of Folk Belief among Texas Coastal Fishermen" (Ph.D. dissertation, University of Texas at Austin, 1968), p. 165.

71. *Galveston Daily News*, November 7, 1943; June 19, 1961; June 6, 1981; September 1–3, 1981.

72. Ibid., August 11, 1969; *Houston Post*, August 8, 1980; N.O.A.A., *National Weather Service Storm Evacuation Map for the Galveston Bay Area* (Washington, D.C.: U.S. Department of Commerce, 1981), n.p.

73. Joseph O. Dyer, *The Early History of Galveston* (Galveston: Springer, 1916), pp. 3–4; Hays, *Galveston*, 1:17–18.

74. "French Refugees in Texas, 1815" (typescript, Barker Texas History Center), pp. 69–73; Hays, *Galveston*, 1:40–41, 43–44.

75. "Houston and Galveston in the Years 1837–8," *Hesperian, or Western*

Magazine (Columbus, Ohio, 1838; reprint for Union National Bank, Houston), pp. 7–8.

76. Frances Harwood, "Colonel Amasa Turner's Reminiscences of Galveston," *Quarterly of the Texas State Historical Association* 3 (July 1899–April 1900): 47.

77. Ibid., p. 46; Joe B. Frantz, *Gail Borden: Dairyman to a Nation* (Norman: University of Oklahoma Press, 1951), pp. 135–138.

78. Feris A. Bass, Jr., and B. R. Brunson, eds., *Fragile Empires: The Texas Correspondence of Samuel Swartwout and James Morgan, 1836–1856* (Austin: Shoal Creek, 1978), pp. 51, 169.

79. *Galveston Daily News*, August 21, 1886.

80. Ibid., October 3–6, 10, 11, 1867; November 26, 1867; May 22, 1868; October 13, 1868.

81. Ibid., June 4, 6, 7, 10, 11, 13, 20, 1871.

82. Ibid., October 3, 4, 1871.

83. *Houston Weekly Telegraph*, September 17, 1875.

84. Ibid., September 17, 24, 1875; *Galveston Daily News*, September 16–19, 21–25, 1875; October 27, 1875; December 7, 10, 1875.

85. Brownson Malsch, *Indianola: The Mother of Western Texas* (Austin: Shoal Creek, 1977), pp. 236–244, 253–254.

86. *Galveston Daily News*, October 20, 1875; June 20, 23, 1876; August 22, 1876; August 14, 1877; May 9, 1878; December 4, 1878; January 1, 1879.

87. Ibid., June 15, 1886.

88. Malsch, *Indianola*, pp. 255–256, 262–266.

89. *Galveston Daily News*, August 21, 1886.

90. Ibid., August 22, 1886; October 20, 1886.

91. Robert Morris Franklin, Papers, Galveston Seawall Committee, 1886–1887, Rosenberg Library; *Galveston Daily News*, January 18, 1887; May 25, 1887; July 19, 1887; August 14, 1887; August 31, 1887.

92. *Galveston Daily News*, May 11, 1894; September 11, 1895.

93. Covey, ed., *Cabeza de Vaca's Adventures*, pp. 54–55.

94. James N. Baskett, "A Study of the Route of Cabeza de Vaca," *Quarterly of the Texas State Historical Association* 10 (January 1907): 249, 257; Cleve Hallenbeck, *Alvar Núñez Cabeza De Vaca* (New York: Kennikat, 1940), pp. 124–127, 260, 266, 271, 284–285, 289–290.

95. Covey, ed., *Cabeza de Vaca's Adventures*, pp. 56–58.

96. Ibid., pp. 60, 125–133.

97. Ibid., pp. 61–63.

98. Oliver's report is included in Albert S. Gotschet, "The Karankawa Indians," in Peabody Museum of American Archeology and Ethnology, Harvard University, *Papers* 1, no. 2 (Cambridge, Mass., 1891): vii–viii, 11–20, 27–32, 45–67.

99. *Houston Post*, June 18, 1978; *Galveston Daily News*, November 13, 1962; Barbara Burger, "Reading History in the Soil," *Rice University Review* 10 (Winter 1975–1976): 20–21.

100. "Karankawa Indians," *The Handbook of Texas*, 3:464.

101. Hays, *Galveston*, 1:17–25.
102. J. Frank Dobie, *Coronado's Children* (Austin: University of Texas Press, 1978), pp. 274–284.
103. "Suppression of Piratical Establishments," *American State Papers: Foreign Relations* 4, no. 290 (Washington, D.C.: Galen and Seaton, 1834): 135.
104. J.J.B., "Early Life in the Southwest—The Bowies," *DeBow's Review* 13 (October 1852): 381; Eugene C. Barker, "The African Slave Trade in Texas," *Quarterly of the Texas State Historical Association* 6 (October 1902): 146–148.
105. "Suppression of Piratical Establishments," pp. 139–140; U.S. Department of State, *Message from the President of the United States Communicating Information of the Proceeding of Certain Persons Who Took Possession of Amelia Island and of Galveston, During the Summer of the Present Year and Made Establishments There, December 15, 1817* (Washington, D.C.: E. de Krafft, 1817), p. 9.
106. W.B., "Life of Jean Lafitte," *Littell's Living Age* 32 (March 6, 1852): 441; Hays, *Galveston*, 1:34; Texas Writers' Project (WPA), "Galveston," p. 45; Sandusky map at the archives of the Rosenberg Library, Galveston.
107. Texas Writers' Project (WPA), "Galveston," pp. 44–45.
108. *Galveston Daily News*, May 25, 1879; January 7, 1884.
109. *Galveston Directory for 1859–60* (Galveston: News Book and Job Office, 1859), pp. 61–63.
110. T., "The Cruise of the Enterprise," *United States Magazine and Democratic Review* 6 (July 1839): 38–42.
111. Hays, *Galveston*, 1:51; W.B., "Life of Lafitte," p. 443.
112. Charles Hamilton, *Great Forgers and Famous Fakes* (New York: Crown, 1980), pp. 121–129.
113. W.B., "Life of Lafitte," p. 445; Charles Adams Guleck, Jr., and Katherine Elliot, eds., *Mirabeau B. Lamar Papers* (Austin: Baldwin, 1925), 2:38, 152.
114. *Galveston Daily News*, October 22, 1922; Dyer, *Early History of Galveston*, pp. 11–12; Jesse A. Ziegler, *Wave of the Gulf* (San Antonio: Naylor, 1938), p. 196; WPA, "Folklore Folder," Barker Texas History Center.
115. *Houston Post*, August 12, 1969; September 9, 1969; June 12, 1980; *Galveston Daily News*, September 15, 1903; January 23, 30, 1970; February 11, 1970; June 11, 1972.
116. Stanley E. Babb, "Caribbean Nocturn," *The Death of a Buccaneer and Other Poems* (Dallas: Turner, 1927), p. 56.
117. Hays, *Galveston*, 1:54–63.
118. Ibid., pp. 63, 65–66; *Galveston Directory for 1859–60*, p. 63.
119. T., "The Cruise of the Enterprise," pp. 40–41; H. Yoakum, *History of Texas* (Austin: Steck, 1935), p. 197. W.B., "Life of Lafitte," p. 443.
120. Brindley, "Jane Long," pp. 13–19; *Galveston Daily News*, February 21, 1932; July 11, 1936.

121. Hays, *Galveston*, 1 : 127, 130–131. See also Juan N. Almonte, "Statistical Report on Texas, 1835," *Southwestern Historical Quarterly* 28 (January 1925): 203–204.
122. "Journal of Lewis Birsall Harris, 1836–1842," *Southwestern Historical Quarterly* 25 (October 1921): 134–136; David G. Burnet to James Morgan, April 21, 1836, Morgan Papers, Rosenberg Library; *Galveston Daily News*, December 20, 1914.
123. *Galveston Daily News*, December 20, 1914; Hays, *Galveston*, 1 : 151–160.
124. Ernest W. Winkler, "The Seat of Government of Texas," *Quarterly of the Texas State Historical Association* 10 (October 1906): 156.
125. *Galveston Daily News*, March 18, 1888; Dyer, *Early History of Galveston*, pp. 24–25; David G. Burnet to James Morgan, June 11, 1836, Morgan Papers, Rosenberg Library.

CHAPTER TWO. THE NEW YORK OF TEXAS

1. Charles W. Hays, *Galveston: A History of the Island and the City* (Austin: Jenkins Garrett, 1974), 2 : 811–814.
2. Ibid., 1 : 170–180; *Galveston Daily News*, February 10, 1963 (article by Lillian Herz); "Legal Documents," December 14, 1836, Samuel May Williams Papers, Rosenberg Library; H. P. N. Gammel, *Laws of Texas* (Austin: Gammel Book Company, 1898), 1 : 1132, 1195.
3. Hays, *Galveston*, 1 : 260; Bob Nesbitt, *Bob's Galveston Island Reader* (Galveston: Nesbitt, 1983), pp. 114–116.
4. Hays, *Galveston*, 1 : 261–262; 2 : 815; *Galveston Daily News*, February 5, 1841; January 2, 1882; April 6, 1890; July 19, 1909; July 9, 1961; February 10, 1963 (article by Lillian Herz); August 11, 1965; Gammel, *Laws of Texas*, 1 : 1482–1483; 2 : 440–447, 586–587; Thomas F. McKinney to Samuel May Williams, November 6, 1838, Samuel May Williams Papers, Rosenberg Library.
5. Hays, *Galveston*, 1 : 327–328, 330, 401–411; Margaret Swett Henson, *Samuel May Williams: Early Texas Entrepreneur* (College Station: Texas A&M Press, 1976), pp. 104, 111.
6. Francis C. Sheridan, *Galveston Island, or A Few Months off the Coast of Texas*, ed. Willis W. Pratt (Austin: University of Texas Press, 1954), pp. vii–viii, 30–32, 35–38, 45–47, 53, 71–76, 92, 100.
7. Ibid., p. 30; Hays, *Galveston*, 2 : 816–823.
8. Hays, *Galveston*, 2 : 822–830; Henson, *Samuel May Williams*, p. 115.
9. Hays, *Galveston*, 2 : 927; Henson, *Samuel May Williams*, pp. 111, 146–147, 162.
10. Jesse A. Ziegler, *Wave of the Gulf* (San Antonio: Naylor, 1938), pp. 146–147; *Galveston Weekly News*, September 14, 1858.
11. *Civilian and Gazette*, October 19, 1838; September 6, 1859; *Daily Advertiser*, February 26, 1842; *Galveston Weekly News*, September 14, 1858; *Galveston Daily News*, September 2, 1869; September 1, 1875; September 15, 1878; September 1, 1882; April 11, 1942.

12. David R. Goldfield, *Cotton Fields and Skyscrapers* (Baton Rouge: Louisiana State University Press, 1982), pp. 86–91, 126.
13. *Galveston Daily News*, November 10, 11, 1886; September 8, 1887.
14. Ibid., May 5, 1876.
15. Keith L. Bryant, Jr., *Arthur E. Stilwell: Promoter with a Hunch* (Nashville: Vanderbilt University Press, 1971), pp. 95–96.
16. *Galveston Daily News*, January 4, 1894.
17. *Thirteenth Census, Manufactures* (1910), (Washington, D.C.: Government Printing Office, 1912), pp. 1215, 1217; Edwin L. Caldwell, "Highlights of the Development of Manufacturing in Texas, 1900–1960," *Southwestern Historical Quarterly* 68 (April 1965): 407–408.
18. Texas A&M Engineering Experiment Station, *An Evaluation of the Industrial Potential of Galveston, Texas* (College Station: Texas A&M, 1959), 76 pp., University of Houston Center for Research in Business and Economics, *Economic Base Study of Galveston County, Texas* (Houston, 1965), 85 pp.; *Galveston Daily News*, January 1, 1980.
19. *Tenth Census, Statistics of Manufacturers* (Washington, D.C.: Government Printing Office, 1880), 2:360, 403; *Galveston Weekly News*, August 4, 1857; September 3, 1861; *Galveston Daily News*, April 11, 1868; May 14, 1876; July 6, 1879; April 23, 1880; *Civilian and Gazette*, January 24, 1851.
20. *Galveston Daily News*, January 9, 11, 1868; December 11, 13, 1868; January 16, 1873; May 12, 15, 16, 31, 1874; June 11, 18, 23, 28, 1874; August 11, 1874; October 27, 1874; April 13, 17, 1875; July 22, 1875; September 1, 1875; March 1, 1891; November 6, 1891.
21. Ibid., February 22, 1879; May 2, 1889; November 2, 1913.
22. Ibid., July 30, 1876; David G. McComb, *Houston: A History* (Austin: University of Texas Press, 1981), pp. 26–29; "Southern Pacific Railroad Grew with the West," *Port of Galveston* 23 (September 1969): 13.
23. *Galveston Weekly News*, August 3, 1852; September 24, 1852; October 12, 1852; April 23, 1853; June 5, 1855; April 22, 1856; April 27, 1858; May 18, 1858; June 15, 1858; July 13, 1858.
24. Ibid., November 22, 1853; August 1, 1854; May 12, 19, 26, 1857; January 11, 1859; February 7, 1860; J. D. Neis to Jacob L. Briggs, March 17, 1859, William Pitt Ballinger Papers, Rosenberg Library; John A. Coplen, "Notes and Fragments," *Quarterly of the Texas State Historical Association* 11 (July 1907): 70–72.
25. *Galveston Daily News*, February 24, 27, 1867; March 1, 1867; December 19, 1871; July 30, 1876; May 22, 25, 1881; Thomas W. Peirce to "My Dear Sir," September 25, 1875, William Pitt Ballinger Papers, Rosenberg Library; S. G. Reed, *A History of the Texas Railroads* (Houston: St. Clair, 1941), 355.
26. *Galveston Weekly News*, August 31, 1858; McComb, *Houston*, pp. 27–29.
27. McComb, *Houston*, p. 33.
28. Ibid., p. 34; *Galveston Daily News*, June 25, 28, 1876; November 29, 1877.

29. McComb, *Houston,* p. 65; *Galveston Daily News,* March 26, 1875; January 11, 1878.
30. *Galveston Daily News,* November 12, 1874; January 11, 1878; L. Tuffly Ellis, "The Revolutionizing of the Texas Cotton Trade, 1865–1885," *Southwestern Historical Quarterly* 73 (April 1970): 496–497.
31. Hays, *Galveston,* 2:679, 685.
32. Keith L. Bryant, Jr., *History of the Atchison, Topeka and Santa Fe Railway* (New York: Macmillan, 1974), pp. 127–133; Reed, *Texas Railroads,* pp. 283–290; Gulf, Colorado and Santa Fe, "Authorization, 1886," Rosenberg Library; Vera L. Dugas, "A Duel with Railroads: Houston vs. Galveston, 1866–1881," *East Texas Historical Journal* 2 (October 1964): 118–127; *Galveston Daily News,* May 2, 1875; March 31, 1876; August 22, 1877; December 9, 1877; August 1, 1880; April 2, 16, 1886; April 27, 1887; April 11, 1917.
33. Reed, *Texas Railroads,* p. 415.
34. *Galveston Daily News,* February 4, 5, 7, 1899; February 7, 1900; August 9, 1902; April 11, 1917; C. P. Huntington to George Sealy, March 31, 1898, George Sealy Papers, Rosenberg Library; Reed, *Texas Railroads,* p. 254.
35. *Galveston Daily News,* October 26, 1911; November 25, 1912; July 13, 1913; August 15, 1914; McComb, *Houston,* pp. 69–70.
36. Charles P. Zlatkovich, *Texas Railroads: A Record of Construction and Abandonment* (Austin: Bureau of Business Research, University of Texas, and Texas State Historical Association, 1981), pp. 70, 71; *Galveston Daily News,* March 18, 1856; September 6, 1859; January 10, 1860; November 30, 1866; October 15, 22, 1867; January 11, 19, 1868; June 25, 1868; December 18, 1938.
37. *Galveston Daily News,* July 22, 1870; February 1, 1871; May 8, 1879; January 13, 18, 1880; December 13, 15, 1884; November 30, 1887; November 18, 20, 1889.
38. Ibid., September 16, 1891; October 19, 1893; November 15, 1893; May 19, 1974.
39. Ibid., November 16, 1893.
40. Ibid., November 15, 1893.
41. Ellis, "Revolutionizing of the Texas Cotton Trade," pp. 483–485, 506–507; Louis Tuffly Ellis, "The Texas Cotton Compress Industry: A History" (Ph.D. dissertation, University of Texas at Austin, 1965), pp. 43, 75–76, 81–82, 87, 106.
42. Charles Hooton, *St. Louis' Isle, or Texiana* (London: Simmonds and Ward, 1847), p. 6.
43. Ferdinand Roemer, *Texas,* trans. Oswald Mueller (San Antonio: Standard Printing, 1935), p. 44.
44. *Galveston Weekly News,* December 7, 1866; *Galveston Daily News,* April 3, 17, 1867; May 1, 1867; November 8, 1868; December 24, 1868; February 11, 1869; May 13, 1869; *Charter and By-Laws of the Galveston Wharf Company* (Galveston: Civilian Book and Job Printing, 1861), 13 pp. in William Pitt Ballinger Papers, Rosenberg Library; "Re-

port of J. H. Hutchings, Esq., President of the Galveston Wharf Company to the Stockholders," Annual Meeting, January 6, 1873, 10 pp., in Ballinger Papers; "Argument of A. W. Terrell in Behalf of the Galveston Wharf Company Delivered before the Committee on Private Corporations of the Constitutional Convention, October 22, 1875" (Austin: Democratic Statesman, 1875), pp. 8–11, in Ballinger Papers; Maury Darst, "The Wharves, Then and Now," *InBetween* 99 (April 1981): 13–14. Bob Dalehite, "History Highlights," *InBetween* 80 (August 1980): 15, gives the original names of the nine wharves of Galveston.

45. *Galveston Daily News*, May 13, 1869.
46. Ibid., April 13, 1871; August 2, 1874; Galveston Wharf Company, "Report of J. H. Hutchings, President, to Meeting of Stockholders, January 15, 1875" (Galveston: Strickland and Clarke, 1875), p. 12.
47. *Galveston Daily News*, August 2, 1874. *See also* ibid., February 25, 1872; March 27, 1874; July 17, 22, 23, 26, 1874; August 4, 13, 1874; October 4, 10, 20, 1874; November 6, 7, 1874; December 23, 1874; January 20, 27, 1875; February 16, 1875; April 23, 1875.
48. Galveston Wharf Company, *A Brief History of the Galveston Wharf Company, Established 1854* (Galveston, 1927), p. 6; *Galveston Daily News*, November 20, 22, 1874; July 1, 1875; October 22, 27, 1875; January 19, 1876; October 20, 1876; January 7, 11, 1878; April 6, 1881.
49. *Galveston Daily News*, December 16, 1880; January 26, 1881; February 3, 1881; November 4, 19, 1881; August 24, 1882; December 28, 1882; January 16, 1883; November 13, 1885; January 21, 1886; February 2, 1886; December 24, 1886; January 22, 1888.
50. Earl F. Woodward, "Internal Improvements in Texas in the Early 1850's," *Southwestern Historical Quarterly* 76 (October 1972): 172–173; *Galveston Weekly News*, May 14, 1849; October 29, 1849; May 6, 1851; July 10, 1855; March 6, 1868; *Galveston Daily News*, May 23, 1868; April 21, 1869; July 21, 1869; June 22, 1870; *Civilian and Gazette*, June 3, 1851; October 21, 1851.
51. *Galveston Daily News*, March 4, 1874; August 16, 1890.
52. Ibid., February 23, 1868; April 25, 1868.
53. Ibid., March 7, 1867; March 6, 1868; June 14, 1868; October 24, 1868; March 11, 1869; April 27, 1869; July 7, 20, 21, 23, 1869; City Council Minutes, April 1868–June 21, 1871, pp. 267, 287.
54. *Galveston Daily News*, July 12, 1870; July 28, 1871; March 18, 1873; March 29, 1876; City Council Minutes, April 1868–June 21, 1871, p. 354.
55. *Galveston Daily News*, July 28, 1871.
56. U.S. Bureau of Statistics, *The Improvement of the Harbor at Galveston* (Washington, D.C.: Government Printing Office, 1884), pp. 2–3, 15.
57. *Galveston Daily News*, December 6, 1874; May 18, 1881; February 8, 23, 1883; October 5, 1883; August 15, 1939.
58. Ibid., February 24, 1880; November 16, 17, 1880; February 6, 1883.
59. Ibid., January 14, 1881; November 9, 1883; December 28, 1883; January

23, 1884; February 27, 1884; March 10, 12, 22, 1884; "Moody, William Lewis," *The Handbook of Texas*, vol. 3 (Austin: Texas State Historical Association, 1976), p. 608.

60. *Galveston Daily News*, May 3, 4, 1884; June 2, 8, 1884; December 11, 1884; James B. Eads, *Improvement of Galveston Harbor: An Argument of Mr. Eads before the Senate Committee on Commerce, May 21 and 22, 1884* (Washington, D.C., 1884), pp. 1–12.

61. *Galveston Daily News*, June 11, 1884; January 28, 1885; February 4, 1885; March 6, 13, 29, 1885; December 7, 11, 29, 1885; Claude H. Hall, "The Fabulous Tom Ochiltree: Promoter, Politician, and Raconteur," *Southwestern Historical Quarterly* 71 (January 1968): 365–366.

62. *Galveston Daily News*, February 28, 1886.

63. Ibid., May 31, 1888; July 20, 1888; August 21, 24, 1888; September 5, 7, 9, 22, 1888; Bernard Axelrod, "Galveston: Denver's Deep-Water Port," *Southwestern Historical Quarterly* 70 (October 1966): 217–227.

64. *Galveston Daily News*, June 4, 1886; March 11, 1887; March 22, 23, 1889.

65. Ibid., December 9, 1888; May 11, 1889; October 1, 2, 4, 1889; December 18, 1889; "Gresham, Walter," *Handbook of Texas*, vol. 1 (Austin: Texas State Historical Association, 1952), p. 735.

66. *Galveston Daily News*, October 3, 1888; August 16, 1890; September 7, 20, 1890.

67. Ibid., February 28, 1892; January 12, 1893; October 14, 1894; January 1, 1900.

68. Ibid., October 4, 11, 1896; February 17, 1897; April 3, 1898; January 1, 1900; February 6, 1900.

69. Dora Fowler Arthur, "Jottings from the Old Journal of Littleton Fowler," *Quarterly of the Texas State Historical Association* 2 (July 1898): 73, 82.

70. Millie Richards Gray, *Diary, 1832–1840* (Houston: Rosenberg Library, 1967), p. 148.

71. Sheridan, *Galveston Island*, p. 53.

72. *Galveston Daily News*, March 5, 1875.

73. *Flake's Bulletin*, June 26, 1865; *Galveston Daily News*, June 2, 26, 1869; August 3, 1870; July 6, 1876; May 30, 1878; City Council Minutes, April 1868–June 21, 1871, p. 374.

74. *Galveston Daily News*, July 11, 1869.

75. Ibid., June 7, 1867; August 26, 1869; June 10, 1874; March 7, 1879; July 10, 1881; May 19, 1899.

76. Ibid., September 29, 1868; September 7, 1872; June 28, 1873.

77. Ibid., May 31, 1877; July 22, 1877; June 4, 1880.

78. Ibid., May 22, 1873; April 11, 1875; January 6, 1876; March 11, 1876; October 28, 1877; August 30, 31, 1891.

79. Maggie Abercrombie, "Sketch of Galveston County," *American Sketch Book* 6, no. 5 (1881): 340, 342.

80. *Galveston Daily News*, August 13, 1881; January 2, 1882; June 11, 1883;

August 2, 1883; Howard Barnstone, *The Galveston That Was* (New York: Macmillan, 1966), pp. 96–97.

81. *Galveston Daily News*, March 9, 1878; December 28, 1882; February 4, 1883; July 1, 4, 1883; Barnstone, *Galveston That Was*, pp. 126–127.

82. *Galveston Daily News*, July 21, 1884; February 1, 1888; Barnstone, *Galveston That Was*, p. 127.

83. *Galveston Daily News*, September 23, 1894.

84. Ibid., July 5, 1889; September 5, 1894; June 25, 26, 1898.

85. Ibid., July 24, 1898.

86. Ibid., April 10, 1966 (article by Lillian Herz); Tom Le Vrier, "Mary Clayton Interview," *InBetween* 49 (June 1979): 7; Robert A. Nesbitt, "The Legend of Nicholas Clayton," *Port Galveston* 27, no. 6 (1974): 5, 7, 15–16; Barnstone, *Galveston That Was*, pp. 89–91, 98, 113, 116, 132, 156–157, 160, 164–165.

87. Nesbitt, "Legend of Nicholas Clayton," pp. 15–16.

88. *Texas Almanac, 1982–1983* (Dallas: A. H. Belo, 1981) pp. 187–192.

89. *Galveston Daily News*, January 13, 1940.

90. Frances Harwood, "Colonel Amasa Turner's Reminiscences of Galveston," *Quarterly of the Texas State Historical Association* 3 (July 1899–April 1900): 47–48; Ephraim Douglas Adams, ed., "Correspondence from the British Archives Concerning Texas, 1837–1846," *Southwestern Historical Quarterly* 15 (July 1912): 233; *Galveston Weekly Civilian*, April 6, 1871.

91. Hooton, *St. Louis' Isle*, p. 7.

92. Ibid., pp. 11, 13, 14, 16, 22, 23, 47, 51.

93. *Galveston Daily News*, June 21, 1868.

94. Harwood, ed., "Amasa Turner," pp. 47–48; Hays, *Galveston*, 1: 312–313.

95. *Galveston Daily News*, April 11, 1917.

96. "Galveston, Texas," *DeBow's Review* 4 (November 1847): 403; Ellen Bartlett Ballou, "Scudder's Journey to Texas, 1859," *Southwestern Historical Quarterly* 63 (July 1959): 5.

97. "Romantic Story of Oleander, Galveston's Flower of Profusion," *Port of Galveston* 24 (February 1971): 10.

98. *Galveston Weekly News*, February 24, 1844; November 6, 1847; May 5, 1848; August 9, 1848; October 13, 1848; May 28, 1849; October 12, 1852; December 11, 1855; September 30, 1856; November 24, 1857; December 22, 1857; July 13, 1858; August 31, 1858; *Weekly Civilian and Gazette*, June 1, 1844; November 6, 1847; December 20, 1853; January 25, 1859; *Daily Advertiser*, February 26, 1842.

99. *Galveston Daily News*, March 24, 1871; Alfred H. Belo, *Memoirs of Alfred Horatio Belo* (Boston: Mudge, 1904), pp. 54, 55, 66.

100. *Galveston Daily News*, June 6, 1961; *Civilian and Gazette*, April 15, 1848; June 9, 1848; August 17, 1848; Adele B. Looscan, "Harris County, 1822–1845," *Southwestern Historical Quarterly* 19 (July 1915): 49.

101. *Galveston Weekly News*, April 26, 1853; Ordinance Book, May 5, 1857–March 19, 1866, resolution of October 4, 1859.

102. John Q. Anderson, *Tales of Frontier Texas, 1830–1860* (Dallas: Southern Methodist University Press, 1966), p. 238.

103. Clarence Ousley, ed., *Galveston in Nineteen Hundred* (Atlanta: Chase, 1900), p. 71.

104. William M. Morgan, *Trinity Protestant Episcopal Church, Galveston, Texas, 1841–1953* (Houston: Anson Jones, 1954), p. 7.

105. *Galveston Daily News*, March 26, 1871; Philip Graham, ed., "Texas Memoirs of Amelia E. Barr," *Southwestern Historical Quarterly* 69 (April 1966): 494.

106. Vernon E. Bennett, *An Informal History of the First Baptist Church, Galveston, Texas* (Galveston, 1970), pp. vi, 1; Records of Proceedings of the First Baptist Church of Galveston, Texas, Rosenberg Library, pp. 9, 10, 18, 31, 102.

107. First Baptist Church, *Historical Sketch of the First Baptist Church of Galveston, Texas* (Galveston: News Steam Job Press, 1871), pp. 4, 8–10; George Fellows to "Dear Brother Sawyer," October 1844, F. E. McCoy Papers, Rosenberg Library.

108. Joe B. Frantz, *Gail Borden: Dairyman to a Nation* (Norman: University of Oklahoma Press, 1951), pp. 129, 152, 155–156, 157–159, 173, 176, 198, 203–220.

109. Joseph O. Dyer, *The Old Artillery Company of Galveston* (Galveston: Dyer, 1917), pp. 2–5, 8; *Galveston Daily News*, April 21, 1872; December 5, 1915.

110. *Galveston Daily News*, December 4, 1885.

111. *Civilian and Gazette*, January 15, 1861; Earl W. Fornell, *The Galveston Era: The Texas Crescent on the Eve of Secession* (Austin: University of Texas Press, 1961), pp. 288–289; Walter L. Buenger, "Secession and the Texas German Community: Editor Lindheimer vs. Editor Flake," *Southwestern Historical Quarterly* 82 (April 1979): 389, 395.

112. Fornell, *Galveston Era*, p. 296.

113. *Civilian and Gazette*, April 30, 1861; Sallie to "My dear friend," May 4, 1861, James P. Bryan Papers, Barker Texas History Center; Ruby Lee Garner, "Galveston during the Civil War" (Master's thesis, University of Texas at Austin, 1927), pp. 38–39.

114. Carland Elaine Cook, "Benjamin Theron and French Designs in Texas during the Civil War," *Southwestern Historical Quarterly* 68 (April 1965): 448–450.

115. *Civilian and Gazette*, May 14, 1861; July 2, 9, 1861; Louis Tuffly Ellis, "Maritime Commerce on the Far Western Gulf, 1861–1865," *Southwestern Historical Quarterly* 77 (October 1973): 167.

116. Paeder Joel Hoovestol, "Galveston in the Civil War" (Master's thesis, University of Houston, 1950), pp. 7–8; Record Book, J.O.L.O. Observatory, April 22–December 27, 1861, Rosenberg Library, pp. 50, 51, 54, 128–129, 159.

117. *Galveston Daily News*, July 13, 1879; Francis R. Lubbock, *Six Decades in Texas*, ed. C. W. Raines (Austin: Ben C. Jones, 1900), p. 319.

118. Hoovestol, "Galveston in the Civil War," p. 20; Texas Writers' Project, American Guide Series (WPA), "Galveston: A History and Guide" (manuscript at Barker Texas History Center), pp. 63–64.

119. G. T. Maelling to Oscar M. Addison, October 3, 1861, Oscar M. Addison Papers, Barker Texas History Center.

120. Lubbock, *Six Decades*, pp. 347–348, 350, 606–607.

121. *Galveston Weekly News*, April 15, 1862.

122. Ibid., May 6, 21, 1862; Hoovestol, "Galveston in the Civil War," p. 20; Lubbock, *Six Decades*, pp. 386–387.

123. John Franklin Smith to Justina Rowzee, June 28, 1862, John Franklin Smith Papers, Barker Texas History Center.

124. *Galveston Weekly News*, October 8, 1862; Charles C. Cumberland, "The Confederate Loss and Recapture of Galveston, 1862–1863," *Southwestern Historical Quarterly*, 51 (October, 1947), 111–115.

125. William Pitt Ballinger, Diary, February 23 to November 17, 1862 (typescript, Barker Texas History Center), p. 79.

126. Cumberland, "Confederate Loss and Recapture," pp. 116–118; *Galveston Weekly News*, October 15, 1862; November 26, 1862; December 10, 1862.

127. *Galveston Weekly News*, October 22, 1862; December 10, 17, 1862; Lubbock, *Six Decades*, p. 422; Hoovestol, "Galveston in the Civil War," p. 31.

128. *Galveston Weekly News*, December 10, 1862; Garner, "Galveston during the Civil War," pp. 49–50.

129. *Galveston Daily News*, December 25, 1888 (report by F.W.B.).

130. Diary of a Union Soldier, January 1 to December 31, 1863, manuscript, Rosenberg Library.

131. Lubbock, *Six Decades*, p. 486; Texas Writers' Project (WPA), "Galveston," p. 66; William Watson, *The Adventures of a Blockade Runner* (London: Unwin, 1892), p. 172; *Galveston Daily News*, August 6, 1876.

132. *Official Reports of the Battle of Galveston and Sabine* (Houston: E. W. Cave, 1863), pp. 2–4; Garner, "Galveston during the Civil War," p. 60; Texas Writers' Project (WPA), "Galveston," p. 67.

133. Texas Writers' Project (WPA), "Galveston," pp. 68–69; *Galveston Daily News*, December 25, 1888 (report by F.W.B.).

134. *Galveston Daily News*, December 25, 1888 (report by F.W.B.).

135. *Galveston Weekly News*, January 7, 1863.

136. Cumberland, "Confederate Loss and Recapture," pp. 124–126.

137. Ibid., p. 127; *Official Reports*, p. 7; Hays, *Galveston*, 2:564.

138. *Galveston Daily News*, August 6, 1876 (article by Sioux).

139. *Official Reports*, p. 11; Texas Writers' Project (WPA), "Galveston," p. 71.

140. H. A. Trexler, "The 'Harriet Lane' and the Blockade of Galveston," *Southwestern Historical Quarterly* 35 (October 1931): 109, 117; Cumberland, "Confederate Loss and Recapture," pp. 127–130.

141. Trexler, "The 'Harriet Lane,'" pp. 111, 121–123; David P. Marvin, "The Harriet Lane," *Southwestern Historical Quarterly* 39 (July 1935):

17–19; Philip C. Tucker, 3rd, "The United States Gunboat Harriet Lane," *Southwestern Historical Quarterly* 21 (April 1918): 360–362, 375; *Galveston Daily News*, May 27, 1884.

142. *Galveston Daily News*, May 2, 1906.

143. Ibid., February 15, 16, 1893.

144. Ibid., March 5, 1876; Alwyn Barr, "Texas Coastal Defense, 1861–1865," *Southwestern Historical Quarterly* 65 (July 1961): 23, 30; Garner, "Galveston during the Civil War," p. 90.

145. Hays, *Galveston*, 2:580–582; Texas Writers' Project (WPA), "Galveston," p. 71.

146. Rebecca W. Smith and Marion Mullins, eds., "The Diary of H. C. Medford, Confederate Soldier, 1864," *Southwestern Historical Quarterly* 34 (October 1930): 128–129.

147. Barr, "Texas Coastal Defense," pp. 23, 30; Smith and Mullins, eds., "Diary of H. C. Medford," p. 122; Samuel E. Asbury, "Extracts from the Reminiscences of General George W. Morgan," *Southwestern Historical Quarterly* 30 (January 1927): 199–202; *Galveston Daily News*, December, 25, 1888 (report by F.W.B.); *Galveston Weekly News*, June 24, 1863; September 30, 1863; November 4, 1863.

148. Ellis, "Maritime Commerce," pp. 188–222.

149. Watson, *Adventures of a Blockade Runner*, pp. 168–169.

150. Ibid., pp. 271–272.

151. Benjamin F. Sands, *From Reefer to Rear Admiral* (New York: Stokes, 1899), pp. 271, 272, 277–278; *Flake's Bulletin*, June 8, 1865.

152. John Franklin Smith to Justina Rowzee, May 19, 1865, John Franklin Smith Papers, Barker Texas History Center.

153. Lawrence F. Hill, "The Confederate Exodus to Latin America," *Southwestern Historical Quarterly* 39 (October 1935): 107.

154. *Galveston Weekly News*, June 7, 14, 21, 1865; *Flake's Bulletin*, June 15, 20, 1865; July 1, 1865.

155. *Flake's Bulletin*, September 11, 1865; I. D. Waters to "William," July 25, 1865; William Pitt Ballinger Papers, Barker Texas History Center.

156. *Flake's Bulletin*, August 29, 1865.

157. Ibid., July 19–22, 28, 1865; August 2, 5, 19, 1865; *Galveston Weekly News*, February 15, 1865; July 26, 1865.

158. *Flake's Bulletin*, October 20, 1865; November 6, 1865; *Galveston Daily News*, January 25, 1867; June 9, 11, 12, 18, 19, 21, 1867; July 28, 1870; August 3, 17, 18, 23, 1870; *Civilian and Gazette*, November 23, 1865; Stephen Franklin Shannon, "Galvestonians and Military Reconstruction, 1865–1867" (Master's thesis, Rice University, 1975), pp. 153–154, 169–172, 206–207; Hays, *Galveston*, 2:689.

159. *Galveston Daily News*, May 29, 1870.

160. Ibid.

161. Shannon, "Galvestonians and Military Reconstruction," pp. 219–220; *Galveston Daily News*, September 6, 1870; December 4, 1873; January 20, 21, 1874.

162. *Flake's Bulletin*, August 18, 1865; November 29, 1865; December 13,

1865; *Civilian and Gazette,* November 23, 1865; *Texas Almanac, 1982–1983,* p. 189.

CHAPTER THREE. THE OLEANDER CITY
1. H. A. Wallace Recollections, Barker Texas History Center.
2. *Flake's Bulletin,* June 28, 1865.
3. *Seventh Census of the United States, 1850* (Washington, D.C.: Armstrong, 1853), pp. 503–504; *Eighth Census, 1860, Population of the United States* (Washington, D.C.: Government Printing Office, 1864), pp. 486–487; *Ninth Census, 1870, Population of the United States* (Washington, D.C.: Government Printing Office, 1872), 1:271.
4. Andrew Forest Muir, "The Free Negro in Galveston County, Texas," *Negro History Bulletin* 22, no. 3 (1958): 68–69; *Civilian and Gazette,* November 4, 1840.
5. *Civilian and Gazette,* August 17, 1848.
6. Ibid., September 23, 1851.
7. Mary M. Brown to "Dear Sister Hannah," February 10, 1855, John Henry Brown Papers, Barker Texas History Center.
8. Muir, "Free Negro," p. 68; Paul Dean Lack, "Urban Slavery in the Southwest" (Ph.D. dissertation, Texas Tech University, Lubbock, 1973), p. 145.
9. *Civilian and Gazette,* November 4, 1840; September 23, 1851; October 21, 1851; *Galveston Weekly News,* October 7, 1856; Harold Schoen, "The Free Negro in the Republic of Texas," *Southwestern Historical Quarterly* 41 (July 1837): 93; Lack, "Urban Slavery," pp. 73, 100–101.
10. *Galveston Weekly News,* January 5, 12, 19, 1958; March 9, 1858.
11. Muir, "Free Negro," p. 70.
12. Lack, "Urban Slavery," pp. 29, 30, 34, 48.
13. *Galveston Weekly News,* April 15, 1863.
14. Ibid., January 10, 1860.
15. Fred Robbins, "The Origins and Development of the African Slave Trade in Galveston, Texas, and Surrounding Areas from 1816 to 1836," *East Texas Historical Journal* 9 (October 1971): 153–161; S. W. Cushing, *Wild Oat Sowing: or the Autobiography of an Adventurer* (New York: Fanshaw, 1857), p. 150.
16. Earl W. Fornell, "A Cargo of Camels in Galveston," *Southwestern Historical Quarterly* 59 (July 1955): 40–45.
17. *Galveston Daily News,* July 5, 1865; May 9, 1886; December 25, 1888 (article by F.W.B.).
18. *Flake's Bulletin,* June 20, 22, 29, 1865; *Galveston Daily News,* June 28, 1865; January 17, 1866; Ordinance Book, May 5, 1857 to March 19, 1866 (in City Secretary's Office, City Hall, Galveston), see June 28, 1865.
19. *Flake's Bulletin,* August 19, 1865; *Galveston Daily News,* March 16, 1867.
20. *Galveston Daily News,* January 31, 1866; June 4, 1867.
21. Ibid., January 26, 1877.
22. *Flake's Bulletin,* September 8, 1865.

23. "Daniel Ransom," Works Projects Administration manuscripts, slave stories, Barker Texas History Center.

24. *Galveston Daily News*, January 8, 1867; Claude Elliott, "The Freedmen's Bureau in Texas," *Southwestern Historical Quarterly* 56 (July 1952): 3, 18–24.

25. Randall B. Woods, "George T. Ruby: A Black Militant in the White Business Community," *Red River Valley Historical Review* 1 (Autumn 1974): 269–270, 272–274, 278–280.

26. For articles and advertisements about antebellum schools see: *The Daily Advertiser*, February 26, 1842 (Galveston University); *Galveston Weekly News*, May 11, 1844 (Galveston Female Academy); November 15, 1845 (Galveston Seminary); February 2, 1858; May 11, 1858 (St. Mary's College); *Civilian and Gazette*, June 1, 1844 (F. Dean's School); December 17, 1845 (Wallbridge Collegiate Institute, Galveston Female Institute); December 5, 1846 (Public School); November 20, 1847; January 24, 1851 (Male and Female Seminary). See also Alton Hornsby, Jr., "The Freedmen's Bureau Schools in Texas, 1865–1870," *Southwestern Historical Quarterly* 76 (April 1973): 398–402, 409–410; Elliott, "Freedmen's Bureau," pp. 7, 24.

27. *Flake's Bulletin*, September 13, 1865; November 11, 1865.

28. *Galveston Daily News*, February 11, 1871.

29. Ibid., May 4, 1871.

30. Ibid., September 6, 1871; October 5, 1871; October 2, 1874; April 27, 28, 1875; February 11, 1877; December 16, 1880; June 2, 14, 1881; August 31, 1881; September 7, 1881; October 11, 1881; November 13, 1881; January 2, 1882.

31. Ibid., February 22, 1867; May 8, 1870.

32. Ibid., June 23, 1872; June 10, 1875; January 20, 1876; February 29, 1876; David G. McComb, *Houston: A History* (Austin: University of Texas Press, 1981), p. 110.

33. *Galveston Daily News*, October 5, 8, 9, 1891; January 17, 1896.

34. Ibid., March 27, 1867; May 3, 5, 1867; June 10, 1869; October 6, 1870; June 5, 1872; June 1, 1877; March 19, 1879; May 15, 1879; June 22, 1879; March 3, 1893.

35. Ibid., August 25, 1884; December 21, 1893.

36. Ibid.

37. Ibid., July 6, 1878; November 23, 1883.

38. Ibid., February 29, 1876; Maud Cuney Hare, *Norris Wright Cuney: A Tribune of the Black People* (Austin: Steck-Vaughn, 1968), introduction; Virginia Neal Hinze, "Norris Wright Cuney" (Master's thesis, Rice University, Houston, 1965), pp. 1–9, 12–15, 21–22.

39. Hinze, "Cuney," pp. 25, 47–48; Hare, *Cuney*, pp. 42–44; *Galveston Daily News*, March 16, 1883; April 3, 1883; March 5, 1889; July 21, 1889.

40. Hinze, "Cuney," pp. 55–58, 129, 137–138.

41. Hare, *Cuney*, p. 31.

42. City Sexton, *Record of Interments of the City of Galveston, 1859–1872* (Houston: Gregory, 1976), pp. 5–30, 201.

43. *Galveston Daily News,* January 6, 1876; December 30, 1881.
44. Greensville Dowell, *Yellow Fever and Malarial Diseases, Embracing a History of the Epidemics of Yellow Fever in Texas* (Philadelphia: Medical Publications Office, 1876), pp. 5–6, 12, 18; Ashbel Smith, *Yellow Fever in Galveston, Republic of Texas, 1839,* ed. Chauncey D. Leake (Austin: University of Texas Press, 1951), pp. 21–23; Ashbel Smith to Guy M. Bryan, July 19, 1879, Guy M. Bryan Papers, Barker Texas History Center; *Galveston Daily News,* August 15, 1939.
45. Charles W. Hays, *Galveston: History of the Island and the City* (Austin: Jenkins Garrett, 1974), 1 : 342.
46. Nicholas Descomps Labadie to Anthony Lagrave, December 27, 1839, Nicholas Descomps Labadie Papers, Rosenberg Library.
47. *Galveston Daily News,* March 13–15, 1867; July 20, 1867; September 14, 1867.
48. Ibid., June 27, 29, 1867; July 5, 7, 1867; Dowell, *Yellow Fever,* pp. 57, 147.
49. Dowell, *Yellow Fever,* pp. 27–28.
50. *Galveston Daily News,* July 30, 31, 1867; August 2, 3, 21, 22, 1867; September 1, 3, 10, 1867; October 16, 1867; Thomas Seargent to Annie M. Seargent, August 13, 1867, Thomas Seargent Papers, Rosenberg Library; Anne Lois Moore Buckhorn, "The Yellow Fever Epidemic of 1867 in Galveston" (Master's thesis, University of Houston, 1962), pp. 43, 47, 52, 126.
51. *Galveston Daily News,* September 17, 1867; July 13, 1888.
52. Amelia Edith Barr, *All the Days of My Life* (New York: Appleton, 1913), pp. 261, 267–271, 281.
53. Ibid., pp. 282, 284, 285, 300; Philip Graham, ed., "Texas Memoirs of Amelia E. Barr," *Southwestern Historical Quarterly* 69 (April 1966): 497.
54. Barr, *All the Days,* p. 268.
55. Hays, *Galveston,* 2 : 704–705; Howard Association Records, 1854–1882, Rosenberg Library. *Galveston Daily News,* September 27, 1853; November 30, 1867; September 30, 1870; June 9, 1907; April 11, 1917.
56. *Galveston Daily News,* August 10, 1867; September 6, 14, 18, 1867; October 1, 10, 1867.
57. Howard Association Records, 1854–1882, ff 17.
58. *Galveston Daily News,* August 30, 1853; September 20, 1853.
59. Ibid., October 1, 2, 8, 9, 10, 1870; Dowell, *Yellow Fever,* p. 18.
60. *Galveston Daily News,* September 7, 9, 10, 13, 16, 1873; October 1, 26, 1873; September 27, 30, 1876; October 3, 6, 1876; Dowell, *Yellow Fever,* p. 18.
61. Smith, *Yellow Fever,* pp. v, 1–6.
62. *Galveston Daily News,* February 13, 1867; Smith, *Yellow Fever,* p. 7; Julius R. Brown to Clara, September 23, 1871, and Brown to "Pa," October 21, 1871, John Henry Brown Papers, Barker Texas History Center.
63. Ruth Ann Overbeck, "Alexander Penn Wooldridge," *Southwestern Historical Quarterly* 67 (January 1964): 336.
64. Elizabeth Silverthorne, *Ashbel Smith of Texas* (College Station: Texas

A&M Press, 1982), pp. 209–211; "Proceedings of the Texas State Medical Association," *Texas Medical and Surgical Record* 1 (June 1881): 233, 235; *Galveston Daily News*, March 4, 1880; September 26, 1880.
65. Overbeck, "Alexander Penn Wooldridge," p. 340.
66. *The University of Texas Medical Branch at Galveston: A Seventy-five Year History by the Faculty and Staff* (Austin: University of Texas Press, 1967), pp. 15–19, 23.
67. *Galveston Daily News*, August 25, 1868; November 26, 1868; August 13, 1869; October 6, 1869; March 18, 1870; April 19, 1871; Ordinance Book, May 5, 1857 to March 19, 1866, January 2, 1865; Matilda Charlotte Fraser Houstoun, *Texas and the Gulf of Mexico; or Yachting in the New World* (London: John Murray, 1844), 1:269–270.
68. *Galveston Daily News*, April 13, 1867; June 3, 1868; October 4, 1870; January 21, 1871; March 22, 1871; May 10, 1879; June 10, 1886; August 1, 1891; March 2, 1898; July 14, 1899.
69. Ibid., July 25, 1868; March 21, 1875.
70. Martin V. Melosi, *Garbage in the Cities: Refuse, Reform, and the Environment, 1880–1980* (College Station: Texas A&M University Press, 1981), p. 24.
71. *Galveston Daily News*, March 21, 1887.
72. Ibid., August 6, 1869; September 12, 1869; October 1, 1869; March 30, 1872; January 24, 1875.
73. Ibid., October 6, 1880; September 25, 1884; September 30, 1893; December 9, 1897.
74. Ibid., November 9, 1869; April 22, 1870; March 18, 1873; June 23, 1874; August 11, 1875; July 2, 1876; April 5, 1878; November 9, 1878; *History of the Galveston Fire Department* (Galveston: Finck, 1906), pp. 33–45.
75. *Galveston Daily News*, January 15, 1880; October 5, 1880; November 18, 1881; January 14, 15, 1882; June 30, 1882; July 7, 1882; January 16, 24, 27, 29, 1884.
76. Ibid., June 17, 1884; September 22, 25, 1885; October 9, 1885; *History of the Galveston Fire Department*, p. 109.
77. *Galveston Daily News*, November 13, 17, 1885; *History of the Galveston Fire Department*, pp. 71, 73.
78. *Galveston Daily News*, November 14, 17, 1885; December 4, 1885.
79. Ibid., November 14, 1885.
80. Ibid., November 17, 21, 24, 1885; April 4, 1886.
81. Ibid., December 4, 1885; January 2, 1887.
82. Ibid., May 28, 1861; January 31, 1867; July 3, 13, 1870; August 2, 1870; October 6, 1870; August 26, 1871; October 13, 1871; August 21, 1872; November 30, 1877; November 13, 1879; April 19, 21, 24, 1883.
83. Ibid., September 8, 1857; July 18, 22, 24, 1875; July 30, 1876; April 11, 1878; November 27, 1879.
84. Ibid., March 17, 1881; October 8, 1881; January 19, 24, 1882; January 22, 1887; February 23, 1887; March 18, 1887; April 3, 18, 1887; September 24, 1887; March 16, 1888; April 20, 1888; June 17, 1888; May 31, 1889; June 22, 1889; June 6, 1895.

85. Ibid., June 22, 1889; July 20, 1889; January 1, 1890; October 7, 1890; May 14, 1891; August 16, 1892.
86. Ibid., June 18, 1892; February 14, 1893; April 4, 1893; January 20, 1895; June 6, 1895; September 1, 1895; August 15, 1939.
87. Ibid., August 29, 1941; August 30, 1943; April 7, 1944; March 9, 1947; April 12, 1952; February 27, 1955; January 28, 1965; April 22, 1965.
88. Ibid., March 17, 1878; March 17, 1881; October 7, 1893; October 15, 1896; September 2, 1899; August 16, 1959.
89. Ibid., January 13, 15, 1882; September 10, 1882; February 12, 1886; January 1, 1890; February 14, 1891; May 25, 1938.
90. Ibid., October 20, 1870.
91. Ibid., May 16, 1867; August 16, 1870; February 3, 1871; June 20, 21, 1871; December 12, 1871; April 13, 1872; July 19, 1877; October 5, 1880; March 12, 1887; January 6, 1893; February 22, 1893.
92. Ibid., July 16, 1868; September 8, 9, 1869; January 13, 1871; July 9, 1872; August 29, 1873; July 12, 1874; October 4, 1876; October 28, 1898.
93. Ralph A. Wooster, "Wealthy Texans, 1870," *Southwestern Historical Quarterly* 74 (July 1970): 27, 34.
94. Jesse A. Ziegler, *Wave of the Gulf* (San Antonio: Naylor, 1938), p. 202; *Galveston Daily News*, February 2, 1871.
95. William P. Hewitt, "The Czechs in Texas: A Study of the Immigration and the Development of Czech Ethnicity, 1850–1920" (Ph.D. dissertation, University of Texas at Austin, 1978), pp. 28, 32, 46–47; Henry R. Maresh, "The Czechs in Texas," *Southwestern Historical Quarterly* 50 (October 1946): 237–238; *Galveston Daily News*, October 29, 1869; November 3, 1869.
96. Moritz Tiling, *The German Element in Texas* (Houston: Tiling, 1913), pp. 12–14, 55; Henry B. Dielmann, "Emma Altgelt's Sketches of Life in Texas," *Southwestern Historical Quarterly* 63 (January 1960): 363–365.
97. *Galveston Daily News*, January 29, 31, 1871; May 2, 1871; April 27, 1872; May 2, 1877; May 4, 1880; May 2, 1883; April 22, 1897; Margaret Sealy Burton, "I'm Telling You," letters to Jesse Ziegler, typescript, Letter 9, Barker Texas History Center.
98. *Galveston Daily News*, March 29, 1923.
99. Ibid., March 5, 1898; July 11, 1936; July 2, 1961; *Henry Rosenberg* (Galveston: Rosenberg Library, 1918), pp. 3, 20, 89–90, 94, 123.
100. *Galveston Daily News*, July 31, 1867; March 28, 1868; November 23, 1886; November 13, 1889; Jane A. Kenamore and Michael E. Wilson, eds., *Manuscript Sources in the Rosenberg Library* (College Station: Texas A&M University Press, 1983), p. x.
101. *Galveston Daily News*, January 1, 1861; July 29, 1865; August 22, 1865; February 20, 1867; April 13, 1867; May 28, 1867; September 29, 1867; November 21, 22, 1867; March 31, 1868; March 9, 11, 13, 14, 1875; Joseph S. Gallegly, "The Renaissance of the Galveston Theatre: Henry Greenwall's First Season, 1867–1868," *Southwestern Historical Quarterly* 62 (April 1959): 442–444.
102. *Galveston Daily News*, December 15, 1876; April 20, 1880; January 29,

1882; January 23, 1883; September 10, 1884; February 22, 23, 1887; April 16, 18, 1888; February 6, 1892; December 5, 6, 1894; January 3, 4, 1895.

103. *Galveston Daily News*, July 4, 1867; September 4, 1872; March 18, 1873; December 31, 1876; March 4, 1880; December 31, 1882; April 2, 1891.

104. Ibid., December 30, 1877; November 8, 1883; January 10, 1885; December 3, 1885; January 17, 1887; February 7, 1894; December 31, 1898.

105. Ibid., April 6, 1878; *Flake's Bulletin*, November 19, 1865.

106. Ibid., April 3, 30, 1867; March 5–7, 1869; August 4, 1869; February 24, 1872; July 4, 6, 1872.

107. Ibid., April 5, 1867; June 19, 1867; October 29, 1870; *Civilian and Gazette*, November 4, 1840; September 9, 23, 1851.

108. *Galveston Daily News*, June 2, 1867; June 30, 1868; October 21, 1868; November 12, 1868; May 23, 1869; July 24, 1870; February 2, 1871; March 31, 1871; May 5, 1871; July 11, 1872; March 5, 1874; October 4, 11, 13, 15, 1874; July 20, 25, 1877; April 30, 1879; May 1, 7, 1879; June 14, 15, 21, 22, 1879; July 8, 1879; September 30, 1879; August 29, 1880; January 19, 1881.

109. Isaac H. Kempner, *Recalled Recollections* (Dallas: Egan, 1961), p. 59.

110. *Galveston Daily News*, March 13, 1874; April 13, 1879; May 18, 1879.

111. Ibid., August 21–30, 1884; September 4, 11, 21, 1884; December 12, 1884; May 30, 31, 1889; June 9, 1889; March 27, 30, 31, 1891.

112. Ibid., August 8, 1873; March 13, 1874; April 13, 1879.

113. Ibid., June 15, 1873; August 8, 1873; March 10, 1874; June 2, 1874; March 8, 21, 1879; April 13, 1879; December 16, 1898.

114. Ibid., June 13, 1867; July 24, 1869; October 17, 1889; June 18, 1893.

115. James V. Reese, "The Early History of Labor Organizations in Texas, 1838–1876," *Southwestern Historical Quarterly* 72 (July 1968): 1, 6–8, 11–14.

116. *Galveston Daily News*, July 31, 1877; August 1–4, 16, 1877; September 2, 3, 1881.

117. Ibid., August 28–30, 1885.

118. Ibid., August 30, 31, 1885; September 1, 1885.

119. Ibid., October 20, 21, 1885; November 4, 6–10, 12, 15, 1885; February 6, 17, 1886; April 28, 1886.

120. Ibid., July 9–15, 20, 1894.

121. Ibid., August 31, 1898; September 2–4, 8, 9, 13, 17, 23–28, 1898.

122. Ibid., January 1, 1896; Vera Lea Dugas, "Texas Industry, 1860–1880," *Southwestern Historical Quarterly* 59 (October 1955): 170, 183.

123. *Galveston Daily News*, February 21–23, 1895; March 4, 27, 28, 1895.

124. Allen Clayton Taylor, "A History of the Screwmen's Benevolent Association from 1866–1924" (Master's thesis, University of Texas at Austin, 1968), pp. 7, 31–44, 53–55, 58–59, 83–84, 106–110.

125. *Galveston Daily News*, March 22–24, 1867; June 30, 1867; November 27–30, 1867; May 26, 1869; April 16, 1873; November 17, 1876; March 22, 1877; October 26, 1880; February 13, 1893; November 14, 1899.

126. Ibid., October 15, 1881; December 10, 1881; November 18, 1884; January 4, 17, 1885; December 19, 1885.

127. Ibid., June 25, 1875; February 11, 1891; September 8, 1892; May 21, 1893; January 12, 1896; May 31, 1896, June 10, 1896; May 23, 1897.

128. Ibid., July 6, 1873; September 8, 1875; June 19, 1879; July 2, 1884; March 7, 1885; April 4, 29, 1887; May 1–4, 1887.

129. Ibid., July 4, 1869; May 5, 1880; August 24, 1884; July 10, 12, 24, 26, 27, 1881; May 20, 1888; May 1, 1890; July 28, 1891; August 10, 12, 1894; September 23, 1895.

130. Ibid., May 15, 1874; see also December 16, 1883; September 10, 1893; September 30, 1894.

131. Ibid., January 8, 9, 1867; February 5, 1867; February 4, 1868; September 28, 1870; July 13, 1871; June 1, 1875; July 30, 1883; May 19, 1887; May 28, 1889; September 13, 1896; April 11, 1942; Ziegler, *Wave of the Gulf*, pp. 183–184.

132. *Galveston Daily News*, July 11, 1876; March 30, 1888; May 14, 1888; September 17, 1888; September 10, 1894.

133. Ibid., January 21, 1890; December 25, 1892; December 1, 3, 15, 17, 1893; February 23, 1896.

134. Ibid., December 7, 1869; October 7, 1889; *Flake's Bulletin*, January 26, 1866.

135. *Galveston Daily News*, September 1, 1895; Randy Roberts, *Papa Jack: Jack Johnson and the Era of White Hopes* (New York: Free Press, 1983), pp. 10–11; Henry W. Rhodes, ed., *Charter of the City of Galveston and Revised Ordinances* (Galveston: Strickland, 1893), p. 31.

136. *Galveston Daily News*, March 3, 1875; January 26, 1876; March 15, 1889.

137. Ibid., September 20, 1890; December 7, 1891; September 21, 23, 1893.

138. Ibid., April 11, 12, 1884; December 24, 1894.

139. Ibid., January 19, 20, 23, 25, 1895; September 30, 1898; August 23, 1899.

140. Roberts, *Papa Jack*, pp. 3–8, 12–16; *Galveston Daily News*, May 9, 1900; February 26, 1901; March 3, 11, 22, 28, 31, 1901; December 26, 1908; November 27, 1909.

141. *Galveston Daily News*, October 19, 1870; March 25, 1880.

142. For samples see *Galveston Daily News*, February 23, 1867; February 25, 1873; May 2, 1873; March 18, 1875; July 4, 1878; June 20, 1879; April 22, 1882; February 11, 1891; Walter E. Grover, "Recollections of Life in Galveston during the 1880's and 1890's," typescript, Walter E. Grover Papers, Rosenberg Library, p. 13.

143. *Galveston Daily News*, January 30, 1867; June 27, 1880; September 19, 1888; April 2, 1897.

144. Ibid., September 12, 1891.

145. Ibid., October 4, 1873.

146. Ibid., October 21, 1870.

CHAPTER FOUR. THE GREAT STORM AND THE TECHNOLOGICAL
RESPONSE

1. E. B. Garriott, "The West Indian Hurricane of September 1–12, 1900," *National Geographic* 11 (October 1900): 384–388; Isaac M. Cline, *Storms, Floods and Sunshine* (New Orleans: Pelican, 1945), p. 94; *Galveston Daily News*, September 12, 1900; October 14, 1900.

2. Garriott, "West Indian Hurricane," pp. 387, 391; Cline, *Storms, Flood and Sunshine*, p. 94; *Galveston Daily News*, July 28, 1901.

3. Morrison and Fourmy, *General Directory of the City of Galveston, 1901–1902* (Galveston, 1901), p. 5; Clarence Ousley, ed., *Galveston in Nineteen Hundred* (Atlanta: Chase, 1900), pp. 23, 26, 31, 45; *Galveston Daily News*, October 7, 1900; June 15, 1901.

4. Dennis S. Mileti, Thomas E. Drabek, and J. Eugene Haas, *Human Systems in Extreme Environments: A Sociological Perspective* (Boulder: Institute of Behavioral Science, University of Colorado, 1975), pp. 39–44, 57, 59, 66, 71–73, 100, 114–115.

5. Joseph L. Cline, *When the Heavens Frowned* (Dallas: Mathis, Van Nort, 1946), p. 47; *Galveston Daily News*, October 15, 1876.

6. Patrick B. Mullen, *I Heard the Old Fishermen Say: Folklore of the Texas Gulf Coast* (Austin: University of Texas Press, 1978), pp. 43, 50, 56; William Watson, *The Adventures of a Blockade Runner* (London: Unwin, 1892), p. 114.

7. *Galveston Daily News*, May 2, 1880.

8. I. Cline, *Storms, Floods and Sunshine*, pp. 92–93; "Galveston Weather Office Celebrates Centennial," *Port of Galveston* 24 (March 1971): 8; *Galveston Daily News*, September 8, 1900; August 16, 1903.

9. *Galveston Daily News*, September 12, 1900; John D. Blagden to "All at home," September 10, 1900, John D. Blagden Papers, Rosenberg Library; "Ella Belle Ramsay," Works Progress Administration, Slave Stories, Barker Texas History Center.

10. J. Cline, *When the Heavens Frowned*, pp. 50–61; J. Cline, *Storms, Floods and Sunshine*, pp. 94–97; *Galveston Daily News*, September 13, 25, 1900.

11. Ousley, ed., *Galveston in Nineteen Hundred*, p. 115; *Galveston Daily News*, May 25, 1901; April 24, 1932.

12. John Newman letter, August 31, 1934, Barker Texas History Center.

13. I. Cline, *Storms, Floods, and Sunshine*, pp. 97–98; J. Cline, *When the Heavens Frowned*, p. 59.

14. J. Cline, *When the Heavens Frowned*, p. 59; Frank T. Harrowing, "The Galveston Storm of 1900" (Master's thesis, University of Houston, 1950), p. 55; John Edward Weems, *A Weekend in September* (College Station: Texas A&M Press, 1957, 1980), pp. 72, 120.

15. Harrowing, "The Galveston Storm," pp. 77–80, 85; Ousley, ed., *Galveston in Nineteen Hundred*, pp. 48–50.

16. Harrowing, "The Galveston Storm," pp. 54, 72, 85, 86; Ousley, ed., *Galveston in Nineteen Hundred*, p. 45; U.S. Board of Engineers for Rivers and Harbors, *Effect of Storm on Jetties and Main Ship Channel at Galveston, Texas* (Washington, D.C.: U.S. Government Printing Office,

1900), pp. 1–4; *Galveston Daily News*, September 14, 1900; November 4, 1900; February 5, 1901.

17. *Galveston Daily News*, August 8, 1909.

18. James Patrick McGuire, *Julius Stockfleth, Gulf Coast Marine and Landscape Painter* (San Antonio: Trinity University Press and Rosenberg Library, 1976), pp. 8, 12–13.

19. Marx to Henry Cohen, September 18, 1900, Henry Cohen Papers, Barker Texas History Center.

20. City Council Minutes, Storm Meetings, pp. 2–3; *Galveston Daily News*, September 10, 1900.

21. Ibid.

22. Ousley, *Galveston in Nineteen Hundred*, p. 36; *Galveston Daily News*, September 10, 12, 1900; *Houston Post*, September 10, 1900.

23. Galveston Daily News, September 10–13, 1900; October 3, 1900; November 3, 1900; Ousley, ed., *Galveston in Nineteen Hundred*, 37–38.

24. Albert E. Smith, *Two Reels and a Crank* (Garden City: Doubleday, 1952), 126–129.

25. *Galveston Daily News*, September 30, 1900; November 30, 1900; December 16, 1900.

26. Ibid., September 13, 14, 1900.

27. Ousley, ed., *Galveston in Nineteen Hundred*, p. 117.

28. Ibid., p. 117; *Galveston Daily News*, September 11–13, 1900; *Houston Post*, September 13, 1900.

29. Red Cross, "Report of Fannie B. Ward," in *Report of Red Cross Relief, Galveston, Texas* (Washington, D.C.: Journal Publishing Company, 1900–1901), pp. 50–51.

30. *Galveston Daily News*, September 16, 1900.

31. Ibid., September 16, 25, 1900; William Crosthwait, *The Last Stitch* (New York: Lippincott, 1956), p. 122; Nathan C. Green, *The Story of the Galveston Flood* (Baltimore: Woodward, 1900), pp. 289–290.

32. *Galveston Daily News*, September 16, 1900.

33. Ibid., December 16, 1900; February 10, 1901; Red Cross, *Report*, p. 48.

34. *Galveston Daily News*, September 17, 22, 25, 28, 1900; October 14, 1900; *Houston Post*, September 25, 1900.

35. J. Cline, *When the Heavens Frowned*, p. 63.

36. H. M. Trueheart to G. Arthur Hilton, September 17, 1900, Henry M. Trueheart Papers, Rosenberg Library.

37. H. M. Trueheart to Charles M. Williams, November 26, 1900, Henry M. Trueheart Papers, Rosenberg Library.

38. H. M. Trueheart to D. C. Jenkins, September 20, 1900, Henry M. Trueheart Papers, Rosenberg Library.

39. Crosthwait, *Last Stitch*, pp. 123–124; Ousley, ed., *Galveston in Nineteen Hundred*, p. 36; *Houston Post*, September 13, 1900; *Galveston Daily News*, December 2, 1900.

40. Ousley, *Galveston in Nineteen Hundred*, p. 258; *Galveston Daily News*, September 18, 1900; November 21, 1900.

41. Red Cross, *Report*, pp. 17, 59, 61; *Galveston Daily News*, September 18, 24, 1900.

42. Red Cross, *Report*, pp. 10–12, 50–55; *Galveston Daily News*, September 26, 1900; November 12, 14, 1900.
43. *Galveston Daily News*, January 10, 1901; February 9, 1901.
44. Ibid., November 28, 1900; Central Relief Committee, *Report of the Central Relief Committee for Galveston Storm Sufferers, Galveston, Texas, May 2, 1902* (Galveston: Clarke and Courts, 1902), pp. 5–6, 9, 11.
45. Central Relief Committee, *Report*, pp. 1–3; *Galveston Daily News*, January 1, 1901.
46. *Galveston Daily News*, September 9, 10, 1901.
47. Ibid., January 18, 1887; February 3, 1887; March 11, 1887; June 24, 1887; August 14, 31, 1887; September 19, 1900; October 28, 30, 1900; January 20, 1901.
48. Ibid., December 1, 1900.
49. Ibid., November 6, 1900; City Council Minutes, Storm Meetings, p. 3; Bradley Robert Rice, *Progressive Cities: The Commission Government Movement in America, 1901–1920* (Austin: University of Texas Press, 1977), pp. 7–8.
50. Rice, *Progressive Cities*, pp. 8–10, 14–16; *Galveston Daily News*, May 25, 1905; August 15, 1907; April 11, 1917; October 21, 1917.
51. Rice, *Progressive Cities*, p. 9; *Galveston Daily News*, September 19, 1901; April 11, 1917.
52. Rice, *Progressive Cities*, p. 12; *Galveston Daily News*, January 15, 1901.
53. *Galveston Daily News*, February 21, 1895; April 26, 1895; February 2, 1897; June 9, 1897; June 6, 1899.
54. Ibid., October 2, 1900; November 6, 1900; February 5, 1901; City Council Minutes, January 1898 to September 1901, pp. 580, 581, 625, 745.
55. *Galveston Daily News*, December 19, 1900; February 5, 1901.
56. Ibid., January 24, 1901; February 5, 1901; City Council Minutes, January 1898 to September 1901, pp. 654–655.
57. *Galveston Daily News*, February 6, 1901.
58. Rice, *Progressive Cities*, pp. 13–14; Isaac H. Kempner, *Recalled Recollections* (Dallas: Egan, 1961), p. 31.
59. Rice, *Progressive Cities*, p. 16; *Galveston Daily News*, September 19, 1901; March 26, 28, 1903; City Council Minutes, January 1898 to September 1901, p. 767.
60. Stanley K. Schultz and Clay McShane, "To Engineer the Metropolis: Sewers, Sanitation, and City Planning in the Late Nineteenth-Century America," *Journal of American History* 65 (September 1978): 389–411; *Galveston Daily News*, September 27, 1901.
61. *Galveston Daily News*, January 31, 1902; July 22, 1954; George Sessions Perry, "Galveston," *Saturday Evening Post* 223 (November 25, 1950): 114.
62. Kempner, *Recalled Recollections*, p. 33.
63. *Galveston Daily News*, April 26, 1895; May 12, 1923.
64. Ibid., December 3, 1901; City Council Minutes, September 18, 1901 to May 5, 1903, p. 63.
65. Board of Engineers, "Report on the Seawall," Rosenberg Library; City

Council Minutes, September 18, 1901 to May 5, 1903, pp. 120–125; *Galveston Daily News*, January 26, 1902.

66. *Galveston Daily News*, December 7, 13, 1901; January 26, 31, 1902; May 21, 1902; September 1, 1903.

67. Ibid., January 29, 31, 1902; February 3, 4, 1902; October 18, 1904; September 1, 1905.

68. Ibid., April 5, 17, 1901; February 15, 1903; Kempner, *Recalled Recollections*, p. 32.

69. *Galveston Daily News*, February 8, 1903; February 20, 1904; Harrowing, "The Galveston Storm," pp. 139–140, 151.

70. *Galveston Daily News*, November 29, 1902; February 24, 1903; May 10, 1903; October 25, 1905; *Houston Post*, August 21, 1904; W. Watson Davis, "How Galveston Secured Protection against the Sea," *Review of Reviews* 33 (February 1906): 203–204.

71. *Galveston Daily News*, August 10, 1902; December 16, 1903; April 28, 1904; Bob Dalehite, "History Highlights," *InBetween* 83 (September 1980): 13.

72. *Galveston Daily News*, October 21, 1917; October 1, 1919; September 27, 1951; July 5, 1962; Bob Nesbitt, *Bob's Galveston Island Reader* (Galveston: Nesbitt, 1983), p. 102; Albert B. Davis, *Galveston's Bulwark against the Sea: History of the Galveston Seawall* (Galveston: U.S. Army Engineering District, 1961), pp. 5, 11, 12–14, 18–19.

73. *Galveston Daily News*, February 19, 1904.

74. Ibid., May 30, 1903.

75. Ibid., August 23, 1904; Texas Writers' Project, American Guide Series (WPA), "Galveston: A History and Guide" (manuscript, Barker Texas History Center), p. 3.

76. *Galveston Daily News*, September 10, 1911.

77. S. C. Griffin, *History of Galveston, Texas: Narrative and Biographical* (Galveston: Cawston, 1931), pp. 79–80; *Galveston Daily News*, September 21, 1902; December 8, 10, 12, 16, 1903; February 20, 1904.

78. *Galveston Daily News*, April 14, 1905; November 11, 1905; January 21, 1906; April 7, 1907; Nathanial R. Helms, "When Galveston Raised Its Grade," *InBetween* 111 (October 1981): 23–25, 27.

79. *Galveston Daily News*, September 1, 1908; March 19, 1910; September 1, 1910; January 1, 1911; April 11, 1917; Samuel B. Graham, *Galveston Community Book* (Galveston: Cawston, 1945), pp. 98–100; Minutes of the Grade Raising Board, September 16, 1905, Edmund R. Cheeseborough Papers, Rosenberg Library; Edmund R. Cheeseborough to Lindon W. Bates, May 13, 1910, letterpress, Edmund R. Cheeseborough Papers, Rosenberg Library; Nesbitt, *Bob's Reader*, pp. 103–105.

80. *Galveston Daily News*, June 19, 1903; June 15, 1905.

81. Ibid., August 27, 1906; November 30, 1906; June 14, 1909; November 7, 1909.

82. Ibid., September 23, 1911; City Ordinances 1901–1910, pp. 295–296, 354, 497–499.

83. *Galveston Daily News*, May 30, 1915.

84. Vernon E. Bennett, *An Informal History of the First Baptist Church, Galveston, Texas* (Galveston, 1970), p. 101.
85. *Galveston Daily News*, July 19, 1918.
86. Ibid., April 20, 1924; October 13, 1939; December 9, 1939; October 19, 1952; February 2, 1955.
87. Ibid., January 13, 1903; December 20, 23, 1903; August 7, 1906; January 20, 24, 25, 1907; February 3, 5, 1907; March 3, 1907; May 8, 1907; June 25, 1907; August 3, 1907; September 9, 1907.
88. Ibid., May 5, 1907; March 14, 1908; November 6, 1908; January 1, 1910; November 19, 26, 1911; April 7, 1922.
89. Ibid., August 7, 1906; January 26, 1909; November 26, 1911; August 11, 1974.
90. Ibid., September 17, 1911; November 23, 29, 1911; December 5, 6, 1911; September 26, 1936; November 1, 1936; Herb Woods, *Galveston-Houston Electric Railway* (Glendale, Calif., 1976), pp. 9–24, 37.
91. *Galveston Daily News*, May 25, 26, 1912.
92. Ibid., April 2, 1935; December 1, 1938; January 25, 1956; March 21, 1957; January 17, 1960; July 26, 1961; April 29, 1964.
93. Ibid., July 22, 26, 1909; November 3, 1912.
94. Ibid., July 22–24, 26, 1909; *Houston Post*, July 22, 1909.
95. *Galveston Daily News*, September 12, 1915.
96. Ibid., October 25, 1936.
97. Ibid., August 18, 23, 1915.
98. Ibid., August 18–21, 1915.
99. Ibid., August 27, 1915.
100. Nellie Watson to "Billy" (Golda Willis), August 21, 1915, Nellie Watson Letter, Rosenberg Library.
101. Ibid.
102. *Galveston Daily News*, August 17, 23, 25, 1915.
103. Ibid., August 18, 19, 27, 1915; September 12, 1915.
104. Ibid., August 26, 1915; September 2, 14, 19, 1915; November 7, 1915; February 13, 1916.
105. Ibid., February 12, 1916; December 9, 1916; February 10, 1917; April 7, 25, 1922.
106. Ibid., September 12, 1915.
107. Ibid., September 14, 17, 1961; January 19, 1962; August 5, 1962; November 28, 1962; Joel Barna, "KGBC in 1961—Heroics on the Airways," *InBetween* 106 (July 1981): 21; Millicent Huff and H. Bailey Carroll, "Hurricane Carla at Galveston, 1961," *Southwestern Historical Quarterly* 65 (January 1962): 293–294.
108. *USA Today*, August 18, 19, 1983; November 7, 1983; *Fort Collins Coloradoan*, August 19, 21, 1983; *Galveston Daily News*, August 19–22, 1983.

CHAPTER FIVE. THE FREE STATE OF GALVESTON

1. David G. McComb, *Houston: A History* (Austin: University of Texas Press, 1981), pp. 66–67.
2. *Galveston Daily News*, June 13, 1915.
3. David G. McComb, "The Houston-Galveston Rivalry," in *Houston: A Twentieth Century Urban Frontier*, ed. Francisco A. Rosales and Barry J. Kaplan (Port Washington, N.Y.: Associated Faculty Press, 1983), p. 18; *Texas Almanac, 1967–1968* (Dallas: A. H. Belo, 1967), p. 472; *Texas Almanac, 1982–1983* (Dallas: A. H. Belo, 1981), p. 424.
4. McComb, *Houston*, pp. 78–80; Isaac H. Kempner, *Recalled Recollections* (Dallas: Egan, 1961), p. 35.
5. *Galveston Daily News*, April 11, 12, 14, 15, 1901.
6. Robert Nesbitt, "Fortress Galveston: United States Coast Guard Has Been a Protector of Galveston Almost since the City Was Founded," *In-Between* 110 (September 1981): 24.
7. *Galveston Daily News*, March 16, 21, 1898; April 30, 1898; May 1–3, 27, 1898; June 8, 10, 1898; July 22, 1898; October 28, 29, 1898; Robert Nesbitt, "Fortress Galveston, Part III: Galveston and the Spanish American War," *InBetween* 104 (June 1981): 29–31.
8. Nesbitt, "Fortress Galveston, Part III," p. 31; *Galveston Daily News*, January 1, 1911; March 12, 19, 1911.
9. *Galveston Daily News*, November 24, 1912; April 8, 1913; September 2, 1913; January 25, 1914; April 5, 9, 1914.
10. Ibid., February 24, 26, 27, 1913; March 1, 1913; April 23, 25, 26, 1913; November 27, 1914; December 1, 3, 1914.
11. Ibid., February 2, 4, 15, 27, 1899; *Texas City Daily Times*, October 2, 1909; March 30, 1914.
12. *Galveston Daily News*, April 13, 1899; May 23, 1899; November 16, 1899; *Texas City Daily Times*, February 7, 1909; May 1, 8, 1909; November 4, 1910; April 28, 1911.
13. *Texas City Daily Times*, February 24, 25, 1913; March 5, 7, 20, 1913; April 21, 28, 1913; May 3, 1915.
14. Ibid., August 28, 29, 1915; September 1, 13, 14, 1915; *Galveston Daily News*, August 27, 1915.
15. *Galveston Daily News*, April 19, 20, 1917.
16. *The City Times*, November 9, 1918.
17. McComb, *Houston*, pp. 111–112.
18. *Galveston Daily News*, November 16, 1917; January 1, 1919; April 15, 26, 1919; January 14, 1927; February 25, 1927; February 23, 1935; July 15, 1940; September 24, 1940; January 16, 1941; March 16, 1941; April 30, 1944; December 10, 1944; August 17, 23, 1945; November 13, 1945; Nesbitt, "Fortress Galveston, Part III," p. 32; "Galveston Airport Enlarged for Army Use," *American City* 56 (June 1941): 72.
19. Ida M. Blanchett, "POW's in Galveston County," *InBetween* 105 (July 1981): 13–15; *Galveston Daily News*, May 29, 1941; December 9, 10, 31, 1941; January 8, 29, 31, 1942; May 6, 23, 1942; June 19, 28, 1942;

October 2, 1942; November 28, 1942; May 8, 1943; August 15, 16, 1945; July 2, 1946.

20. *Galveston Daily News*, September 15, 1946; June 4, 11, 1947; September 2, 1953; January 6, 1955; October 22, 23, 1957; Nesbitt, "Fortress Galveston, Part III," p. 33; Nesbitt, "Fortress Galveston, Coast Guard," pp. 26–27.

21. *Galveston Daily News*, August 15, 16, 1917; December 4, 1917; February 1, 1918; May 30, 1918; June 4, 1918.

22. Ibid., June 7, 28, 1918; July 11, 1918; February 25, 1919; January 2, 21, 1920; February 15, 1920.

23. Ibid., June 28, 1887; June 1, 2, 9, 11, 1899; October 14, 1899; January 25, 1900; January 8, 1912; ? Cohen to Henry Cohen, October 13, 1905, Henry Cohen Papers, Barker Texas History Center.

24. Kempner, *Recalled Recollections*, p. 26.

25. Rhoads Murphey, *Shanghai, Key to Modern China* (Cambridge: Harvard University Press, 1953), p. 7.

26. Granville Price, "A Sociological Study of a Segregated District" (Master's thesis, University of Texas at Austin, 1930), pp. 2–85, 102; *Galveston Daily News*, July 12, 1935; June 30, 1939; Bob Dalehite to author, October 1, 1982 (personal letter).

27. *Galveston Daily News*, July 23, 1937; November 23, 1939; March 13, 1941.

28. Ibid., April 12, 1941; May 23, 1942; November 20, 1942; December 30, 1942; January 9, 1943; March 16, 17, 1943; April 24, 1943.

29. Ibid., September 5, 1943; January 14, 1944; February 2, 1944; May 6, 1944; August 18, 1944; February 21, 1945.

30. Ibid., January 29, 1946; May 7, 26, 27, 1947; May 5, 6, 1948; June 24, 1948; October 13, 14, 1948; August 9, 1951; February 10, 11, 20, 1953; May 21, 1953; June 27, 1953; August 3, 4, 1953.

31. Ibid., May 12, 1955; June 1, 1955; February 1, 1956; May 23, 1956; August 5, 1956; November 28, 1956; January 3, 1957; May 29, 1957; "Sin in Galveston," *Time* 65 (May 23, 1955): 26; "Sin with System," *Newsweek* 45 (May 23, 1955): 33.

32. William S. Red, ed., "Allen's Reminiscences of Texas, 1838–1842," *Southwestern Historical Quarterly* 17 (January 1914): 287.

33. *Galveston Daily News*, December 26, 1907.

34. "Prohibition Movement," *The Handbook of Texas*, vol. 2, ed. Walter Prescott Webb (Austin: Texas State Historical Association, 1952), p. 415; *Galveston Daily News*, April 16, 18, 1918.

35. *Galveston Daily News*, December 11, 1930.

36. Ibid., May 4, 1931; February 14, 1932.

37. Ibid., March 12, 1923; January 7–10, 12, 1924; July 16, 19, 1924; December 23, 1924, March 12, 1925; July 8, 1925; February 12, 1929; October 18, 1929; April 23, 1930; January 12, 1940.

38. Ibid., October 30, 1929; February 26, 1930; April 11, 1930; March 14, 15, 24, 1931; April 19, 1931.

39. Ibid., May 31, 1931; November 11–13, 1931.

40. Ibid., April 19, 1931; August 13, 14, 25, 1931; February 14, 1932.
41. Janice Williams, "The Galvez and the Gambling Years," *InBetween* 76 (June 1980): 15; Otis Skains, oral history interview by Robert L. Jones, June 4, July 17, 1980, transcript, Rosenberg Library, p. 7.
42. Skains interview, p. 10; *Galveston Daily News*, March 1, 7, 20, 1928; November 15, 16, 1928.
43. *Galveston Daily News*, September 23, 1884; March 11, 1899; August 4, 1905; March 25, 1907; January 29, 1911; April 26, 1912; June 14, 1923; July 21, 1939; July 13, 1946.
44. Ibid., May 16, 1926; June 8–10, 13, 1926; June 6, 15, 1927; May 26, 1929; June 13, 15, 1933; April 21, 1934; June 20, 1936; July 24, 1939; August 24, 1961; Harold Scarlett, "Galveston's Gaudy Years," *Houston Post, Tempo Magazine*, August 10, 1969, p. 9; William A. Ward, "Casinos for Galveston: A Natural—Or Snake Eyes, Part I," *InBetween* 147 (March 1983): 11; Paul Burka, "Grand Dame of the Gulf," *Texas Monthly* 11 (December 1983): 168.
45. Ibid.
46. *Galveston Daily News*, June 13, 15, 1933; July 9, 1933; August 7, 1939; September 14, 21, 1941.
47. Ibid., October 6, 16, 19, 1937; January 26, 1938; May 18, 1938; September 5, 1940; September 15, 23, 24, 29, 1942; October 2, 3, 6, 7, 24, 1942.
48. Ibid., October 25, 1942.
49. Ibid., October 11–13, 26, 1929; August 30, 1931.
50. Ibid., August 5, 1931.
51. Ibid., April 21, 22, 30, 1933; Alan Waldman, "Big Sam and Papa Rose," *InBetween* 55 (August 1979): 29.
52. *Galveston Daily News*, June 9, 1935; July 25, 26, 1935; August 4, 1935; March 11, 12, 1936; May 27–29, 1936.
53. Ibid., May 7, 8, 1937; January 3, 1938; January 15, 1939.
54. Ibid., December 26–31, 1938; January 5, 1939.
55. Ibid., December 31, 1938; January 5–7, 10, 1939.
56. Ibid., January 22, 25, 26, 28, 1939; February 4, 1939; November 9, 1939; February 23, 1940; March 20, 1941; April 29, 1941; August 14, 1941; November 7, 9, 1941; November 10, 1942; December 3, 1942; February 9, 19, 1943.
57. Ibid., April 28, 1903; May 12, 1909; April 6, 1911; May 14, 1913; May 8, 1917; May 14, 17, 1919; May 11, 1921; May 2, 10, 13, 1929.
58. Ibid., August 30, 1884; February 1, 1891; December 15–17, 1901; April 24, 1926; July 13, 1930; June 26, 1938; October 2, 1938; November 5, 1944; "Sealy, John," *The Handbook of Texas*, 2:586.
59. Ibid., June 8, 1947; Thomas T. Barker, Jr., "Partners in Progress: The Galveston Wharf Company and the City of Galveston, 1900–1930" (Ph.D. dissertation, Texas A&M University, 1979), pp. 52, 116, 178–179.
60. James C. Maroney, "The Galveston Longshoremen's Strike of 1920," *East Texas Historical Journal* 16 (1978): 34–38; *Galveston Daily News*, May 15, 1920; June 2, 1920; August 1, 1920.

61. *Galveston Daily News,* June 4–6, 8, 9, 11, 16, 29, 1920; August 8, 11, 1920; September 18, 19, 30, 1920; October 1, 3, 1920.
62. Ibid., January 6, 1921; Maroney, "Galveston Longshoremen's Strike," p. 34.
63. *Galveston Daily News,* January 15, 1922; February 21, 22, 1922; March 10, 1922; July 8, 1967; August 11, 1967; "Abandoned Concrete Ship Inspires Fantasies," *Port of Galveston* 19 (May 1966): 11.
64. *Galveston Daily News,* January 22, 1920; July 31, 1932; October 1, 1933; October 1, 1934; March 23, 1937; December 16, 1941; April 11, 1942; July 4, 7, 1943; June 1, 6, 1945; August 18, 1946; March 4, 1948.
65. Ibid., July 22, 1928.
66. Barker, "Partners in Progress," pp. 132, 138–139; Galveston Wharf Company, *A Brief History of the Galveston Wharf Company, Established 1854* (Galveston, 1927), 38 pp.
67. *Galveston Daily News,* February 18, 1939; March 11, 1939; September 13, 1940; September 22, 1940; November 30, 1940; November 17, 1944.
68. Ibid., July 21, 1944; September 1, 1944; August 9, 10, 1946; May 27, 1947; June 10, 11, 1947; September 3, 1947; October 24, 1947; November 13, 1947; December 14, 1947; January 9, 1948; May 12, 1948; May 4, 1949; City Council Minutes, June 29, 1944–January 31, 1946, pp. 94–95.
69. George E. Marcus, "Law in the Development of Dynastic Families among American Business Elites: The Domestication of Capital and the Capitalization of Family," *Law and Society* 14 (Summer 1980): 869.
70. "Kempner, Harris," *The Handbook of Texas,* vol. 1, ed. Walter Prescott Webb (Austin: Texas State Historical Association, 1952), p. 945; Kempner, *Recalled Recollections,* pp. 14–17.
71. Marcus, "Law in the Development of Dynastic Families," pp. 870, 875–878; Harris Weston, oral history interview by Louis J. Marchiafava, August 29, 1981, transcript, Rosenberg Library, pp. 3–7; Kempner, *Recalled Recollections,* p. 12.
72. Harris L. Kempner, oral history interview by Robert L. Jones, June 17, 18, 1980, transcript, Rosenberg Library, p. 19; *Galveston Daily News,* July 27, 1969.
73. *Houston Post,* April 24, 1976; Alan Waldman, "The Jews of Galveston," *InBetween* 77 (July 1980): 13, 15, 17; (August 1980): 27–29.
74. A. Stanley Dreyfus, *Henry Cohen, Messenger of the Lord* (New York: Block, 1963), pp. 20, 41–42, 57, 59, 73; Ann Nathan and Harry I. Cohen, *The Man Who Stayed in Texas* (New York: McGraw-Hill, 1941), pp. 141–142, 252–253; Ronald A. Axelrod, "Rabbi Henry Cohen and the Galveston Immigration Movement, 1907–1914," *East Texas Historical Journal* 15 (1977): 24–32; *Galveston Daily News,* January 2, 11, 1894; June 13, 14, 1899; February 8, 1914; September 27, 1914; June 13, 1952. See also Bernard Marinbach, *Galveston: Ellis Island of the West* (Albany: State University of New York Press, 1983).
75. Harris L. Kempner, "Speech to the Harvard Business School Club of

Houston, September 27, 1981," typescript, Rosenberg Library, pp. 8–9; I. H. Kempner, *Recalled Recollections*, p. 40.

76. *Galveston Daily News*, July 31, 1898; June 2, 1907; March 10, 1910; May 28, 1911; June 9, 11, 28, 1911; Marsha Walker with Hyman Block, "The Grand Opening, the First Time, 1910," *InBetween* 75 (May 1980): 24.

77. "Moody, William Lewis," and "Moody, William Lewis, Jr.," *The Handbook of Texas*, vol. 3 (Austin, Texas State Historical Association, 1976), pp. 608–609; *Galveston Daily News*, March 22, 1923; July 4, 1926; January 1, 1932; February 23, 1969.

78. Pauline N. Wortham, oral history interview by Robert L. Jones, August 19, 1980, transcript, Rosenberg Library, pp. 8–9.

79. W. L. Moody IV, oral history interview by Robert L. Jones, September 9, 11, 1980, transcript, Rosenberg Library, pp. 11–12; "Dear Billy" from W. L. Moody, Jr., September 19, 1945, in the oral history file, Rosenberg Library.

80. Sara Weston, oral history interview by Louis J. Marchiafava, August 29, 1981, transcript, Rosenberg Library, p. 12.

81. *Galveston Daily News*, March 30, 1913; May 1, 1929; May 9, 1950; June 29, 1956; December 12, 1971; March 24, 1972.

82. Ibid., May 13, 15, 1929; July 11, 1933; May 11, 15, 1935.

83. Ibid., July 4, 1926; February 28, 1936; W. L. Moody IV, interview, pp. 9–10.

84. *Galveston Daily News*, May 31, 1954; July 22, 25, 29, 1954; July 1, 1956; December 18, 1966; *Houston Post*, July 24, 1977.

85. *Galveston Daily News*, July 1, 2, 1956; December 5, 1956; July 3, 1957; June 17, 1958; September 29, 1959; March 24, 1969; April 11, 1969; October 1, 6, 17, 20, 22, 31, 1970; November 1, 1970; January 16, 19, 20, 22, 1971; May 6, 1972; September 7, 13–15, 21, 1972; October 28, 1972; November 3, 1972; April 5, 1973; November 20, 1973; March 26, 1974; June 5, 1979.

86. Ibid., April 13, 1960; December 8, 22, 1961; November 15, 1963; March 25, 1965; May 30, 1967; February 9, 1968; June 15, 1968; November 13, 1971; November 27, 1972; June 25, 1976; Alan Waldman, "The Moving Force behind the Strand: The Moody Foundation," *InBetween* 135 (September 1982): 39; Third Conference on Urban Design, October 1981, flyer in Edward Protz file, oral history file, Rosenberg Library.

87. Waldman, "Big Sam and Papa Rose," p. 29.

88. *Galveston Daily News*, January 19, 1971.

89. Ibid., December 8, 1963; James Presley, *A Saga of Wealth—The Rise of Texas Oilmen* (New York: Putnams Sons, 1978), p. 244.

90. Isaac H. Kempner to Cecile Kempner, June 14, 1942, Kempner Papers, Rosenberg Library.

91. Isaac H. Kempner to Cecile Kempner, August 22, 1948, Kempner Papers, Rosenberg Library.

92. I. H. Kempner, *Recalled Recollections*, p. 70; H. L. Kempner interview, pp. 25–26; *Galveston Daily News*, November 27, 1938.

93. *Galveston Daily News*, December 23, 1933; January 16, 1935; October

16, 20, 1942; May 5, 11, 1946; July 13, 1947; February 8, 12, 1948; September 18, 1949; June 27, 1951.

94. Ibid., October 6, 1928; October 16, 1942; Bob Dalehite, "History Highlights," *InBetween* 77 (July 1980): 5; Tax Court Memorandum Decisions, "Estate of Sam Maceo" (Commerce Clearing House), pp. 262–265, 268.

95. Jack Lait and Lee Mortimer, *USA Confidential* (New York: Crown, 1952), pp. 215–217; Scarlett, "Galveston's Gaudy Years," pp. 8–12.

96. Waldman, "Big Sam and Papa Rose," p. 47; *Galveston Daily News*, June 27, 1951.

97. *Galveston Daily News*, August 19, 22, 23, 27–29, 31, 1930.

98. Ibid., March 21, 1951; June 6, 1951.

99. Ibid., January 17, 1937.

100. Ibid., July 5, 1940.

101. Ibid., June 24, 1948.

102. "Texas Pleasure Dome," *Time* 58 (July 9, 1951): 20.

103. *Galveston Daily News*, January 24, 1938.

104. Ibid., September 21, 1949; "Gambling in Texas," *Time* 61 (January 12, 1953): 74; William J. Burns, oral history interview by Steve Waspen, November 19, 1977, tape recording, Rosenberg Library, n.p.

105. *Galveston Daily News*, May 13, 14, 1941; May 11, 12, 1943; May 14, 1947; June 27, 1951; July 17, 1951.

106. Ibid., May 11, 1955; September 8, 25, 1955; March 9, 1956; March 19–23, 1958; April 3, 1958; June 26, 1958.

107. Ibid., May 29, 1957; March 21, 1958.

108. Ibid., June 8, 1947; Barker, "Partners in Progress," pp. 52, 116, 178–179.

109. *Galveston Daily News*, April 27, 1909; May 19, 1909.

110. Ibid., August 4, 1909; August 18, 1910; August 15, 1911; August 11, 1912; July 24, 1913; July 30, 1914; July 4, 5, 1916.

111. Ibid., August 9, 1911; February 10, 1918; September 23, 1921.

112. Ibid., February 12, 1902; February 19, 1917; June 1, 1922; June 2, 1934; February 20, 1949; May 14, 1950; February 14, 1952; May 22, 1977.

113. Ibid., April 5, 7, 1916; May 13, 1946; May 4, 10, 1964; May 1, 2, 1965; April 7, 1969.

114. Ibid., June 14, 1914; May 16, 27, 29, 1916; June 4, 16, 1916; July 29, 31, 1919.

115. Ibid., August 24, 1919.

116. Ibid., December 19, 1948; June 19, 1964; July 15, 1966 (see picture); April 3, 17, 1966.

117. Ibid., May 12, 1920; May 21, 1922; January 26, 1923; May 23, 1927; January 23, 1928; June 18, 1931; June 30, 1938; *Austin-American*, April 7, 1927.

118. Robert C. Cotner, et al., *Texas Cities and the Great Depression* (Austin: Texas Memorial Museum, 1973), pp. 138–140, 143, 146–150; Dianne Treadway Ozment, "Galveston during the Hoover Era, 1929–1933" (Master's thesis, University of Texas at Austin, 1968), pp. 66, 73,

91, 156, 164; United Community Funds and Councils of America, *A Survey of the Social Work Agencies of Galveston, Texas* (New York, 1938), pp. 12, 15, 28–30, 32, 40, 49, 51–52, 83, 92; City Council Minutes, June 23, 1931–July 10, 1933, p. 287; *Galveston Daily News*, February 12, 1930; December 12, 1930; March 9, 13, 1934; January 5, 1938; March 26, 1938.

119. *Galveston Daily News*, March 17, 1901; April 8, 1903; October 15, 1911; September 12, 1913; October 19, 1913; January 21, 1914; February 7, 1914; December 2, 1914; August 31, 1915; July 30, 1918; April 11, 1937.

120. Ibid., January 12, 1940.

121. Ibid., December 19, 1939; March 22, 1940; February 23, 1941; September 17, 1941; November 21, 1941; February 28, 1943; April 8, 1943; February 3, 10, 1946.

122. Ibid., August 22, 1961; September 2, 1962; August 11, 1982; "Editorial," *InBetween* 132 (July 1982): 5.

123. *Galveston Daily News*, February 24, 1909; March 1, 1912; March 19, 1915; May 19, 1917; December 14, 1918; July 27, 1919; April 14, 1933; January 20, 25, 1938; February 28, 1943; April 12, 1950; August 18, 1955.

124. Ibid., June 4, 12, 1955; August 18, 1955.

125. Ibid., May 4, 1905; August 6, 1911; December 29, 30, 1948; January 3, 4, 1950; January 2, 1951; January 2, 1952; December 24, 28, 1952; January 3, 1955; December 19, 1955; December 9, 1956; December 16, 1957; April 20, 21, 1958; December 15, 1958; December 14, 1959; July 1, 1960; July 8, 1968; Matthew Drummond, "The Bowl That Failed," *InBetween* 142 (December 1982): 31–33.

126. *Galveston Daily News*, November 5, 1948; December 4, 5, 1951; April 9, 1953; June 10, 1955; December 30, 1955; August 2, 3, 1957; March 14, 1964; Tax Court Memorandum, Estate of Sam Maceo, pp. 272, 281–282, 310–311, 365–367; James Letsos, Sr., oral history interview by Robert L. Jones, October 1, 1980, transcript, Rosenberg Library, p. 21.

127. *Galveston Daily News*, April 13, 1951; May 11, 1951; June 1, 2, 5, 1951.

128. Ibid., June 8, 1951.

129. Ibid., June 16, 1951; Isaac H. Kempner to Cecile Kempner, June 10, 1951, June 18, 1951, Kempner Papers, Rosenberg Library.

130. *Galveston Daily News*, November 29, 1951; December 12, 1952; January 1, 6, 1953; November 3, 1954; March 24, 1956.

131. Ibid., August 1, 1956; January 2, 1957; May 2, 1957; June 9, 10, 1957.

132. Ibid., June 11, 1957; Will Wilson, oral history interview by Robert L. Jones, October 6, 1980, tape recording, Rosenberg Library.

133. *Galveston Daily News*, June 11–15, 18–22, 27, 1957; August 18, 1957.

134. *Galveston Daily News*, September 25–27, 1957; October 3, 1957; November 2, 1957; July 30, 1958; October 23, 1958; November 8, 1958; April 2, 1959; January 3, 1969.

135. Ibid., April 15, 17, 1959; March 13, 1960; October 14, 1961; March 11, 1962; January 23, 1966; Alan Waldman, "Isle of Illicit Pleasures: Decline and Fall," *InBetween* 55 (August 1979): 43–44.
136. *Galveston Daily News*, August 1, 1962. In 1984 the Galveston electorate defeated a proposal for the return of casino gambling, 7,992–4,632 (*Galveston Daily News*, January 22, 1984).

CHAPTER SIX. GALVESTON ISLAND: ITS TIME HAS COME . . . AGAIN
   1. *Texas Almanac, 1982–1983* (Dallas: A. H. Belo, 1981), pp. 184, 189, 192; *Galveston Daily News*, March 21, 1967. (The title of this chapter is taken from the advertisements of Galveston's Park Board.)
   2. *Galveston Daily News*, February 15, 1963; May 12, 1964; July 3, 1968; May 8, 1970; March 22, 1979; December 29, 1979; November 5, 24, 1981; August 4, 8, 1982; December 6, 1982; January 6, 1983; November 16, 1983; "Last Passenger Train Out of Galveston," *Port of Galveston* 20 (April 1967): 19; Tom Le Vrier, "The Last Picture Show," *InBetween* 42 (March 1979): 20–21.
   3. *Galveston Daily News*, November 21, 1937; November 22, 1938; December 16, 1938; January 31, 1939; April 1, 1939; August 13, 1939; July 25, 1941; January 10, 1945; February 13, 1946; March 21, 1946; September 10, 1947; May 18, 1948; February 2, 1949; August 11, 1957; October 13, 1963; July 3, 1964; October 22, 1964; November 20, 1964; December 31, 1964; August 2, 1966; February 12, 1978; March 22, 1980; "Devoy Reports on Feasibility of Offshore Super-Terminal," *Port of Galveston* 25 (September 1971): 6, 15; "A Superport for Texas?" *Port of Galveston* 27 (January–February 1974): 2–3, 9–11.
   4. *Galveston Daily News*, August 23, 1961; November 10, 1963; August 16, 20, 30, 1964; November 19, 1964; April 12, 1965; May 21, 1965; April 15, 1966; October 5, 6, 1966; December 18, 1966; April 15, 1973.
   5. Ibid., October 30, 1912; June 11, 1926; January 4, 1931; May 23, 1940; March 8, 1942; June 14, 1944; May 29, 1948; February 24, 1955; January 25, 1963; May 21, 1963; September 27, 1963; December 8, 1963; June 30, 1965.
   6. Ibid., April 2, 1964; November 7, 1965; Marsha Walker, "Sea Arama Zza-Zza: Grand Old Lady of the Sea," *InBetween* 77 (July 1980): 4–5, 12–13.
   7. Helen Smith, "Old Red, a Landmark in Texas History," *InBetween* 131 (July 1982): 16, 21, 22; Bob Nesbitt, *Bob's Galveston Island Reader* (Galveston: Nesbitt, 1983), pp. 97, 106–107.
   8. *Galveston Daily News*, May 17, 1887; January 31, 1913; June 1, 1915; July 2, 1941; April 8, 1949; June 7, 1952; December 15, 1953; March 2, 1961; May 30, 1961; July 3, 1963; September 29, 1963; April 19, 1964; May 11, 1965; October 29, 1968; November 21, 1969; February 19, 1977; April 6, 1978; January 23, 29, 1982; Sealy and Smith Foundation, *Historical Review of the Medical Branch of the University of Texas and the Sealy and Smith Foundation for the John Sealy Hospital at Galveston, Texas* (Galveston, 194-), p. 32; Nesbitt, *Bob's Reader*, p. 107.

9. *Galveston Daily News*, November 14, 1955; May 6, 1957; April 11, 1963; August 21, 1976; February 12, 1977; March 3, 1982; Joel Barna, "Looking for a Cure to Salmonellosis," *InBetween* 106 (July 1981): 11.

10. *The University of Texas Medical Branch at Galveston: A Seventy-five Year History by the Faculty and Staff* (Austin: University of Texas Press, 1967), pp. 41–42.

11. Ibid., pp. 284–294; James S. Hanna, *What Life Was Like When I Was a Kid* (San Antonio: Naylor, 1973), p. 71; Truman G. Blocker oral history interview by Nonie K. Thompson, March 4, 1980, transcript, Rosenberg Library, pp. 4–5, 8–9; John H. Clouser, oral history interview by Robert L. Jones, April 22, 25, 1980, transcript, Rosenberg Library, p. 44.

12. *Galveston Daily News*, February 21, 24, 26, 1942; June 9, 1942; August 2, 1942; November 14, 1943; July 16, 1944; June 9, 1951; February 17, 1955; *University of Texas Medical Branch*, pp. 163–171.

13. *University of Texas Medical Branch*, p. 260.

14. Ibid., pp. 179–180; Red Cross, *Texas City Explosion, April 16, 1947* (Washington, D.C., 1948), p. 6; *Galveston Daily News*, April 17, 1947.

15. *Galveston Daily News*, January 1, 1945; Ernst Behrendt, "What Really Happened at Texas City," *Popular Science* 166 (April 1955): 268, 272.

16. *Galveston Daily News*, April 17–29, 1947; May 1, 10, 19, 29, 1947; June 17, 21, 22, 1947; October 12, 1947; October 10, 1948; June 11, 1949; April 14, 1957; November 4, 1960; Elizabeth L. Wheaton, *Texas City Remembers* (San Antonio: Naylor, 1948), pp. 1–10, 59, 63; Red Cross, *Texas City Explosion*, pp. 5–18; *Report of Fire Prevention and Engineering Bureau of Texas and National Board of Fire Underwriters* (New York, Dallas, 1947), pp. 5, 7, 37–43.

17. *Galveston Daily News*, February 9, 1958; June 8, 1958; January 15, 17, 1965; August 11, 1965; September 29, 1965; March 16, 1966; April 3, 1966; July 26, 1966; August 18, 1966; December 4, 10, 11, 1966; July 19, 1967; September 15, 17, 1967.

18. Ibid., August 30, 1962; November 18, 1963; August 5, 1965; June 14, 1968; June 11, 1977; August 19, 1979.

19. Ross M. Lamar, oral history interview by Robert L. Jones, August 28, 1980, transcript, Rosenberg Library, pp. 31–32.

20. *Galveston Daily News*, October 8, 1911; July 26, 1953.

21. Ibid., August 8, 1952; January 31, 1953; January 31, 1954; January 29, 1955; May 4, 1955; October 5, 1956; February 20, 21, 1958; October 23, 1958; August 7, 1959; November 13, 1960; March 22, 24, 1964; March 25, 1965; February 4, 1982.

22. Ibid., October 19, 1968; Sandy Sheehy, "The Mitchell Saga," *InBetween* 60 (November 1979): 21.

23. Sheehy, "Mitchell Saga," p. 21; "Man of the Year," *InBetween* 64 (January 1980): 25–28; Dana Blankenhorn, "Galveston's Greatest Developer: R. E. "Bob" Smith," *InBetween* 76 (June 1980): 23–25; James Presley, *A Saga of Wealth—The Rise of Texas Oilmen* (New York: Putnam's Sons, 1978), pp. 243–244, 246.

24. *Galveston Daily News*, December 4, 1965; May 22, 1966; June 27, 1967;

April 24, 1968; February 23, 1969; August 9, 1970; June 5, 18, 1971; October 16, 1972; December 10, 1972; February 6, 1983; Joel Barna, "Eckert's Bayou—Armistice Approaching in an Environmental War," *In-Between* 98 (April 1981): 1–4; Steven Long, "On the Record: George Mitchell," *InBetween* 155 (June 1983): 16.

25. *Galveston Daily News*, January 6, 1972; April 22, 1982; March 8, 1983.
26. Ibid., September 9, 1976; May 13, 1979; May 28, 1983; Robert J. Mihovil, "The Mitchell Project," *InBetween* 116 (December 1981): 22–23; Robert J. Mihovil, "George Mitchell Invests in a Dream," *InBetwen* 117 (January 1982): 7, 14.
27. *Galveston Daily News*, February 1, 1957; April 15, 1959; Howard Barnstone, *The Galveston That Was* (New York: Macmillan, 1966), p. 24.
28. *Galveston Daily News*, August 17, 22, 1962; June 2, 1966.
29. Ibid., March 9, 1967; September 30, 1967; January 30, 1970; April 27, 1973; October 14, 1973; December 1, 1973; Peter Brink, oral history interview by Mary M. Love, September 12, 1980, transcript, Rosenberg Library, pp. 3–4, 18–20.
30. Margaret Sealy Burton, "I'm Telling You," letters to Jesse Ziegler, typescript, Letter 14, Barker Texas History Center; Pete Fredriksen, "Supernatural Tales of Local Spooks That Go Bump in the Night," *InBetween* 112 (October 1981): 27.
31. *Galveston Daily News*, June 22, 27, 1968; July 13, 1968; October 10, 1968; March 16, 1969; May 1, 9, 1969; June 24, 1969; January 13, 1971; November 28, 1974; Barnstone, *Galveston That Was*, pp. 55–56.
32. Gianni Longo, Jean Tatge, and Lois Fishman, *Learning from Galveston* (New Brunswick: Institute for Environmental Action, 1983), pp. 53, 55.
33. *Galveston Daily News*, June 30, 1974; October 4, 1974; March 2, 1976; May 27, 1976; July 7, 1977; February 3, 1978; March 8, 1979; May 5, 1979; August 2, 1979; January 4, 1983; Margie Cosgrove, "Isle Historic Districts," *InBetween* 118 (January 1982): 9; Donald J. Lehman, *Lucky Landmark: A Study of Design and Survival* (Washington, D.C.: Superintendent of Documents, 1973), pp. 1, 3, 6.
34. *Galveston Daily News*, November 30, 1975; December 14, 1981; December 5, 1982; *Houston Post*, March 31, 1977; Babette Fraser, "The Whiteside Years: The Ax Falls," *InBetween* 82 (September 1980): 22–25; Galveston Historical Foundation Minutes, September 5, 1974; October 16, 1974; December 11, 1974.
35. "Elissa Arrives at New Home in Galveston Bay," *Port of Galveston* 32 (July 1979): 14; Babette Fraser, "Here's Elissa," *InBetween* 87 (November 1980): 13–15, 28–29; Marsha Walker, "Elissa," *InBetween* 114 (November 1981): 12–18.
36. Karen Lord, "Elissa: The People Who Make Her Over," *InBetween* 118 (January 1982): 8; Nick Horvath, "Working on a Square Rigger," *In-Between* 151 (May 1983): 12–13; *Galveston Daily News*, September 8, 1982.
37. *Galveston Daily News*, March 2, 1951; January 13, 1961; May 22, 1983;

Houston Post, July 9, 1980; W. H. Sandberg, oral history interview by Robert L. Jones, August 20, 29, 1980, transcript, Rosenberg Library, p. 30.

38. *Galveston Daily News,* June 27, 1961; November 3, 1963; October 7, 1965; January 26, 1967; January 4, 1972; "Jumbo Dry Dock Arrives at Todd Galveston," *Port Galveston* 35 (March–April 1982): 5.

39. *Galveston Daily News,* April 29, 1962; May 3, 1976; May 1, 1978; April 27, 1981.

40. Ibid., June 7, 1964; May 19, 20, 24, 1974; November 15, 24, 1975; December 2, 1975; January 17, 1976; February 19, 29, 1976; March 4, 1976; April 3, 7, 20, 27, 1976; September 25, 29, 1976; December 22, 23, 1976; January 14, 16, 1977.

41. Ibid., June 19, 1965.

42. Ibid., June 19, 1965; April 1, 11, 1970; November 17, 1970; June 1, 1976; July 25, 1980; October 28, 1980; November 12, 1981; December 3, 1981; April 7, 1982; Joel W. Barna, "A Silent Violence," *InBetween* 80 (August 1980): 15–18; Joel W. Barna, "The Big Ones: The Top Ten Air Polluters," *InBetween* 82 (September 1980): 16–17.

43. *Galveston Daily News,* April 18, 1967; August 7, 8, 1968; July 2, 1969; August 18, 20, 1971; April 2, 1975.

44. Ibid., June 3, 1933; December 12, 1937; June 8, 1947; September 3, 1947; July 22, 1949; November 19, 28, 1950; April 5, 1951; June 14, 15, 1963.

45. Ibid., January 22, 1966; October 12, 1967; November 10, 1967; Lloyd Victor Urban, "Estimates of Physical Exchange in Galveston Bay, Texas" (Master's thesis, University of Texas at Austin, 1966), p. 1; Luther J. Carter, "Galveston Bay: Test Case of an Estuary in Crisis," *Science* 167 (February 20, 1970): 1103, 1106.

46. *Galveston Daily News,* January 14–16, 19, 1970; February 13, 14, 1970; Richard Starnes, "Galveston: The Island That's Killing Itself," *Field and Stream* 75 (August 1970): 6.

47. *Galveston Daily News,* February 19, 20, 1970; March 28, 1970; April 4, 25, 1970; February 14, 1971; April 15, 1972; May 5, 1973; June 27, 1973.

48. Ibid., January 14, 1951; February 27, 1955; November 18, 1963; February 22, 1970; March 23, 1974; Edwin Shrake, "Dredging Up A Texas Squabble," *Sports Illustrated* 27 (August 14, 1967): 43, 46, 48; *Texas Almanac, 1982–1983,* p. 151.

49. *Galveston Daily News,* November 2, 6, 7, 9, 10, 19, 24, 27, 1979; January 9, 18, 1980; February 20, 1980; *Houston Post,* April 22, 1980; October 25, 1980.

50. *Galveston Daily News,* June 29, 1891; May 12, 23, 1962; February 27, 1973; August 22, 1975; July 16, 1976.

51. Ibid., February 4, 1979; August 5, 1982; *Houston Post,* October 18, 1981; Sheaffer and Roland, Inc., "Barrier Island Development Near Four National Seashores," Report to the Council on Environmental Quality (Chicago, 1981), p. 1; "Sea Level Rise Conference Document: Projections, Impacts, and Responses" (Washington, D.C., March 30, 1983), pp. 5–1, 5–9, 5–10; "Highlights," *Science 83* 4 (June 1983): 10.

52. *Houston Post,* April 23, 1978; October 16, 18, 1981; *USA Today,* May 27, 1983.

53. *Galveston Daily News,* April 29, 1884; June 1, 1885; September 5, 1885; January 13, 1893; August 3, 1897; January 2, 1898; August 31, 1909; February 4, 1910; March 15, 1910; September 1, 1922; October 1, 1922; October 1, 1934; February 3, 1939; August 15, 1939; July 9, 1950; May 21, 1968; June 5, 1974.

54. Ibid., September 9–11, 1887; August 10, 1889; May 23, 1899; July 25, 1937; September 11, 1966; March 20, 1970; March 31, 1977; January 1, 1982.

55. Ibid., May 27, 28, 1958; June 7, 1959; July 17, 1959; October 5, 1959; May 6, 1961; June 16, 1962; May 2, 5, 1963; January 31, 1964; March 31, 1964; June 10, 1967; July 9, 10, 1970; June 16, 1977; March 2, 3, 17, 1978; March 21, 1980.

56. Ibid., July 20, 21, 1941; April 2, 19, 1963; April 22, 1965; June 7, 1968; September 6, 1979; December 4, 1981; March 12, 1982.

57. Ibid., December 21, 1886; June 26, 1891.

58. Ibid., November 29, 1871; February 12, 13, 1879; June 27, 1936; August 8, 1961; October 15, 1964; April 24, 1966; City Council Minutes, June 29, 1944 to January 31, 1946, p. 231; Robert L. Jones, "LeRoy Colombo— The Lifeguard Who Would Not Quit," *InBetween* 98 (April 1981): 9–11.

59. Nathanial R. Helms, "Beach Patrol," *InBetween* 105 (July 1981): 26–29; "Where's Gordo," *InBetween* 79 (July 1980): 3, 5; Nesbitt, *Bob's Reader,* p. 8; *Galveston Daily News,* September 8, 1974; June 10, 1980.

60. *Galveston Daily News,* January 4, 1963; August 12, 1965; April 2, 1975; February 28, 1982; Joel W. Barna, "Living in Galveston: Hazardous to Your Health," *InBetween* 78 (July 1980): 16–17.

61. *Galveston Daily News,* May 1, 1966; July 6, 7, 1971.

62. Ibid., July 21, 1971; January 28, 1978; September 8, 1982.

63. Ibid., September 27, 1964; March 3, 1968; October 12, 1969; September 19, 1977; April 1, 1979; *Houston Post,* April 16, 1982.

64. *Galveston Daily News,* March 29, 30, 1978; December 1, 1978; February 2, 1980; April 8, 1981; July 23, 1981; September 10, 1981.

65. Ibid., March 31, 1968; September 30, 1974.

66. Ibid., January 15, 1974; Nathanial R. Helms, "Wino," *InBetween* 112 (October 1981): 6–7.

67. *Galveston Daily News,* July 5, 1976; March 28, 1979; November 7, 1980; March 14, 1982.

68. Ibid., May 28, 1980; June 15, 1980; July 23, 1980; October 22, 1980; January 9, 11, 14, 16–18, 1981; April 9, 1981; October 2, 30, 1981; January 27, 1982; February 2, 1982.

69. Ibid., October 4, 11, 1907; June 16, 1922; City Ordinances, 1901–1910, June 28, 1906, p. 275.

70. *Galveston Daily News,* June 16, 17, 23, 1922.

71. Ibid., August 3, 1928; May 8, 1931; October 16, 1931.

72. Ibid., October 23, 30, 31, 1931; November 4, 5, 13, 21, 1931; January 28,

1932; City Council Minutes, June 23, 1931–July 10, 1933, p. 359; Clouser interview, pp. 19–20.

73. *Galveston Daily News*, January 15, 1922; February 20, 1922; September 4, 1922; June 4, 11, 1926; August 6, 26, 1926.

74. *City Times*, October 1, 1904; March 24, 1917.

75. Ibid., January 15, 1921; *Galveston Daily News*, November 10, 1931; *Galveston Sentinel*, February 22, 1935.

76. *Galveston Daily News*, June 16, 1943; May 9, 1950; February 7, 1952; January 18, 1955; March 15, 1955.

77. Ibid., September 17, 1954; September 16, 1955; June 29, 1956; November 2, 1957; June 11, 1958; City Council Minutes, September 21, 1950 to September 6, 1951, p. 444; Leon M. Banks, oral history interview by Robert L. Jones, April 24, 1980; May 2, 6, 1980, transcript, Rosenberg Library, pp. 24, 47.

78. *Galveston Daily News*, August 19, 20, 1954; June 16, 1955; June 8, 1956; January 8, 24, 1961; April 10, 1961; August 4, 1961; January 16, 1964; November 15, 1964; March 30, 1967; February 27, 1969; May 28, 1981.

79. Ibid., June 15, 1907; May 13, 1962; October 29, 1977.

80. Ibid., March 12, 13, 15, 1960.

81. Ibid.; Kelton Sams oral history interview by Robert L. Jones, April 4, 1980, transcript, Rosenberg Library, pp. 1, 3; Griffith D. Lambdin, oral history interview by Robert L. Jones, May 29, 1980, transcript, Rosenberg Library, p. 18.

82. Lambdin interview, pp. 23–24; *Galveston Daily News*, April 6, 1960.

83. *Galveston Daily News*, July 7, 8, 15, 1960; September 21, 1960; October 7, 1960; June 15, 1966; July 20, 1967; November 17, 1971; April 21, 1981. The black population has been the largest and most influential minority in the history of Galveston. There have been small numbers of Chinese and, most recently, Vietnamese. Hispanics, however, have constituted the second largest minority for the city—18 percent in 1980. It is difficult to track their history in Galveston because of the lack of information in the historical sources, and because the U.S. Census Bureau took cognizance of this minority only in the 1970 and 1980 census data. An oral history interview in 1980 by Robert L. Jones with two-term councilman Paul Quintero (Rosenberg Library) points out that Hispanics live all over Galveston, many are upwardly mobile, some have become involved in politics, and most reject radical activity.

84. Ibid., October 5, 1958; November 15, 1960; March 14, 1962.

85. Ibid., October 5, 7, 1958; May 7, 13, 1959; July 15, 1959; January 27, 1960; April 16, 17, 20, 1960; November 15, 1960; May 18, 1982.

86. Ibid., April 12, 1961; May 10, 1961; June 30, 1961; August 13, 1961; October 27, 1961; August 11, 1963; Edward Schreiber oral history interview by Robert L. Jones, July 23, 1980, transcript, Rosenberg Library, p. 2.

87. *Galveston Daily News*, May 17, 1961; June 25, 1965; April 3, 1966; De-

cember 9, 1966; July 2, 1979; March 2, 1980; March 27, 1981; April 5, 1981; *Houston Post*, January 14, 1979; February 8, 1979; March 29, 1981.

88. *Galveston Daily News*, June 1, 1981; *Houston Post*, March 29, 1981; Jan Coggeshall, "Slashing the Life from the City's Budget," *InBetween* 84 (October 1980): 19–21.

INDEX

Addison, Oscar M., 16, 74
Adoue, Bertrand, 112, 134, 171, 182
Alden, Capt. James, 73
All American City Award, 214
Allen, Augustus C., 42
Allen, John K., 42, 43
Allen, John M., 44
Allen, W. Y., 159
Allison Doura, 146–147, 148
Altgelt, Emma, 105
Amateis, Louis, 106
American National Insurance Company (ANICO), 171, 172, 191
Apffel Park, 208
Architecture: and N. J. Clayton, 63–65; and fire (1885), 101–102; and iron front buildings, 69; and stilts, 28
Armstrong, T. D., 214
Ashton Villa (James M. Brown House), 198–199
Association of Concerned Taxpayers (ACT), 214–215
Atchison, Topeka and Santa Fe Railroad, 52, 127, 144–145, 189; building preserved, 199; and strike, 111–112; and water well, 103
"Auia," 5
Aury, Louis, 34
Austin, Stephen F., 6
Austin, Valery, 137
Austin, William T., 137
Automobiles, 143–144, 206

Babb, Stanley E., 38
Backenstoe, Kid, 160

Baker, Charles, 74
Baker, Mosely, 42, 43
Balinese Room, 174–175, 176; and gambling raids, 178, 186–187; reopened, 197
Ball, George, 92
Ballinger, William P. H., 75, 81–82
Barnstone, Howard, 3, 198
Barr, Amelia, 95
Barton, Clara, 133
Bates, Lindon W., 142–143
Bathing Girl Review, 181
Baylor, George W., 22
Beaches: and automobiles, 206; and bathhouses, 63–64; and bathing suits, 62, 180–181; and crime, 208–209; and drownings, 207–208; and festivals, 180–182; and groins, 205–206; and lifeguards, 207–208; and loss of sand, 16, 29, 149, 205–206; and Pleasure Pier, 190; and pollution, 204–205; and sand dunes, 16; sounds of, 17; and surfboards, 206–207; and tar, 15; and tourism, 17–18, 44, 61–65; unstable nature of, 6, 18, 149, 205–206. *See also* Crime; Marine life; Wildlife
Beach Hotel, 64–65, 102, 103
Beauregard, Pierre G. T., 100
Beauty contests, 181–182
Beggs, Ken, 190–191
Belo, Alfred H., 60, 69, 104
Benson, John, 21
Bergen, Edgar, 176
Bernhardt, Sarah, 107
Bertolino, Charles, Sr., 207

Bettison's Fishing Pier, 145
Biaggne, Frank L., 177, 178, 184, 212
Bishop's Palace (Gresham House), 65
Blacks: and boxing, 116–118; and churches, 90; and civil rights, 87; and Freedmen's Bureau, 88; and "Juneteenth Day," 85; and lynchings, 91; as police officers, 82; and public housing, 182–183; and riots, 24, 153–154; and schools, 89–90; and segregation, 89–90, 182–183, 210–214; and slavery, 35, 84–86, 88; in sports, 116–118, 212; and unions, 111–112
Blagden, John D., 124
Block, Hyman, 171
Blum, Leon, 112, 151
Bolivar Peninsula, 8, 13, 39, 122, 154, 187, 189
Booth, Edwin, 107
Borden, Gail, Jr., 49, 57, 71–72, 96; and customshouse, 27
"Bottoms," 209
Bowie, James, Resin, and John, 35
Bowman, Peter, 197
Bradbury, David, 57
Bridges, 53–55, 127, 144–145, 189
Briggs, Mrs. Frank, 144
Brindley, Anne A., 198
Brink, Peter H., 198
Brown, James M., 198
Brown, Rebecca, 198
Brown, William, 40
Bryan, W. F., 178
Burmah Agate, 204
Burnet, David G., 40–41
Burns, William J., 12, 178
Burr, David H., 6
Byrne, Christopher E., 65, 157, 158, 181–182

Cabeza de Vaca, Alvar Núñez, 31–33
Calandra, Mike, 165
Calder, R. J., 40
Camels, 86–87

Campbell, Glen, 162
Campbell, James and Mrs. James, 36
Campeachy, 35, 36, 37
Campeche Banks, 22
Camp Wallace, 10–11, 154
Carancahua Reef, 33
Cartwright, Herbert Y., 165, 178–179, 184
Cary, "Major," 85
Causeway, 144–145
Central Relief Committee (1900), 128–129, 133–135
Chew, Beverly, 35
Choynski, Joe, 118
Churches, 70–71, 90; and blessing of the shrimp boats, 201; and vice, 175, 178
City government: city manager plan, 214; commission plan, 134–137
City Party, 178
Civil War, 73–82; and Battle of Galveston, 76–78
Clampett, George, 213
Clark, Marvin J. "Big Jim," 160, 161
Clayton, Mary Lorena, 65
Clayton, Nicholas J., 64–65
Cleveland, Grover, 60–61
Climate, 23–31; and folklore, 123. *See also* Hurricanes
Clinch, James, 163
Cline, Isaac M., 123–126
Cline, Joseph, 124–126, 132
Clough, George Roy, 158, 179, 212
Clouser, John H., 211
Cohen, Henry, 65, 128, 170, 211
College of the Mainland, 195
Colombo, LeRoy, 207
Colquitt, Oscar B., 142, 145
Commercial and Agricultural Bank, 45
Commission government, 134–137
Connally, Ben, 212
Cooper, H. S., 171
Corbett, James, 117
Cotton business, 47; and blockade running, 79–81; and compresses, 55; and railroads, 51, 52; and ship

loading, 113–114; and shipments, 132
Cotton Carnival, 179–180
Cotton Jammer's Association, 114
Crime, 74, 86, 91, 108–111, 161–166, 208–210. *See also* Gambling; Narcotics; Prohibition; Prostitution
Crotty, John, 114–115
Cuney, Norris Wright, 91–92, 114

Dalehite, Bob, 2
Daniel, Price, 185
Daugherty, Joseph, 86
Davie, John P., 103
Davis, Edmund J., 83
Deep Water Committee, 59–61, 134–136
De la Rosa, Paul, Jr., 209
Depression (1930's), 182
Devoy, C. S. "Chuck," 202
"Dickens Evening on the Strand," 200
Dickenson, Jane, 108
Dickinson, Grady, 213
Die Union, 69, 73
Diseases, 92–97
Dismukes, Jack, 190
Douglas, Mary Walker, 40
Dowell, Greensville, 94, 98
Dyer, Cleyborne, 88
Dyer, Mrs. Isadore, 69
Dyer, Joseph O., 27, 37

Eads, James B., 59, 60
Eaton, Benjamin, 70
Economy: and depression (1930's), 182; and manufacturing, 48–49, 112; in 19th century, 47–49; and oil companies, 48, 151, 189. *See also* Cotton business; Fishing business; Gambling; Oyster business; Prohibition; Prostitution; Shell business; Shrimp business; Tourism; University of Texas Medical Branch
Edwards, Monroe, 86
Ehlinger, Joseph, 27–28

Elba, 110
Electricity, 104; and 1900 hurricane, 127
Elissa, 200–201
Ellzey, Pee Wee, 164
Evans, John, 60
Evia, José de, 5

Farragut, David G., 75
Faye, Alice, 163
Fellows, George, 71
Fertitta, Anthony J., 187
Fertitta, Frank, 164
Fire department, 100–102
First Baptist Church, 70
Fisher, Rhoads, 37
Fishing business, 22–23. *See also* Mosquito fleet; Oyster business; Shrimp business
Flagship Hotel, 190
Flake, Ferdinand, 73, 82, 87
Fleschig, Emil Richard, 109–110
Fly, Ashley W., 135–136
Forbes, Henry, 110
Ford, Walter C., 195
Fort Crockett: construction of, 152; and German prisoners, 154; and 1915 hurricane, 147, 148; sale of, 154; and seawall, 140; in World War I, 153–154; in World War II, 154
Fowler, Charles, 58
Fowler, Littleton, 61
Frankovich, Mitchell, 160
Fraser, George W., 178–179
Fraser, Matilda Charlotte, 99
Freedmen's Bureau, 88–89
Fulton, Robert L., 102

Galveston: becomes city, 42–44; descriptions of, 1–2, 35–36, 40, 44, 55, 105; early maps of, 5–6; early names of, 5
"Galveston" (song), 162
Galveston and Brazos Navigation Company, 57
Galveston and Western Railroad, 53

Galveston Artillery Company, 72, 83, 112
Galveston Athletic Club, 117
Galveston Bay, 8, 11–12, 55–56
Galveston Chamber of Commerce, 49
Galveston Chess and Whist Club, 106
Galveston City Company, 43, 56; and "wharf privileges," 56
Galveston City Railway Company, 63–64
Galveston College, 173, 195
Galveston Cotton Exchange, 49
Galveston Cotton Mill, 112
Galveston Daily News: beginning of, 69; and blacks, 87, 213; and 1885 fire, 102; and Galveston Wharf Company, 51; and W. C. Jones, 136; and 1900 hurricane, 127; and segregation of schools, 89–90
Galveston Historical Foundation, 198–199
Galveston Historical Society, 106
Galveston, Houston and Henderson Railroad, 50–51
Galveston-Houston Electric Railway, 144–145
Galveston Independent School District, 89–90, 191, 212–213; and employment, 191; and integration, 212–213
Galveston Island: description of, 6, 8; geography of, 6–7; geology of, 10
Galveston Island State Park, 13, 206
Galveston, LaPorte and Houston Railroad, 53
Galveston Lyceum, 106
Galveston Medical College, 98
Galveston Pavilion, 63–64
Galveston Rowing Club, 114
Galveston Wharf Company: beginning of, 56; dissolved, 168–169; and *Galveston Daily News*, 51, 56; and grain elevators, 49; as mo-

nopoly, 56–67; and C. Morgan, 51; and Sealy family, 166
Gálvez, Bernardo de, 5
Galvez Hotel, 147, 171
Gambling, 161–162, 164–166; abolished, 186–187; early, 70; and Maceo family, 176–177, 184–185; raids and, 176–177
Garbage, 99–100, 203
Garrison, Homer, 177
Garten Verein, 105–106; restored, 199
Gates, A. J., 42
Geography: and Cabeza de Vaca, 32; and Galveston Bay, 8; maps, 5–6
Geology, 6, 8, 10–11, 17–18
Germans, 105–106; in World War II, 154. *See also Die Union;* Fleschig, Emil Richard; Garten Verein; Henniker, Charles
Gillespie, George L., 60
Goedhart, P. C., 142–143
Goldbeck, Cora, 126
Goss, O. J. "Windy," 164
Gould, Jay, 51, 52
Grade raising, 138–139, 142–143
Grand Opera House, 107–108
Granger, Gordon, 81, 84
Grant, Ulysses S., 119
Gray, Millie Richards, 61
Green, Howard, 183
Greenwall, Henry, 90, 107–108
Gregory, Kye, 160
Gresham, D. C., 60
Gresham, Walter, 60, 65, 135
Griffin, Charles, 82, 95
Griffin, "Sin Killer," 90
Groesbeck, John D., 43
Gulf, Colorado and Santa Fe Railroad, 52

Haden, W. D., 19
Hall, James and Mary, 88
Hall, Warren D. C., 24, 36, 39
Hanna, Mark, 153
Hansen, Charles W., 146
Harbor, 8, 57–61. *See also* Galveston Wharf Company; Port

Hardin, William, 42
Harris, Frances K., 214
Harris, Lewis, B., 40
Harris, Mollie, 108–109
Harris, Phil, 162–163
Harrison, Benjamin, 92
Hausinger, Lee, 164
Haviland, James E., 82
Hawkins, Charles, 40
Hays, Anthony, 86
Hebert, Paul O., 74
Hegwood, Henry S., 210
Henniker, Charles, 109
Herrera, José Manuel de, 34
Herzik, Gus, 204
Hill, Charles R., 202
Hispanics, 39, 40, 44, 119, 152,
    182–183, 255 n.83
Historic preservation, 197–201
Hobby, William P., 167
Holbrook, Ray, 206
Hollywood Dinner Club, 176, 187
Hooton, Charles, 55, 68
House, Thomas W., 78
Housing conditions, 182–183
Houston, Sam, 40, 41, 45, 61, 73
Houston: and Galveston, 11, 47, 48;
    and quarantine, 97; and rivalry,
    51; and ship channel, 28, 150
Howard Association, 96
Howell, C. W., 58
Huckins, James, 70–71, 96
Huddleston, Dave, 19
Hughes, Jonathan, 71
Humboldt, Alexander von, 6
Hunter, Robert H., 23
Huntington, Collis P., 53
Hurford, O. P., 48
Hurricanes, 26–31, 149; 1900,
    121–134; 1909, 145–146; 1915,
    146–147; 1961 (Carla), 26, 149;
    1983 (Alicia), 26, 149
Hutchings, Robert K., 195

Indianola, 29, 30
International Longshoremen's Asso-
    ciation, 167

International Pageant of Pul-
    chritude, 181
Interurban, 144–145
Irvine, R., 80
Islander East, 190

Jack, William H., 42
Jamaica Beach, 33, 190
James, Harry, 162
Jarvis, Howard, 214
Jetties, 58–61; and 1900 hurricane,
    127
Jews. *See* Kempner family; Cohen,
    Henry
John Sealy Hospital, 191; and 1915
    hurricane, 147; and Texas City
    explosion, 193, 195; and venereal
    disease clinic, 158
Johnson, Andrew, 82
Johnson, Jack, 117–118
Johnston, Albert Sidney, 82
Johnston, Walter L., 158
J.O.L.O., 73
Jones, Levi, 43, 93
Jones, Walter C., 128, 129, 135–137,
    151
Junemann, Charles and Mrs.
    Charles, 109–110

Karankawa Indians: archeology and,
    33; and battle with Laffite, 39;
    and battle with Long, 38; and
    Cabeza de Vaca, 31; and can-
    nibalism, 33; description of,
    32–33
Kelso, Walter, 165
Kempner, Cecile, 174
Kempner, D. W., 171
Kempner, Harris (elder), 169
Kempner, Harris and Eliza, Fund,
    171, 192, 198
Kempner, Harris L. (son of Isaac),
    175, 213
Kempner, Isaac H. (son of Harris),
    169–170; and ANICO, 171; and
    Balinese Room, 174–175; and
    city finances, 138–139; as com-

Kempner, Isaac H. (*continued*) missioner, 137, 166; death of, 171; and Deep Water Committee, 134–135; and "Galveston Spirit," 137; and gambling, 185–186; and oil stocks, 151
Kempner, R. Lee (son of Harris), 165
Kempner, Ruth Levy, 187, 213, 214
Kempner, Stanley, 106
Kempner family, 169–171
Kerr, Gordon E., 204
Kinsolving, George H., 117
Kirchem, Theodore G., 164
Kirwin, James M., 130, 170, 211
Knights of Labor, 111–112
Kopperl, Moritz O., 143
Kotton Karnival Kids (KKK), 180
Kugle, William H., 158
Ku Klux Klan, 170, 211
Kyle, W. J., 50

Labadie, Nicholas, 93
Labor organizations, 111–114; and dock strike (1920), 167
Lachinsky, Sam, 163–164
Lackland, Frank D., 154
Laffite, Jean, 34–37; and hurricane, 27; and Karankawas, 39; and treasure, 37–39
La Harpe, Bénard de, 5
Lamar, Mirabeau B., 37
Lambdin, Griffith D., 213
Lamour, Dorothy, 181
Lange, Herman C., 137
Langtry, Lily, 107
Larsen, Klaus L., 146
Lasker, Morris, 112, 128, 134
Layton, Robert E., 214
Lea, Albert M., 77
Lea, Edward, 77
League of Women Voters, 214
Leake, Chauncey D., 192–193
LeBlanc, "Frenchy," 168
Lee, Robert E., 81, 118–119
Leonard, Charles H., 82
Lera, Leo, 165–166
Levy, Ben, 128–129
Levy, E. S., and Company, 188

Lewis, Joe E., 162
Lincoln, Abraham, 73
Lipton Tea Company, 201
Liselle, Peter, 15
Little Susie (railroad), 53
Lobit, J. S., 151
Lockhart, W. B., 89
Lombardo, Guy, 162
Long, Ann, 39
Long, James, 36, 38
Long, Jane Wilkinson, 24, 39
Lowe, Robert, 127
Lubbock, Francis, 74
Lynn, Arthur T., 86–87
Lyon, James E., 190
Lyons, Tom, 177

McCarthy, Glenn, 187
McCluskey, "Dave," 22
Maceo, Rosario (Rose): arrested for murder, 164; and charity, 176; early life of, 161; death of, 184; estate of, 185; opens Hollywood Dinner Club, 162
Maceo, Sam: character of, 175–176; early life of, 161; death of, 184; and Internal Revenue Service, 184–185; and J. Mitchell, 196; and narcotics arrest, 163; opens Hollywood Dinner Club, 162
Maceo, Vic, 165
Maceo family, 174. *See also* Gambling
McKinley, William, 153
McKinney, Thomas F., 45; and "Charter War," 44; and founding of city, 42–43
McKinney and Williams Company, 45, 56
McVitie, W. A., 128
Maelling, G. T., 74
Magic Harbor, 189
Magnolia Homes, 183
Magruder, John B., 51, 76–79, 81
Mail service, 70
"Maison Rouge," 35
Malhado, 5, 32
Manyhan, Tom, 117

Marine life: "granduquois," 20; jewfish (junefish), 20, 22; oysters,
18–19; Portuguese men-of-war,
14; rays (devilfish), 20; redfish,
20; red snapper, 22; red tide (algae), 15; sargassum (seaweed),
14–15; sawfish, 20; sharks, 21–
23; shells, 14, 61; shrimp, 19;
Spanish mackerel, 19–20; tarpon,
19; toredo (shipworm), 14, 53, 54;
turtles, 15; whales, 15–16
Massey, James C., 198
Maury, Matthew F., 31
Menard, Michel B., 42; and found-
ing of city, 42–44; and Galveston
Wharf Company, 56
Menard, Peter J., 70
Messina, Tony, 163, 165, 166, 177
Mexico: and customshouse, 39; and
prisoners at Galveston, 41
Military, 72, 151–152, 153–156
Miller, Celia, 91
Miller, Glenn, 162
Miller, Mary, 90
Mills, Robert, 45
Mina, Xavier, 34
Minor, Farrell D., 135
Minor, Lucian, 134
Miranda, John, 165
Mitchell, Christie, 23, 196
Mitchell, Cynthia, 197
Mitchell, George, 195–197
Mitchell, Johnny, 174, 196
Mitchell, Maria, 196
Mitchell, Mike, 196
Moller, George H., 94
Moller, Jens, 139
Moody, Shearn, 172, 183
Moody, Shearn, Jr., 173
Moody, William L., 59, 171–172;
and Cotton Carnival, 179–180;
and Cotton Exchange, 49; and
Deep Water Committee, 59; and
1900 hurricane, 137; yacht of,
used, 129
Moody, William L., Jr., 172–173;
and ANICO, 171; death of, 184;
and Galveston Wharf Company,

168–169; and I. Kempner, 170–
171; and Maceos, 174; and oil
stocks, 151
Moody, William L., III, 172–173
Moody Bank, 137, 173
Moody family, 137–138, 171–174
Moody Foundation, 173; and Ash-
ton Villa, 199; and higher educa-
tion, 195; and the Strand, 198;
and University of Texas Medical
Branch, 191
Moore, James W., 96
Moran, Johnny, 24
Moreland, Isaac N., 42
Morgan, Charles, 51–52; and sand-
bars, 57
Morgan, James, 28
Morgan Line, 29–30, 56. *See also*
Morgan, Charles
Morris, Seth Mabry, 143, 192
Morrison and Fourmy Company,
122
Mosquito Fleet, 54, 201
Musey, George, 160, 161, 164
"My Galveston Gal" (song), 162
Mystic Merry Makers (MMM), 180

Narcotics, 207–209; and Sam
Maceo, 163
Narváez, Pánfilo de, 31
Nation, Carrie, 159
Nelson, Miss Frankie, 114
Newman, John, 126
New Orleans: and cotton business,
47; and quarantine, 97
Newspapers, 69. See also *Die
Union; Galveston Daily News*
Nichols, Ebenezer, B., 56
Nimmo, Joseph, 58
Noble, Alfred, 138, 142
Noble, Ray, 162
Norman, A. P., 137
Northen, Mary Moody, 173
Nounes, John L. "Johnny Jack," 160,
164

Offatt's Bayou, 26, 203, 204
Oldenberg, William, 101

Oleander Park, 115
Oleanders (plant), 69, 100
Oliver, Alice Williams, 33
Ormond, Mrs. E. W., 113
O'Rourke, J. M., 139–142, 148
Ostermeyer, Henry, 126
Ousley, Clarence, 129
Owens, Theodore "Fatty," 160–161
Oyster business, 18–19

Pareskivopoulis, Savva and Katina,
   196
Parsutte, Maxie, 164
Peete, George W., 29
Peirce, Thomas W., 51
Pelican Island, 6, 44, 86, 195–196
Pepper, Nat, 214
Perry, Henry, 34
Phillips, Harry T., 164–165
Police, 24, 110; and beach, 208; and
   black officers, 82, 212; and jails,
   110–111; and labor unions, 111;
   and nude swimming, 62; and
   prostitutes, 108–109, 157, 158;
   and vagrancy, 87, 108, 109, 209.
   See also Burns, William J.; Biag-
   gne, Frank L.; Messina, Tony;
   Texas Rangers; Wilson, Will
Pollution, 64, 202–204
Population: growth of, 66–68, 83,
   188; and 1900 hurricane, 122; and
   slaves, 85
Port, 8, 47, 168, 201–202; and effect
   of jetties, 61. *See also* Galveston
   Wharf Company; Harbor
Price, Granville, 155–157
Prohibition, 159–161, 175, 176
Prostitution, 151, 153, 155–158;
   after Civil War, 91, 108–109;
   Rabbi Cohen and, 170

Quinn, Ollie J., 161, 162
Quintero, Paul, 210

Races: and biracial politics, 89; and
   early mixture of, 44. *See also*
   Blacks; Hispanics; Mexico

Ragsdale, Clyde B., 178
Railroads, 49–53
Ramsey, Ella Belle, 124
Ransom, Daniel and Ellen, 88
Raynor (prizefighter), 116
Reagan, Ronald, 215
Reconstruction, 82–83
Red Cross: and 1900 hurricane, 133
Red Fish Bar, 18, 28
Reed, Walter, 93
Renshaw, W. B., 75, 77
Richardson, Willard, 56, 69
Riley, Caroline, 108–109
Riley, J. M., 108
Ripley, Daniel, 128
Ripley, H. C., 54, 138
Robert, Henry M.: and beaches,
   205; and causeway, 144; and grade
   raising, 134, 138; and harbor, 60;
   and seawall, 134, 138; and Texas
   City, 153
Rob Roy, 80–81
Roemer, Ferdinand, 55–56
Roosevelt, Franklin D., 207
Rosenberg, Henry, 106; and Gulf,
   Colorado and Santa Fe Railroad,
   52; and sandbars, 58
Rosenberg Library, 2, 3, 106, 173
Rowzee, Justina, 74
Ruby, George T., 88–89, 91
Runge, Julius, 112
Rybka, Walter, 200

Saccarap, 68–69, 87
St. Patrick's Church, 29, 142
Saloons, 25, 153; and vice district,
   108
Sams, Kelton, 213
Sands, Benjamin F., 81
San Luis Hotel, 197
San Luis Pass, 8, 189
Santa Anna, Antonio López de, 40,
   41
Santa Fe Railroad. *See* Atchison,
   Topeka and Santa Fe Railroad
Sayers, Joseph D., 135
Schreiber, Edward, 214

Scott, Bill, 21
Screwmen's Benevolent Association, 113
Scurry, Thomas, 130, 132
Sea-Arama, 190–191
Sea Isle, 190
Sealy, George, 166; and Galveston Cotton Mill, 112; and Gulf, Colorado and Santa Fe Railroad, 52; and medical school, 99; and Southern Pacific Railroad, 53
Sealy, George, Jr., 166; death of, 184; and Galveston Corporation, 169; and Phillips murder, 165
Sealy, John, 166; and Central Relief Committee, 128; and Deep Water Committee, 134; and Galveston, Houston and Henderson Railroad, 51; and University of Texas Medical Branch, 98–99, 191
Sealy, John, Jr., 166; and Galvez Hotel, 171
Sealy, Rebecca, 99
Sealy and Smith Foundation, 166–167, 191
Sealy family, 166
Seawall, 138–142; and beach loss, 205; early concerns for, 30
Seeligson, Henry, 59
Seguin, Juan N., 42
Selma, 168
Serio, Sam, 185
Sharks, 21–23
Shell business, 18–19
Sheridan, Francis C., 44–45
Sherman, Sidney, 50
Shrimp business, 19
Simmons, Teri, 213
Sinclair, William H., 48, 64
Singer, Jacob, 177
Smith, Albert E., 129
Smith, Mrs. Ardie, 157
Smith, Ashbel, 96–98
Smith, Jared A., 60
Smith, John Franklin, 74
Smith, Leon, 76–77
Smith, Preston, 203

Smith, R. E. "Bob": and G. Mitchell, 196; and yacht basin, 189
Smith, R. Waverly, 135, 166
Smith, Thomas "Nicaragua," 79
"Smokey Row," 116
Somerville, Albert, 52
Southern Pacific Railroad, 53
Spanish: early explorations of, 31–33; and Laffite, 35; and Mexico, 34; name for Galveston, 5
Splash Day, 180
Sports: baseball, 115–116, 148, 183–184; bicycling, 104, 114, 127; and blacks, 116–118, 212; boating, 114–115; boxing, 116–118; football, 116; Oleander Bowl, 184; Shrimp Bowl, 184; "sporting houses," 116; surfing, 206–207
Steinmetz, George, 139
Sterett, William G., 127
Stewart, Maco, 43
Stewart Beach, 206, 213
Stilwell, Arthur E., 48, 53
Stockfleth, Julius, 127
Strand, the: and 1885 fire, 101; and historic preservation, 197, 198
Streets: design of, 43; drainage of, 100; early activities on, 44–45; lighting of, 69, 104; names of, 43; and 1900 hurricane, 126, 132; pavement of, 68, 69, 104; pigs on, 99; sanitation of, 99; sidewalks of, 69, 104
Stringfellow, H. M., 31
Stuart, Ben C., 21
Stull, Virginia, 213
Sullivan, John L., 117
Swartwout, Samuel, 28
Sydnor, John S.: and navigation company, 57; and slave sales, 86

Tacquard, Jacques, 103
Teachworth, Walter, 214, 215
Telegraph, 70, 83; and 1900 hurricane, 127, 132
Telephone, 104; and 1900 hurricane, 127, 132

Templeton, Fay, 107
Terry, B. F., 50
Texas City: development of, 152–153; and explosion, 193–195; and fossils, 10; and growth of port, 150–151; and 1915 hurricane, 146, 153; and U.S. Army, 152
Texas Medical College, 98
Texas Rangers, 167, 176–177
Texas Revolution, 40–41; statue to, 106
Theaters, 107–108
Theron, Benjamin, 73
Thompson, Clark W., 172
Three-legged Willie (Robert M. Williamson), 68
Throckmorton, Peter, 200
Tiki Island, 190
Todd Shipyards, 168, 201
Tourism, 61–65, 179–184, 189, 190, 198–201, 207–208
Treaccar, H. H., 211
Treasure, 37–38
Tremont Hotel, 45, 82
Tremont Opera House, 107, 117
Trentham, Marjorie, 199
Trinity Protestant Episcopal Church, 70
Trueheart, Henry M., 132–133
Truman, Harry S., 185
Tucker, Sophie, 162
Turf Club, 175, 185
Turner, Amasa, 27, 68
Turner Association, 105
Typographical Union, 111

University of Texas Medical Branch (UTMB), 191–193, 197–199; donations to, 166; and "Old Red," 65, 98–99; as storm refuge, 193; students of, 191, 192
Ursuline Convent (Academy): destroyed, 65; in 1900 hurricane, 126, 132
U.S. Coast Guard: at Fort Point, 154; and prohibition, 160

U.S. Quarantine Station, 29
U.S.S. Enterprise, 36–37
U.S.S. Harriet Lane, 76–78
U.S.S. South Carolina, 73–74; old shell from, 78
U.S.S. Westfield, 77, 78
U.S. Weather Service, 29, 123; and hurricane definition, 26

Vandiver, Frank, 1
Voight, O. E. "Dutch," 159–160; allied with Maceos, 161, 162, 176; car of, used by murderer, 165

Wainwright, Jonathan M., 77, 107
Wainwright, Marie, 107–108
Wallace, H. A., 84
Walton, John H., 44
Water supply, 8, 25, 100–104; and 1900 hurricane, 127, 132
Watson, Mrs. M. J., 86–87
Watson, Nellie, 147
Watson, William, 80–81
Weather. *See* Climate; Hurricanes; U.S. Weather Service
Webb, James, 162
Weissmuller, Johnny, 180
Westcott, Leander H., 111
Weyer, Henry, 109–110
White, David, 42, 43
White, Mose, 91
Whiteside, Emily, 199–200
Whorton, Evangeline, 200
Wigley, O. B., 143
Wildlife, 11–12; alligators, 12; ducks, 12–13; migratory flyway, 13; mosquitoes, 16; pelicans, 13–14; rattlesnakes, 12; seagulls, 14
Williams, Henry H., 45, 56
Williams, Isaac G., 82
Williams, Samuel May, 42, 43, 45; and "Charter War," 44; and Galveston and Brazos Navigation Company, 57; house of, preserved, 198

Williamson, Robert M., 68
Willis, Golda, 147
Wilson, Will, 186–187
Wilson, Woodrow, 170
Wolvin, August B., 152–153
Women's Health Protective Association, 182

Wood, Evans, 146–147
Wood, Leonard, 153

Yellow fever, 92–97

Ziegler, Jesse A., 37, 105